LISTER HILL

Fred W. Morrison Series in Southern Studies

Lister Hill

Statesman from the South

Virginia Van der Veer Hamilton

The University of North Carolina Press

Chapel Hill and London

© 1987 The University of North Carolina Press

All rights reserved

Manufactured in the United States of America

Library of Congress Cataloging-in-Publication Data

Hamilton, Virginia Van der Veer.

Lister Hill: statesman from the South.

(Fred W. Morrison series in Southern studies)

Bibliography: p.

Includes index.

1. Hill, Lister, 1894–1984. 2. Politicians—

Alabama—Biography. 3. Legislators—United States—

Biography. I. Title. II. Series

F330.3.H55H36   1987   328.73′092′4 [B]   87-1863

ISBN 0-8078-1744-9

FRONTISPIECE

Senator Lister Hill, 1894–1984

CONTENTS

ILLUSTRATIONS

M A P S

ACKNOWLEDGMENTS

Within the intimate community of natives and longtime residents of Alabama, many matters are resolved on the basis of friendly acquaintance or mutually beneficial alliance; due to the circumstances of this kind, I came to write this book. I was introduced to Senator Lister Hill by my father, McClellan ("Ted") Van der Veer, an editorial writer for the old *Birmingham Age-Herald* and later editor of the *Birmingham News*. These widely circulated and influential newspapers staunchly and consistently supported Hill throughout his Senate career; their loyalty and enthusiasm far exceeded that of Hill's hometown newspapers in Montgomery. Although I had been in no way involved in this journalistic decision-making, my kinship gave me entrée to Alabama's senior senator when I became a neophyte reporter for the Washington bureau of the Associated Press. During my tenure in this role, Hill always hid himself behind the typically extravagant, courtly language ("My, you lookin' pretty today! How's your daddy and yo' sweet mother?") with which he greeted visiting constituents and every woman. I had no idea that this almost comic facade concealed a tough, consummate politician.

After I left Washington and entered the academic world, I seldom saw Senator Hill. But during his retirement, he read my study of the Alabama career of his fellow New Dealer, political rival, mentor, and sometime friend, Hugo L. Black. Hill expressed mild disappointment that I had not mentioned his role in the creation of the Tennessee Valley Authority; otherwise, however, my book on Black must have impressed him favorably. By then I was a member of the faculty of the History Department of the University of Alabama at Birmingham, whose Medical Center had benefited enormously from Senator Hill's ability to obtain federal funds for buildings, research, library development, and numerous other health-related enterprises. I was urged to write a biography of Lister Hill by the then president of this university, Dr. S. Richardson Hill. Dr. Hill also served as chairman of the board of the National Library of Medicine in whose reorganization and massive modernization Senator Hill had played a leading role.

In typical Alabama fashion, these interwoven factors—Hill's grateful remembrance of my father's editorials; his close working relationship with Dr. Hill and with his predecessor, Dr. Joseph Volker; his interest in the University of Alabama at Birmingham and the National Library of Medicine; and the fact that I had written a book on Hugo Black—evidently motivated Senator Hill to grant me sole access to his Papers. At this stage, I was not certain that I wished to attempt such a task. The prospect of tackling Hill's congressional career (almost five times the length of Black's Senate career) and of making my way through his mammoth reservoir of Papers (1,875,000 pieces, according to the professional librarians who accessioned this collection) would daunt even the most venturesome scholar. Furthermore, at the outset I doubted that Hill's career would contain any dramatic and challenging illustration (comparable to Black's alliance with the Ku Klux Klan) of the eternal political question of whether ends justify means; in this regard, I now believe my initial assumption to have been incorrect.

Bringing this project to fruition required more years than I care to confess, interspersed though it was with other responsibilities such as teaching, administrative duties, and researching and writing other books. But throughout this experience, I was heartened by the support and tolerance of those who sponsored this project. The National Library of Medicine provided funds to enable me to interview many of those who worked with Hill in the preparation and passage of health-related legislation. The University of Alabama at Birmingham contributed funds and assistance for research and word-processing services, the sabbatical leave that enabled me finally to complete this book, and a grant to aid in its publication.

I am grateful to members of Senator Hill's family, particularly to his daughter, Henrietta Hill Hubbard, and to his nephew, Luther Lyons Hill Jr., for generous assistance in hunting up family photographs and for sharing information on family history. A number of history graduate students helped me sift through mountains of Hill Papers and run down elusive dates, middle initials, and factual details; among them, Berdine Rittenhouse, Ron Hammon, Norma Walter, Edwin L. Brown, Anne Tyler, Terry Flanders, Bill Ivey, Cathy Reynolds, and Claire Datnow. As always, members of library staffs provided indispensable support, particularly Tinker Dunbar and Mary Claire Britt, of the University of Alabama at Birmingham, and Mimi Jones, of the Alabama Department of Archives and History. Katharine Watson, a member of the staff of the History Department of the University of Alabama at Birmingham, made a crucial contribution by enduring an author's constant, often picayune revisions in order to put this manuscript into final form. As he had done many times before, my husband, Larry, patiently nurtured me through the agony of composition.

But when all else is said and done, I remain primarily indebted to the man whose life and political career I have attempted to chronicle. At the end of his strenuous 1944 campaign for reelection, Hill complained to his campaign manager, Roy Nolen: "The story ought to be told. . . . it is a historical chapter which should be put in black and white for all time."[1] To aid any future historian who might essay this task, Hill left a monumental written record, one that (unlike Justice Black) he never attempted to edit, purge, or partially destroy. When I began to search out his story, it was all there, the accomplishments, the flaws, the trivia. This book emerged primarily from this rich resource.

After Hill's retirement from the Senate, the *Montgomery Advertiser*, evidently recanting its past doubts about Hill's political course, predicted: "When a dispassionate history of Alabama during the decades of Hill's service is written, our guess is that the Senior Senator will be recorded as Alabama's greatest public servant of the 20th Century."[2] In the hope that this is such a history, I submit Lister Hill's long career to the reader's judgment.

Virginia Van der Veer Hamilton
University of Alabama at Birmingham
May 1986

L I S T E R   H I L L

The Preparation

1 8 9 4 — 1 9 1 6

In Montgomery, the past outranks the present. Alabama's white-domed, pillared seat of government, a graceful, modest echo of the nation's capitol, still dominates Montgomery's skyline from atop a rise known as Goat Hill at the head of a broad avenue. Lest Montgomerians tend to forget, the old capitol serves as a constant sentinel of the past, reminding them of memorable happenings in this setting . . . when Jefferson Davis stood on its steps to take his oath as president of the Confederate States of America . . . when Yankee troops marched through these streets three days after Appomattox . . . when chiefs of state, Grover Cleveland and both Roosevelts, came to visit . . . when daring Zelda Sayre, before she married F. Scott Fitzgerald, rode up Dexter Avenue in a rumble seat, wearing only a flesh-colored bathing suit . . . when the Freedom Riders stepped from their bus . . . when Rosa Parks refused to ride in the back of another bus . . . when George Wallace defied federal judges and presidents of the United States . . . when Martin Luther King Jr. led thousands of voting-rights marchers from Selma to this capitol. Although scattered across two centuries, to Montgomerians these events seem telescoped. When did all this happen? Yesterday. Just yesterday.

"In union there is strength"

On 27 December 1894 or, as Montgomery measures time, about midway between the visits of Grover Cleveland and Teddy Roosevelt, Lister Hill was born in this city. His parents must have rejoiced that wintry day over the arrival of a black-haired, male child to fill the void left five years earlier by the death of their first-born son. Scarcely had the excitement over the birth of a boy subsided than the household bustled anew. As family lore has it, Lilly Hill announced to her surprised husband, "Doctor, I don't believe we are entirely finished."[1] Whereupon the doctor delivered an unexpected twin, red-haired and female. She would be named Amelie for her grandmother but would be destined to bear the family sobriquet of "Baby" throughout her long life.

The Hills would rear Amelie to conform to the traditional mold for southern ladies of privileged station. She and her older sister, Lillian ("Sister" to her family), were to be carefully supervised by their mother in the expectation that they would develop from beguiling, obedient girls to popular belles and soon thereafter to capable and dedicated wives, mothers, and homemakers. Whatever qualities of leadership or dominance either possessed would be carefully concealed beneath this facade, or channeled into acceptable avenues such as heading the Red Cross or the Junior League. Neither Amelie nor Lillian would ever question that such was their destiny.[2]

But a boy, born in this bloodline of ambitious male achievers, would find that almost unlimited opportunities beckoned. In choosing a name for his son, Luther Leonidas Hill Jr. plainly signaled his hope that this child would follow in his footsteps. After earning two medical degrees in New York and Philadelphia by the age of twenty-one, Dr. Hill had studied for six months at King's College Hospital, London, under the famed British surgeon, Sir Joseph Lister. Awed by his mentor, the young Alabama physician wrote to a friend: "My venerated master, Lord Lister, is the greatest genius of the world."[3] Now on his way to becoming a medical leader in his own right, Dr. Hill seized the earliest possible moment to begin to exert a towering influence over his son. Throughout his life, Joseph Lister Hill would strive to live up to the rigorous challenge and high expectations embodied in a name chosen for him by the father he feared and revered.

His name would prove a considerable asset. At first he would be "Joe" to his schoolmates (and always to his irreverent younger brother, Luther).[4] Joe Hill—such a mundane name. When he first entered politics at the state university and in the city affairs of Montgomery, he would sign himself J. Lister Hill. Eventually he would drop the "J" altogether. *Lister Hill*. Short enough to fit into a headline. Easily pronounced and remembered. Unusual but not highfalutin. Hinting of education and genteel birth. Calling to mind the great surgeon. As Lister's grandfather, who had been the first to bear the sonorous name of Luther Leonidas Hill, once reflected: "There is power in names."[5]

Only two men, both master politicians, would dare to poke fun at his name to Lister's face—Alabama Governor Bibb Graves ("Lister the blister") and Franklin D. Roosevelt ("Listerine!"). Informed of his namesake, Lord Lister wrote to Dr. Hill to wish for the boy a life of "health, goodness, and usefulness."[6] Shortly after their births, Lister and Amelie received their names formally when they were christened in the Roman Catholic faith of their devout mother.[7]

What did his ancestry presage for Lister Hill, born in the first capital of the Confederacy near the turn of the twentieth century? Strong men and women on both sides of his family had seized opportunities open to early and aggressive white migrants to this southwestern frontier. Only briefly did a great civil war retard their upward progression. Through his mother's line, Lister descended from Jewish immigrants who had made their way from Europe to the southern United States in the early nineteenth century. If the boy were to become a doctor, his father may have reasoned, his partly Jewish ancestry and his Catholicism would be no deterrents. But when Lister chose, instead, a public career, his atypical background and early religious affiliation would prove barriers that he would be forced to conceal or remove.

Partly to overcome this problem, Lister Hill, as a public figure, would identify primarily with his Hill progenitors, descendants of a Welshman who had migrated to North Carolina in 1687 and whose son had fought for American independence. In maturity, he would bear a striking resemblance to the tall, stern-visaged males of the Hill line with their prominent noses, unflinching gazes, determined mouths, and bald heads. Like his great-grandfather and grandfather in the Hill line, both of whom had been impassioned and persuasive Methodist preachers, Lister, too, would become an eloquent, if sometimes perfervid, orator.

Upon occasion, the Hills had also displayed a stubbornly independent cast of mind. In 1825, Lister's great-grandfather, the Reverend William Wallace Hill, a self-educated preacher, was threatened with expulsion from his church for daring to advocate that representation in the conference of the Methodist Episcopal church of North Carolina be widened to include laymen and local ministers. Formally charged with "trying to sow dissension," William Hill replied with such a thundering denunciation of "spiritual tyranny" that a church committee quickly acquitted him.[8] Despite this vindication, the Reverend Mr. Hill soon left the Methodist Episcopal church to join a new branch of Methodism whose members espoused more democratic church governance. These reformers organized the Methodist Protestant church, admitted lay representatives to their conference, and dropped the title of bishop in favor of that of president.[9]

Largely because of his participation in this denominational tempest, William Hill decided in 1829 to pack up his family and move to the new state of Alabama. Family tradition has it that this journey was "more in the nature of a flight."[10] William settled his wife, Nancy Bowen Hill, the pious daughter of a Quaker preacher, and their children, eventually nine, in the planter community of Greensboro at the northern edge of Alabama's Black Belt, so named for its rich, dark soil. Like many other early migrants to this fertile crescent, he accumulated cotton acreage, slaves, and wealth. Absorbed in these new opportunities, William did not serve as a fulltime minister but remained active in the Methodist Protestant church as an elder and president of its Alabama conference. On special occasions, such as the dedication of a large, new sanctuary in Montgomery, he was called upon to demonstrate his oratorical fervor. At his death in 1849, William Hill was among Alabama's largest and wealthiest planters.[11]

To symbolize his strong defense of reform and dissent, William Hill named his eldest son Luther Leonidas.[12] Like his father, Luther Leonidas became a preacher. Assigned in 1859 to the large Montgomery Methodist Protestant Church, the Reverend Luther Leonidas Hill thundered his denunciation of such popular frivolities as pigeon shooting, card games, and waltzing ("a fashionable disguise for public hugging").[13] But although he voiced such conventional views of his day on social transgressions, he dared to depart from orthodoxy on the most volatile national issue of the nineteenth century. A planter and slaveowner as well as minister, Luther Leonidas Hill assumed a political stance that was anathema to the majority of his fellow Alabama planters by openly supporting Stephen A. Douglas, who favored local option on the issue of slavery in the territories, rather than John C. Breckinridge, an unequivocal advocate of slavery's expansion.[14]

Until Alabama seceded, Luther Leonidas Hill spoke out for remaining within the Union. Even after the firebrand William Lowndes Yancey led Alabama to make its fateful decision, the Reverend Mr. Hill continued to hope that the slavery issue could be peaceably resolved. Yet when the Civil War broke out, he, like many other onetime opponents of secession, volunteered to serve the Confederate cause. But when deafness barred him from being an officer, he refused to serve in the ranks, bluntly informing the recruitment officer: "If I'm too deaf to give orders, I'm too deaf to take them."[15]

As a consequence, Luther Leonidas spent the war years on his plantation. Wisely he refrained from converting his store of gold coins, issued by the United States Mint, into Confederate bonds. When peace came, he had lost his slaves, horses, and mules but, unlike most southern planters, he possessed $10,000 in gold in addition to the family silver and jewels, all successfully hidden during the Union occupation of Montgomery. Accepting the verdict of Appomattox realistically, he lost little time in forming a cotton partnership with the Reverend Charles W. Buckley, a Northerner who had come South as chaplain of a black Union regiment and remained in Montgomery to supervise black work contracts, serve as superintendent of schools for the Freedmen's Bureau, and become a "carpetbagger" member of the Reconstruction convention of 1867. Because his work with the Freedmen's Bureau also gave Buckley access to the valuable and scarce commodity of mules, he saw to it that the Hill plantation had both freedmen and mules to plant, weed, and harvest cotton. From 1868 to 1872, Buckley served as a Republican representative to Congress from Alabama's Second District. Half a century later, Luther Leonidas Hill's grandson, Lister, would be elected to represent this same congressional district.[16]

In years to come, the Reverend Luther Leonidas Hill's lack of a war record and his somewhat hasty alliance with a former enemy would prove something of an embarrassment to his descendants. His son, Dr. Hill, felt this stigma keenly. His grandson, Lister, whether ignorant of the circumstances or embroidering the truth, would always claim that *both* his grandfathers had fought for the Confederacy.[17]

Prior to the war, a devastating personal tragedy had afflicted Luther Leonidas Hill. His first wife, Mary Helener Walton Hill, and six of his seven children had died in the scarlet fever epidemic of 1856. Only a newborn baby, Walton, had survived. Eventually the bereaved husband and father took up life anew, courting Laura Sarah Croom, whose Baptist forebears had also moved to Alabama from North Carolina. Laura, an orphan at nine, had been sent by her well-to-do relatives to be educated at private schools in Richmond, Virginia, and New York City, a worldly experience for a southern girl of her day. Among her classmates at the fashionable Abbott School in New York had been Jennie Jerome, the future mother of Winston Churchill.[18]

Upon her return to Alabama, Laura Croom caught the eye of the widowed minister, seventeen years her senior. After a long and proper courtship, during which she never allowed him to address her by any more intimate term than "Miss Laura," she consented in 1861 to marry Luther Leonidas Hill.[19] Before their wedding, Luther Leonidas gave Laura a diamond necklace and earrings valued at $10,000. To honor his wives equally, he commissioned an elaborately carved marble monument from Italy, at a cost of $10,000, to mark the graves of Mary and her little ones in Montgomery's Oakwood Cemetery.[20]

Eventually Luther Leonidas also replenished his family. He and Laura had twelve children, four of whom died in infancy. Comfortably situated but not as affluent as before the war, the Hills occupied a modest cottage in Montgomery and spent holidays and vacations in a rustic country house at Rosemary Hill, their plantation east of that city.[21]

Almost every evening after supper, Luther Leonidas, who had been educated by plantation tutors, gathered his flock around a table to drill them in a variety of subjects from higher mathematics to the King James version of the Bible, translations of Greek and Latin classics, or the works of Molière, Mark Twain, and other literary greats. Laura taught her children manners and the fine points of English. Unacquainted with such a concept as vacation, the Hills kept their children close about them, conducting their evening classes twelve months a year. As patriarch of what he liked to call his "tribe," Luther Leonidas imprinted upon the minds of his children his own trinity of virtues: love, discipline, and, above all, work. He and Laura must have been gratified by the fruits of this ritual. Of their seven sons, three were to become prominent lawyers, two would become noted physicians, one a highly regarded dentist, and one a dedicated Presbyterian minister.[22]

Luther Leonidas Hill instilled other values in his descendants: frugality, democracy, a modest lifestyle, and, above all, loyalty. To illustrate the advantage of a tight family group, he would give each child a twig to snap, then ask each to attempt to break a bundle of twigs tightly wound together.[23] Evidently he made his point that "in union there is strength." His six sons who remained in Montgomery became renowned for their clannishness. Almost daily they met for a family conference. Once a week they gathered to discuss issues of the day at a stag dinner in one of their homes, each wife striving to outdo the others in bounteousness of food and drink.[24]

For fifty years or more, two of the Hill brothers, William Wallace and Wiley, dominated an important clique in Montgomery politics, tending to favor reform and oppose narrow, entrenched interests in behalf of a broader, more democratic base. In their law practice, William and Wiley preferred plaintiffs to corporate clients and proved gifted at defending those charged with criminal offenses. As Will frequently remarked: "One good juryman is worth twelve good witnesses."[25]

Perhaps this leaning toward reform sprang from the teachings of Luther Leonidas who, upon the occasion of his large funeral in 1893, was described by the *Alabama Journal* as "one who bowed not to power but was ever inclined to the side of the weak." His sons, being urban professionals, members of the South's growing middle class, and inclined by background and rearing to favor social justice, fit the definition of southern progressives. The Hills may also have chosen their political turf for practical reasons. Long-established, wealthy Montgomerians already had their political champions. Those who sought to challenge these defenders of the status quo would be forced to look to the more numerous, poorer whites for support.[26]

When affronted, the Hill brothers demonstrated—often dramatically—their unity, temper, and strong sense of honor. Around the turn of the century, an editorial critical of Wiley appeared in the *Montgomery Advertiser*. Dr. L.L. and another brother vented their clan's anger directly upon its hapless author. While one stood guard, the other assaulted the editor with a cane. For years thereafter, the influential *Advertiser* opposed the Hills politically. In turn, the Hills supported the *Alabama Journal* or any other newspaper that rivaled the *Advertiser*. Dr. Hill, a frequent author of letters to the editor, directed most of these epistles to the *Journal*.[27]

On at least three other occasions, Dr. Hill embroiled himself in disputes threatening or actually involving physical violence. Before his marriage, he had volunteered to serve as a second in a duel, but that encounter never took place. After he became a widely known physician, he became enraged because the concerned family of one of his patients had summoned a distinguished New Orleans doctor for consultation without advising Dr. Hill. To the astonishment and dismay of his fellow physician, Dr. Hill challenged that New Orleanian to a pistol duel. Fortunately for all concerned, the visitor refused to fight. Another, more conclusive encounter became famed in Montgomery's annals of violence. Dr. Hill, who always carried a pistol, shot a druggist on a downtown street following a public argument between the two over a piece of Hill property rented by the druggist. But the gunpowder was old, the wound not fatal, and, thanks to the legal talents of William and Wiley, the doctor was acquitted.[28]

In spite of their father's admonition, financial and political differences began to split the Hills in the early 1930s. Dr. L.L. and his brother, Dr. Robert, fell out over disposition of the hospital that they had founded and did not speak to one another for a decade. Only Will maintained friendly relations with all the other brothers. After World War II, the family divided into "yellow dog Democrats" and "black Republicans." Once tightly bound, the twigs fell apart.[29]

Tough. Determined. Able. Conservative in manner and dress. Sufficient unto themselves. "Not social people." Despite their family quarrels, most male Hills exhibited these characteristics.[30] Midway into the twentieth century, a writer for the *Montgomery Advertiser* summed up their reputation thus: "Characteristically the Hill tribesmen are lean men who work hard, achieve their goals through ability and singleness of purpose and live a long time."[31]

But in spite of their accomplishments and comfortable status in life, these upwardly mobile descendants of Methodist preachers were not originally regarded as patricians of the same stripe as those whose Presbyterian or Episcopalian affiliation indicated a longer family history of formal education or affluence. One Montgomery legend has it that a prominent father forbade his daughter to marry a Hill because that young man was a dentist, a profession then considered socially unacceptable. But Hills did marry men and women of means and higher social status. With the land-holdings of their patriarch as a foundation, they built a real-estate empire of city lots and suburban acreage. By the latter half of the century, the *Montgomery Independent*, describing the Hills, observed "not a poor one in the city."[32] As they acquired wealth as well as political and professional success, descendants of the Reverend Luther Leonidas Hill, whether Democrats or Republicans, were to become unquestioned members of Montgomery's jealously guarded elite.

"This was not a totally sort of Catholic family"

Lister Hill's paternal ancestry typified that of numerous white Alabamians whose forebears had moved to these former Indian hunting grounds in hope of bettering their status in life. But his mother's ancestors, although propelled by this same motivation, represented tiny minorities in the over-whelmingly Protestant South. From colonial to modern times, Jews comprised less than 1 percent of the entire southern population. Only three synagogues existed in antebellum Alabama. Even in relatively cosmopolitan Mobile, census takers in 1850 could find only seventy-two Jewish families.[33] The neighboring port of Pensacola, Florida, had no Jewish synagogue until 1881. Catholics, too, were almost lost in a virtual sea of Baptists, Methodists, and lesser numbers of Presbyterians and Episcopalians. Although Mobile had been founded by the French and nurtured by the Spanish who later occupied this old seaport, Catholics became a religious minority in that city after its American occupation. In all of Alabama, only nine Catholic churches, most of them in the Mobile area, existed in 1860.[34]

Lister Hill's great-grandmother, Bela Weil, came to New York from her birthplace, the Jewish community of Steinsfurt in the then Grand Duchy of Baden.[35] Around 1845, she and her husband, Andrew Horsler, a fellow German immigrant whose origins are obscure but who may have been a Catholic, moved to Pensacola, Florida, to join an established German community.[36] In that rowdy seaport, the Horslers operated the New York House, one of two public inns catering to sailors. These establishments carried on a keen rivalry; at one point the Horslers even filed a slander suit against the proprietors of the other hostelry.[37] Eventually Andrew Horsler obtained an order from a justice of the peace, closing the second inn on the grounds that it was a disorderly house; thereafter the Horslers dropped their suit.[38] One or two years later, Andrew Horsler mysteriously disappeared. Some believed that, while carrying a large sum of money on a trip to St. Louis, he had been robbed and murdered; others wondered if he had been killed by rivals in the tavern business.[39]

Bela, who by then called herself Barbet, struggled to educate her four children, kept roomers, and sold ship equipment. Evidently she prospered. Pensacola records indicate that she bought and improved property and owned her own schooner as well as several slaves.[40] But she contracted two unhappy marriages, one to a William Stein whom she divorced two years later on grounds of desertion; the second to a young sailor, James Madison Langley, by whom she had four more children.[41] During their tempestuous marriage, "Mad" Langley, who had become a bar pilot, was involved in several lawsuits relating to the robberies of a storehouse and a British schooner.[42]

When Federal forces burned and looted Pensacola during the Civil War, many residents fled to inland towns. But Barbet, although perhaps a secret Union sympathizer, stuck it out in the beleaguered city, caring for her younger children while smuggling goods through the Federal lines to the

Confederacy.[43] In 1872, she converted to the Catholic faith, perhaps because other members of her family had already made this switch.[44] In 1876, after several attempts, she obtained a divorce on the grounds that Langley had been unfaithful and had beaten her cruelly.[45] Thereafter she managed her varied enterprises alone. When she died in 1900 at the age of eighty-seven, she was known in Pensacola as Bertha Langley and regarded as a well-to-do businesswoman who had made her own way up in the world.[46] Lister Hill, only six at the time of her death, probably never met his strong-willed and resourceful great-grandmother or had any inkling of the vicissitudes she overcame during the bizarre course of her life.[47] But modern-day scholars of nineteenth-century Pensacola are familiar with the story of Barbet (Bela, Bertha) Weil Horsler Stein Langley and consider her a unique personality in the colorful annals of that port city.

Before the Civil War, Barbet had sent her daughter, Amelia Horsler, to Mobile to be educated at the fashionable Catholic Convent of the Visitation. There Amelia renewed her acquaintance with Mark Lyons, a student at a nearby Catholic institution, Spring Hill College. Mark's Jewish father, Michael Lyons, and his mother, Sophia West Lyons, a Catholic, were also German immigrants who had lived in Pensacola before the war and had known Barbet and her family. When his father died at an early age, young Mark assumed responsibility for his widowed mother and his brother.[48] By the outbreak of the war, he had become an experienced merchant. To win Amelia's admiration, he joined the Confederate ranks in 1862 as a lieutenant. Ten months later, because his mother feared that he would be killed in action, he resigned his commission to embark upon the risky but highly profitable business of bringing goods to the South through the Federal blockade.[49]

Mark and Amelia were married at the home of relatives in Greenville, Alabama, in 1863. Despite the austerities of wartime, Mark provided his bride with a new silk wedding gown, a bonnet with a lace veil, a ring specially designed by a Mobile jeweler, a twenty-five-pound wedding cake, and other luxuries of a prewar ceremony. Drafted in the final year of the war, Mark left his bride and their young son in Mobile and served in the batteries around Mobile until Confederate forces surrendered.[50]

After the war ended, the Lyonses lived for more than a decade in the small community of Pollard, Alabama, where Mark acquired pine lands, exported lumber and naval stores, operated a general store, and represented Escambia County for one term in the Alabama legislature. He, too, had become at least a nominal Catholic. To provide a place of worship for his growing family, he financed the building of a small Catholic church in Pollard.[51] When he moved his family to Mobile in 1881, Mark invested in a variety of enterprises, including hardware, dry goods, an ice factory, and a popular patent medicine called Acid Iron Earth, purported to be a remedy for numerous ailments and "the only tonic free from alcohol." Before he died from cancer at the age of forty-seven, Mark Lyons had accumulated considerable wealth and laid the foundation of a future family dynasty in his adopted city.[52]

Amelia Lyons guided her seven children to maturity from the handsome surroundings of a two-story brick house at the corner of St. Anthony and Conception streets, featuring a winding staircase and a large glass atrium decorated with stuffed birds. Upstairs and downstairs maids, gardeners, cook, butler, coachman, and groom attended the family. Building on the foundation provided by their enterprising father, the five Lyons sons prospered in business, commerce, banking, and law. The eldest, Albert Sidney Lyons, became active in politics, briefly serving as Mobile's mayor and a member of both the Alabama House and Senate.[53] Popular, high spirited, and too rich and powerful to suffer stigmatization, the Lyonses became pillars of Mobile's Catholic establishment and quickly gained acceptance in that city's highest social circles.[54]

Shortly after Mark Lyons's death, his daughter, Lilly, traveled up the Alabama River by steamboat to visit friends in Montgomery. There she met Luther Leonidas Hill Jr., eldest son of Luther Leonidas and Laura Hill, who had returned from his studies with Lord Lister in England. Immediately attracted to this petite visitor clad in mourning, Dr. Hill initially assumed that Lilly was a young widow. One can imagine the consternation in the household of the Reverend Luther Leonidas Hill, still an elder in the Methodist Protestant church, and Laura Croom Hill when young Luther announced his intention to marry a Catholic and to rear a future generation of Hills in that faith. Whether he revealed Lilly's Jewish background at that time is a matter for conjecture. Both Amelia Lyons and Laura Hill vigorously opposed the marriage. "I have reason to believe," the Reverend Luther Leonidas Hill wrote shortly after the wedding, "that the union has been baptized in the tears of both of those mothers."[55]

Despite the objections of their families, Lilly Lyons and Dr. L. L. Hill were married in 1888 at her mother's house, amid lavish gifts and numerous toasts, in a ceremony performed by the Catholic bishop of Mobile.[56] Over the course of more than sixty years, their marriage would endure enough trials and tribulations to justify their mothers' apprehensions. Lilly discovered her husband's quick temper and found him slow to forgive her small transgressions. Both found it difficult to get along with their mothers-in-law; Dr. L.L. clashing with the capable, strong-willed Amelia Lyons and Lilly finding it hard to live, during her early married years, under the same roof with the sternly Calvinistic Laura Hill. But her mother-in-law's Puritanism was not the only philosophical cross Lilly had to bear. To be married to a disciple of the noted agnostic, Robert Ingersoll, must have caused considerable anguish for the doctor's devoutly Catholic bride.[57]

Busy on his rounds by early morning, Dr. Hill returned to his home only to eat, study, discipline his children, and sleep. At his hospital, the doctor worked in close partnership with a dictatorial, red-haired spinster, Claribel McCann, who served as his head nurse. Their long association continued until the doctor's death.[58]

Largely excluded from her husband's professional life, Lilly devoted herself almost entirely to rearing her children, managing her household and numerous black servants, dealing with grocer, vegetable vendor, and iceman, and worshiping at the church that forbade her to seek divorce, even had such a heretical idea entered her mind. She must have felt isolated in provincial Montgomery, far from her family in relatively cosmopolitan Mobile. Even after the immigration tide of the late nineteenth century, Catholics made up only 5 percent of Alabama church members by 1906. Lilly's early married years coincided with the Populist movement during which Jews and Catholics became objects of heightened suspicion and hostility. To avoid this cultural pressure, some Montgomery Jews converted to other faiths. Lilly's church, St. Peter's, the only island of Catholicism in an overwhelmingly Protestant city, had a total membership of around two thousand in 1907; in that era Catholics comprised a little over 5 percent of Montgomery's thirty-eight thousand population.[59]

On the subject of religion, Lilly's openly agnostic husband offered her little or no comfort; indeed the doctor delighted in quoting Ingersoll at home. Undoubtedly her Jewish ancestry was known to some of Lilly's Montgomery contemporaries, few secrets being safe within the small and gossipy circle of the Alabama gentry. Her sense of exclusion from the inner circles of Montgomery society and from her husband's professional interests evidently manifested itself in her demeanor. "I saw poor Mrs. Hill at the market," one matron reported to her daughter. "Her eyes looked like drowned violets." As the years passed, Lilly (so her eldest grandson noted) increasingly assumed—perhaps even enjoyed—"the martyr's role."[60]

Although they encountered difficulties in the course of their long marriage, Dr. Hill and his wife shared a pride in their children and a common interest in their business ventures. Lilly had brought to their marriage a sizable inheritance from her father. Discovering his wife's sound instincts in financial matters, the doctor always consulted her before investing her money or his earnings. Profit was not Lilly's sole concern. It was she who persuaded Dr. Hill to install plumbing in the homes of their black tenants, a gesture that met with much disfavor on the part of fellow landlords in Montgomery. But neighbors and friends admired Lilly for the manner in which she bore her lot in life and for a kind nature that somewhat offset her husband's reputation for brusqueness and temper.[61]

Bright auguries attended the birth of their second son. Lister's roots went deep into the pioneer era of his state. His demanding but devoted father stood ready to guide his son through the formative years, serve as a role model, spur him to achievement, and help remove any obstacles to that success. His wide network of kin, embracing the professionally minded Hills and the wealthy Croom and Lyons families, stretched across a large portion of central and southern Alabama. Lister would grow up with the knowledge that he belonged to that powerful coterie of affluent, educated white men accustomed to holding positions of leadership in Alabama.

Yet certain aspects of his ancestry and rearing set Lister Hill apart from most of his fellows. Brought up a Catholic and educated in the early grades at a small school operated by St. Peter's, he must have shared to some degree his mother's experience of being outside the fold of conventional Montgomery.[62] Furthermore, all four Hill children probably knew that it was not only Catholicism that set them apart from the overwhelming mass of Alabamians. They could scarcely have visited their Mobile relatives— as they did—without sensing (so one of their descendants later put it) that "this was not a totally sort of Catholic family—there's something peculiar."[63] To win political office amid the widespread bigotry of the 1920s, Lister would eventually renounce Catholicism. As a matter of practical politics, he would never publicly acknowledge his Jewish ancestry and would attempt to contain awareness of this fact within the borders of comparatively tolerant Mobile.

In maturity, Lister Hill was to depart fundamentally from the predominant outlook of those born to privileged status in Alabama. By education, manner, and lifestyle, he belonged to this inner circle. But unlike the vast majority of his peers, Lister was to ally himself (except in the politically perilous area of civil rights) with forces dedicated to a more democratic society. Initially he may have embarked on this path because of Will and Wiley Hill's political alliances in Montgomery. Certainly he found Franklin Roosevelt an inspiring example of noblesse oblige. Without doubt, an ambitious young politician could build a strong following in the 1930s by championing New Deal policies in economically destitute Alabama.

But another, less tangible factor also helped to shape Lister's character. Frequently, almost compulsively, he credited his father as having been the major force in directing his destiny, alluding to his mother only as a dedicated homemaker.[64] But Lilly Hill did much more for her son than provide a comfortable home.[65] His heritage from his mother set Lister apart from his peers, even his cousins. Because Lilly insisted that he be reared a Catholic and attend a Catholic school, he personally experienced, at a young and impressionable age, the sensation of being in a minority. This awareness surely heightened when he learned of his Jewish ancestry and understood its social and political implications. To turn his back on both aspects of this heritage must have caused Lister to feel some degree of guilt, even if he excused this action by blaming it on the bigotry of his fellow Alabamians. To make amends to his mother and to salve his conscience, he would have to believe that the accomplishments of his political career would justify such a fundamental compromise.

However complex its origins, his philosophy would be viewed by members of Alabama's establishment as apostasy. Like his independent-minded Hill forebears, who had dared to espouse more democracy in the Methodist church, to plead for remaining within the federal union, and to cross religious barriers in matrimony, Lister, too, would be perceived as heretical by others of his class and community.

"Chance favors only a prepared mind"

Stern Luther Leonidas Hill Jr. ruled his household unequivocally. Should his children incur his ire, sons could expect the switch, daughters the scowl.[66] Early each morning they gathered to watch the doctor set forth on his rounds, always careful to place the tail of his horse over the dashboard of the buggy before sounding his ritual exhortation: "Chin up, tail over the dashboard!" This phrase was to hold a lasting fascination for Lister. Years later he often mystified friends and fellow members of Congress by using it as his own unique form of farewell.[67]

Achieve. Achieve. Relentlessly, the doctor pursued this goal for himself and his boys. "Father" molded Lister's character so forcefully that, to the end of Lister's life, he was never free of paternal influence. Luther Lyons Hill, born two years after his brother, proved to be more like the Lyons family, relaxed and jolly, less dutiful than Lister. On occasion, Luther even dared to challenge his father, something his older brother never did. Both the doctor and his wife openly favored Lister and expected him to bear the full brunt of the burden and the challenge to succeed.[68]

His father took it upon himself to indoctrinate Lister in the Victorian virtues of work and self-discipline that he, as a youth, had absorbed from his own stern and demanding father. To impress upon his son the vital importance of determination, the doctor frequently quoted Cardinal Richelieu's injunction, as the Reverend Luther Leonidas Hill had quoted it to him: "In the lexicon of youth, which fate reserves for a bright manhood, there is *no such word* as fail."[69]

Dr. Hill's formula for success stressed three further essentials: an early start, a superior education, and lifelong application. He did not preach to Lister what he himself had not practiced. After graduating from Professor George Thomas's School for Boys, a strict preparatory academy in Montgomery, he had obtained an appointment to the U.S. Military Academy. But to his bitter disappointment, he failed that institution's physical examination because of defective hearing. (Although forced to abandon his dream of an army career, he was always to keep up—and pass along to his sons—a keen interest in military affairs. Many years later, he would succeed in obtaining a West Point appointment for his younger son and take great pride in his rise to the rank of brigadier general.)[70]

Brooding over his failure to qualify for West Point, young Luther Leonidas indulged in one of his rare lapses from self-discipline. Restless amid the quiet surroundings of Howard College, a small Baptist school in the Black Belt, he and several fellow students angered churchgoers by shooting at rabbits on Sunday morning. Expelled from Howard, the young man sought to appease his father by promising to dedicate himself to his studies if sent to medical school in New York City. To save his son the disgrace of standing trial for "breaking the peace," the Reverend Luther Leonidas Hill agreed.[71]

It was during his stay in worldly New York that this descendant of Alabama Methodist preachers came under Robert Ingersoll's spell. By chance, he heard Ingersoll deliver one of his flamboyant exhortations against religious orthodoxy. "Colonel Bob's" eloquent attacks upon the ideas of eternal damnation, hope of a future existence, and other biblical concepts made a deep and lifelong impression on the medical student. Eventually he left the Methodist Protestant church where his ancestors had preached hellfire and damnation. He memorized long passages from Ingersoll's lectures, frequently quoted them to his children, and prized a picture of the "great agnostic."[72] Daring to profess such beliefs in conventionally religious Alabama, the doctor informed a fellow physician: "I am thoroughly in accord with Mr. Ingersoll when he said John Calvin died the year Shakespeare was born and it was the greatest swap for the world ever recorded."[73]

At nineteen, Luther Leonidas Hill Jr., after only one year of study, received his M.D. degree from the medical department of the University of New York. On a dare from a senior, he had taken—and passed—the final examinations for the normal, three-year program in medicine. But when the young graduate came home, his skeptical father, demanding a practical demonstration of the medical skills that his son had so quickly acquired, ordered him to remove the cataracts from an old black man who lived at Rosemary plantation. While a student, Luther had witnessed a cataract operation but never performed one. If the operation failed, his father threatened not to finance further medical education. After ordering the necessary instruments and studying several books on eye operations, Luther—his father looking on—removed a cataract from one of his patient's eyes. Beginner's luck—or untutored skill—favored Luther. The operation proved a success. He would be allowed to continue his medical studies.[74]

At Jefferson Medical College in Philadelphia, young Dr. Hill studied under Dr. Samuel Gross, the leading American surgeon of that day, stood first in his class, and earned a second M.D. degree. Thereafter he completed a course in eye, ear, nose, and throat at New York Polyclinic Medical School, the first postgraduate medical school in the United States. His preceptor, Dr. John Allan Wyeth, was a native Alabamian whom Dr. Hill held in high esteem despite the fact that the older man had served as physician for the Union Army at Appomattox.[75]

Equipped with the best training offered in America, Dr. Hill persuaded his father to send him to London to study at King's College Hospital under the world-renowned surgeon, Sir Joseph Lister. In that primitive era of surgery, doctors who performed abdominal operations, forbidden by law in England until 1877, were known to scornful fellow physicians as "belly rippers." Although Joseph Lister was England's most skilled surgeon, he refused to perform such operations. The first abdominal operation that Luther Hill ever saw was one that he himself later performed in Montgomery. However, Sir Joseph, with his developments of antiseptic methods, absorbable threading, and the drainage tube, was changing surgery, as Dr. Hill later wrote, "from a near-massacre to a healing art."[76] Long before Lister's pioneering methods of creating sterile conditions in operating rooms had become generally accepted, Luther Hill was to adopt these techniques in his Montgomery hospital. Sir Joseph remained the doctor's lifelong hero. "There was but one Joseph Lister," he wrote in his memoirs. "There will never be another."[77]

Armed with such intensive preparation, Dr. Hill could have practiced in a larger southern city or alongside the most skillful physicians of the East. Instead he elected, at the age of twenty-two, to return to his hometown. Montgomery in the 1880s had only two primitive hospitals, one for blacks and the other for whites; little surgical equipment, no adequately equipped laboratory, and no trained nurses. The new doctor had to perform home operations after ordering relatives of the patient to move the kitchen table to a more suitable room, boil instruments on the stove, and place sheets over the windows to frustrate the curious. His insistence on the "Lister principle" of cleanliness caused a small stir in Montgomery's medical circles where it was not unheard of for a surgeon to spit on his knife and strop it on the sole of his shoe before operating.[78]

Finding such conditions intolerable, Dr. Hill and his younger brother, Robert, established their own hospital, named in honor of their mother. When it opened in 1898, the Laura Croom Hill Hospital had only a few beds, two doctors, two nurses, and a superintendent. It was to grow to fifty beds, staffed by twenty-two nurses. The hospital proved a magnet for rural Alabamians as well as Montgomerians. As a boy, Lister watched patients arrive "more dead than alive" after long, bumpy rides by wagon, buggy, or day coach to this marvelous new facility.[79]

In this hospital, Dr. L. L. Hill exhibited his surgical skills, learned in the East and abroad, for the benefit of younger physicians. He taught twenty-one doctors, including his brother. As his students watched, Dr. Hill would give the name of the operation that he was about to perform, identify the person who had first performed it, specify the date, and, while operating, instruct them in the names and locations of muscles and vessels.[80] On one occasion, he took young Lister to watch him remove a patient's cancerous nose, using ether as an anesthetic. Observing this "ghastly sight," Lister fled the operating room, realizing to his intense shame that he could never follow in his father's footsteps.[81]

Whether this led Lister to have feelings of guilt or unworthiness in adulthood would later become a topic of much speculation. Many who noted the senator's frequent references to his father, coupled with his choice of health legislation as the major emphasis of his career, wondered if, despite his national stature, Lister Hill was still attempting to make amends for the fact that he had not become a noted physician. But although this may have been one factor, Senator Hill's choice evolved out of a much more complex set of circumstances.[82]

Even if he were not destined to be a doctor, young Lister would absorb other lessons from his father's example. He would be aware that Dr. Hill, after making evening rounds, always retired to his library to read literary classics, biographies, history, news of scientific developments in the *British Medical Journal*, the London *Lancet*, or German publications translated by the German-born widow of a fellow physician. His library dominated the commodious, gray stucco house with marble veranda that Dr. Hill had built in 1903 at 422 South Perry Street. In this room, the doctor spent many hours in a chair suited to his 250-pound girth, surrounded by the more than five thousand books and bound medical journals that comprised one of Alabama's largest private collections of that day. Most visitors to this sanctuary found themselves subjected to a soliloquy. Increasingly deaf, Dr. Hill depended upon his portophone, a black box containing an earphone. But the doctor considered this device a nuisance and deemed it more interesting to talk than to hear.[83]

At his massive desk, surrounded by three revolving bookcases and a heavy table piled with current magazines and newspapers, Dr. Hill corresponded with widely known physicians like Joseph Lister, William and Charles Mayo, William Osler, and William Gorgas. Men of superior attainments, it became clear to Lister, did not end their working days at sundown or their education at the conclusion of formal training. Lister also observed that his father had "little time for play" and none whatever to waste on athletics. The doctor, his son realized, "was trying to keep up, trying to keep ahead of the game all the time." Why? Dr. Hill explained this habit by quoting another favorite axiom, Louis Pasteur's advice that "chance favors *only* a prepared mind." Recognizing Dr. Hill's unusual dedication, fellow physicians had elected him president of the Montgomery Medical and Surgical Society in 1887 and head of the Alabama State Medical Association in 1897. Other honors were to follow his most famous surgical achievement.[84]

Through his self-imposed studies, Dr. Hill had taken a special interest in the human heart. He knew that even great surgeons doubted that it would be possible to repair through surgery a wound of the heart. But he had also read that several Italian surgeons had successfully sutured the heart of a dog and, in 1896, of a human. Before dawn one September morning in 1902, Dr. L. L. Hill, forty years of age and in the prime of his career, would get an opportunity to prove to his satisfaction (and probably to his son, Lister) the truth of Pasteur's maxim.[85]

The summons that was to make American medical history came from two fellow physicians who realized that this case was beyond their capabilities. In a rude farm cabin, several miles from Montgomery, Henry Myrick, a thirteen-year-old black stabbed in the heart with an ice pick, lay in critical condition. It was rare that one of Montgomery's physicians should operate upon a black person in a humble cabin. Dr. Hill gave his services liberally to the poor of both races and was one of the few white doctors to practice in Hale's Infirmary, the hospital reserved for blacks. Four doctors assisted him in this historic operation, performed by the light of a kerosene lamp and with chloroform as an anesthetic. The pick had penetrated the left ventricle of Henry Myrick's heart, leaving a wound three-eighths of an inch deep. Dr. Robert Hill thrust his hand through the surgical opening, lifted the heart, massaged it to keep the blood pumping, and held it steady. His brother then passed catgut suture through the wound. Within fifteen days, the patient was permitted to sit up. Eventually Henry Myrick recovered fully.[86]

Luther Leonidas Hill Jr., calling upon the skills learned through formal studies, practice, and self-education, had performed the first successful open-heart surgery, requiring repair of a penetration of the cavity, in United States medical annals. In its day, this feat was as spectacular as the first heart transplant would be more than a half century later.[87] His performance, which he described in a medical journal, brought the heretofore obscure Montgomery surgeon to the attention of fellow physicians nationally and worldwide, vastly broadening his contacts and increasing his evening burden of correspondence. Lister Hill, even after he had become a powerful member of the United States Senate and the nation's leading champion of health legislation, still paid frequent and almost compulsive tribute to his father's achievement.

"Work Wins"

If not medicine, what other career would be suitable? After his son's near disgrace in the operating theater, the doctor must have pondered this question. As Lister recalled many years later: "In that day . . . a young fellow thought in terms of being in a profession . . . that is, if he had a Dad like my father. [A profession] was to serve. [A business] was to make money. A man in a profession had a standing in the community which a man in business didn't have."[88]

In marrying a Catholic, Dr. Hill had unintentionally assured that Lister could never follow in the Hill tradition of Methodist ministry. Even had this not been the case, it was highly unlikely that a disciple of Robert Ingersoll would rear his son to serve an organized church. Evidently a military career did not hold the appeal for Lister that it at first did for his brother, Luther. Law, then, must have seemed an obvious option. In Alabama it was almost second nature for men versed in law to seek political office. Obstacles lay in this path but Dr. Hill had long been conditioned against admitting the possibility of failure. For his son to become governor of Alabama would not satisfy the doctor; Lister must seek *national* stature. No lesser office than that of United States senator was to be Lister's goal; father and son must move quickly and purposefully to lay the groundwork.

Relieved that he was to witness no further operations and always a pliable son, Lister embraced his father's plan enthusiastically. Oratory, that essential art of the southern politician, came naturally to him, perhaps from his pulpit ancestors. At the age of seven, he had memorized William Jennings Bryan's famous peroration in the "Cross of Gold" speech and become familiar with the cadences of other great orators like Daniel Webster, John C. Calhoun, and Henry Grady. In boyhood daydreams, he envisioned himself not only going to Congress but even serving as orator at Montgomery's most emotional occasion, the annual observance of Confederate Memorial Day in Oakwood Cemetery. By the time he was fifteen, the Senate goal had become so firmly fixed in Lister's mind that he believed he had originated it himself.[89]

But first a proper schooling. Having yielded to his wife's insistence that her children's education begin at St. Peter's, Dr. Hill insisted that his boys thereafter follow a path similar to his own. To prepare sons of privileged Alabama families for higher education, Professor John Metcalf Starke, a graduate of the University of Virginia, presided over Starke University

School with the same exactitude that had deeply impressed Lister's father in his school days at Professor Thomas's academy.

Starke boys wore military uniforms and caps and, if caught in mischievous or dilatory behavior, found that their headmaster could wield with authority the mulberry switches he kept under his desk. Some students, like gentle Clifford Durr, were repelled by Professor Starke's whippings and Spartan approach to education. But Lister, already conditioned to obey, never suffered one of Professor Starke's thrashings, knowing that, if so, he would be thrashed a second time when he arrived home. He was not one to sneak out for a forbidden smoke or otherwise to flaunt the rules, as had jaunty Catesby ap R Jones of Selma, who made an unforgettable impression upon his classmates when he arrived at Starke wearing a derby.[90]

After opening each school day with prayer, Professor Starke hammered into his boys the same values that Lister's father stressed at home: loyalty, truthfulness, hard work and, most of all, the joys of accomplishment. Those who failed to master the week's lessons went to Saturday school; anyone unfortunate enough to fail on Saturday suffered a thrashing. Like Dr. Hill, Professor Starke believed in the power of adages to impress young minds. On a tin plate above the blackboard in the "Big Room" was inscribed a comforting message: "For when the Great Scorer comes, he marks not whether you won or lost but how you played the game." But Starke boys knew that their headmaster, in his heart, did not endorse this concept. Professor Starke's most urgent message to his students, repeated again and again, was briefer and more positive: "Work *Wins!*"[91]

Mental agility, as exhibited by those fortunate pupils who could solve arithmetic problems in their heads quickly and correctly, was highly prized at Starke. So was victory in debates and oratorical contests wherein a boy might learn not only to vanquish platform shyness but to exhibit his knowledge of government and great leaders of the past, deliver a spirited rendition of Webster's speech on the union, or champion an unpopular cause like woman's suffrage. Lister wasted little time on sports, following his father's example and in compliance with another of Professor Starke's axioms: "Work first, athletics second."[92]

Four times a day, always coming home for midday dinner, Lister walked to and from Starke School, located on a plot of land almost in the shadow of Alabama's storied capitol. Although Montgomery's founders had named these streets Perry, Hull, Decatur, Lawrence, and McDonough [Macdonough], for the great naval heroes of the War of 1812, this conflict had long since paled by comparison with what Montgomerians always spoke of as "*the* war." After all, *the* war had actually come to Montgomery. White residents took fierce pride in Montgomery's brief tenure as the Confederacy's first capital. As if these things had happened yesterday, they passed from generation to generation family recollections of great moments in the life of the Confederacy and of their plight during the Union occupation of Montgomery. The Reverend Luther Leonidas Hill had been one of the tremendous throng to watch Jefferson Davis take his oath as president of the Confederacy, a crowd so huge that it obscured the hill on which Alabama's capitol stood. Dr. Hill, although only three years old at the time, claimed to remember the day in April 1865 when the first Yankees entered his hometown. Proudly he recalled that he had helped to hide part of his family's gold by wearing it in the hem of his clothing.[93]

As a boy, Lister often heard his father recall the era of Reconstruction when rural blacks had poured into Montgomery to be near the comforting presence of a strong federal garrison and the state headquarters of the Freedmen's Bureau. Dr. Hill had impressed upon his children the indignation that he and fellow white Southerners had felt upon being treated "like citizens of a conquered nation" at a time when black policemen and aldermen shared in Montgomery's governance and black legislators occupied seats in the former Confederate capitol.[94]

Just as loyalty to the Lost Cause was a sine qua non, the great majority of white Montgomerians also accepted without question the concept of blacks as members of a lower caste, permanently confined to the status of servants following their forcible release from slavery. Like many members of the southern gentry, the Hills treated their slaves and later their servants with a mixture of haughtiness and intimacy, oppression and paternalism. William Hill, the first member of his family to migrate to Alabama, had served on a church committee charged with considering the matter of "supplying the gospel to the slaves," a mission the Methodist Protestant church eventually undertook. When William's great-grandson, Lister, became a member of the House of Representatives, he received a letter from a Birmingham waiter hinting at other aspects of the complex relationship between whites and blacks on the Hill plantations (as on many another). The writer, Homer Hill, identified himself as the mulatto son of a faithful body servant of Fabius Hill, one of William's sons. Homer and his brothers and sisters, he told the congressman, still owned the farm land given to their father by Fabius "as payment for long years of service."[95]

William's oldest son, the Reverend Luther Leonidas Hill, having vigorously opposed secession, blamed that fateful decision for his declining fortunes after the Civil War. Frequently he lamented: "If it had not been for that damned William L. Yancey, I'd still have my niggers." To exhort his sons to achieve, the old patriarch often reminded them: "I'd rather see a shiftless nigger than a lazy white boy." In later years, the minister concluded that members of the black race, being "naturally non-progressive," lacked the native ability to rise above the status of manual laborers.[96]

Lister's father, in his attitude toward blacks, mixed the typical paternalism of a privileged, white Southerner with the broader outlook of a physician educated far beyond the provincial bounds of Montgomery. After the automobile age came to Montgomery, the doctor always hired a black chauffeur to drive him on his rounds. When his favorite driver was charged with breaking into the home of a white woman, Dr. Hill engaged his brothers, Will and Wiley, to defend the chauffeur. But even those talented legal pleaders could not save the black man from a one-year jail sentence. His successor disappointed the doctor, who referred to this chauffeur as "D.F." for, he loudly whispered, "damn fool." When the new driver announced that he planned to quit, his angry employer, shaking his walking stick, responded: "Goddamn you, you'll quit when I tell you you can!"[97]

When he recalled Reconstruction, the doctor used even harsher language: "I saw the best citizens in this town forced by Republican bayonets into the voting lines with ignorant, odoriferous negroes and jostled, derided and insulted by their former slaves." But Dr. Hill also served on the then all-white Board of Trustees during Booker T. Washington's term as president of Tuskegee Institute. When these men sat down to lunch at the president's home, the pragmatic Washington tactfully excused himself. Recounting this experience to his family, Dr. Hill said that it was wrong that a man of such stature did not feel that he could eat with whites in his own home. But to most of the doctor's peers in Montgomery, such a concession in racial mores would have been unthinkable.[98]

In his medical practice, the doctor ministered to both races. "Throw a towel over the head," he often said, "and all bodies are the same."[99] Patients of either race, if unable to pay cash, gave the doctor what they could. During hard times and holiday seasons, the Hills' backyard swarmed with chickens and turkeys. Lacking even such a bird as this, a patient might appear with a squirrel or opossum. As a boy, Lister deemed it "quite a feast" when the cook prepared 'possum with sweet potatoes.[100]

Growing up in Montgomery, Lister encountered blacks only as faithful servants. The idea that his hometown would become the cradle of a nationwide civil rights revolution and that the issue of black rights would alter and limit his political career—had the boy ever imagined such eventualities—would have seemed inconceivable.

Lister spent five formative years under Professor Starke's command. In 1911, adorned with medals in oratory and scholarship, he was graduated as senior cadet captain. If he ever chafed under this regimen, he had forgotten this in later years when he importuned fellow alumni to support Starke School's fund-raising efforts, always gratefully recalling that Professor Starke had taught him to accept discipline and to exercise it upon himself.[101]

"Lister Hill is our coming politician"

Dr. Hill chose the University of Alabama as his son's next proving ground. As a ritual part of their progression to maturity, young Alabamians converged on the Tuscaloosa campus in pursuit of knowledge, conviviality, and the opposite sex. Here they acquired a wide range of acquaintance among offspring of middle- and upper-income white Alabamians, thereby, like their parents and grandparents, attaining the sense of belonging to an extended family whose members shared a near unanimity of outlook and enjoyed a similar lifestyle.

The state university also served as a practice field for future Alabama political leaders. Before Lister Hill arrived on campus, future Senator and Supreme Court Justice Hugo Black had whisked through its two-year law school without sparing time for student politics or formal education in the liberal arts. During World War I, John Sparkman, offspring of sharecropper parents, was to stoke university furnaces in order to finance his studies and prepare for a political career that climaxed in 1952 with his nomination as Adlai Stevenson's running mate. In the late 1930s, George C. Wallace, a cocky and ambitious youngster from southeastern Alabama, was to form a close campus friendship here with Frank M. Johnson Jr. from Alabama's hill country. Amid the civil rights turmoil of the 1960s, Governor Wallace and Judge Johnson would become Alabama's chief antagonists and their friendship would perish in mutual acrimony.

What a sense of freedom Lister Hill, at seventeen, must have felt upon emerging from under the constant scrutiny of his father and Professor Starke into the company of seven hundred of his peers. As an almost indispensable prelude to the pursuit of higher education on this campus, he set out to choose a suitable fraternity. Like many another Starke graduate, Lister affiliated with one of the more exclusive Greek groups, Delta Kappa Epsilon. He and other "Dekes" lived in a boardinghouse but, on special occasions, took meals at a famous Tuscaloosa hostelry, the McLester Hotel, where the mulatto Homer Hill (although he did not at that time know Lister Hill's identity) waited upon young, white males sufficiently affluent to afford this luxury.[102] In his freshman year, Lister roomed with a fellow "Deke," Ed Leigh McMillan of Brewton, to whom, on nights when fraternity brothers lay awake contemplating the future, he confided his political ambitions.[103]

On campus Lister encountered other strong male mentors—George H. Denny, the university's autocratic president; the Law School dean Albert J. Farrah, who admonished each student to "live like a hermit and work like a horse," and Thomas Chalmers McCorvey, who taught southern history to several generations of young Alabamians except on those sunny afternoons when he donned his colonel's uniform to command the university corps of cadets. Born in 1851, Professor McCorvey nurtured all the bitterness bequeathed to him by his defeated Confederate forebears, and had vivid memories of Reconstruction when he had been proud to affiliate with the Knights of the White Camellia, a milder version of the Ku Klux Klan.[104]

Professor McCorvey not only reinforced in the minds of his students the ignominy of Reconstruction but he insisted that northern oppression had not ended when Federal troops had been withdrawn from the South. His lectures convinced Lister that the Republican party had exploited his region economically, holding its people down to serve as "hewers of wood and drawers of water" for the industrial North. But the Democratic party, Professor McCorvey believed, represented the "masses" in their never-ending struggle against "predatory wealth." When he got to Congress, Lister resolved, he would right the ancient wrongs inflicted on his region by Republicans, using the same power that had made possible the Federal garrisons and the Freedmen's Bureau.[105]

For a young man with his sights set upon the United States Senate, the heady atmosphere of the state university offered experiences of a more practical nature than lessons from Professor McCorvey. Here one might polish his oratorical skills, make valuable contacts with future supporters from across the state, and master the essential art of remembering names. Before he left the university, Lister could call every one of his fellow students by first name. When he entered the wider arena of politics, he was to store in his prodigious memory thousands of names.

During Lister's undergraduate years, politically minded students embroiled themselves in two issues then agitating the emotions of their
elders—prohibition and woman's suffrage. Before the dry cause had become popular, crowds of curious citizens, young Lister among them,
had gathered along Dexter Avenue to gape at ardent members of the
Women's Christian Temperance Union, their white ribbons fluttering as
they marched toward the capitol, an occasional courageous male in their
ranks.[106] By the second decade of the twentieth century, however, the
"prohi" tide had risen dramatically and such scenes were common. Numerous men, led by former Governor B. B. Comer and Representative Richmond Pearson Hobson, an authentic hero of the Spanish-American War,
had come to appreciate the political potential of this crusade. Lister Hill,
too, boarded the prohibition bandwagon, joining the campus "Comer
Club" and postponing until later in life his adoption of Dr. Hill's ritual of a
few sips of bourbon before retiring to help ensure a good night's rest.[107]
Drawing on all the tricks learned in Professor Starke's competitions, Lister
delivered a rousing oration at a rally of Tuscaloosa prohibitionists. For his
first public address, a young orator could not wish for a more responsive
audience unless he were commemorating Confederate Memorial Day.

To Governor Comer, Congressman Hobson, and Lister Hill, it seemed
appropriate that the federal government should be given the power to
prohibit the manufacture, sale, or transportation of alcohol. For that same
government to order that no female be denied the ballot because of her sex
was another matter altogether. This prospect freshened memories of the
hated Reconstruction; loyal Southerners must guard against renewed federal interference at the ballot box lest any breach in this barrier admit not
only white women but Alabama's almost totally disfranchised blacks.[108]

But what harm could come from allowing women students to vote in
campus elections, especially if they cast their ballots to help form a new
student government association and to elect Lister Hill as its first president? As business manager of the student newspaper, the *Crimson-White*,
Lister occupied an influential position from which to champion the cause
of woman's suffrage on campus. Grateful women students rewarded him
with enough votes to ensure his election in 1914 as first president of
the student government association. Vigilant President Denny, noting the
emergence of this adroit young leader on his campus, predicted, "Lister
Hill is our coming politician," his voice striking its familiar high note on
the word "Hill."[109]

Compared with his first political victory, graduation in May 1914 must have seemed almost anticlimactic. Wasting no time before addressing the next task, Lister spent ten weeks of the ensuing summer at the University of Michigan Law School to attain a head start over fellow law students back home. Upon his return to Tuscaloosa, he earned his law degree in nine months, the youngest graduate in the class of 1915. In that era, those who held degrees from the University School of Law were admitted automatically to the Alabama Bar.[110]

But not so fast. Young men in the Hill family must prove that they could perform at the level of capable students in more prestigious universities outside of the South. For this test, Dr. Hill and Lister chose Columbia University Law School whose dean, Harlan F. Stone, was to become chief justice of the United States. Stone proved to be a flexible dean. Although Columbia offered a three-year law program, he permitted the ambitious young Alabamian to complete these requirements in only one year and six weeks. In 1916, Lister earned his second law degree, again graduating as the youngest member of his class.[111]

In October 1916, twenty-two years of age and having emulated as nearly as possible his father's educational example, Lister Hill returned to the familiar surroundings of Montgomery, a town of around forty thousand, its populace almost evenly divided between whites and blacks. Bales of cotton, piled high in Court Square each fall, symbolized the historic dominance of that crop and Montgomery's almost exclusively agricultural economy. Like Dr. Hill, Lister would make his name nationally known from this base, still as remote from the power centers of the East as when it had been chosen as the Confederacy's first capital.

The new young lawyer entered practice with Bernard Gerson, a young Jewish attorney who had been a fellow student at Starke School and Columbia. His sojourns in Michigan and cosmopolitan New York City had not changed Lister's basically southern values or diluted his respect for the homely virtues and exacting standards instilled in him by Dr. Hill, Professor Starke, and Dean Farrah.[112] Work *did* win. Failure was, indeed, unthinkable. In due course, chance would again favor a prepared mind.

Hill's father, Dr. Luther Leonidas Hill

Hill's mother, Lilly Lyons Hill

Hill children with their nurse. Left to right: *Lister (age six),
Lillian, Luther Lyons, and Amelie.*

Young Lister in costume

As a senior cadet at Starke University School

As a student at the University of Alabama in Tuscaloosa

In World War I

The First Campaign

1 9 2 3

"I stand again in the temple of my fathers"

At their daily get-togethers in the fall of 1916, the six Hill brothers had much to discuss. Would their country soon be embroiled in a European war? Could the Hills retain control of Montgomery's City Hall, wrested from their rivals, the Gunters, only one year earlier? What political toehold could they find for young Lister, elder son of the oldest brother?

Political rivalry between the Hills and the Gunters, begun early in the century, was to continue for two decades. William A. Gunter Jr., grandson of a wealthy cotton grower so embittered by the Confederacy's defeat that he exiled himself permanently to Brazil, led the Gunters, having served as Montgomery's mayor from 1910 to 1915. The second oldest Hill brother, William Wallace, whose father had accepted the Civil War's verdict quickly and realistically, led his family's political faction. "Mr. Will" Hill, most widely acquainted member of the Hill clan, mixed easily with his fellow Alabamians and told a joke with flair.[1]

In addition to their attitudes toward military defeat, the two families had further distinguishable characteristics. The Gunters, being Episcopalians, did not equate liquor with sin and displayed no enthusiasm for legal prohibition. The Hills, sons and grandsons of Methodist pastors, were associated, at least publicly, with the zealous drys. The Gunters drew their support primarily from city dwellers. The Hills dominated the rural beats that surrounded Montgomery. The influential *Montgomery Advertiser*, its fledgling editorial writer Grover C. Hall, city employees whom Mayor Gunter could fire at will, and a majority of the city's old families of wealth supported the Gunters. The Hills drew their political strength from middle- and working-class whites plus a few comfortably well-to-do citizens inclined to favor such typical progressive measures as regulations on child labor and day nurseries for children too young to work alongside their mothers in the West End textile mills.[2]

Neither family concerned itself with Montgomery's miniscule black vote. Shortly after blacks had been disfranchised through the literacy, poll tax, and other intricate provisions of the new state constitution of 1901, one black group had been bold enough to mount a court challenge. Representing the state, the law firm of William A. Gunter and William A. Gunter Jr. had successfully fended off this legal strategem. Nonetheless, the handful of black voters in Montgomery who had managed to retain the franchise, by virtue of their education and outward demeanor, evidently made the pragmatic decision to cast their lot with the well-to-do paternalists associated with the Gunters rather than expose themselves to the more overt hostility of the working-class element of the Hill machine.[3]

Through a deft flanking attack in 1915, the Hills caught their rivals napping and ousted Gunter from the mayor's seat. William Wallace Hill, elected to the Alabama Senate from Montgomery County without opposition from the Gunters, persuaded fellow legislators to pass a bill changing Montgomery's form of government from mayor-council to a commission and barring the incumbent mayor from becoming a candidate for the new commission. He also removed two potent vote-getting machines—the city's fire and police departments—from commission control and placed them, instead, under a Board of Public Safety elected by the Alabama Senate. Having vanquished their rivals, at least temporarily, the Hills prepared to dominate City Hall.[4]

What political plum, then, would best exhibit the talents of a young member of their tribe? In October 1916, the Hill-dominated city commission appointed Lister to the Montgomery City Board of Education. Six months later, his five fellow members elected their twenty-two-year-old colleague to head the board, due primarily to the fact that he was Dr. Hill's son. *Leslie's Weekly*, a national magazine, published a photograph of J. Lister Hill, describing him as the youngest president of a city education board in the country.[5]

Lest Montgomery parents doubt a young bachelor's commitment to their children's education, Hill resolved to launch a long-overdue school construction program. Noting the low salaries of Montgomery's teachers and its poorly equipped schools, the new Education Board president made a mental note that federal aid would be Montgomery's only hope of improving this situation. Addressing a group of black teachers, he advised "my colored friends" to follow the cautious, accommodating, and dedicated example of Booker T. Washington.[6]

Ambitious plans had to be postponed, however, when the United States entered World War I. Montgomery, always susceptible to martial adventures, flamed with war fervor. Hilary A. Herbert, a native Alabamian who had served as Cleveland's secretary of the navy, evoked patriotic fervor at a large rally held in the Grand Theatre. But a younger and more vigorous orator stole Herbert's show. Recalling his own speech on this occasion, Hill said many years later: "I really fought the war at that rally."[7]

Hundreds of Montgomery citizens enlisted in the Fourth Alabama Regiment, later to be famed as the Rainbow Division of the 167th Infantry. Many Alabamians were to die or suffer injury when the Rainbow Division found itself in the thick of battle at Château-Thierry and Saint-Mihiel. Attempting to enlist, Lister found to his dismay that he was too thin to meet Army standards. Dr. Hill appealed to his friend and fellow Alabamian, General William C. Gorgas, surgeon general of the United States Army. This minor barrier was quickly overlooked.[8]

In August 1917, Hill became a private in the Seventeenth U.S. Infantry. Although he was never to face hostile gunfire, he served eighteen months and rose to the rank of first lieutenant. Assigned as defense counsel for soldiers facing court martial, he proved so successful that the Army transferred him to other duties. By the time he and his comrades reached France, World War I was virtually over. Two wartime memories remained with Hill throughout his long life: the sight of caskets containing the bodies of flu victims piled high at Fort Meade, Maryland, and his shock at the discovery that French officers, assigned to train Americans, used cologne rather than soap and water to disguise their bodily aromas.[9]

Military experience, even though brief and uneventful, afforded definite advantages. In service, Hill met a young Texan, Tom Connally. Their wartime friendship would be a bond between the two when they became colleagues in the House of Representatives and, during another world war, on the important Senate Foreign Relations Committee. Of more immediate use, Hill had acquired the valuable political credential of being a war veteran.[10]

Returning to Montgomery, Hill resumed legal practice, this time with a more mature attorney, Joseph Lee Holloway, a Methodist and president of the Rotary Club. Hill, too, joined Rotary, as well as the American Legion, and reclaimed the school board presidency. For two months during the spring of 1920, a storm of controversy shook the public schools of Montgomery County, aroused the ire of Governor Thomas E. Kilby, and made the name of J. Lister Hill known in every hamlet reached by the *Montgomery Advertiser*. Those readers dissatisfied with the *Advertiser*'s circumspect accounts obtained spicier details of this drama, including hints of interracial sex, via Montgomery's active and less restrained rumor mill.

Leading figures in this controversy were William F. Feagin, superintendent of Montgomery County's public schools; Mary Burke, a teacher and the only woman member of the Montgomery City Board of Education, and Hill. Feagin, a former state superintendent of education, enjoyed high political connections and the reputation of a competent administrator. However, nineteen women teachers, led by Mary Burke, appeared before the county board to bring charges of moral unfitness against their superintendent. The all-male board, contending that Feagin had the right to be presented with the names of his accusers and specific, written charges, declined to investigate until these conditions had been met. The teachers, fearing retribution from their superintendent and initially reluctant to have their names made public, refused to comply. A stalemate ensued. Meantime a number of other female schoolteachers in the county came to their superintendent's defense.[11]

With the county board standing firm in its position, the accusers found in Lister Hill, who had previously differed with Feagin over matters of school administration, a sympathetic and activist ally. Under his leadership, they announced that they would divulge their charges at a mass meeting in the courthouse. Nineteen prominent Montgomery men, supporting the county board's position, publicly protested such an unorthodox procedure. Nonetheless, crowds overflowed the courthouse to hear the charges against Feagin. The superintendent, although invited, did not appear.[12]

Acting as spokesman for the women and several of their male supporters, Hill read the names and affidavits of eight white women teachers who attested that the superintendent had made sexual advances to them, and of two men who alleged that Feagin had had sexual relations with black women teachers. Then, in a speech freighted with emotional allusions to the "most precious gift of God to man—Southern womanhood" and references to Feagin's "negro concubine" and "negro wench," Hill appealed to the crowd to help "drive this vulture William F. Feagin from the confines of our people." Applause filled the courtroom.[13]

Two days later Feagin resigned, after professing innocence of any "serious charge" against his character, protesting that he had been denied a fair trial, and contending that he had been "unrelentingly pursued" by political foes. His complaints engendered considerable support. The county board, although accepting Feagin's resignation, issued a formal statement protesting "the methods employed," reiterating its position that Feagin "was at least entitled to no less consideration than would be given to the humblest criminal," and alluding to the motives of the superintendent's critics as "good, bad, selfish, and political." Governor Kilby, labeling the mass meeting "a character lynching bee," stung the Hill faction to publish a pamphlet containing a stenographic account of that occasion. The charges against him ended Feagin's hopes of becoming president of Alabama Polytechnic Institute at Auburn; instead his friend Kilby named him head of the State Convict Department. (Feagin would reemerge on the Alabama scene in the 1930s as an aide to Governors B. M. Miller and Bibb Graves, next as an ally of the anti-New Deal interests, then in 1944 as an advocate of Lister Hill.)[14]

Eventually this brouhaha subsided, becoming part of the immense storehouse of Montgomery legend. Mixed motives had caused Hill to take a leading part in this controversy; his past differences with Feagin, a desire for public attention, and a commitment to protect "Southern womanhood." But he chose not to remind voters of the Feagin case during his first political campaign three years later. Perhaps, upon reflection, he thought it best not to recall the manner in which this matter had been brought to a head. Or perhaps he believed that his role as champion of "the most sacred heritage of our noble women" had already become fixed in the memory of many teachers and other working women who found themselves entitled to vote in 1920.

But the champion of female virtue in the school board case had opposed Alabama's ratification of the Nineteenth Amendment, choosing to side with those women who successfully fought such action by their state. He did not oppose woman's suffrage, Hill told two hundred supporters of the Montgomery Anti-Ratification Association in 1919, but he believed that *federal* action in behalf of their voting rights would imperil an even more important principle—states' rights. "The principle of states' rights," he told this friendly audience, "was the principle for which our fathers fought and bled and died. Shall we be false to them? God of our fathers be with us yet—lest we forget—lest we forget." As customary in southern politics, Lister used this emotional appeal to dignify his and his listeners' real objection: federal action might open the polls not only to white women but to blacks as well. He pointedly reminded two hundred opponents of ratification that Carrie Chapman Catt, national leader of the suffragists, had stated publicly: "The fight for woman suffrage is no white woman's fight; it is every woman's fight." In raising the time-honored cry of states' rights to cloak objection to a racial issue, Hill set forth upon a well-worn path that he and his political adversaries would continue to follow.[15]

At some point in his preparation for the future, Hill made an essential concession to political reality. Publicly affirming his belief in Protestantism, he announced to members of the Court Street Methodist Church: "I stand again in the temple of my fathers."[16] Some family members believe that both Lister and his brother forsook Catholicism while students at the University of Alabama or even earlier. Others think that Lister made this decision just prior to being elected president of the school board in 1917. Since it is highly unlikely that Montgomery citizens would have permitted a known Catholic to direct the affairs of their public schools, the latter date would appear to have been timely. However, during Hill's first campaign for Congress, opponents whispered that he had announced his conversion to Methodism as late as 1921.[17]

Dr. Hill's open agnosticism and frequent recitations of Ingersoll's philosophy surely made this decision easier for his sons. Thirty years later, Lister could still quote from memory what he described as Ingersoll's "beautiful expressions," including this: "I belong to the Great Church which holds the world within its starlit aisles; that claims the great and good of every race and clime; that finds with joy the grain of gold in every creed. . . ." In maturity, Lister would also express more conventional religious views and always maintain his Methodist church membership. However, Sunday morning would more often find him at work than at church.[18]

But Amelie, who with her sister remained a devout Catholic, remembered years later the pain that Lister caused their mother by leaving her church. "She *hated* it," Amelie recalled. Other Montgomery Catholics bitterly resented this defection. Almost a quarter of a century later, a member of St. Peter's Church vowed: "Lister may get the votes of Catholics, Jews, and niggers outside Montgomery but he'll *never* get the Catholic vote of Montgomery." As Hill undoubtedly realized, the Catholic vote of Montgomery was inconsequential compared with the votes of Alabama's overwhelmingly Protestant majority.[19]

"They were claiming you to be a Catholic"

For one who aspired to succeed in Alabama politics during the 1920s, this shift had been a necessity. The Ku Klux Klan, revived during the war under the guise of patriotism, was building rapidly toward its peak Alabama membership of around eighty-five thousand in 1926. Although Klansmen terrorized Asians, blacks, Jews, and any hapless individuals whose personal habits they disapproved, their primary targets were Catholics. When farm people moved to industrial Birmingham in search of livelihood, they came into contact and competition with numerous Catholic immigrants from southern and eastern Europe, also attracted to the prospect of jobs in coal mines and steel mills. Natives, predominantly of Anglo-American stock and fundamentalist persuasion, perceived these newcomers as intruders in their job market and Protestant community. Under the anonymity of the hood and claiming the sanctities of patriotism and Protestantism, they indulged their penchant for violence.

Native-born industrial workers provided the base for Alabama's largest klavern, Robert E. Lee Klan No. 1 in Birmingham. But the Klan also appealed to thousands in Montgomery and the rural bastions of south Alabama. Hooded and robed mobs who flogged other citizens at will created a virtual reign of terror in some rural counties. Amid this climate, Hugo L. Black, an enterprising young Birmingham lawyer scornfully decried as a "Bolshevik" by many business and political leaders because he won whopping damage claims for injured workmen, joined the Klan in the belief that it could mobilize enough votes to vault him from relative obscurity to political prominence. In Montgomery, Bibb Graves, neighbor and sometime friend of the Hills, served as cyclops of the local Klan klavern as a prelude to his election as Alabama's governor in 1926. Anticipating Graves's ascension to power, Hill had already instructed his father: "Tell the Colonel [Graves] how much you love him."[20]

Many other Alabamians in public life became Klansmen for reasons of political expediency during the 1920s. Probably hundreds in the lower white elements that supported the Hill machine in Montgomery joined the Klan. But William Hill, leader of that faction, publicly supported William Gunter when Gunter faced—and defeated—a Klan-backed rival in a heated race for mayor of Montgomery in 1927. Lister, unlike many of the politically ambitious, did not affiliate with the Klan.[21] Lilly Hill, never reconciled to her son's defection from her church, would surely have been devastated had he allied himself, even for ambition's sake, with a virulently anti-Catholic organization. Furthermore, even if he had pretended to share its religious prejudices, the Klan, which admitted only "white, Protestant, Gentile, native-born Americans," might well have questioned some of Lister's credentials.

An attorney, a veteran, a civic leader, and belatedly a Methodist, Hill awaited the intervention of chance. His wait proved brief. In March 1923, John R. Tyson of Montgomery, a former chief justice of the Alabama Supreme Court, died during his second term of office as representative of Alabama's Second District in Congress. After Judge Tyson's death, members of this family endorsed Lister Hill, who had worked with the judge against ratification of the suffrage amendment and who, like Judge Tyson, opposed the political interests of the Alabama Power Company. In early April, Hill, twenty-eight years of age, announced his candidacy for the Democratic nomination to fill the unexpired term and chose Tyson's son-in-law, Kenneth Murphy, to be his campaign manager.[22]

Nine counties, stretching from Montgomery to the sand dunes of the Gulf of Mexico, made up Alabama's Second Congressional District (see Appendix, Map 1). Until the Creek War of 1813–14, this had been part of a vast Indian hunting ground. The first clashes between Creeks and white settlers had erupted within what was to become the Second District. Storming a wooden stockade known as Fort Mims, angry Creeks indiscriminately slaughtered most who had taken refuge there.

Rallying to avenge the killing of women and children at Fort Mims, American troops invaded Creek lands, scourged villages, destroyed crops and herds, and left an estimated one thousand warriors dead within their last stronghold, a bend where the Tallapoosa River curved like a horseshoe. Helpless to resist further, Creek leaders signed a treaty with General Andrew Jackson, who had directed the assault at Horseshoe Bend, agreeing to yield two-thirds of present Alabama and to move west of the Mississippi River.

White pioneers streamed into Alabama, transplanting the cotton and slavery culture of older southern states to its river bottoms and Black Belt. Small slaveholders and those too poor to own slaves planted corn, wheat, and cotton on small farms in northern Alabama and in a southeastern area called the Wiregrass by men who struggled to clear its tough undergrowth. Migrant herdsmen allowed hogs and cattle to range through the piney hills of south-central Alabama, which no ambitious planters or farmers bothered to claim. The Second District contained a strip of rich Black Belt soil, a portion of the Wiregrass, and a large swath of the infertile piney hills.[23]

Except for Montgomery, by then a city of almost fifty thousand, this district was sparsely populated. Two-thirds of its residents lived on farms. Since the Civil War, poverty had blighted the lives of most of these farmers. Malaria also sapped their energy. "I've got the chills and fever," was a common complaint. Joining what one historian would later term "the one-gallused rebellion," many embraced the Farmers' Alliance in the 1880s and bolted Democratic fealty in the 1890s to support Populist candidates for the legislature and governorship.[24]

But Democrats, manipulating black votes, stamped out the flames of Populism in Alabama. Then, to end the widespread fraud associated with black voting and to protect against further white insurgency, party leaders rewrote Alabama's constitution in 1901, erecting such complex barriers to voting that black voters disappeared almost immediately. By the 1920s, virtually all blacks, including those who comprised almost one-fourth of the population of the Second District, had been barred from taking part in the political process. Eventually, the cumulative poll-tax and literacy restrictions would disfranchise more poor whites than blacks.

In eight counties of the Second District, 10 to 17 percent of all citizens were illiterate. But in Wilcox, a Black Belt county where blacks outnumbered whites 4 to 1, *one-third* of the population could neither read nor write. Ignorance, poverty, boredom, and frustration combined to make these predominantly rural counties, Crenshaw in particular, fertile ground for the dark excitement promised by the Klan in the mid-1920s.[25]

During the spring planting season of 1923, Hill campaigned along the unpaved roads of this district in an open Dodge, leaving trails of dust behind him. When squalls blew in from the nearby Gulf of Mexico, he put up the car's rain curtains and struggled to guide it through the muddy ruts.[26] Like Populists of the past, he assured white farmers that he favored a platform to help the economically destitute. He would work for better schools, paved roads, lower freight rates, and a bonus in the pocket of every war veteran. He would vote to allow the nation's most innovative private entrepreneur, Henry Ford, to convert a wartime nitrate plant and dam at Muscle Shoals, Alabama, to production of low-cost fertilizer to renew their eroded and worn-out soil. He promised those who had left farms for industrial payrolls that he would support their right to join unions and to bargain for reasonable hours and decent conditions of work. He pledged to seek regulation of child labor and restrictions on immigration to keep out "pauper labor" and "undesirable and dangerous aliens."[27]

Ray Rushton, an able and prominent Montgomery lawyer but a lackluster politician, and William B. Sanders, a little-known Troy physician, also sought the congressional seat. Of the three, Rushton was by far the most politically experienced and widely known. He had served as Montgomery alderman and city attorney; for seven years he had headed the Montgomery County Democratic Executive Committee. Although he had run unsuccessfully for the United States Senate in 1913 and 1920, Rushton confidently expected to win an election in which his hometown would figure prominently.[28]

Both in their fifties, Rushton and Dr. Sanders probably thought it foolhardy of young Hill to aspire to Congress in his initial foray into politics. If so, they reckoned without the Hill family's connections and determination. Friends and kinsmen quickly launched a vigorous letter-writing campaign in Hill's behalf. Kenneth Murphy assured former Tyson supporters that Hill was best qualified to carry on the judge's policies. Frank M. Beck, a Montgomery friend, importuned members of the Disabled Veterans of Alabama to support a fellow comrade-in-arms. Frances Nimmo Greene urged newly enfranchised women of the Second District to rally around "virile young men" who had defended their country, particularly one who had supported women students in their fight to vote in campus elections at the university. The Reverend Bob Jones, a budding evangelist just embarking on the road to national prominence, entreated his followers to vote for a fellow dry.[29]

Family members pitched in. Amelie entered the exciting world of politics, accompanying her brother to rallies and courting women voters. Two Lyons uncles, Joseph and LeBaron, sought votes from friends in Baldwin County across the bay from Mobile. William Wallace Hill wrote clients, fellow attorneys, and judges in small towns like Troy, Georgiana, and Greenville. As a political asset, "Uncle Will," widely viewed in south Alabama as a lawyer of integrity, was second in importance only to Dr. Hill.[30]

In an era of highly personal relationships between doctors and patients, a politician could wish for no more potent ally than a widely known physician who got around the countryside and treated hundreds of patients. Almost a half century later, Lister Hill would reflect: "In those days, your doctor had more influence than anybody because when you were in trouble they answered the call . . . whether you had money to pay or not . . . muddy roads, cold weather, or no."[31]

Mining his rich lode of gratitude and professional comity in behalf of "my boy," Dr. Hill wrote to patients who had "the Hill trademark" on them, nurses whom he had trained and who revered him as he had revered Joseph Lister; fellow physicians, dentists, pharmacists, hospital workers, and county health officers. Dr. Hill's reputation as a surgeon to whom other doctors referred their patients far exceeded that of Dr. Sanders. "People everywhere feel bound to you by the strongest obligations," one correspondent advised Dr. Hill. "No love is greater than that of the person who feels that the 'old Dr.' saved my wife or my child." As if to corroborate this·statement, another wrote: "You operated on the wife of the writer, hence we would like very much to do something for your son." From tiny Oak Hill in Wilcox County, yet another of the family's admirers entered this judgment: "I like the Hills. They make good doctors, good preachers, and I believe will make good legislators."[32]

To emphasize his devotion, Dr. Hill often accompanied Lister by train to whistle stops like Florala, Georgiana, Castleberry, and Red Level. When his son orated at a high school commencement or a commemoration of Mother's Day, the doctor, earphone cocked, sat in the audience and joined vigorously in its applause.[33]

But disquieting rumors filtered into country stores, cafés, and court-houses of the Second District. "They were claiming you to be a Catholic," reported an alarmed supporter in Georgiana. He had been told, he wrote, that Lister had joined the Methodist church two years earlier "for political purposes" but that he remained a secret Catholic. Spread as if by strong breezes from the Gulf, this rumor reached Opp, Brantley, Evergreen, Greenville, McKenzie, and other small clusters of population. From Luverne, a friend reported to Dr. Hill: "Rushton is saying that the Catholics of Mobile are spending $200,000 in Lister's campaign and that your wife was Catholic." Another correspondent demanded to know: "What is Mr. Hill's religion? Will his love and respect for his Mother have any influence [sic] on him while in Washington in regard to Catholicism?"[34]

Hastily, the Hills moved to deflect the potentially damaging effects of such gossip. William Wallace Hill reminded his friends that Lister's grand-father and great-grandfather had been noted Methodist preachers. Dr. Hill mailed out numerous copies of a small book containing the sermons and a brief sketch of the life of the Reverend Luther Leonidas Hill. The candidate himself intensified his speech-making from Methodist and Baptist pulpits and testified to his Methodist fealty in the *Alabama Christian Advocate*, a Methodist paper, and the *Alabama Baptist*. Through this latter means, the rumors were laid to rest in Red Level, as Dr. Hill learned from a friend who wrote: "All our people sware [sic] by their church paper."[35]

Fighting bigotry with bigotry, Hill informed a voter in Opp that Rushton, while a member of the Alabama legislature in 1919, had "made a speech in behalf of the Roman Catholic Church of Rome, Italy." Kenneth Murphy charged that Rushton, although a Baptist, had the support of "the biggest Catholics in Montgomery" because he, like they, opposed federal aid to education. Employing the frequent excuse that Hill was "out of town," the campaign manager took it upon himself to respond to numerous questioners that Hill had been a Methodist "years before the campaign started and he has never been a member of any other church." When confronted, Hill equivocated. Without mentioning his Catholic upbringing, he reiterated over and over that he was a member of the Court Street Methodist Church, advising the doubtful to contact his pastor.[36]

After the primary, one of Dr. Hill's professional colleagues in Atmore attempted to address this delicate matter with finesse. To a friend in Brewton, Dr. A. P. Webb wrote: "Mr. Hill may have been affiliated with his mother's church during his infancy, childhood, and early young manhood. I am not in a position to say. . . . I cannot believe that he is such a religious hypocrite that he would desert his mother's faith for political reasons. So far as the strain of Jewish blood in Mr. Hill's veins is concerned, I remember that Jesus Christ was a Jew. . . . The pedigree of all of us will not bear too close inspection."[37] When the new Democratic nominee received a copy of this letter, he responded: "Your rejoinder . . . is a crushing knock-out . . . a masterful presentation of our side of the case."[38]

"We had better begin to groom [Lister] for the Presidency"

Gossip about Hill's ancestry and religion remained confined to whispers and personal letters; in public he and Rushton sought a higher plane. At his father's suggestion, Hill focused on two main appeals: more fertilizer, produced at Muscle Shoals, and better schools, funded by the federal government. Rushton was quick to counter that "dangers infest such a course" as federal aid to education. Not so, Hill retorted. Such money would be under *state* control.[39] But almost a quarter century later, Hill would decide that Rushton's old prediction might come true. That decision would alter the course of his senatorial career.

Better to attack, however, than to defend. Especially if one could impress upon voters that Rushton, in his law practice, had represented the interests of that political albatross, the Alabama Power Company. Before a large Montgomery crowd, Hill claimed that Rushton had helped Alabama Power acquire control of the city's street railway system, thereby bringing on a fare increase from five to eight cents. In other speeches and in letters, he charged that Rushton had lobbied against bills to remove the power company's tax exemptions. Rushton, attempting to cloak his longtime association with the power company, insisted that he had tried for twelve years to save the Montgomery Light and Traction Company from being acquired by "monopolies." To support his claimed independence from Alabama Power, Rushton announced that he too favored operation of Muscle Shoals by Ford rather than other power interests. "Rushton is trying his best to get away from the [Alabama Power] company," Hill reported gleefully to a friend.[40]

Compared to accusations of secret allegiance to big corporations or the Church of Rome, other issues paled. Hill favored the soldiers' bonus; Rushton opposed it. Hill supported national prohibition; Rushton had opposed the Eighteenth Amendment but, after its passage, had reluctantly affirmed his allegiance to this new law of the land. Hill believed that federal judges should be nominated in primaries; Rushton favored taking this choice out of the hands of the "unthinking masses" by allowing party conventions to select judges. Seeking a simpler issue, Rushton pleaded with the electorate to choose "a level head" over a mere boy. But Hill had prepared his answer to this: remember that youthful men like Patrick Henry, Thomas Jefferson, James Madison, and Alexander Hamilton were among our nation's Founding Fathers; remember, too, that leadership in Congress is based on seniority, not age.[41]

From remote Troy, Dr. Sanders attacked the "arrogance" of the two Montgomery candidates in ignoring him and objected to the obvious fact that Montgomery County voters controlled the outcome of the Second District race. Perhaps sensing a rural trend, the doctor announced he was ready "to measure hat bands" with Lister Hill. But both Sanders and Rushton faced a formidable array of veterans, women, physicians, patients, druggists, nurses, health officers, judges, attorneys, clients, "Dekes," drys, and friends and relations of the large Tyson, Lyons, Croom, and Hill families. Hill also courted a less visible element of the electorate, following the advice of one sage to "remember the patch breeches fellow, they vote."[42]

Rain fell over most of the Second District on 16 July 1923, driving many a hard-scrabble farmer in from his fields. The primary took place under Democratic rules adopted in 1915 for the ostensible purpose of eliminating costly runoff elections. Faced with three or more candidates for the same post, voters were required to indicate both their first and second choices. The person with the highest total of first- and second-choice votes won. This arrangement had benefits other than economy. As its prohibitionist instigators had hoped, the system could permit the candidate of a minority of voters to win an election.[43]

But to the surprise of Montgomery editors who expected a close race, there would have been no need for a runoff in the Second District. Hill received almost as many first- and second-choice votes as Rushton and Sanders combined. In his first try for elective office, he piled up support in rural beats as well as in Montgomery. He carried every county in the district, outpolling Rushton in crucial Montgomery County 3 to 2.[44] The *Montgomery Advertiser*, which had supported Rushton, hailed the new Democratic nominee as "a brilliant young attorney." Family members exulted. Not entirely in jest, Joseph Lyons wrote Dr. Hill: "We had better begin to groom [Lister] for the Presidency."[45]

Although newspapers took no note of it, the limited electorate of the Second District had been a major factor in Hill's victory. Out of a total population of just over 300,000, fewer than 18,000 qualified or bothered to take part in the primary. It was not impossible for an energetic young candidate, along with his friends, connections, and large family, to conduct a personal solicitation of a majority of these white voters. Hill's success was a prime illustration of the Alabama tradition that a candidate's friends and neighbors could play a major role in his political fortunes.[46] But another factor had been crucial to Hill's unexpected victory. Years later, after many other campaign successes, he insisted that one person, above all, had launched him in politics. "It was those small town doctors who elected me," Hill remembered. "My *father's* friends."[47]

This victory had been long in the making. In Lister's boyhood, Dr. Hill and Professor Starke had conditioned him to work and to win. As a young man, he had set out to acquire the politician's tools—oratory, a law degree, a war record, a broad acquaintance, and a widely publicized start in public service. He had reiterated the obligatory, traditional views of a white southern politician on the touchy matter of federal interference at the ballot box. He had spoken of blacks in the typical demeaning parlance of his day. He had rid himself openly of the political handicap of Catholicism. It had not been necessary to deny publicly his Jewish heritage. In accordance with the code of the times, suspicions of this sort had been confined to whispers and rumor. By dint of single-minded dedication to his goal and by making fundamental but politically essential concessions, Lister had launched his career in national politics.

Governor W. W. Brandon called a special election in the Second District for a day in mid-August when farmers would have their crops "laid by." As customary in the one-party Alabama politics of that era, the election was a mere ritual. Without opposition, the Democratic nominee was officially elected to the Sixty-eighth Congress.[48] Lister Hill would serve in that body for almost a half century.

CHAPTER 3

The Young Congressman

I 9 2 3 — I 9 3 2

"Just keep working and working"

August 1923. When news of the death of Warren Harding reached a hamlet in the Vermont hills, Calvin Coolidge, his father officiating, took his oath to become thirtieth president of the United States. (How had the elder Coolidge known that he could administer the presidential oath to his son, curious reporters later asked. "I didn't know I couldn't," that laconic Yankee replied.) President Coolidge returned to a drowsy seat of government where income taxes were negligible, parking spaces plentiful, even on F Street, and the politically ambitious coveted, above all, an invitation to the salon of Evelyn Walsh McLean. Tourists and newcomers to the capital, not being on Mrs. McLean's social list, might catch a glimpse of power as dashing Nicholas Longworth, Republican leader of the House, whizzed up Pennsylvania Avenue in his electric car.[1]

Hard-pressed for news that fall after the stir over Harding's unexpected death had subsided, photographers and motion-picture cameramen focused on the youngest member of the House of Representatives. The likeness of a "baby congressman" who had not yet celebrated his twenty-ninth birthday appeared in theaters and newspapers over the nation. "If you go to a movie, you are almost certain to see Lister as they have him in Pathé and International both," a friend reported to one of Hill's Mobile cousins. "He looks alright [sic] but not as good as Rudolph Valentino."[2]

Kenneth Murphy, who was to serve as his secretary, and the congressman's sister, Amelie, accompanied Hill to Washington where the Hills took rooms at a hotel near the capitol. Keeping close tabs on his progeny, Dr. Hill plied the new congressman with political and personal advice, written on prescription pads, and suggested remedies for any illnesses

49

Lister and Amelie might contract in the miasma of the Potomac. Amelie passed time pleasantly with her friend Bertha Underwood, wife of Senator Oscar W. Underwood who had lost his bid to be Democratic presidential nominee in 1912 but was to make a second try for the nomination in 1924.[3] Underwood, along with two seasoned House members from Alabama, William Bankhead and Henry Steagall, helped to initiate the newcomer into the mysteries and proprieties of Congress while that body was in session or during the long train ride to and from Washington. On his office walls, Hill enshrined photographs of his mentors: his father; University of Alabama president George Denny; Columbia Law School dean Harlan F. Stone; John Nance Garner, Democratic leader of the House; and his heroes of the past, William Jennings Bryan, Alexander Hamilton, and the political figure whom he professed to admire above all, Thomas Jefferson. To refresh his memory of the philosophical differences between these latter two (and emulating his father's routine), Hill retired to his hotel room at night to read Claude Bowers's new and popular study, *Jefferson and Hamilton*.

But the fledgling congressman's most pressing task was to imbue his two-man staff with the Hill work ethic. "First things first and get it all finished before you sleep," he demanded. *He* could not sleep, he told them, if one piece of work remained undone. Every letter and memorandum must be answered on the day received. White parents in the Second District must be congratulated upon the births of their babies; wires must be sent to the bereaved. Not content with a mere signature, Hill added handwritten notes and underlined passages in letters to assure his correspondents that they had his personal attention. "Just keep working and working and you are bound to win," he advised a West Point cadet. Not even Christmas slowed this frenetic pace. "Send me all Christmas cards," the congressman ordered from Montgomery. "I have gotten a batch of them here and I am telephoning, seeing or writing the senders. . . . you know my mind is energetic and I like to know what is going on."[4]

Noting the unusual industriousness in Hill's office, Capitol Hill observers joked: "If you write him, he will wire you. If you wire him, he will phone you; if you phone him, he will come to see you." After two years of this regimen, Murphy, accustomed to his father-in-law's more leisurely approach to governance, sought other employment. His successor, Robert Frazer, a naive, barely nineteen-year-old native of Greenville, Alabama, judged suitable by Dr. and Mrs. Hill, was to prove more malleable. The loyal Frazer would endure this test of stamina for fifteen years.[5]

Other than keeping up with births and deaths in their districts and seeking new post offices, Hill and his colleagues bore a light load. Affairs of state seldom occupied Congress more than a month or two, leaving members free to tend political fences or try for higher office. To Underwood's bitter disappointment, he failed again in 1924 to win the Democratic presidential nomination, even though members of his delegation, including Lister Hill, appointed a delegate-at-large by former Governor B. B. Comer, entranced radio listeners and earned a place in political legend for their tenacious battle cry, "Alabama casts twenty-fo' votes for Oscar W. Underwood." But of more significance to Hill's future, he first glimpsed Franklin Roosevelt, as the crippled New Yorker made his way to the platform to nominate Alfred E. Smith, and heard Roosevelt's vibrant voice that would later reassure a frightened nation.

To impress his constituents, Hill called at the White House to present a lavalier for Mrs. Coolidge and a watch fob for the president fashioned from arrowheads found at Fort Mims. The young congressman made an elaborate presentation during which he praised Andrew Jackson for the prompt and conclusive manner in which that Democratic hero had exacted vengeance from the Creeks at Horseshoe Bend. (Recalling his speech to Coolidge years later, Hill again praised Jackson: "Old Andrew had a way of winning.") But when Hill finished this accolade, the president simply gestured to the gifts and then to his desk. "Put 'em there," said Coolidge. "Thank you." Hill always remembered Coolidge as "a man of taciturnity."[6]

Upon entering the House, Hill had won a coveted committee assignment. Not only would a seat on the Military Affairs Committee give him an opportunity to attract army bases for his district and state but, of even more importance, this committee would help to decide the future of the government's wartime nitrate plants and uncompleted hydroelectric dams on the Tennessee River near Muscle Shoals, Alabama, a topic of great interest to all who farmed impoverished soil. Synthetic nitrogen, no longer needed for explosives, could be a vital aid to these farmers in the form of cheaper fertilizer. To engage in the lively controversy over Muscle Shoals would involve a Washington neophyte in more substantive matters than presenting old arrowheads from Fort Mims to President Coolidge.

The Muscle Shoals issue was to be debated in Congress until 1933. During the decade in which he was deeply involved in these negotiations, Hill gradually moved away from his original position favoring use of these facilities by private enterprise for the manufacture of fertilizer. Eventually he would become a co-sponsor with Nebraska's Senator George W. Norris of the act establishing the government's multifaceted Tennessee Valley Authority (TVA). Although Hill would later look back with pride upon his role in establishing TVA, he had initially been reluctant to back Norris's bold concept, capitulating only when its adoption appeared inevitable.

In his campaign, Hill had promised impoverished farmers of the Second District that he would support Henry Ford's grandiose scheme to buy the nitrate plants (for a fraction of their original cost) and lease the dams, when completed by the government, for one hundred years. This plan, Hill told the House, was the "greatest offer ever made by a citizen to his Government."[7] But the seasoned Norris and some of his fellow progressives suspected that "Uncle Henry," while paying lip service to fertilizer, was actually planning to use cheap power, generated by government-built plants, to produce auto parts and other industrial products.

Although they disagreed about Ford, Hill and Norris shared a determination not to turn over this project to the Alabama Power Company. That utility had previously shown no interest in bidding on these facilities, but Ford's offer had alerted its officials to the possible emergence of a major hydroelectric competitor in their own backyard. Reversing itself, the company offered to lease the site for fifty years and to complete the dams at its own expense. Alabama Power's offer, however, contained no promise to produce fertilizer. Hill found this bid "woefully lacking."[8]

After Ford suddenly withdrew his offer in late 1924, Hill announced his preference for another private bidder, the American Cyanamid Company, which had the backing of the powerful American Farm Bureau Federation. While his committee considered this new proposal, Hill worked closely with Chester Gray, the Farm Bureau's Washington lobbyist, and its president, Edward A. O'Neal, a fellow Alabamian. Eventually the committee also rejected this private bid because a majority feared that the cyanamid company, too, had great interest in cheap power but little commitment to fertilizer.[9]

Gradually Congress moved toward the Norris approach. Hill deplored this trend. Private operation, he wrote a north Alabama correspondent, "holds out much more hope for the farmers and the people of the Tennessee Valley than does government operation." He expressed his preference for private operation even more explicitly in a minority report that he prepared but, evidently upon second thought, decided against submitting to the House. For the government to produce fertilizer and power, Hill warned in this document, would set a dangerous precedent that might discourage individual enterprise and eventually destroy America's industrial supremacy.[10]

With a north Alabama colleague, Representative Miles Allgood, Hill called on President Herbert Hoover to discuss what might be done with Muscle Shoals. After the two Alabamians had outlined their plans for fertilizer production, the president asked: "Well who could I get to operate that thing?" Years later, Hill, having elected to forget his own initial hesitancy about government operation, remarked scornfully: "That was Hoover's thinking."[11]

In 1932, as this long controversy neared its climax, Hill attempted to devise a compromise between government and private operation. By then chairman of the subcommittee concerned with Muscle Shoals, he sponsored a bill providing for limited government operation of the power plants, coupled with leasing the nitrate plants to a nonprofit organization such as the Farm Bureau. The Hill bill would have given the federal government no authority to build transmission lines; thus power sales could have taken place only at the switchboard. When Congress adjourned in July, both the Hill bill and another Norris proposal died. The Nebraskan was content to wait until the presidential election in the fall. It might produce a president who, unlike his stubborn predecessors Coolidge and Hoover, would actually champion the program that Norris had fiercely advocated for a decade.[12]

"I may follow suit"

Such intricate political maneuvering could not have been the sole concern of a young bachelor member of Congress, no matter how work-oriented. What a catch Lister Hill must have been! Young women in Washington, wishing to make the acquaintance of "the rising young statesman from Alabama," invited him to Sunday night supper parties in their mothers' parlors. One Montgomery belle confessed that she had faked excuses to talk to him "because I liked the vibrations of success and ambition that surround you." For years—even after Hill's marriage—a secret female admirer sent him a white gardenia on the opening day of Congress. Other young ladies wrote coy letters to which he replied gallantly but cautiously, thanking "My dear Miss Mary Lou" or "My dear Miss Sue Ellen" for your "lovely" letter. Parents occasionally used a more direct approach, dispatcl:ing nieces or daughters to Washington accompanied by a request that their congressman show them through the Capitol. "Of course," Hill wrote his father in a rare moment of candor, "Mrs. B. wants me to show her [daughter] more than the capitol."[13]

What advantages could matrimony afford over the freedom to spend one's evenings gadding about Washington in Robert Frazer's new Model-T coupe, which they had christened "Vivian," to hear Fritzi Scheff sing "Madame Modiste" at Poli's, or to watch the shocking Countess Cathcart perform at the Belasco? But shortly after his thirty-third birthday, Hill's defenses began to weaken. In early February 1928, he confided to a newly engaged friend in Texas that a "very beautiful and charming young lady" was trying to persuade him to marry her. "If yours works out all right," Hill ventured, "I may follow suit." Of a trusted confidant in Alabama, he inquired: "Do you advise such a step on my part or not?"[14]

Suddenly the matter was resolved. To the surprise of Hill's friends and constituents, the *Montgomery Advertiser* reported on its front page an unconfirmed rumor of his engagement. Three days later, on 20 February, Lister Hill married Henrietta Fontaine McCormick, of Eufaula, Alabama, in the presence of a small gathering of family and friends at the ancestral home of the bride's grandmother in Columbus, Georgia.[15]

In the matter of background, so important to the southern gentry, Henrietta McCormick was an eminently suitable mate. Her ancestors included pioneer settlers of Eufaula, a prosperous cotton-trading village on the western bank of the Chattahoochee River, as well as the first mayor of Columbus, Georgia, on the eastern bank. One of her grandfathers had fought for the Confederacy to the bitter end, having stood with Robert E. Lee as silence fell over Appomattox. The other, a physician, was a close friend of Dr. Hill. Henrietta had been reared within the safe cocoon of a privileged childhood, shielded by parents, household servants, the Episcopal church, and the knowledge that she belonged to the leading citizenry of Eufaula and Columbus. Her father, head of a wholesale grocery firm and as stern a disciplinarian as Dr. Hill, had read aloud to Henrietta and her sister in the evenings from novels by suitable authors such as Scott, Dickens, and Thackeray. Her lively mother had inculcated in Henrietta the impeccable taste and genuine artistry of a southern lady in such household matters as arranging flowers, preparing foods, choosing decor, and entertaining guests.[16]

To fill the interim between Henrietta's girlhood and marriage, the McCormicks had sent their daughter to St. Mary's School in Raleigh,

North Carolina, where other southern girls from similar circumstances received the polishing touches for womanhood. When she returned from St. Mary's, Henrietta was introduced to the highly eligible Lister Hill within the closely guarded confines where the southern establishment arranged proper mates for its younger generations. She had already been impressed by hearing this promising young man deliver an eloquent tribute on Mother's Day.[17]

To "catch" this longtime bachelor and thwart her Washington rivals, Henrietta occasionally visited the capital, ensconcing herself in the Gordon Hotel at Sixteenth Street near the White House, a slightly decayed but severely respectable hostelry whose corridors reeked with the aroma of cooked cabbage. When Lister took an evening off from work, he would borrow "Vivian" and drive Henrietta to view the Potomac from Hains Point. Lister's family, jealous of his increasingly serious interest in Henrietta and aware that she had no dowry other than her aristocratic lineage, displayed little enthusiasm for this romance. Nonetheless, after driving Henrietta to Hains Point one raw winter evening, Hill asked Robert Frazer to help him select a ring.[18]

As a romantic setting for her wedding, Henrietta chose the imposing mansion built by slave labor for her Columbus forebears, the Fontaines, who had started the first cotton mill in that Georgia community. Fashioned after a Greek temple with Doric columns, the Fontaine home overlooked the Chattahoochee River. As had other brides in that family, Henrietta descended its mahogany circular staircase to a drawing room, embellished with gold-framed mirrors and black marble mantel, where Lister and his best man, Dr. Hill, awaited her.[19]

Earlier that day, Henrietta's plans for a quiet wedding had been interrupted by the unexpected appearance of the entire United States Army Band that had come from nearby Fort Benning to serenade the future wife of a prominent member of the House Military Affairs Committee by playing "The Stars and Stripes Forever." Its director, with an eye to congressional favor, thus honored a promise he had once joshingly made to bachelor Congressman Hill.[20]

The band provided a stirring prelude to the start of a long and, to all appearances, a devoted union. In sophisticated Washington, where the extramarital dalliances of many of his colleagues became common gossip, Hill was reputed to be one senator who preferred home life to the cocktail circuit. If occasionally he enjoyed the stimulating company of an intellectual or flashy, politically minded woman, he kept such friendships discreetly private. As he expressed it to his Uncle Will, "a man in public life has got to be like Caesar's wife 'above suspicion.' "[21]

His unexpected marriage dismayed many a young lady in Washington and Alabama, none more so than Amelie, who had served as her brother's hostess for Wednesday afternoon "at homes" as well as an enthusiastic campaigner during the five years he had served in Congress. A half century later, Amelie still vividly recalled her feelings of jealousy and displacement. Now a new hostess would entertain for Lister Hill. Henrietta Hill must be ready at a moment's notice to produce luncheon, tea and cookies, dinner, or breakfast for the visiting constituents, Washington friends, relatives, and overnight guests whom her husband frequently invited to their modest apartment. Hill, work always his first priority, arrived home for a late dinner, left early the following morning, and spent most Saturdays and many a Sunday in his office. Thus the rearing of their daughter, Henrietta, born a year after their marriage, and their son, Luther Leonidas III (later changed to Luther Lister but always "Pal" to his father), born seven years later, fell almost entirely to Henrietta Hill. If she found such responsibilities burdensome, she may have confided this to her closest Washington friend, another pretty, young Alabamian, Josephine Foster Black, whose husband, Senator Hugo Black, also required that his wife perform these traditional roles to perfection.[22]

"Romanist Hill"

Hill was to retain his congressional seat with ease. What Alabama voter could resist a young legislator who persuaded Congress that the War Department should pay for headstones on the unmarked graves of veterans of the Confederacy (as well as of those who had served the Union), insisted that a portrait of Robert E. Lee be displayed at West Point along with the academy's other past superintendents, and successfully sponsored a bill to establish the Gorgas Memorial Institute in Panama, named for General William C. Gorgas, the famed Alabamian who had sanitized the Canal Zone?

But Hill focused most of his energy on his major power base. He arranged for Montgomery to be placed on the airmail route. He secured an appropriation for a modern building to replace its old Victorian post office on Dexter Avenue; construction of this imposing structure would provide much-needed jobs during the Great Depression. As soon as he took his seat on the House Military Affairs Committee, he set out to rescue Maxwell Field, a small airplane-repair base commanded by a major, from the "abandon" list. The War Department considered Maxwell too close to the city to become an air base. But Hill proved so adept in securing federal funds for Maxwell that, as he put it years later, "they couldn't very well abandon it."[23]

In 1928, Hill persuaded the Army to move the Air Corps Tactical School from Langley Field, Virginia, to a permanent home at Maxwell. Even during the depression era of the 1930s, he prodded the federal government to spend nearly seven million dollars at Maxwell. This dependable payroll would help many a Montgomery merchant weather the depression. (After World War II, the tactical school would be expanded to become the Air University, and Maxwell would be designated an Air Force base. By 1962, Maxwell and its companion facility, Gunter Field, would represent a federal investment of nearly $117 million and employ one of every sixteen civilians in Montgomery.) During Hill's first two decades in Congress, Montgomerians appreciated his efforts. As early as 1925, a friend reported: "The town is singing your praises."[24]

Rural constituents, too, benefited from their congressman's energy. The Second District acquired more post offices than any other district in Alabama; new rural postal routes stretched to many a remote farmhouse. Not only did these country folk know the name of their congressman; chances were good that he knew *their* names. One lifelong resident of Opp marveled that Hill could "call more names of people in my own town in 5 minutes than I could in 10." A friend in Luverne assessed his former college classmate as "a democrat . . . a gentleman . . . a brilliant orator . . . and the poor man's friend." Such abilities discouraged potential opponents. Hill was unopposed in seven Democratic primaries. In 1932, a Republican and a Socialist made the futile gestures of running against him in the general election. An independent candidate filed against him in 1936. Altogether these challengers polled fewer than two thousand votes.[25]

But the Alabama political scene in the late 1920s was not as tranquil as might be surmised from Hill's secure hold on the Second District. Thousands of plain whites, exhorted by drys, veterans, and the Klan, forged a loose coalition that succeeded in 1926 where the frustrated Populists of the 1890s had failed. They placed their candidates Bibb Graves, a south Alabama progressive, in the governor's chair and Hugo Black, the workingman's advocate, in the United States Senate and ensconced many other

members of their slate in lesser offices and the state legislature. This
landslide, if allowed to proceed, threatened to upset the uneasy balance
achieved in the aftermath of black disfranchisement whereby reform-
minded whites who yearned for a share in political power had been permitted access to executive offices while Black Belt elements that favored the
status quo had remained entrenched in a malapportioned legislature.[26]

To ensure that they would be supported by the Klan's highly disciplined
bloc of voters, both Graves and Black had joined that order. Although he
polled less than one-third of the total vote, Black became Democratic
Senate nominee under the "minority primary" rule that awarded this prize
without a runoff to the leading vote-getter in a field of three or more.
Thereby a rank outsider had prevailed over such prominent Alabamians as
John H. Bankhead Jr., scion of a wealthy political dynasty; Thomas E.
Kilby Jr., a prosperous steel manufacturer and former governor; and James
J. Mayfield, a former justice of the Alabama Supreme Court.[27]

Ambitious Representative Hill must have been startled by the unexpected appearance in the Senate of the hitherto little-known Black, just
forty years of age. What effect was it to have upon Hill's aspirations that
Alabama's Senate seats, traditionally reserved for men of his own station
in life, were now held by Black and J. Thomas Heflin, both of whom had
sprung from modest family surroundings in the Alabama hills to the Senate
largely by appeals to the emotions, fears, prejudices, and aspirations of
plain, white folk?

The issue of religion in politics reached its climax in 1928 as American
voters actually entertained the possibility of installing a Catholic, Alfred E.
Smith, in the White House. Only through monumental efforts would loyal
Alabama Democrats be able to deliver their state's electoral votes to
Smith. Resorting to their old rallying cry of white supremacy and raising
the specter of Reconstruction, Democrats addressed the task of preserving their one-party system and its precarious power balance by out-
demagoging Republican appeals to Protestantism and prohibition.

Black and Graves kept prudently silent during this campaign, fearing to
breach Democratic regularity yet not daring to offend their recent supporters by openly stumping for a Catholic and a wet. But Heflin, ranting
against Catholics in general and Smith in particular, made the fatal political mistake of openly declaring his intent to vote against the Democratic
nominee. "I will vote against Al Smith, so help me God!" Heflin told a
crowd in Dothan shortly before election day. Such apostasy roused Dr. Hill
to take to the airwaves to excoriate Heflin and his cohorts as "political

tomtits and chickadees [who] would . . . destroy the white man's rule in Alabama."[28]

Lister Hill, barely on the lower rungs of the congressional ladder, had no intention of emulating the feckless Heflin. National Democratic leaders in Congress would never award choice committee posts to one who had defected from their ranks. Powerful Democrats in Alabama threatened to bar bolters from their party's future primaries, thereby blocking the road to the United States Senate. With his own congressional seat a virtual sinecure, Hill set forth in a 1927 Hudson sedan, a gift from his father, to stump the state for Smith. In so doing, he would alienate many former supporters, including prohibitionists, the vast majority of Alabama's Protestant ministers, and prominent leaders such as J. Bibb Mills, superintendent of the Alabama Anti-Saloon League; M. E. Lazenby, editor of the *Alabama Christian Advocate*; and Bob Jones, the evangelist. On his prescription pad, Dr. Hill jotted a note of caution to his son: "Don't forget that you can never make peace with the Catholics." But to Lister the alternative of deserting his party was unthinkable.[29]

Campaign oratory was the best, often the only, show in small Alabama county seats. Crowds expected speakers to declaim, exaggerate, and wave their arms after the platform manner of William Jennings Bryan, who had stumped Alabama during the senatorial election of 1920 in an unsuccessful effort to help defeat his old political enemy, Senator Underwood. Urged to deliver "enthusiastic, aggressive speeches," Hill set out to cover, in two hours, the bravery of Confederate soldiers, the horrors of Reconstruction, corruption in the Republican party, betrayal of the farmer, prohibition, Catholicism, and "the negro [sic] question." Included in this latter topic would be mention of black delegates at the Republican convention of 1928 and of desegregation in the Commerce Department under Secretary Herbert Hoover, with the result that white women "sit side by side with black men in their work." After such a speech in Montgomery's Grand Theatre, wherein Hill invoked the shades of Robert the Bruce, that storied warrior for Scottish independence, and of John Tyler Morgan, the ex-Confederate general who had represented Alabama in the Senate for thirty years, Marie Bankhead Owen reported with satisfaction, "very few dry eyes in the audience."[30]

But bigotry, as a political weapon, could cut both ways. In Huntsville, Hill suffered minor embarrassment when a minister accused him of having been drunk at an American Legion meeting. Denying such misconduct, Hill pronounced firmly: "I never take a drink. I am a teetotaler." But as the

campaign neared its zenith, whispers of his Catholic background finally
broke into print via a sensational circular distributed by the Klan on the
streets of Alabama towns and cities. In the space of one page, its authors
sought to shock voters and to elevate their fears of Tammany Hall, secret
Catholic plots, and, most disturbing of all, miscegenation. The circular
bore the photograph of a white woman, said to be the wife of a black man
in New York. On her lap she held "triplets," two white and one black. This
state·of affairs, the circular implied, could be blamed upon Al Smith, who
had been Speaker of the New York Assembly when a bill forbidding
interracial marriages had died in committee, and upon his Alabama supporter, "Romanist Hill . . . a pseudo-Methodist . . . born and raised in the
Roman Catholic Church." After Hill's election to Congress, the circular
charged, one of his first acts had been to appoint a Catholic "altar boy" to
West Point.[31]

Compelled to respond, Hill denounced as "an infamous and cowardly
lie" the statements that he was "Romanist Hill," who had for religious
reasons appointed boys to military academies and supported Smith, and
that he approved mixing of the races. He had named only Protestants to the
academies, he insisted, "but they have been appointed on their merit and
not because of their religion." Omitting any mention of his Catholic upbringing, he declared that he was a steward in Montgomery's Court Street
Methodist Church, a 32nd-degree Scottish Rite Mason, a Knight Templar,
a Shriner, and a Knight of Pythias. As a loyal Democrat, he would continue to support the ticket and to denounce Republican "rottenness . . .
enmity and hostility to the South and our people."[32]

When this heated campaign ended, Democrats had managed to keep
their state in that party's column by the slim and perhaps contrived margin
of seven thousand votes. Electoral votes of five other southern states had
gone to Hoover in the first breakup of the Solid South since the end of
Reconstruction. In Alabama, an organization of former servicemen, led by
Major Frank M. Dixon of Birmingham, had been active in behalf of the
Democrats. But party loyalists like W. B. Oliver, chairman of the State
Democratic Committee; Jesse B. Hearin, an executive of the Montgomery
Chamber of Commerce; and even William Gunter, who had regained the
mayoralty of Montgomery in 1919, gave more credit for this narrow
victory to Lister Hill, the busiest and most effective Democratic speaker in
the state. Dixon and Hill would take part in many future campaigns but
would come to differ sharply on the issue of party loyalty. Hill's competi-
tive instincts had been fueled by the meteoric rise of Hugo Black, less than

nine years his senior. Now he, rather than the silent Black, had become a hero in the eyes of party regulars.[33]

With Heflin having imperiled his political future by deserting the Democratic nominee, would 1930 be an opportune time for Lister Hill to move up to the Senate? John Bankhead Jr., still smarting from his 1926 defeat by the upstart Black, planned to run against Heflin. Why not make this Democratic primary a three-man race? Since his first election to the House, Hill had been laying the groundwork to achieve his boyhood ambition. For years, friends and supporters had spoken of his elevation to the Senate as a virtual certainty. "You will get to the Senate in a walk," one had predicted as early as 1925. J. Bibb Mills, offering to distribute one of Hill's speeches in 1926 to lay the groundwork for a Senate race, had instructed: "[I] want your name to be a household word in all the prohibitionists' homes in the state. So make your speech a little longer but don't make it so long that the folks won't read it."[34]

Hill went so far as to write out a proposed announcement of his Senate candidacy. Focusing on Heflin, he described this probable opponent as a "Judas" who had betrayed his party "for $250 a speech." But after further thought, he and his father decided that Heflin, given the opportunity, would train his formidable oratorical talents on Hill's onetime Catholicism. Frank Glass, publisher of the *Montgomery Advertiser*, confirmed Dr. Hill's fears that Heflin would have Lister's "Catholicism to work on." The *Advertiser*, Glass advised the doctor, would prefer to support "a good and available man . . . without the handicap of Catholicism."[35]

In December 1929, Alabama Democratic leaders temporarily changed the rules of the game by carrying out their long-awaited threat to bar from running under their emblem any person who had voted Republican in 1928 or had openly opposed Democratic nominees. Excluded from his party, Heflin gathered remnants of the anti-Smith forces, courted Republican voters, and planned to run on an independent ticket as a self-styled "Jeffersonian Democrat." Hill and his father, polling their statewide network of physicians, county health officers, probate judges, "Dekes," relatives, and acquaintances, next considered whether or not Lister should oppose John Bankhead Jr. in the 1930 primary. Urging the Hills to enter this fray, a school principal responded: "Why should we now compromise and turn over to a back number the natural reward that the general—LISTER HILL—deserves? He can defeat Bankhead, after which he will have a walkaway over Heflin."[36]

But Hill let this chance pass him by. He would risk possible defeat by mounting a challenge to one of the "royal Bankheads"; most of his advisers rated such a race as a tossup. Furthermore, the spectacle of two regular Democrats tangling in the primary might seriously split his party and help reelect Heflin. Even if he should succeed in the task of defeating Bankhead, he would still have to face Heflin and the Catholic issue in the general election. Perhaps it would be more prudent to wait; after all he was only thirty-five. "You are a young man," one adviser wrote, "and can afford to defer your ambitions for years." Several correspondents urged Hill to bide his time until 1932 and take on Black instead.[37]

Bankhead had opposition in the primary after all. Frederick I. Thompson, a progressive-minded newspaper publisher in Mobile, waged a vigorous but unsuccessful campaign. Had Hill's decision not to challenge Bankhead been a crucial failure of nerve and a serious error in judgment? He agonized over this question. Later he confessed to William Hill that he had missed a "golden opportunity." If he had announced first, Thompson might never have entered the race. Never again would he find such an "easy" opponent as the once-defeated John Bankhead Jr. Now, in order to gain a Senate seat, he would be forced to take on a powerful incumbent instead of the outcast Heflin or the untried Bankhead. As for running against Black, Hill confided to his uncle, "he and I represent too much the same people and agree too well. . . . I really do not know an issue I could raise with him."[38]

The wily Black played his cards well. With both the Klan and the drys on the wane, he realized that he must forge new political alliances if he were to remain in the the Senate. As the election between Bankhead and Heflin neared its climax, Black began to make eloquent speeches in behalf of the man who had been his major opponent in 1926. Bankhead won easily. On the Senate floor, Black defended Bankhead against Heflin's claims that the election had been fraudulent and that he had been illegally excluded from the Democratic ballot.

In exchange for his vigorous campaign for Bankhead, Black elicited pledges of support from conventional political forces such as Alabama's Democratic party machine and the *Birmingham News*, which heretofore had bitterly opposed him. Taking note of Black's powerful new allies, as well as his original strength within the ranks of labor, drys, and the Klan, Hill refrained from challenging him in 1932. By again defeating Thomas Kilby, Black renewed his tenure in the Senate, further entrenching himself in a position which, had Alabama politics run a traditional course, might have been bestowed upon Lister Hill.[39]

First campaign for Congress, 1923

"Baby Congressman," 1923

With Henrietta on their wedding day, 20 February 1928,
in Columbus, Georgia, surrounded by the U.S. Army Band

With President Roosevelt at the signing of the act creating
the Tennessee Valley Authority, 18 May 1933. Fourth from right,
Congressman Hill; third from right, *Senator George W. Norris.*

Hill's constituency: Alabama audience for a political speech, 1930s

Editorial cartoon by Daniel Fitzpatrick in the St. Louis Post-Dispatch *after the 1938 election to the Senate of Lister Hill from Alabama and Claude Pepper from Florida*

With President Roosevelt at Tuskegee Institute, 1940. Backseat, left to right:
Roosevelt, Alabama governor Frank Dixon, and Senator Hill.

*Exhibiting typical oratorical fervor for the unseen audience
over the new medium of radio, early 1940s*

The Making of a New Dealer

1 9 3 3 — 1 9 3 7

"There's only one Lister Hill"

In January 1933, Franklin D. Roosevelt, smiling and waving to Alabama farm families who had risen before dawn to line his route, came to see Muscle Shoals for himself. Shortly after the 1932 presidential election, Lister Hill had called upon the president-elect at Warm Springs, Georgia, to urge a firsthand tour of the Tennessee River Valley. Following this inspection, Roosevelt accepted Hill's invitation to visit Montgomery. As host, Hill had instructed his uncle and his sister to arrange a dinner of Alabama quail for the president-elect and, for the press corps, "nice things to eat and plenty of liquid refreshments—you know how much [newspapermen] enjoy liquid refreshments." Standing where Jefferson Davis had taken his oath, Roosevelt paid tribute to the Confederate president and, tactfully adopting the parlance of Montgomery, spoke of "the war between the states." Observing this skillful performance, Hill felt positively exhilarated. "After being treated as the red-headed step child of the nation for all these years," he rejoiced, "the South is indeed to have a new deal." The sight of their young congressman escorting the nation's new leader also impressed Alabamians. "You should have heard the many complimentary things said about you around the hotel lobbies," a friend reported.[1]

Not yet forty years old, Lister Hill was still impressionable during the heady era when the New Deal took shape. He would observe from the vantage point of his secure House seat the ferment led by Roosevelt. Washington bustled under this new president. At long last, Hill reported to friends and relatives, a "real leader" had replaced "weak, incompetent" Hoover, who had "floundered around and seemed absolutely incapable of even any show of leadership." Roosevelt "captivated" Hill. "I have never known a more charming, delightful man," he informed his father. Further-more, the new occupant of the White House promised to be a master politician, blessed with "courage and . . . the faculty of using other men's brains."[2]

Hill soon realized that Roosevelt and Norris would have their way on Muscle Shoals. To attempt to block them would be futile and damaging to his standing with this new administration. He would keep urging Roosevelt to "our views," he assured the alarmed owner of a north Alabama lumber company. But when Roosevelt announced his comprehensive program for development of the Tennessee Valley, embodying Norris's ideas for flood control, navigation, reclamation, power, and industrial growth, Hill wired the president-elect: "Your plan becomes more dazzling all the time." As chairman of the House subcommittee charged with considering the fate of Muscle Shoals, Hill offered a bill emphasizing commercial manufacture of fertilizer and allowing private companies to lease power lines before per-mitting the government to construct new lines. But Roosevelt insisted upon Norris's version. Hill, having exhausted his arguments for a more limited federal role, accompanied Norris to the White House where they and the president agreed upon a name—Tennessee Valley Authority.[3]

TVA was created by combining bills introduced by Hill and Norris. Hill's 1933 version differed markedly from that he had proposed earlier. Norris had won a sweeping victory both on the issue of experimental fertilizer studies and on unrestricted construction of transmission lines. Hill admitted that the bill approved by House and Senate conferees vested Roosevelt with the power to do "nearly anything he wants" both as to nitrates and electricity.[4] It had taken Hill seven years to come around to Norris's visionary approach to development of the Tennessee Valley; fur-thermore, he had acceded only when he realized that Norris and Roosevelt would prevail. But preferring to forget his earlier fulminations against government activism, Hill proudly claimed to have helped to create TVA.

Hill's pragmatic decision paid off handsomely. For a few weeks after the TVA Act passed Congress in May 1933, he was deluged with letters from Alabamians who feared that the new agency would ruin their Alabama Power Company stocks and thereby plunge numerous widows and retired schoolteachers into pauperhood. But most Alabamians, caught up in the excitement of developing their great river basin, soon forgot their initial fears about putting the federal government in the power business.

As that government undertook to build a series of dams to harness the once unruly Tennessee River, one of the nation's most severely depressed areas started to blossom. New industries, the "Great Lakes of the South," barge traffic, jobs, fertilizer, conservation practices, and cheap electricity were to uplift the lives of the hitherto isolated and predominantly rural people of north Alabama. After the Rural Electrification Administration (REA) stretched power lines to these remote areas, Hill and Norris, visiting a newly electrified farm home, observed tears of joy in the eyes of its occupants. Such citizens, barely aware of the role played by Norris, would give Hill much of the credit for their new prosperity; the Tennessee Valley region would become his main area of political strength.

In 1935, Hill emerged as an equal partner with Norris in defending TVA from fresh attack. Private utility, coal, and railroad interests, supported by many Republicans, had proposed changes in the basic TVA law that Norris feared would virtually kill TVA. Hill led a successful floor fight to defeat these amendments. Then he countered with pro-TVA amendments that sheltered the Authority within the accepted commerce power of the federal government. In 1937, Hill succeeded to the chairmanship of the House Military Affairs Committee, chief legislative guardian of TVA.[5]

Roosevelt and Norris had given Hill his first taste for the exhilarating possibilities of a New Deal. After this lesson, Hill would prove much more responsive—even occasionally bold—as Congress authorized other federal ventures into hitherto uninvaded aspects of American society. Joining the congressional majority that authorized the first New Deal, Hill supported enormous public works and employment programs, government regulation of banking, the unwieldy experiment known as the National Industrial Recovery Act, and the expenditure of millions of tax dollars to cut back agricultural production and to help save farms and homes from mortgage foreclosure. He even offended many fellow veterans in 1934 by voting against their bonus, heeding Roosevelt's warning that such an expenditure might imperil the nation's recovery program.[6]

In Alabama and Washington during the 1930s, Hill encountered a number of other contemporaries who confronted the process of governance with boldness and imagination. Bibb Graves had dramatically demonstrated, as governor of Alabama from 1927 to 1931, that he could institute progressive programs in taxation, education, and road building as well as abolish the leasing of convicts as cheap, captive labor for private industry. This "little brown hickory nut of a man," with his chew of tobacco, Yale law degree, and captivating personality, endeared himself to the majority of Alabama voters by the remarkable record of his first administration and by his generosity with personal favors.[7] In 1934, Alabamians returned

Graves to the governorship, making him the first chief executive of Alabama in the twentieth century to serve two terms. Although Hill never involved himself publicly in gubernatorial races, he had favored Graves over his opponent, Frank Dixon, by then a prominent Birmingham lawyer allied with defenders of the status quo.

On the national scene, another Alabamian demonstrated that a relatively new and little-known senator could capture the nation's attention by espousing a radical antidote for unemployment. Putting forth his notion of a thirty-hour work week, Hugo Black stung New Dealers to counter with their own panacea, the ill-fated National Recovery Administration (NRA). Black was never to convince Roosevelt that a thirty-hour work week would alleviate the depression, but his revolutionary proposal helped to break the ice for the Fair Labor Standards Act of 1938. By bringing himself dramatically to White House attention, Black had taken his initial step toward becoming Roosevelt's first Supreme Court nominee. During the 1930s, this son of a small-town merchant, who had used the Klan as a vehicle to political power, discovered that Lister Hill, although from a more privileged background, shared his concern for the underdog. Not as daring or innovative as Black, Hill found himself drawn to this feisty, strong-minded colleague. Each man, however, had reservations about the other. Black evinced an attitude of superiority when discussing philosophical and political matters with Hill. Privately, Hill assessed Black as acting primarily in his own interest rather than from "any sense of loyalty, friendship, righteous obligation. . . ." In 1935, Hill confided to a friend: "Hugo Black was always the attorney for Hugo Black." But when they ceased to be potential political rivals, Hill and Black developed a close personal bond.[8]

Amid Washington's political and social circles or as visitors to the capital, Hill encountered other forward-looking Southerners, like Representative Maury Maverick of Texas; Brooks Hays of Arkansas, then an official of the Resettlement Administration; H. C. Nixon, a fellow Alabamian and one of the Vanderbilt Agrarians; and Francis Pickens Miller of Virginia, secretary of the Foreign Policy Association and founder of a citizens' group known as the National Policy Committee. Miller envisioned thousands of lay people, whom he called the "political yeomanry," engaged in discussion and debate on national issues. Crisscrossing the South, Miller discovered a surprising number of kindred spirits. In 1935, he molded them into the Southern Policy Committee, with Nixon as chairman and himself as secretary, to encourage discussion of southern issues and to promote progress in that region. Hill lent his name to the Southern

Policy Committee but seldom attended its meetings. Perhaps prudence dictated that he not affiliate too intimately with an organization that publicly opposed the poll tax and called for an end to "lynch law."[9]

During 1936 and 1937, however, Hill and Brooks Hays organized a weekly supper group in Washington and importuned southern members of Congress like John McClellan of Arkansas, Claude Pepper of Florida, and Lyndon Johnson and Maury Maverick of Texas to listen to such speakers as Henry A. Wallace and Harry Hopkins. (Not always successfully. Bluntly declining one such invitation, a Georgia Democratic congressman replied: "If there is one thing for which I have a distinct aversion, it is hearing Mr. Hopkins speak.") However, a great many "forward-looking Southerners" gathered at Hall's Restaurant for what Hill called the "Hall's Restaurant Southern Association" where they discussed tenancy, soil erosion, rural electrification, and other southern issues under the large painting of a naked woman over the bar. Led by Hill, this group persuaded fellow Democrats to include a statement deploring tenancy in their 1936 national platform.[10]

Following his reelection, Roosevelt named Hill to a special committee on farm tenancy headed by Agriculture Secretary Wallace. Hill chaired its steering committee that helped to frame and enact the Bankhead-Jones Farm Tenant Act of 1937, establishing the Farm Security Administration (FSA) to aid tenants in becoming landowners by means of low-interest government loans. By taking a lead in this innovative but sparsely financed program, Hill would be decried as a "spender" by large landowners who preferred that their labor force remain in the status of cheap, plentiful tenants. Shortly after his election to the Senate, Hill would describe FSA as one of the finest chapters in American history and urge that it be raised from an emergency agency to permanent status. But it would be another world war, rather than another government agency, that would profoundly change the status of tenants.[11]

By the spring of 1937, Hill, a fourteen-year veteran in Congress, had risen to the important post of chairman of a major committee and been freshly reelected to the House Democratic Steering Committee. ("A compliment from the White House," the *Alabama Journal* noted proudly.) Responding to the overwhelming national mood of isolationism, the new head of the House Military Affairs Committee, along with his Senate counterpart, the American Legion, and the secretaries of war and of the Navy, put forth a plan to "take the profits out of war" by conscripting industry as well as soldiers and taxing wartime profits heavily. Such a plan,

Hill told constituents back home, would prevent wars of aggression and avoid any repetition of the "ballooning" wartime profits that had created instant millionaires during World War I. Passage of a new and sterner neutrality law took precedence over this concept, but Hill would continue, even after United States entry into the war, to push for the concepts of universal national service and for barriers to wartime profiteering.[12]

On the homefront, his efforts bore more immediate fruit. Hill stunned Birmingham boosters by obtaining a new 1.5 million-dollar veterans hospital for Montgomery. "Montgomery was almost as surprised to receive the hospital as Birmingham was to lose it," commented the *Alabama Journal*. Some Alabama editors hinted that Birmingham may have lost this political plum because of its leadership's open hostility to the New Deal. But the Second District gave full credit to its alert congressman, with his important committee post, close ties to the military establishment, and friendship with Roosevelt. The grateful Montgomery Chamber of Commerce honored Hill at a banquet; the *Greenville Advocate* declared: "The various Alabama cities that bid for the new veterans hospital now realize that there's only one Lister Hill."[13]

Small wonder that Hill, with praise such as this ringing in his ears, should look toward larger horizons. In 1936, he had again refrained from challenging Bankhead and that formidable political clan, continuing to hope that an unexpected vacancy would occur in one of Alabama's senatorial posts. Barring such an eventuality, he would be forced to run against either Bankhead or Black. In the summer of 1937, Black, his name affixed to the administration's wage and hour proposal and its major proponent in the Senate, appeared to be the more vulnerable. The Black-Connery bill, an outgrowth of Black's original thirty-hour proposal, alarmed southern industrialists and timber owners with its plan to set federal standards for wages and work hours and to ban the labor of children under sixteen.

With Black coming up for reelection in 1938, anti-New Deal forces in Alabama pondered whether they might be wiser to back the more cautious New Dealer, Lister Hill, than to launch a hopeless candidate of their own philosophical persuasion. Between Black and Hill, New Deal opponents preferred Hill as "the lesser of two evils."[14] Would Hill risk his seniority in the House, key committee post, and safe congressional district to accept these uncongenial supporters and attempt to oust his friend and fellow Rooseveltian from the Senate? But how else to achieve the long-sought goal?

"Carry the cause to the people"

In August 1937, Roosevelt startled the Senate and the nation by nominating Hugo Black to the Supreme Court. This totally unexpected news struck Alabama political circles "like a bombshell," raising momentary hopes in the minds of men like Tom Heflin; Congressmen Frank Boykin of Mobile, Sam Hobbs of Selma, Joe Starnes of Guntersville, and Henry Steagall of Ozark; State Senator J. Miller Bonner of Wilcox County; and industrialist Donald Comer and attorney James A. Simpson of Birmingham. But the most likely contender for this vacancy was in Europe touring World War I battlefields with the American Battle Monuments Committee. Frantically Dr. Hill sought to convey this long-desired information to his son by transatlantic telephone. Meantime the doctor made his own announcement: "I feel safe in saying [Lister] will be a candidate." When this welcome news finally reached Hill in London, he wired his own intention to seek Black's seat and immediately sailed for home. Wags in Montgomery circulated a tongue-in-cheek story that their congressman had drowned: "Lister couldn't find a boat quick enough, so he started swimming back!"[15]

Finally Hill had a clear shot at a Senate seat. It must have seemed almost miraculous that Black, who had emerged from nowhere to claim a Senate seat in 1926, was no longer an obstacle to his own political advancement. Lo and behold, Franklin Roosevelt, with a clever stroke of his pen, had removed that rival from Alabama politics. Scanning the political horizon, Hill could see no serious challenger except Heflin.[16]

Bibb Graves, urged by supporters of both Hill and Heflin to appoint one of these men for the remaining eighteen months of Black's term, adroitly sidestepped this choice, ignoring a message from Washington that Black and "The Boss" [FDR] wanted Hill appointed. Calling a special Democratic primary for 4 January 1938, Graves placed this responsibility on the voters. Meantime, he named his wife, Dixie, to Black's seat where, the governor said candidly, she would not face any important decisions before January. After the primary, she would meekly step down, allowing her husband to appoint the voters' choice to the Senate prior to an April special election to fill the remaining eight months of Black's term.[17]

Like Hill, Heflin had been reared by a stern physician. But, unlike the innovative and ambitious Dr. Hill, Heflin's father had been a typical rural doctor, comfortably well-to-do by hill-country standards. By requiring his son to work in the fields alongside blacks, Dr. Heflin had inadvertently provided Tom with the opportunity to acquire his greatest political gift:

storytelling. Mimicking black dialect and inventing guileless blacks ("Uncle Rufus," "Aunt Cindy") as butts of imaginary tales became Heflin's political forte. To add lyricism to his speech-making, Heflin threw in melodious lines from Shakespeare and, to sanction his views, carefully selected passages from the Bible. His flowing hair, ample girth, and costume—striped trousers, Prince Albert coat, double-breasted waistcoat, bow tie, broad-brimmed hat, and yellow shoes—dramatized Heflin's act. Most Alabama voters relished this show. To rural folk, Heflin *looked* like a senator. They guffawed at his stories and applauded when he voiced their sentiments on the subject of race ("I believe . . . that God almighty intended the negro to be servant to the white man") and male dominance ("I do not believe there is a red-blooded man in the world who in his heart really believes in Woman's suffrage. . . . every man who favors it ought to wear a dress"). His gut appeals and showmanship had won Heflin eight terms in the House and two elections to the Senate.[18]

During twenty-six years in Congress, Heflin had sponsored no more significant legislation than the resolution creating Mother's Day to honor, as he put it, "the good angel of the fireside, the queen of the American home." In general, he was a loyal Democrat, a friend of the cotton farmer (hence one of his nicknames, "Cotton Tom"), an ardent patriot, and an unswerving follower of Woodrow Wilson before and after World War I. But amid the resurgent nativism of the 1920s, Heflin had hit upon a fresh theme that brought him to the attention of audiences across the nation. At Klan-sponsored rallies, Heflin railed against what he described as a Catholic plot to draw the United States into war against Mexico.[19]

Challenged on the Senate floor by Catholic colleagues, Heflin embroiled himself even more deeply in this issue. Although he insisted that he opposed political, not religious, aspects of Catholicism, Heflin epitomized bigotry to most Americans. In 1928, Heflin attacked his party's nominee, Alfred E. Smith, as a threat to the reigning trinity of rural southern politics: prohibition, Protestantism, and segregation. For openly opposing Smith, he had been severely and, many thought, unjustly punished when Alabama Democratic leaders allowed the unfaithful to return to their fold as voters in 1930 but not as candidates.

Forced to run for reelection to the Senate as an independent, Heflin suffered almost inevitable defeat at the hands of the Democratic candidate, John Bankhead Jr. He demanded and got a long, costly Senate investigation of this election, but Bankhead, strongly supported by the pragmatic Black, won this contest also. Heflin made another unsuccessful attempt to return to Congress in 1934 as representative of Alabama's Fifth District. Sympathetic friends then arranged for him to be appointed to a $6,000-a-year federal sinecure in Washington. But when he heard that Black's seat was up for grabs, the old fire horse threw over these traces and bolted for Alabama. In poor health, a heavy drinker, and sixty-nine years of age, Heflin prepared for his last hurrah.[20]

Hill's family, practiced in the art of advancing Lister's career, geared up to promote their relative to the long-desired position of senator. Dr. Hill, his brother Dr. R. S. Hill, and his son-in-law Dr. E. W. Rucker, called upon their patients and on other physicians for support. Lister's uncles, William Hill, who held the key political post of probate judge of Montgomery County, and Wiley Hill, and his cousin T. B. Hill Jr., wooed fellow lawyers and judges. Mrs. Albert Thomas, chairman of the women's division of the campaign, reminded hundreds of her friends: "Remember Tom Heflin opposed woman's suffrage!" Ex-servicemen, Woodmen of the World, and members of other fraternal organizations were exhorted to support a fellow veteran and lodge member.[21]

But the art of personal politics, so successful in the Second District, could not deliver sufficient votes to carry an entire state. This task required money and organization. Campaign funding would be no problem: the determined Dr. Hill stood ready to provide out of his own pocket up to $100,000 if necessary, an unheard-of sum in the Alabama politics of the 1930s. However, Dr. Hill demanded careful management and strict accounting of his money. At one low point in campaign finances, Hill, hesitant to approach his father, sent Robert Frazer to ask for more funds. Reluctantly the doctor reached into his big safe and pulled out $5,000 in moldy, World War I Liberty Bonds. Referring to a sewage drain that ran through the center of Montgomery, he chastised Frazer: "You and Lister must be throwing my money in the Genetta ditch!" Years later, Clarence Allgood, charged with responsibility for expenditures, recalled that this campaign had cost considerably less than $10,000. Nonetheless the doctor frequently demanded of Allgood: "Son, you getting receipts for all this money?"[22]

To manage his campaign, Hill turned to Roy Nolen, whose political expertise he had come to appreciate in the 1928 campaign when Nolen had directed the Speakers Bureau for the Alabama Democratic party. In 1930 Hill had again witnessed Nolen's political wizardry as the major architect of John Bankhead Jr.'s victory over Heflin. Through Hill's influence, Nolen had been appointed in 1933 to a strategic political watchtower, the postmastership of Montgomery. To the knowledgeable, Nolen's appointment had signaled Hill's intent to seek statewide office. But almost five years were to pass before Nolen would get the go-ahead openly to organize Alabama for Hill. Meantime the postmaster kept up with legislators, lobbyists, members of the governor's staff, and politicos over the state. Grover Hall Jr., observing Nolen at work, judged him Alabama's most accomplished political agent, "stable, sage, crafty and a man who understands the sweet uses of patience," the perfect counterpoise to Hill's "spitfire attack, stormy syllogisms." As soon as he heard of Black's nomination, Nolen told William Hill that this power vacuum was "made to order for Lister."[23]

Until illness in the late 1940s forced Nolen to disengage from political activity, he served as Hill's main informant on Alabama politics. Almost every day—sometimes twice a day—the postmaster wrote Hill a lengthy letter relaying the most minute details of Montgomery gossip and reporting every nuance in the state's political affairs. In their otherwise frank correspondence, Nolen and Hill devised a private code to denote those whom they most frequently discussed. "Bibbo the Builder" was a joshing reference to former Governor Graves, who ran his own political show and competed with Hill for the post of Alabama's number one Rooseveltian. The nickname "Brooklyn overseer" connoted Hill's and Nolen's belief that Frank Dixon had links with large corporations and absentee ownership. Other characters in their correspondence included "Caesar" (Speaker William Bankhead); "Jawn" (Senator John Bankhead); "Marble Columns" (Justice Black); "Bishop" (the Montgomery journalist Atticus Mullin); "First Avenue and Twentieth Street" (the anti-New Deal leadership in Birmingham); and "the cause" (their own viewpoint).[24]

"Roy Nolen worshipped Hill," a colleague remembered years later. "He was nervous as a cat when Lister was in a campaign." An ardent New Dealer, Nolen urged his candidate to take stands on issues with broad, popular appeal. "Roy was a conscience for Hill," another friend recalled. "He kept him pushed and stirred up legislatively." Hill, with his penchant for slogans, adopted two of Nolen's favorite sayings as his own: "let's keep our faces to the rising sun and the shadows will fall behind" and "carry the cause to the people." Friends whom Hill frequently exhorted to support "the cause" interpreted this term to mean the human weal in general and the New Deal in particular.[25]

As cotton whitened in the fields, Heflin and Hill took their campaigns to county seats and small towns. Radio was too impersonal a medium for the local politics of 1937. Voters wanted to *see* the old gladiator and the young New Dealer, to while away a few Saturday hours consulting a roadside palm reader, shucking peanuts, or swapping mules, hounds, hogs, and chickens as the beloved cadences of southern oratory swirled above their heads.

Heflin's fame as a tub-thumper spurred Hill to embellish his own style. "When [Hill] started talking," a friend remembered, "he was like a holiness speaker weaving a trance." Hill reminded audiences that Heflin had opposed woman's suffrage, the Bankheads, "the party of our fathers," and, by his absurd charges against Catholics and Jews, had embarrassed his state. Facing unemployed coal miners and steelworkers in north Alabama, Hill pledged to fight the "Big Boys" of Birmingham and those mysterious, faraway enemies who had devised the arbitrary system that kept the price of Birmingham steel three to five dollars a ton higher than that of Pittsburgh.[26]

Rural voters waited expectantly for Hill's famous perorations, especially the legend of the Scottish king, Robert the Bruce. As Hill recounted this story, Robert, on his deathbed, had ordered that his heart be removed from his body and borne by his knights to the Holy Sepulcher. When Turks attacked the Scots bent on this mission, the Earl of Douglass had hurled the casket containing the heart of Robert into the midst of the enemy. Lister's vibrato rendition of Douglass's battle cry—"Lead on, heart of Bruce, we follow thee!"—thrilled his listeners, women in particular. Recalling Hill's platform style years later, Frazer wrote: "In the old days we hurled the gory heart of Robert [the] Bruce in every face in Alabama, while John T. Morgan stood guard with a shotgun to see that nobody put out the light in the capitol dome." In other favorite summations, Hill would roar: "I'm for the red, white and blue forever!" or "When election day comes, we gonna *call the roll*! Folks like you and me gonna register our influence on this government. Yes boys, we're gonna *call the roll*!" As a political pundit for the *Montgomery Advertiser* once put it, "If your boy Lister Hill ain't an orator, I'm Tom Heflin's choice for the next Pope." But more sophisticated city audiences sometimes hinted that Hill's elocution sounded dated to their ears. Hearing snickers at "the tears in Lister's voice," a friendly observer advised that Hill's speech-making "smacked a bit too much of the old ten-twent'-thirt' style of oratory."[27]

Anti-Catholicism as an issue in American politics had peaked in 1928, then slowly receded. In the Heflin camp, most allusions to Hill's Catholic upbringing were confined to letters and whispers. (One letter writer, recalling that Hill had made charges that "the people did not believe" against William Feagin because Feagin had differed with "the alter [*sic*] boy," urged Heflin to revive this old quarrel.) But Heflin himself openly spread word of a whisper campaign that his opponent had been a Catholic and a "choir boy." Feigning tolerance, Heflin said: "I am against dragging that issue into the campaign. . . . it does not matter whether my opponent is or is not a Catholic. A man's religion is his own affair." But by 1937, the Klan, which had fanned the fires of religious prejudice, had fallen from political power. Nor was race a live issue with both candidates avowing opposition to a federal antilynching bill. Somewhat at a loss for a bugaboo, Heflin appealed to impoverished farmers to oppose "this great Ajax of the Hill dynasty, Lord Lister of the Aristocracy of the Dollar."[28]

Although they relished such verbal fusillades, many in Alabama's limited electorate found pocketbook issues more compelling, at least for the moment, than any appeals Heflin might concoct to stir the ever-smoldering fires of racism, bigotry, class animosity, and resentment of meddlesome outsiders. Behind Hill they sensed the larger shadow of Franklin Roosevelt to whom they had given 86 percent of their votes only one year earlier. Had it not been for Roosevelt, would their state have enjoyed a major share of the revitalizing Tennessee Valley Authority? Had not FDR, with his pet scheme of a Civilian Conservation Corps, put their sons to work cutting trees and clearing forests? Was it not Roosevelt who had brought electricity to their rural homes, liberated them from the tasks of cooking over wood stoves, lifting heavy "sad irons," and pumping water from wells, and even made it possible for them to enjoy the miraculous diversion of radio? Had not they and thousands like them escaped from the demeaning dole to the more respectable payrolls of his Works Progress Administration (WPA)? Were not Birmingham's miners and steelworkers strengthened in their efforts to secure higher wages and better work conditions now that the New Deal had sheltered unions under the protective eye of the National Labor Relations Board?

While Tom Heflin had languished in political exile, Lister Hill had helped to bring about all these changes that had directly bettered their lives. Perhaps Congressman Hill *had* gone a bit far by supporting Roosevelt's plan to bring a recalcitrant Supreme Court to heel but, looking at the overall picture, could not most Alabama voters forgive this excess of zeal? With the Court itself changing and their own Hugo Black now on the high bench, despite the brouhaha over his onetime Klan membership, was it not like beating a dead horse to argue this issue?

Furthermore, Roosevelt and Hill offered to these underpaid and over-worked people the hope of yet another benefaction. While Alabamians pondered their choice for senator, a coalition of Republicans and southern Democrats stood guard at the gates of the House Rules Committee to prevent consideration of the administration bill to require that many indus-tries raise their minimum pay immediately to at least twenty-five cents an hour (and soon to forty cents) and shorten their work week to forty-four hours (and eventually to forty). The vast majority of southern members of Congress, responding to pressure from business and industrial interests back home, stood fast against federal intrusion to elevate the low wage structure of their region.[29]

Although Hill had never declared in favor of the Black-Connery bill, he now campaigned for wage-hour legislation and hinted that, if need be, he would again support FDR's unpopular plan to enlarge (opponents said "pack") the Supreme Court. The administration's proposal for federal regulation of wages and hours, Hill told an audience in Troy, would be "the death knell of the sweatshop and . . . [of] exploitation, for gain, of Ameri-can children in the factory." Furthermore, if a majority on the high court should continue to perform "legislative . . . rather than judicial functions," Hill pledged that he "would fully meet my obligations as a member of the Senate." To take such openly controversial stands seemed uncharacteristi-cally bold. Behind the scenes, Hugo Black encouraged such audacity. To Justice Black, Hill reported: "I am hewing right down the line as vigor-ously as I can, as you suggested."[30]

Heflin, facing crowds of overalled men, wobbled on the subject of Roosevelt but minced no words in opposing federal wage- and hour-scales and frightening his listeners with images of industrial collapse, higher wages for farm labor, and higher prices for everything that farmers had to buy. Southern folk lived in the open, Heflin argued, and thus did not require the same wages as the "aliens and foreigners" of New England. Leaders of Alabama's farm hierarchy, Edward A. O'Neal and J. Litt Edwards of the Farm Bureau Federation, Frank Earle of the Alabama Agricultural Association, and heads of almost every county affiliate urged their restive followers to disregard Heflin's dire predictions and remember that the New Deal had helped them to become landowners or to refinance their mortgages. Hill asked farmers to ponder how much more produce they could sell if industrial workers received higher wages. Nonetheless many sympathetic farmers continued to regard old "Cotton Tom" as one of their own, another poor fellow who had received a raw deal.[31]

Supporters of both candidates seemed strangely unenthusiastic about their choices. After listening to a Heflin speech, a Hill spy reported that the Farm Bureau, despite its public stance, had arranged the applause. Offering lukewarm endorsement to Hill, the *Birmingham News* and the *Birmingham Age-Herald*, strong Bankhead organs, made it plain that they opposed his stands on the Court and the wage-and-hour bill but foresaw even more danger in "having the state's business entrusted to a lovable clown." The *Birmingham Post*, too, supported Hill feebly. After some initial hesitation, the *Anniston Star* came out for Hill. The *Montgomery Advertiser* endorsed its hometown candidate but took care to mention that it did not wholly agree with Hill's views. "The wage-hour bill is what is hurting," a friend advised Hill. Calling upon Montgomerians to support Hill, Mayor Gunter admitted that he and the Hills had disagreed in the past but assured his followers that "none of this unpleasantness exists at this time."[32]

Most Alabama industrialists, timber owners, and business leaders considered a Heflin victory their best bet against the threat of federal work standards but seemed slightly embarrassed by the antics of their standard bearer. Lest Heflin be accused of "economic royalist" backing, the "big mules" prudently kept a low profile. (Bibb Graves saddled Alabama businessmen and industrial leaders with the label "big mules" because, he explained, he had seen many wagons heavy with hay pulled by little mules while the big mules, tied to the back, munched away at the load.) Atticus Mullin, the *Montgomery Advertiser*'s gossipy political columnist, surmised that the "Big Boys" backed Heflin only in hope of slapping FDR; if their man should defeat Hill, they planned to pick another candidate to defeat Heflin for the full Senate term to start in 1938.[33]

In December, Congress faced another showdown over wage-hour legislation. Administration allies forced this measure out of the House Rules Committee and onto the floor. Opponents countered with a successful move to send the bill back to committee. In the Alabama delegation, only Hill and a seemingly reluctant Speaker Bankhead (who had to be reminded to cast his vote by the House clerk) supported the administration's bill. By this uncharacteristically rash action, Hill staked his senatorial hopes on the belief that a majority of Alabama voters would not buy Heflin's argument that milder climate justified cheaper wages.[34]

As voting day neared, Hill held the face cards. Organized labor, including mine, steel, and railroad workers and the Alabama Federation of Labor, endorsed him as did the big machines headed by Graves and

Gunter. Senator Bankhead, victor over Heflin in the bitter electoral contest of 1930, made a crucial contribution by announcing that he would find Hill a more congenial colleague than his old antagonist. Voters in north Alabama readied themselves to express their gratitude for the transformation of the Tennessee Valley. Above all, Franklin Roosevelt lent his implicit support after Hill appealed to Hyde Park for help. Pictures of Roosevelt and Hill adorned campaign posters. Hill rode with Roosevelt as the president's train rolled back from Miami to Washington in December. "The inference is obvious," observed the *Washington Herald*. In essence, the senatorial contest boiled down to one central issue: despite Roosevelt's recent setback on the Court fight and the nation's still faltering economy, would voters in this Deep South state send another ardent New Dealer of the Hugo Black stripe to the Senate?[35]

Undertaken so spiritedly in August, the senatorial campaign sputtered to a close. Hill, claiming that he was urgently needed at a special session, commuted between Alabama and Washington. Heflin, exhausted by his oratorical efforts, contracted pneumonia. During the final weeks of the campaign, the "fleshy, feverish old man" lay bedridden, unaware that election day had come and gone. His illness, his age, and the haunting memory of his 1928 defection from the Democratic party helped to seal Heflin's fate. On 4 January 1938, fewer than 150,000 of Alabama's voters bothered to go to the polls. This light turnout represented only slightly more than 10 percent of Alabama's voting-age population, heavily disfranchised by the poll tax, race, illiteracy, poverty, and apathy. Of those who did appear at voting booths, 61 percent supported Hill. He won all but twelve of Alabama's sixty-seven counties, including the Tennessee Valley and most of north Alabama; every Black Belt county except one; Montgomery (by a vote of over 20 to 1) and the rest of his old congressional district, and the metropolitan centers of Birmingham and Mobile with their sizable labor contingents. Heflin carried his home county, Chambers; part of his old congressional district; four counties in southwestern Alabama dominated by timber and sawmill interests; one Wiregrass county; and two poor and sparsely populated counties in central Alabama (see Appendix, Map 2).[36]

As the *Birmingham News* interpreted it, the election had been a victory "for the New Deal, Rooseveltism, Democracy, and the WPA; a defeat for Economic Royalty, KKKism, and the Power of a Good Joke." Relieved to find a southern state still safely in line for the New Deal, James A. Farley, chairman of the Democratic National Committee, wired Hill, "the Union is safe." A jubilant Bibb Graves interpreted the results for Roosevelt: "Keep on keeping on, Americans are with the New Deal." The president himself telephoned to congratulate Hill. The *Washington Evening Star*, noting that Hill's advocacy of the wage-hour bill "did not hurt him a bit," predicted that this victory would give other southern members of Congress "something to think about."[37]

Hill's victory was followed that May by the thumping reelection of another native Alabamian and ardent New Dealer, Senator Claude Pepper of Florida. These two victories, a Pittsburgh labor journal rejoiced, showed that "even in the South labor can deliver the goods."[38] Such strong expressions of support by rank-and-file Southerners broke the congressional logjam and led to passage of the Fair Labor Standards Act of 1938, forcing immediate pay raises for millions and ending child labor. Observing the dramatic effect of this federal law upon the South, Hill must have recalled with satisfaction the vow he had made as a student of Professor McCorvey.

True to his promise, Graves appointed Hill to the Senate less than one week after the primary. In the April special election to complete Black's term and in the regular May Democratic primary to choose a candidate for the ensuing six years, no one opposed Senator Hill. In the November election, Hill overwhelmed a little-known Republican.[39]

Generously supported and constantly prodded by his father, Lister Hill had achieved his boyhood dream with relative ease. As Dr. Hill had promised, sound preparation, an early start, self-discipline, hard work, and chance had all been factors in this accomplishment. Hill had also enjoyed an unusual luxury for a politician. Financed solely by his father in all his campaigns, he had not found it necessary to become indebted to special interests. Reflecting on this good fortune, Hill wrote Nolen in 1940: "The sweetest thing about my service both in the House and in the Senate has been that I have been absolutely independent and free as far as anybody being able to come to me and say they had put up money, etc., for my election." Describing himself as "a virgin on this [money] score," Hill confided to his campaign manager that he hoped to "hold fast to [this virginity] in the future." But even for one with such a generous father, total financial independence would not prove feasible in the future.[40]

Having ventured far from the confines of Montgomery before his thirtieth birthday, Hill had been young and flexible enough to be educated in a national context rather than in the narrow, parochial viewpoint held by the majority of his hometown peers. Amid the innovative atmosphere of the New Deal, he had responded to a number of stimuli. No compassionate person could have been impervious to the needs of the majority of his Alabama constituents, bogged in tenancy, dietary deficiencies, and ignorance. Bold thinkers like Norris, Henry Wallace, Francis Miller, Bibb Graves, and Black had stirred Hill's imagination and illustrated the power of strong-willed individuals to influence the course of government. But one colossus above all, the squire of Hyde Park, exemplar of the aristocrat as democrat, daring proponent of governmental noblesse oblige, had fired up Lister Hill, erased his initial misgivings, and transformed him into an ardent New Dealer, willing to commit himself to total adherence to Roosevelt's programs. Years later, when one of Hill's staff members offered him the draft of a speech containing the line, "here to do the people's wishes," Hill instantly corrected him: "No, no! Here to *lead* the people for their own best interests."[41] He had absorbed this from Franklin Roosevelt.

Usually cautious, Hill had refrained from putting his name up for the Senate until only the aging, infirm, politically rejected, and often ridiculed Heflin stood in his way. It had not been necessary to make the painful choice of whether to attempt to oust his friend and fellow progressive, Hugo Black, from the Senate by means of an unnatural alliance with enemies of the New Deal. Prodded by Hugo Black and Roy Nolen, inspired by Roosevelt, he had put caution aside to come out strongly for a wages-and-hours law. Building on his statewide network of kinship and friendship, he had enlarged his political base to include the grateful citizenry of the Tennessee Valley, the increasingly politicized elements of organized labor, and, at least publicly, leaders of organized agriculture. Hill won his Senate seat in an era when economic rather than demagogic considerations swayed most Alabama voters. With most Alabama voters having wearied of their nativistic excesses by the late 1930s, his Catholic upbringing and partially Jewish ancestry appeared to be dead and almost forgotten issues. But ahead lay a vastly more complex, combustible, and exhaustive test of political acumen.

The Wartime Years

1 9 3 8 – 1 9 4 4

"The Bankheads can't have their cake and eat it too"

His colleagues welcomed the new senator from Alabama with spirited applause when Hill took his seat in the upper chamber 12 January 1938. By their warm greeting, senators also expressed their relief that they were to be joined, not by a cantankerous old clown, but by a vigorous and legislatively experienced member just turned forty-three years of age, thus among the Senate's five youngest members. After Hill had served only one year in the Senate, fellow Democrats signaled that they regarded him as a comer by choosing him as assistant whip, the third most important post in party ranks. In January 1941, Hill would become whip, charged with helping Democratic leader Alben Barkley of Kentucky in such crucial matters as determining the order in which bills were to be considered and seeing to it that Democrats were fully represented on the floor for major debates and votes.

For a freshman senator who moved so quickly into a leadership role, what other opportunities might lie ahead? Grover Hall Jr., political columnist for the *Montgomery Advertiser*, predicted that Hill would someday take over the powerful role of majority leader. Earlier, Harlan Miller of the *Washington Post* had advanced an even more titillating possibility, describing Hill as a "modern . . . streamlined Southern senator of a type apt to be the first twentieth century [southern] president." This columnist noted that Hill differed from the "classic Southern senator" in that he considered the twentieth century more important than the nineteenth. Less than a year later, Miller again touted Hill, along with two more experienced legislators, Pat Harrison of Mississippi and James Byrnes of South Carolina, as a southern senator of presidential caliber. "The USA must elect a Southern president one of these years," Miller urged, "or [the South] will stop breeding anything but regional Huey Longs." Many Alabama editors proudly reprinted Miller's estimate of their senator. The *Florala News* theorized that Hill, being young, could serve in the Senate for many years and "still be White House material."[1]

Personal friends, such as Alabama's Lieutenant Governor Albert A. Carmichael, the Montgomery journalist Gould Beech, and the devoted Nolen, also began to hint at this possibility. In 1940, Nolen reminded Hill that few men of independent cast of mind remained on the national scene, with Hugo Black on the Court, Norris "in the evening of his career," and the passing of that political maverick, William E. Borah. "You have a real mission in the world," Hill's campaign manager urged. Beech, searching through biographies of great men, reported that he could not find another recent American who had displayed such statesmanship and political savvy and achieved such high stature by the age of forty-three. In 1942, a Cullman insurance salesman and dark-horse contender for Alabama's governorship would also advance this possibility. "I'm a Lister Hill for President in '44 booster right now," James E. Folsom wrote Hill. Hill, too, spoke openly to his longtime, trusted secretary, Robert Frazer, about his chances to reach the White House. Years later Frazer recalled: "He was going for the top."[2]

But no matter what national notice he would attract, Hill had conformed to the conventional political behavior of a southern senator less than three weeks after he entered the Senate. Although a rank newcomer, he acceded to an urgent request from his old army friend, Tom Connally, that he make his first speech in the Senate even before receiving his committee assignments. Hill joined the filibuster against a proposed antilynching law that called for federal prosecution of a state or local officer if a prisoner in his custody were killed by a mob. As had Hugo Black before him, Hill concentrated on procedural objections to the Costigan-Wagner bill, a technique he would attempt to follow in later civil rights debates. It would be difficult, he argued, to convince a jury from the same voting constituency that had *elected* these law officers to convict them of willful negligence, thereby subjecting them to fines or imprisonment. Furthermore, Hill rationalized, states might, as during prohibition, take the position that a federal law absolved them of all responsibility. It would be "cruel injustice," he pleaded, to condemn the South when lynchings in that region had declined from 231 in 1892 to eight in 1937, indicating that Southerners had "about" solved this problem on their own.[3]

In the windup of his maiden speech, Hill treated the Senate to one of those remarkably convoluted sentences with which he virtually hypnotized Alabama voters:

> Mr. President, when we weigh the pending measure, when we look beyond and behind it and see the real reason that brings it here, when we consider all the unfortunate and perhaps tragic possibilities that might grow out of its passage, and its absolute futility to in any way do what its authors claim for it, I would ask all true friends of the negro, I would ask all liberal-minded members of this body who believe in the great human welfare program and who would save that program, all who would heal wounds rather than open them, all who would help people rather than condemn them, all who would save our American institutions rather than destroy them, all who would forget the dark, bitter days of the past and would lead mankind into the sunlight of a new day, with its hope and its promise, to join hands and send this measure down to the tongueless silence of dreamless dust.[4]

No wonder that two years later Democratic strategists, eager to display continuing southern loyalty to their party, would agree that an orator such as this should place Franklin Roosevelt's name in nomination for an unprecedented third term. As Hill explained in 1939 to his friend Jonathan Daniels, editor of the *Raleigh News and Observer*, Congress was no longer divided along Democratic-Republican lines but between New Dealers and a coalition of Republicans and anti-New Dealers, most of the latter from the South. Although Hill had told Daniels that he was at a loss to explain this bitter southern opposition to a president who had done so much for their region, he clearly understood that he and even such cautious advocates of change as William and John Bankhead Jr. had aroused the ire of economic forces resentful of federal intrusion into hitherto unregulated spheres.[5]

Frank Dixon, elected Alabama's governor in 1938, represented the interests of his state's dissident Democrats. Hill led FDR loyalists. Both elements desired to control Alabama's delegation to the 1940 Democratic convention and professed to back the virtually hopeless favorite-son candidacy of Speaker William Bankhead. But Hill's friends suspected that Dixon and his followers, in favoring an uninstructed delegation, meant to give Bankhead only token support, then trade their votes to John Nance Garner or some other anti-Roosevelt candidate.

Hill and Nolen urged party loyalists to enter the delegate race pledged to remain diehard supporters of the New Deal. "The delegation must be for Bankhead," Hill directed Nolen, "but it must also be for the New Deal." With the exception of occasional pro-Roosevelt statements by Henry Steagall and Representative John Sparkman from Huntsville, other members of Alabama's congressional delegation did everything possible to escape a showdown between New Dealers and anti-New Dealers. The Bankhead brothers, one fancying the presidency and the other concerned about his own reelection in 1942, proved fearful of offending monied interests and avoided an all-out commitment to Roosevelt. "You stand alone," Nolen advised Hill.[6]

Through the winter and spring of 1940, internecine warfare raged in the ranks of those who labeled themselves Alabama Democrats. "It is an awfully hard job," Hill complained to Nolen, "waging a fight when you do not have lieutenants and captains and . . . are so badly lacking in the munitions of war. . . . think of it, almost an entire state press against you and not a penny with which to buy radio time." But the chiefs of the two factions did not operate alone: the Roosevelt team also included former Governor Graves, Lieutenant Governor Albert A. Carmichael, and the astute strategists Nolen, Richard Rives, and Marc Ray ("Foots") Clement; Dixon had assistance from, among others, Marion Rushton, Gessner McCorvey, James E. Simpson, Harry Ayers, Sam Hobbs, and Hill's old adversary in the school board controversy, William F. Feagin.[7]

So long as Speaker Bankhead remained a possible contender, both sides cagily hid their real intentions under a cloak of loyalty to a fellow Alabamian. To Nolen, Hill confided his puzzlement over how "to let the Bankheads know they can't have their cake and eat it too. . . . they have either to go 100% with us and the New Deal . . . or else . . . go with the New Deal haters." To hearten his friend, Nolen frequently reminded Hill that the great majority of Alabamians were "more solid for Roosevelt . . . and the continuous responsibility of Government for Human Welfare than ever before." Sentiment for drafting Roosevelt in remote counties like Conecuh and Escambia, Nolen reported, was "overwhelming." Fired up, Hill responded that it would be "nothing short of an outrage to let [the anti-New Dealers] win in a state as wholeheartedly New Deal as is Alabama." He was disgusted, Hill told his campaign manager, with the "pussyfooters and those who betray the New Deal for their selfish hides."[8]

As March approached, Hill and Nolen began to plan how to persuade William Bankhead to withdraw as a possible Roosevelt opponent, thus leaving the anti-New Dealers with no alternative except FDR. Bibb Graves was summoned to Washington for a showdown; the White House was advised as to the Bankheads' equivocation, with the unspoken threat that a victorious Roosevelt might block William's reelection as Speaker and withhold his support from John in his Senate race. Thus confronted, the Bankheads cast their die. "My candidacy," the Speaker announced, "will not be in opposition to [Roosevelt's] nomination." William further urged that Alabama elect only delegates favorable to the New Deal. Proudly, Hill confided to Nolen: "I myself wrote the statement from the first word to the last."[9]

The Bankheads' capitulation had not been accidentally timed. At the behest of Hill and Nolen, the Speaker had waited until after the deadline for further entries into the delegate race; it was too late for the anti-Roosevelt forces to rally behind new candidates. With the path now clear for a New Deal victory in Alabama, Hill openly committed himself to a third term "for the cause of human welfare and the advancement of our people."[10]

With Roosevelt remaining coy, a host of other Democratic hopefuls, including Speaker Bankhead, Vice President Garner, Secretary of State Cordell Hull, Governor Paul McNutt of Indiana, Senators Byrnes, Burton K. Wheeler, and Scott Lucas, and the estranged former chairman of the Democratic National Committee, James A. Farley, awaited word of the president's intent. But FDR, Hill noted, was "wise enough to keep his own counsel while delegation after delegation fall [sic] in line for him."[11]

In May 1940, Alabama Democrats elected a convention delegation dominated by New Deal loyalists. Hill, Steagall, John Bankhead Jr., and Lieutenant Governor Carmichael, all professing loyalty to Roosevelt, won the statewide contest for delegates-at-large. John Bankhead, his name closely associated with the popular Speaker and preferred by anti-New Dealers over the other three leading candidates, had proved to be the top vote-getter, followed by Hill. But within the delegation, Hill had more backers than the senior senator and was to be elected chairman. Harry Ayers, the Anniston publisher who had been persuaded by Governor Dixon to run for delegate-at-large, and a fifth candidate, also opposed to Roosevelt, had trailed badly. Ayers explained to readers of his newspaper that, in opposing two senators, a House member, the lieutenant governor, all "with vast patronage to bestow," as well as the organized farm and labor vote, he had been up against the "strongest vote-getting combination" in Alabama history. A fellow editor, Ed Field of the *Selma Times-Journal*, complained that Hill had exploited William Bankhead's popularity to "deliver Alabama into the hands of the third termers." But Hill told Nolen with great satisfaction: "Well, we have got the delegation and we have got the Chairmanship. . . ."[12]

"That speech cooked him"

When fifty thousand Democrats, prepared to "draft" Roosevelt, gathered in the steamy Chicago stadium that July, FDR supporters angrily shouted down an anti-third-term plank. At Bankhead's request, Alabama's delegates abandoned plans to honor their native son by placing him in nomination when the name of their state was called first on the roll. They hoped that Roosevelt, to reward Bankhead for his loyalty, would tap the Speaker as his running mate. But an adamant FDR would insist upon having his own choice, Henry Wallace, on the ticket. Bankhead, who served as temporary chairman and keynoter of the convention, was to die in September a disappointed man.

Rather than yield the honor of nominating Roosevelt to his home state, as customary, the chairman of the Alabama delegation, who had seen to it that his state had sent a majority of New Deal loyalists to Chicago, had been picked by Roosevelt himself to place his name before the convention. Back in May, Nolen had foreseen just such an opportunity. Alabama's twenty-two votes may look "feeble" compared to the vote of larger states but "they can't take away Alabama's first place on the call," Nolen reminded Hill. "Why can't you nominate [FDR] right off the bat?" the campaign manager suggested.[13]

What an opportunity for a freshman senator to be heard by the nation and further his dream of attaining the presidency! Had not Roosevelt himself, by nominating Al Smith at the Democratic conventions of 1924 and 1928, set the stage for his own nomination in 1932? With Robert Frazer holding the stopwatch, Hill practiced his speech over and over until he could deliver it in eleven minutes. As his boss left for Chicago, Frazer pleaded: "Brisk and bouncy now; please don't drag it!" But when Speaker Bankhead introduced this "brilliant, young senator," Hill—never before nervous on a podium—was "petrified" by the gravity of the moment and the prospect of a huge nationwide radio audience. How could a man warm up these listeners, seen and unseen, in only eleven minutes? [14]

Addressing the third-term issue indirectly, Hill evoked the memory of Roosevelt's leadership, courage, and compassion during the Great Depression and urged delegates to rally behind this strong, experienced leader as the nation faced the possibility of war. But his oratory obscured this message. He spoke deliberately, rolling every syllable lovingly on the tongue ("ad-min-is-tra-ti-on," "his-to-ry"), inventing syllables where none existed ("ow-ah," "gre-at," "ah-nd"). His convention audience, waiting to be roused to a pitch of high enthusiasm, seemed hypnotized, interrupting only once to snicker at a particularly grandiloquent sentence. To hold his listeners in a trance might be considered an enviable ability in rural Alabama politics; to do the same to these rowdy Democrats and millions listening via radio proved disastrous. Hill managed to present Roosevelt's name in eleven minutes but, to Robert Frazer and the senator's friends and family cringing before their radios, the speech seemed interminable.[15]

Southern listeners, so rudely shocked in 1928 to hear Al Smith's harsh Brooklyn twang over the airwaves, noticed nothing unusual in Hill's oratory that evening. It reminded many an Alabamian of his famous "call the roll" speech. One member of the radio audience in his home state was put in mind of "great orators of other days."[16] But millions throughout the rest of the nation, predisposed to scorn a southern inflection, guffawed at the dramatic pauses and oratorical flourishes that Hill had absorbed from his pulpit ancestors, William Jennings Bryan, and Professor Starke. As at the 1924 Democratic convention, Alabama became a national laughingstock.

From the anti-Roosevelt press, stinging reaction ensued. Franklin P. Adams, the *New York Post* columnist, marveled that Hill made "two syllables blossom where only one once grew"; if Roosevelt could live down that nominating speech, Adams wrote, "I'll believe there is nothing he can't do." Bluntly the *New York Sun* characterized the speech as "the worst exhibition of oratory in the prehistoric form that has been heard in this country in this century." *Time* described Hill as having laid back his head and brayed. The *Norfolk Ledger* compared Hill's delivery to that of a "specialty in a minstrel show." The senator's political enemies in Alabama snickered. "Major Squirm," columnist for *Alabama* magazine, an organ of anti-New Deal business interests, joked: "I can never forget that blow-off because my radio ain't been worth a hoot since." Editor Edmund Blair of the *Pell City News* mocked: "Of all the silly, mauldin [sic] peculiar accented, exaggerated public speeches, his takes the well-known fur-lined gravy bowl. . . ."[17]

The urbane Roosevelt, subject of it all, ordered an aide, General Edwin ("Pa") Watson, adept in matters of tact, to compose a "beautiful reply" to Hill's letter enclosing a copy of his nominating speech. "I of course was at my radio," FDR wrote, "and heard every word you said, and understood the depth and genuineness of your feelings." Such a delicately worded message probably did little to heal Hill's wounds. What did this fiasco portend for his political future, not only in Alabama but on the national scene? In the face of such ridicule, could a southern politician, accustomed to meeting audiences face to face and mesmerizing them by his ardor and lyrical cadences, ever hope to project his appeals to his constituents and the entire country through the impersonal medium of radio? "That speech cooked him," thought the disheartened Frazer.[18]

Within Hill's inner circle, the nominating speech (like the subjects of his Catholic upbringing and Jewish ancestry) became a taboo topic, never mentioned in the senator's presence. Hill spoke of it to only a few intimates. Roy Nolen tried to provide his friend with an excuse by quoting Hugh Johnson's advice: "A man must never let anybody crowd him into making a major speech when he is tired." Fervently Hill responded: "How true this is. How well I know it. Unless the speech can be made right it is better not to make the speech." Although he would be compelled to use radio in order to reach more voters, Hill was never to feel entirely comfortable with this political medium. Pleased with his extemporaneous speech to a live audience in 1941, he told Nolen: "You can have your radio talks with their polish and quiet demeanor and their culture. I will take nature in the raw. I will look the bulls in the eye." During Hill's 1944 campaign for reelection, Nolen cautioned him not to apologize for his radio delivery: "The senator has long since forgotten Chicago," his campaign manager insisted. However the memory of his humiliation in 1940—the first major failure of his life—would lurk in Hill's subconscious for years to come. But his pompous oratorical style in the nominating speech was not to be the ultimate barrier to Hill's ambition.[19]

"Now has come the time for action"

Fortunately his zeal for reelecting Roosevelt and preparing the nation for war diverted Hill from his embarrassment. Seeking votes for FDR in Pennsylvania, Ohio, and Illinois, and finding that Pullman porters, taxi drivers, barbers, railroad workers, and stenographers almost universally admired and supported the president, Hill relayed this to Roosevelt in a typically extravagant comparison: "It was said of the Master—'and the common people loved him.'" With Hitler on the march, Roosevelt was as indispensable to the United States as Churchill to England, Hill urged, and as Lincoln had been to the federal union and George Washington to the American Revolution.[20]

But that "inexperienced" Republican nominee, Wendell Willkie, "glamor boy of Wall Street" and arch foe of the Tennessee Valley Authority, represented to Hill yet another envoy from the South's "ancient enemy." Willkie, the dark horse, had given Republicans and anti-New Dealers a glimmer of hope. In Alabama, dissident Democrats found it tempting to rally behind this charismatic political newcomer but most, remembering the banishment of Heflin in 1928, prudently kept their voting intentions to themselves. Reporting to Hill from his Montgomery watchtower, Nolen predicted: "We will . . . crack up this Wilkie [sic] and the most monumental special interest-greed octopus our wool hat boys and squirrel shooters in this nation have ever had a chance at." In November, Roosevelt swept the nation and the South, carrying Alabama by 251,000 votes to 42,000 for Willkie.[21]

With FDR safe, Hill could turn his full attention again to the Senate where he had been rewarded for his diligence, ability, and tact by key assignments. He served on the committees on Military Affairs and on Education and Labor, both carry-overs of his longtime interests in the House, as well as the committees on Commerce and on Interstate Commerce. The Commerce Committee handled waterway legislation; the Interstate Commerce Committee dealt with the complex and thorny issue of freight rates. In 1942, he also became chairman of the Committee on Expenditures in the Executive Department, a potential watchdog over all government activities.

From the vantage point of the Commerce Committee, Hill pushed for development of another major waterway system in Alabama. The Coosa and Alabama rivers, joining near Montgomery to flow to Mobile, offered a potential for electric power production almost as great as that of the Tennessee. But with the nation facing the possibility of war, 1940 was no year to battle for another TVA. Instead, Hill persuaded the Commerce Committee to approve a resolution calling on Army engineers to review their negative assessment of the Coosa-Alabama development. If dams could be built with public money to supplement existing private dams, Hill was willing to agree that his old adversary, the Alabama Power Company, be allowed to lease and purchase additional horsepower from government dams. This development would stimulate industry in towns along these streams, such as Gadsden, as well as increase property values and recreation facilities. Three years later, Congress would authorize this long-sought waterway. So as not to neglect western Alabama, Hill joined John Bankhead Jr. in backing the long-sought project of a canal to link the Tennessee and Tombigbee rivers into another unified waterway to emerge at Mobile. Mindful of the vocal hostility toward him in Mobile, Hill wrote his uncle, Joseph Lyons, in 1940: "I want those folks down there [in Mobile] who are knifing me to know that I will be a member of the U.S. Senate for at least four more years."[22]

His seat on the Interstate Commerce Committee gave Hill an opportunity to join the southern crusade against freight-rate differentials. Led by Bibb Graves, southern governors had pressed upon Roosevelt since 1934 their complaints that this rate structure, by penalizing shipments from the South, perpetuated their region's status as a raw-material economy. As a subcommittee chairman in 1939, Hill began hearings on rate discrimination. He urged western congressmen to support an investigation of territorial differentials by the Interstate Commerce Commission (ICC) and told business leaders in Atlanta that freight-rate inequities crippled southern progress. His efforts came to fruition when the Transportation Act of 1940 included a proposal by Hill and Representative Robert Ramspeck of Georgia authorizing an ICC investigation. To influence the outcome of these hearings, Hill persuaded Roosevelt to appoint ICC commissioners friendly to the South. Although this investigation would not bear fruit until 1945, in that year the ICC, describing the old system as "unjust and unreasonable," mandated uniform class rates east of the Rockies.[23]

But in a nation being slowly drawn toward war, peacetime projects took a back seat to an overriding concern with the international crisis. The issue of American preparedness offered Hill a welcome, new political topic, one on which he could expound wholeheartedly. Military readiness was a congenial stand for one who had adapted so splendidly to Professor Starke's regimen, volunteered so persistently for service in World War I, supported TVA with its potential for supplying power to vital, war-related industries, peppered his state with bases, training fields, and similar installations, and strongly supported General Billy Mitchell's fight for an independent and more powerful air force. (When Hill had been ranking Democrat on the House Military Affairs Committee in the 1930s, he had unsuccessfully urged Roosevelt to listen to Mitchell's arguments. "My boy," FDR had responded. "You forget . . . we have the two best friends in the world . . . the Atlantic Ocean and the Pacific Ocean.")[24]

In 1940, Hill had also helped officials of Reynolds Metals Company

enter the hitherto closed field of aluminum production to challenge the
monopoly held by the Aluminum Company of America. R. S. Reynolds
had informed him that the United States was far behind Germany in
aluminum and magnesium alloys needed for airplanes in a "light metals"
war. With Hill's aid, Reynolds won approval to purchase cheap electric
power from TVA and obtained financing for his new venture from the
Reconstruction Finance Corporation at 4 percent interest with the plants as
collateral. Grateful to Hill, Reynolds christened the Alabama plant site,
which introduced competition into the aluminum industry, Listerhill. One
year later, Hill proudly described the pouring of the first aluminum "in
competition with the most gigantic monopoly in America." To Nolen, he
confided his disappointment that no mention of this appeared in the *Montgomery Advertiser*. "Suppose . . . it had been an Alabama Power Company event," he speculated. "What mighty displays there would have
been." Hill also induced the Army Chemical Warfare Service to locate a
plant at Huntsville to take advantage of cheap electricity to produce gas.
"We didn't want to use gas in that war," he recalled years later, "but if the
Germans started using gas, we were going to be ready to gas them. . . ."[25]

During his fourteen years on the House Military Affairs Committee, Hill
had become strongly convinced that his nation's military establishment
needed to be enlarged, strengthened, even consolidated. This attitude
aroused little, if any, opposition from his constituents, the majority of
whom were descendants of immigrants from the British Isles, militarists by
inclination, and sympathetic to people who had, like their own ancestors,
experienced military defeat and occupation. In his views on rearmament,
Hill found himself back in harmony with most of his regional colleagues in
Congress. Despite their disaffection with New Deal economic policies, the
majority of southern legislators rallied behind Roosevelt's foreign policy in
the late 1930s and early 1940s, motivated both by inclination and by the
hope that huge economic benefits could accrue to their underdeveloped
region as the result of a national push to rearm.

Upon taking his seat on the Senate Military Affairs Committee, Hill had
quickly joined those members opposed to the views of Chairman Robert
Reynolds. That North Carolina isolationist, by contrast with most southern
senators, believed that there would be no war in Europe, that the United
States could do business with Hitler, and that, even if hostilities should
break out, America must not become involved. In 1940, Hill, acting for
the committee majority, sent to the Senate the first peacetime draft to
extend the terms of those called into service earlier. The southern bloc

provided crucial support when this amendment passed Congress only four months before Pearl Harbor.[26]

In early 1941, Hill vigorously supported Roosevelt's proposal to arm those governments whose defense the president believed essential to American interests. Ardently he advocated the use of American ships, manned by American crews, to convoy these supplies and even to enter combat zones and belligerent ports to deliver them safely. Fervor heightened Hill's rhetoric. Failure to enact lend-lease would mean "a Munich for the world"; isolationists like Gerald Nye and Burton Wheeler, who opposed further revision of the 1937 Neutrality Act, were "false prophets," comparable to "the Quislings of Europe."[27] In his zeal, Hill even dared to address another national radio audience. As the apex of that speech, he resorted to a few lines of doggerel, climaxed by his favorite campaign war cry:

> Now has come the time for action
> Clear away all thought of faction
> Out from vacillating shame
> Every man no lie contain
> Let him answer to his name
> CALL THE ROLL![28]

In March 1942, Hill pressed Roosevelt to name someone of the stature of General George C. Marshall, General Douglas MacArthur, or Admiral William E. Leahy as chief of an overall staff of American air, land, and naval officers to map grand strategy. FDR, somewhat exasperated, summoned his zealous supporter to the Oval Office. "My dear boy," the president protested, "I have had . . . [an overall staff] ever since December seventh!" The *Wall Street Journal* speculated that, by bringing this issue to the fore, Hill sought Roosevelt's attention in hopes that he might be named to succeed Henry Stimson in the important post of secretary of war. Did Hill actually seek a place in the Roosevelt administration because he feared a strong test at the polls in 1944? Would he have sacrificed his Senate seniority for the limited tenure of a cabinet member? Stimson himself, by delaying his desire to retire until Truman had assumed the presidency, made these questions moot.[29]

After this visit, Hill still remained dissatisfied with his commander in chief's relationship to his military advisers. General Marshall and British observers, too, worried over Roosevelt's blithe manner of dealing informally and often separately with his military chiefs. But as the war intensi-

fied, Hill, Marshall, and other advocates would see their cherished concepts embodied in a joint chiefs of staff for American forces, the combined
chiefs of staff to direct the Allied war effort, and a supreme commander to
head the D-Day invasion of western Europe.

Although a unified military strategy did emerge, Hill was never able to
persuade Congress to enact a universal service law to empower the president "to have the right number of right people in the right places at the right
time," whether on farms, in industry, or in the armed forces. In 1942 he
had again argued that his proposed National Service Act, patterned after
similar laws in England and Canada, would result in "equal burdens and
equal sacrifices for all and war profits and war benefits for none." Roosevelt favored this concept but deemed it premature. Hill had to content
himself with less sweeping measures to commandeer a broader spectrum
of Americans for war service. He was proud that he, although always a
southern gentleman of the old school where ladies were concerned, had
been co-author of bills that created the temporary Women's Army Auxil-
iary Corps (WAACS) and permitted women doctors to serve as members of
the Army Medical Corps and that he had warmly supported higher ranks
and pay for Army and Navy nurses.[30]

At least the Japanese attack on Pearl Harbor ended the debate over
American involvement. Proudly describing to an Alabama friend the
"calm manner" in which Congress had responded to Roosevelt's declaration of war on Japan, Hill concluded, with relief, "we are at last a united
American people."[31]

But underneath this appearance of loyalty, anti-Roosevelt feelings remained as heated as ever. When the congressional elections of 1942
indicated a national drift away from the New Deal, Foots Clement saw this
as an omen of the future. "We must accept the [1942] results as a *fair
warning*," Foots advised Hill. "*Maybe the Pendulum is swinging*." Roosevelt must "recast his leadership and substantially reshape his administration," Hill responded, lest his enemies "take over the government and,
worse still . . . write the peace."[32]

In an effort to forestall further erosion of New Deal loyalty in Alabama,
Hill's friends arranged that the Senate's majority whip be invited to address
a joint session of Alabama's legislature in January 1943. The death of Bibb
Graves a year earlier had left no doubt as to who was Roosevelt's number
one advocate in Alabama. Hill made the most of this opportunity to
reaffirm his New Deal loyalty, promote his own reelection, and chastise
those "club room Caesars and curbstone Napoleons" who critized Roose-

velt's conduct of the war. Roosevelt, he declared, had broken many of the "shackles" foisted upon the South by eastern industrialists and Republicans. Pointedly he reminded FDR's critics, "small in number but loud of voice and powerful in propaganda," that not even Republicans—"the ancient foe"—had advocated repeal of a single major New Deal measure. Alabama newspapers, most of them approvingly, spread Hill's message throughout the state. But in Alabama, as elsewhere in the country, New Deal enthusiasm had already crested; hereafter Hill and other Roosevelt supporters would find themselves increasingly on the defensive.[33]

"B²H²"

With the country fully engaged in war, Hill focused in 1943 on the possible aftermath of an eventual Allied victory. His new colleague, Joseph H. Ball, a young newspaper reporter appointed by the Minnesota governor, Harold Stassen, had arrived in Washington in 1940, idealistic and innocent enough to believe that a freshman could quickly play a leading role in the Senate. Elected on his own in 1942, Ball set out to put the United States on record in favor of the establishment, during wartime, of an organization to keep the peace. He attracted to this cause three kindred spirits, his fellow Republican, Harold H. Burton of Ohio, and two Democrats, Carl Hatch of New Mexico, and Harry Truman of Missouri. But Truman, deep into the thicket of investigating corruption in war industries, had no time for this effort. Its three authors then invited Lister Hill to lend party and geographical balance, as well as his persuasive talents, to this cause. If these relatively new members could convince the Senate to take such a positive approach in its advisory role on treaties, perhaps Roosevelt could avoid a repetition of the debacle that had followed World War I. Were they calling for a new League of Nations, a reporter inquired. Hill responded sharply: "Please don't bring that in. This has no relation to the League of Nations. Nothing like it."[34]

Roosevelt, "ridden by the memory of Wilson's defeat" on that hotly debated issue, feared to commit himself this early to support a plan that might arouse the quiescent isolationists. When its sponsors announced their intent to offer a formal resolution to put the Senate on record favoring formation of a new world body, an alarmed FDR summoned these self-appointed policymakers to the White House for an unusual Sunday afternoon meeting and tried to persuade them not to raise the issue so soon.

When they emerged, Hill, never one to challenge authority and always susceptible to FDR's blandishments, told reporters that the senators might agree to delay. But Ball refused to be deterred by the caution of Roosevelt, Hull, and the Senate Foreign Relations Committee chairman, Tom Connally, or by Burton Wheeler's promise of a "long, bitter fight." He introduced the resolution two days after his visit to the White House. A clever reporter promptly nicknamed it B²H².[35]

Administration strategists decided to bottle up this potentially troublesome topic in Connally's committee until public opinion could be aroused, then to offer a more vaguely worded resolution. During the summer of 1943, Hill and his three colleagues, their wives, and members of their staffs undertook to rally Americans in support of their bold concept. They spoke to internationalists and peace groups, women's organizations, mass meetings, and over the radio. Why wait? To delay, Hill argued, would only strengthen economic rivalries, nationalistic feelings, and party differences. Peace-loving nations should move immediately to form a collective world security system with the power to enforce its decrees. Important organs of opinion, including the *New York Times*, *Washington Post*, and *New Republic*, agreed that the time to consider peace plans had come.[36]

While Connally stalled, J. William Fulbright quietly persuaded the House to pass a less specific resolution calling for American participation in an international peacekeeping organization. Senators were furious, a *Time* correspondent reported to his editor, that "a freshman Congressman from a rube state like Arkansas [should] grab the ball and run for a touchdown when they have not been able to cross the goal line in twenty years."[37]

Spurred by a Gallup poll reporting that 78 percent of the American people favored the Fulbright resolution, Roosevelt gave Connally the go-ahead to proceed in the Senate. In October, Connally presented his own resolution, weaker than B²H², stronger than that of Fulbright, calling for "international authority" but omitting any mention of an international peacekeeping force. Ball and his colleagues, joined by ten other senators including Truman and Pepper, pleaded for a stronger commitment. Pepper offered amendments to specify an organization with the power to use military force. Eventually senators agreed to a compromise. They would support a new world peacekeeping body but evade the vital issue of machinery to enforce its decrees. Hill was the first of the B²H² senators to announce his willingness to go along with this watered-down version.[38]

The Senate passed the Connally resolution 5 November 1943. By prodding the public, Ball, his three Senate co-sponsors, Fulbright, Pepper, and other leaders of this movement had set the stage for international postwar cooperation. But as Hill reminded those who wrote to congratulate him, the Connally resolution had been only "a first step." He and fellow supporters of a United Nations must not relax their efforts until such an organization, with the United States as one of its leaders, came into being.[39]

Compared to Ball and Fulbright, Hill had been a cautious advocate of postwar internationalism, prepared to delay when FDR asked, quick to compromise with Connally, and not inclined, like Pepper, to push a controversial plank. His role in B²H² typified Hill's senatorial style. Work behind the scenes. Negotiate. Make concessions if necessary. Don't risk losing the whole ball game; settle for the possible. In the end, prevail.

"Creating racial disturbances"

Hill's stand for a strong military establishment and a postwar organization of "United Nations" to settle future disputes peacefully had received general approbation from constituents back home. But more controversial issues of the war years foreshadowed an epic struggle to come. Early in his Senate career, Hill had proposed that Congress should enact not only a wartime Selective Service Act, but a program of federal aid to education to mobilize the nation's youth for peacetime pursuits. Education, like road building, could not be provided by states alone, Hill felt; it required a national effort. No nation could be strong unless it educated its people in vocational and professional skills as well as in literacy, he pleaded in 1941 before a receptive audience at the National Education Association meeting in Boston.[40]

At his father's suggestion, Hill had put forth this same idea in his 1923 campaign against Ray Rushton. As had Rushton, opponents in the early 1940s hastened to warn that federal financial aid would lead to federal control and, although they did not mention this publicly, to school integration. Hill replied, as he had twenty years earlier, that this money would be spent by state departments of education that would not condone federal interference in the internal affairs of their schools.[41]

In 1943, Hill, along with two fellow Democrats, Senator Elbert Thomas of Utah, and Representative Robert Ramspeck of Georgia, sponsored a bill to allot federal education funds to states on the basis of need. Southern states, especially, were to benefit from this formula. Thus, Hill argued, ten

million federal dollars each year would flow back to help compensate
Alabamians for the high cost of buying goods manufactured in the North,
thereby lessening the regional inequality that Professor McCorvey had
taught him to resent. But faced by a reelection campaign, Hill eventually
put this bill aside. The *Montgomery Advertiser* stated the opposition's case
as plainly as it dared: "Once a subsidy is given, it becomes a club that
forever is compelling. . . . Rather than give the subsidy up, we will finally
have to allow the federal government to educate our young. And that
means . . . of course you know."[42]

If southern opposition halted federal aid to education, surely no patriotic
legislator would dare to go on record as denying brave soldiers their right
to vote. Yet in the background of this seemingly innocuous matter lay
another issue involving race. To a proposed soldier vote bill, some members of Congress, including Estes Kefauver, then a representative from
eastern Tennessee, and Senator Pepper, offered an amendment to exempt
GIs from the necessity of poll taxes, not only in federal elections but even
within the hitherto sacrosanct boundaries of party contests.[43]

In Alabama, the poll tax had stood since 1901 as the major barrier to
voting by the poor of both races. Not only must this tax be paid months
prior to election day, but it cumulated yearly for voters between the ages of
twenty-one and forty-five, a longer cumulative period than that of any state
except Georgia. At the Alabama poll-tax rate of $1.50 per year, the maxi-
mum cumulative amount was $36. Persons over forty-five were exempt
from further poll taxes but, in order to vote, had to prove payment of the
poll tax for the past twenty-four years. Largely due to the poll tax, fewer
than 20 percent of Alabama's eligible voters had participated in the presidential election of 1940. As Representative Sam Hobbs of Selma expressed it to a friend, the poll tax, with its cumulative feature, ensured
"rule by those who are fit to rule."[44]

Hill voted against the final version of the soldier bill because it contained an anti-poll tax provision. He insisted that only constitutional
amendments could change voting qualifications. Supporters mustered sufficient votes to pass this bill but, by the time it reached Roosevelt's desk for
signature, the southern party primaries of 1942 had already taken place.[45]

This victory wetted the appetites of poll-tax foes for its total abolition.
Pepper and Representative Lee Geyer of California introduced companion
bills to achieve this purpose. In the Senate, southern opponents, no longer
constrained by patriotism, immediately resorted to the filibuster. After
Southerners had manned this ancient barricade for eight days, anti-poll-tax

forces sought to close off debate through the cloture rule. But cloture could be invoked only by a two-thirds majority of senators present and voting. Eight Southerners absented themselves so that a quorum would not be available for this vote. An obdurate majority leader Barkley ordered his sergeant at arms to "arrest" these absentees, among them Senate whip Lister Hill, whose duty it was to assist the majority leader in rounding up members for quorum calls.[46]

Although this anti-poll-tax bill passed the House, it eventually died in the Senate. The two sides agreed that, if the cloture vote failed, this bill, which so distracted the Senate from wartime concerns, would be withdrawn. In the final day of debate, Hill put forth the same objections he had raised earlier and informed the Senate that the Alabama legislature had adopted a unanimous resolution warning that this issue was "creating racial disturbances." When Barkley failed to achieve cloture, "Dr. Win-the-War" Roosevelt, needing southern support, thought it prudent not to pursue such a touchy matter in the midst of war.[47]

Hill, too, had practical reasons for his stand against a law that Pepper, representing a more hybrid and liberal constituency, dared to sponsor. As Hill frankly told his friend and fellow Alabamian, Virginia Durr, a leader in the fight against the poll tax: "If you will guarantee that this thing will pass, I'll vote for it, because the kind of people that will be voting after the poll tax is off, they'll be the kind of people that will be voting for me. But unless you guarantee it's going to pass both the House and Senate, I can't do it."[48]

Ahead of Hill loomed another campaign. Already opposition forces in Alabama were planning his defeat. Stop going around the country talking about idealistic matters like a postwar United Nations, the editor of an Alabama labor newspaper advised. "You are going to have a hard time getting reelected," he wrote the senator, "and will need all the friends you can get."[49]

"Foots"

To keep in touch with sentiment in his state, Hill relied chiefly on Roy Nolen but also, increasingly, on a new, younger adviser, Marc Ray Clement, who had proved in that traditional political classroom, the University of Alabama, to be a master at this game. A country doctor's son from Arkansas, Clement had come to Tuscaloosa in the early 1930s, following in the big steps of his brother, Charles B. Clement, captain of Alabama's 1930 Rose Bowl football team. Charlie Clement had been known on campus as "Big Foots," Marc Ray as "Little Foots." When his brother moved to Georgia, Marc Ray acquired sole title to the nickname of "Foots." Although he had come to Alabama to study law, more exciting pursuits diverted Foots. Occasionally Coach Hank Crisp appealed to Foots to keep another country boy from Arkansas in line so that Paul ("Bear") Bryant would not stray too often from the Crimson Tide's training camp. But campus politics intrigued Foots more than football or law school. In the margins of law books, he jotted the names of those young politicians who showed promise of winning campus elections.[50]

During the mid-1930s, the university brimmed with ambitious young men struggling to pay their tuition by waiting on tables at Pug's eatery, Rex Drugstore, or Mrs. Veal's boardinghouse, persuading sororities and fraternities to buy their dairy products from Perry Creamery or some competing dairy, renting cars for U-Drive-It, or, like Carl Elliott, among the poorest of the poor, working for the WPA and living on "Poverty Ridge." But political jobs, like editor or business manager of the *Corolla* or the *Crimson-White* or manager of the Cotillion Club that brought big bands like Kay Kyser to Tuscaloosa, paid better than Pug's or U-Drive-It. Campus political machines fought for these jobs. None was so successful as the one Foots founded by linking the politically astute Kappa Alphas with Greek groups like Pi Kappa Alpha, "Deke," Phi Gamma Delta, and Pi Kappa Phi and with nonfraternity men who lived in barracks and women students from dormitories. The heavyset Arkansan took campus politics seriously: one had to plan two or three years ahead to select those likely politicians who greeted hundreds of fellow students by name, evinced a sincere concern for the popular weal (as did their mentors, FDR and Bibb Graves) by participating in the campus chapter of Young Democrats and the A-Club, got along well with their fellow National Guardsmen at summer camp, and needed jobs to stay in school.[51]

Foots, closely allied with fellow campus kingmakers John Horne from Barbour County and Bob Jones from Jackson County, sponsored the first campaigns of such political comers as Kenneth Roberts and Carl Elliott, who, along with Jones, were to be elected to Congress in the 1940s. Future journalists like Carroll Kilpatrick and Gould Beech and men who would later become powers in state politics, like Aubrey Dominick, Billy Partlow, George Le Maistre, Jim Smith, Young Boozer, and Hugh Merrill, came under Foots's influence on campus. No detail escaped their leader's notice. When Bob Jones, to celebrate his victory in a race for business manager of the *Corolla*, donned his best blue jacket and white trousers, Foots upbraided him for showing off after an election.[52]

Men whom he tutored never lost a political contest while Foots masterminded his university machine. But after he graduated from the Law School, Foots put his considerable talents to work primarily on behalf of one political figure, Lister Hill. His Tuscaloosa law partner, George Le Maistre, had introduced Foots to Hill during the 1938 campaign. Clement assisted Frank Dixon that year in his successful race for governor but, disliking the tone of Dixon's administration, devoted himself increasingly to build a statewide network for Hill, using the Young Democrats whom he had led at the university during the Great Depression as its base. When Roy Nolen became ill in the 1940s, Foots became Hill's number one campaign manager. He was to serve in this role until his death in 1961.[53]

Those who came under Foots's tutelage remember him as the best organizer they ever met, a "political genius" who loved evenings of intrigue at Montgomery's Elite Restaurant and Sunday night strategy sessions when political strings were pulled, who could easily call seventy-five people around a banquet table by name, and who "could lean on you harder than anybody in the world." To Foots, a political campaign, with its myriad details, complex maneuvers, and tricks of organization, was a zestful challenge, a bigger and better game than Monopoly. Not as much of an idealist as Roy Nolen, Foots played politics for the joy of it. But he prided himself that he rarely, if ever, asked his senator for any reward in the form of money, an appointment, or a favor, although (too fat to qualify for service in World War II) he did accept an appointment as statewide organizer of Alabama's War Bond drive. Foots Clement was to prove indispensable to Lister Hill, especially in the hotly fought 1944 campaign. "The Senator would almost blindly follow anything Foots would suggest," Hill's longtime administrative assistant, Don Cronin, recalled.[54]

With the aid of Nolen and Clement, Hill fashioned a formidable network of thousands of Alabamians—those for whom the senator had performed favors, those who courted favor, those attracted to power, and those few who sometimes placed broad, humane considerations above purely personal gain. Political supporters who aspired to favors or to bask in the glow of power proved easy to find. But to round up those Alabamians willing to be associated with the label "liberal" was a more difficult and delicate undertaking.

Liberalism in Alabama had crested in 1938 when politicians like Hill,

Bibb Graves, John Bankhead Jr., and Congressman Luther Patrick of Birmingham, had agreed to sponsor or take part in the Southern Conference for Human Welfare (SCHW). This new organization had been formed by some of those active in Francis Pickens Miller's Southern Policy Committee in response to Roosevelt's concern for what he termed "the Nation's number one economic problem." With the active help of the New Deal, SCHW leaders attacked old southern bugaboos like the poll tax, lynching, freight-rate differentials, tenancy, and even referred obliquely to racial injustice. When this assemblage of New Dealers, idealists, labor leaders, prominent blacks, a few Socialists, a handful of Communists, and perhaps a dozen fellow travelers met in Birmingham that year, its open challenge to segregated seating provided those who favored the status quo with the ammunition they sought. Frightened by the ensuing row, prominent politicians like Hill, Patrick, Bankhead, and even Claude Pepper dissociated themselves officially from the SCHW. Pepper continued quietly to encourage this organization but Hill, so one historian put it, "was never heard from again." Thereafter, with racial customs headed toward postwar change, the designation of "liberal," fashionable in the thirties, was to become a political liability.[55]

Hill's organization took care to identify other progressive thinkers through personal contact and recommendation. Richard Rives, Wiley Hill's law partner, introduced Hill to John C. Godbold, a younger lawyer of similar political views. Through his contacts with organized labor, Hill met William Mitch, of the United Mine Workers, and Barney Weeks, of the Alabama Labor Council. Journalists, too, proved a rich source of political allies. Hill won the almost unqualified admiration of editors such as Charles Dobbins of the *Montgomery Advertiser*; Neil Davis of the *Lee County Bulletin*; Barrett Shelton of the *Decatur Daily*; Frederick I. Thompson, owner as well as editor of papers in Mobile and Montgomery, and James E. Chappell and McClellan ("Ted") Van der Veer of the *Birmingham News*. These men introduced Hill to promising, younger journalists such as Walling Keith, Paul Duncan, and Gould Beech. Hill wooed these opinion-makers for "the cause" by introducing them to prominent New Dealers and sending them position papers and copies of bills pending before Congress. "One cannot serve his fellow man better than to challenge him and put him to thinking," Hill had written Grover Hall in 1938. "Hill set in to educate me," Neil Davis remembered.[56]

But Hill had less success in courting other Alabama journalists. His relationship with Grover Hall and his son, Grover Jr., who would succeed to his father's old post as editor of the *Montgomery Advertiser* in 1947, was always tentative and unstable. Although Hill and Harry M. Ayers, owner of the *Anniston Star*, shared many common viewpoints, the senator could not always rely on the support of the independently wealthy Ayers, who had been on Frank Dixon's side in the 1940 split between Alabama's pro- and anti-New Dealers. John Temple Graves II, the widely read, front-page columnist for the *Birmingham Age-Herald*, was originally cordial to Hill but would sour on the New Deal in the mid-1940s. Prior to Graves's change of heart, Hill dealt cautiously with this journalistic prima donna whose column, he told Nolen, "is a potential pistol at my head each morning."[57]

Journalists may have committed themselves for or against Hill on philosophical grounds, but other Alabamians rallied to him in order to be close to a senator who could dispense federal jobs and Public Works Administration funds, obtain commissions in the military, and arrange valuable business favors like airline routes, radio station licenses, and the right to issue mortgages backed by the Federal Housing Administration. Hill, like other politicians, used his patronage power to reward the faithful and court former enemies. Henry J. Willingham, nominated by Hill and Bankhead to the potent job of collecting federal taxes in Alabama, kept careful track on a state map of those whom he appointed to be field representatives and stenographers in strategic political areas. Clarence Allgood, nominated by his senators to be referee in bankruptcy of the U.S. District Court in northern Alabama, helped to advise Hill, Clement, and Nolen on their choices of deputy marshals, United States attorneys, federal judges, even those to be awarded temporary roles in rationing food and gasoline for the Office of Price Administration.[58]

Because they enjoyed associating with a political winner, Thomas N. Beach and Rufus Lackey, prominent Birmingham insurance executives, supplied Hill with personal and financial support. In Montgomery, Ed E. Reid, politically minded executive director of the Alabama League of Municipalities, and Lieutenant Governor Carmichael were known as Hill men. No detail of building his network escaped Hill's attention. He pressed Willingham to raise the pay of a loyal supporter in the Wiregrass. He and Bankhead arranged that an attractive young matron from south Alabama, Dorothy Vredenburgh, would become secretary of the Democratic National Committee, a titular post she was to hold for forty years. J. Bibb Mills, once the leader of Alabama prohibitionists, and H. C. Sanders, a former Troy police chief, both of whom had helped Hill win his first congressional election, were appointed Senate doorkeepers and retained on the federal payroll long after illness prevented them from performing their ritual duties. Partly out of compassion but also to please Heflin's supporters, Hill arranged to restore his needy old antagonist to the federal payroll. Hill even kept up an appearance of cordiality with college friends who had chosen a different political path. Who knew when a man might change his allegiance? Many warned Hill, as had the labor newspaper editor in Mobile, that in 1944 he was to need every friend he could muster.[59]

"How you, ole fellow, ole fellow, ole fellow?"

Approaching his fiftieth birthday, Hill had acquired power and learned to manipulate it. Under Roosevelt's spell, he had broadened his political philosophy. Tall, bald (to his acute dismay) like his Hill forebears, clad in his customary dark suit and tie, white shirt and stiff collar, he no longer looked like a "baby congressman" but like a mature senator, his only outward eccentricity being a tendency to imitate FDR by turning up his hat brim at a rakish angle. Hill's lifestyle was as conservative as his dress. Henrietta Hill attended to the rearing of "Little Henrietta" and "Pal," making sure that they did not disturb their father on evenings when he had work to do or wanted to read Alabama newspapers, biographies of Thomas Jefferson or Jefferson Davis, Leo Tolstoy's *War and Peace*, Arnold Toynbee's *Study of History*, or a currently popular book such as Walter Prescott Webb's *Divided We Stand*, with its thesis of growing northern preponderance in the United States. Lister and Henrietta Hill were seldom seen on Washington's cocktail circuit; the senator preferred to entertain at small home dinners or Sunday breakfasts where open-minded Alabamians mingled with ardent New Dealers like Hugo Black, Jonathan Daniels, Thomas Corcoran, Aubrey Williams, Henry Wallace, and Clifford and Virginia Durr.[60]

In futile efforts to keep current with the endless demands made on a prominent senator who might accumulate as many as twelve thousand requests, Hill intensified his work habits. Constituents marveled at the rapid, seemingly personal responses they received from Hill; even out-of-state correspondents got swift attention. But all this efficiency took its toll upon Hill and his staff. Only Roy Nolen, Henrietta Hill, and those who worked for Hill realized the personal burden of such a load. Hill frequently complained to his trusted campaign manager: "Here Robert [Frazer] and I sit on a beautiful spring day grinding away with letter after letter—all of them with some vexing problem." Or "We worked last night until half past eight. Heaven knows what time we will finish tonight."[61]

Frazer, his health almost wrecked by fifteen years of this regimen and aggrieved that his salary in 1941 was limited by law to thirty-nine hundred dollars a year, resigned that year to assume a more lucrative government job. In a temporary mood of bitterness, Frazer later wrote Hill that he had found the motto, "Heaven helps him who helps himself," more realistic than "Work Wins."[62]

His successor, Walling Keith, a Birmingham journalist, found that his new boss had "a memory as long as an elephant's and as keen as a razor and is accustomed to a most exacting secretary." Fresh from Alabama's more leisurely pace, Keith tried without success to persuade the senator not to work so many nights in the frantic months following Pearl Harbor. "I don't know how long [Hill] can go on doing everything," Keith wrote Nolen. "It can't keep up—but I don't know how it can be stopped." Alabamians now flooded Hill's office with requests for wartime contracts, commissions for sons called into service, even allotments of scarce sugar with which to manufacture soft drinks. His idea of a National Service Act, Hill reflected, would have helped to lessen such a flood of demands for special favor.[63]

Although still a compulsive workhorse, Hill often confided to Nolen that he was "dead tired" and "simply worn out." He had realized his lifelong dream of becoming a United States senator only to find himself so overwhelmed with his duties as whip and often as acting majority leader, his five committees, his mail, and a never-ending stream of visitors that "it is difficult for me not to be miserable." Exasperated and disillusioned by his constituents' wartime greed, Hill wrote Nolen: "Every contractor in Alabama is expecting a fat, juicy contract. Is there anything to get the people of Alabama to think of me as their Legislator rather than as a grab-bag artist?" When his patience wore thinnest, Hill himself questioned whether he could keep up this pace. "I am like a man in a quagmire," he told Nolen. "The more I struggle, the deeper I get. I am afraid that by 1944 I will be lost."[64]

Don Cronin, who was to be Hill's longest-serving and last administrative assistant, recalled that Hill worked on sunny Saturday afternoons, many a Sunday, even the Fourth of July. (Writing to Nolen on a Saturday before Easter, Hill noted: "It is after 3 P.M. and I am trying not to keep the girls too late.") When his telephone rang late at night, Cronin was never surprised to hear a familiar voice demand abruptly: "Colonel, let me read you what I just read in the *Montgomery Advertiser*." Carroll Kilpatrick, Washington correspondent for the *Birmingham News* in the early 1940s, also received late night calls from Hill, suggesting a story for his newspaper or wanting to talk to someone about America's military needs. Hill and Tommy Corcoran frequently gossiped over the phone until almost midnight. Hugo Black, an ardent tennis player, tried to persuade his friend to take up golf or "something that will give you both recreation and release from constant mental strain." Hill permitted himself an occasional fishing trip with "Uncle Will" Hill or with a political buddy like Clarence Allgood to bait his hook, row the boat, and disentangle his line whenever the senator threw it over a tree. But above all, Hill relished the sport of politics.[65]

Among Capitol Hill office workers, Senator Hill was widely reputed to be one of the most exacting employers in Congress, demanding that his staff be unfailingly punctual and "tend toward perfection." Those who worked under Hill learned that he had inherited the fiery Hill temper and had a vocabulary with which to express it. Like FDR, he was inclined to pit one member of his staff against another to accelerate their work and see which one survived. "You were allowed a mistake every now and then, but not many," Cronin remembered. "You had to give 101%." Hill's staff worked under a Victorian taskmaster who seldom accepted honoraria for speeches, paid his wife's expenses when she accompanied him on official junkets, and often startled and offended small donors by returning their campaign contributions. Their aloof, sometimes tyrannical boss, although generous with favors, proved loath to grant pay increases, never seeming to realize that loyal workers deserved monetary appreciation. These were human flaws, however, one of Hill's speech writers later reflected, not to be held against the senator's long record of accomplishment.[66]

Colleagues seldom saw this side of Lister Hill. Fellow Democrats found their whip tactful, patient, good-humored, and almost unfailingly courteous, a leader who preferred to work behind the scenes or in committees rather than to make heroic appeals on the floor. Hill attempted to model himself upon those senators whom he most admired: thinkers like Carl Hatch and Bob La Follette Jr.; a man of rectitude like George Aiken; and that gutsy fighter against wartime fraud and corruption, Harry Truman. But George Norris remained Hill's role model in the Senate. "My highest privilege, so far as politics are concerned," Hill wrote Nolen in 1941, "has been to know Franklin D. Roosevelt and George W. Norris."[67]

Among his fellow Southerners, Hill found fewer men to admire. Although he had received crucial support from John Bankhead Jr. in 1938, Hill had an uneasy relationship with the senior senator from his state, based more on expediency than friendship or mutual admiration. Richard Russell resembled Hill in looks and mannerisms but not in basic philosophy. Claude Pepper, although a fellow New Dealer, differed markedly from Hill in his almost reckless disregard for the consequences of his outspoken liberalism. Casting about for a mentor from his own region, Hill fixed upon a courtly, sternly moral, military-minded, old progressive who saw no reason to disturb the racial status quo in the South. "You, George W. Norris, and Franklin Roosevelt have been my political mentors," he wrote to FDR's old boss, former Navy Secretary Josephus Daniels, whom Hill regarded in 1944 as "the greatest living Southerner."[68]

Visiting constituents met another Lister Hill, courtly, folksy ("How you, ole fellow, ole fellow, ole fellow?"), effusive to the point of being corny (to every middle-aged man, accompanied by his wife, the question, "Is this your daughter?" to every bald-headed male, "Boll weevils get in your hair?"). Younger visitors received an especially vigorous welcome. One student reported to her family back home that "Senator Hill grabbed my hand and shook it through the whole conversation; I thought he was going to shake the charms off my bracelet!" Young, ambitious Douglass Cater, calling on his famous fellow Montgomerian, received a long, orotund lecture on the benefits of youth and felt himself enveloped by a "sort of farrago of language, a verbosity that kind of concealed him from you." Cater sensed that, by this act, Hill intended to cloak an inability to deal comfortably with people whom he did not know well. Fellow members of the Alabama delegation who served with Hill in Congress for many years and journalists whom he sought to influence remembered that Hill was not given to intimacies, never a "toucher," and that "people didn't get to him closely." Thus it had been, Bob Jones mused after having served thirty years in the House, with most great politicians.[69]

CHAPTER 6

The Crucial Test

1 9 4 4

"The racial issue . . . is burning like a bale of cotton at the core"

"Nothing makes a man stronger in political life than to occasionally defeat an opponent," Hill's longtime Montgomery friend Jesse B. Hearin counseled in the fall of 1943. As head of the Production Credit Corporation, a low-interest agricultural lending agency managed by farmers, Hearin often traveled through rural Alabama, Mississippi, and Louisiana. He observed Deep South farmers, laborers, merchants, timber owners, and small businessmen, spurred by the demands of war, "enjoying a substantial prosperity the like of which they have never dreamed of." But in Alabama's Black Belt, Hearin also encountered those "who were oppressed and poor a few years ago now rich and arrogant and bitter in their denunciation of all who had made it possible for them to become rich."[1]

Prominent among these disaffected were Walter Randolph and fellow leaders in Alabama's Farm Bureau Federation whose attitude toward Hill had deteriorated from dutiful support in 1937 to barely concealed hostility. By staunchly defending the Farm Security Administration against attempts to destroy its programs to aid small landowners and because of his association with an administration that imposed agricultural price ceilings, Hill had antagonized not only the Farm Bureau but also P. O. Davis and other powerful figures in the Alabama Extension Service, a federally financed and covertly political network of farm agents with headquarters at Auburn University that worked closely with the farm lobby on behalf of large agricultural interests. In league with these farm spokesmen, leaders of Associated Industries of Alabama, including many representatives of eastern-owned corporations, were determined to eliminate the last of Ala-

113

bama's powerful New Deal triumvirate that had once included Bibb Graves and Hugo Black. If rank-and-file farmers could be persuaded to put aside their traditional antipathy to the monied interests of Birmingham, the forces of big industry and big agriculture hoped to control the legislature, cut corporate taxes, fight organized labor, court further outside investors, send an anti-FDR delegation to the 1944 Democratic convention, and eventually displace not only Hill but even such a lukewarm Roosevelt supporter as John Bankhead Jr.[2]

But with Roosevelt still occupying the White House, the war going well, the homefront making money, labor unions stronger, dirt farmers comparatively prosperous, and postwar upheaval merely a cloud on the horizon, Hearin found that "the PEOPLE still back the administration." All things considered, he advised Hill: "I hope Jimmy Simpson will run against you. I KNOW you can defeat him now. . . . and only Heaven knows what may happen six years from now."[3]

The senator was not so sanguine. Military victory, Hill sensed, would dispel the unity with which Americans had faced their most dangerous foreign enemy. Inevitably, too, a commanding figure would pass from the American scene. The death of Bibb Graves in 1942 had left Alabama's New Deal adherents demoralized and temporarily leaderless. The end of the era of Franklin Roosevelt was certain to create a national leadership void.

Furthermore, Hill's traditional opponents in Alabama, exemplified by Ray Rushton in 1923 and by the big business, industrial, utility, textile, and lumber interests that had reluctantly backed Tom Heflin in 1937, would surely intensify their counterattack. As Ray Rushton's nephew, J. Frank Rushton Jr., of Birmingham, vice president of Associated Industries of Alabama, pledged in an address to the Montgomery Chamber of Commerce early in 1943, this congeries, now joined by big agriculture, was determined to reverse the trend toward centralized government and return to a pre-New Deal America with few, if any, restraints upon individual incentive for profit. "Good God!" exclaimed Hearin, the small farmers' advocate, after attending this gathering. "How could a man of Mr. Rushton's intelligence say or feel that no progress has been made in America for the past 'twenty-seven' years as he once expressed it, or since the election of Woodrow Wilson as he again measured the dark (?) days that have fallen upon us?"[4]

But how were these reactionaries to persuade dirt farmers and blue-collar workers, who had tasted the benefits of TVA, rural electrification, stronger unionism, small farm loans, the minimum wage, and the shorter work week, that further "creeping socialism" would constitute not a boon but a menace? To douse the flames of Populism in the late nineteenth century, Alabama's Democratic establishment had invoked white supremacy and played upon emotional memories of the Confederacy's defeat. After World War I, Klansmen and drys had used nativistic appeals to weld Alabama's overwhelmingly white, Protestant, and provincial voters into a successful political machine. To save Alabama from going Republican in 1928, Hill himself had sounded some of these time-tested tocsins. But as another war approached its end, the senator feared that the bugaboo of race would now be employed against him.

Roosevelt's 1941 executive order creating a Fair Employment Practices Committee (FEPC), coupled with the threat of federal laws against lynching and poll taxes, had provided the bait with which anti-New Dealers hoped to lure the Alabama electorate away from "that man." On a simpler and more personal level, the activities (real and fancied) of Eleanor Roosevelt in behalf of black Americans riled thousands of white Southerners. Complaining to Hill, one indignant Alabamian voiced the sentiment of many fellow citizens: "Folks are for Roosevelt in Alabama but not for Mrs. R. Her too friendly attitude on the rights of negroes [*sic*] is not only disgusting but is an affront to Alabama folks, women especially. The FBI says it cannot find any 'Eleanor Clubs' but I can find a host of negroes [*sic*] who believe in her teachings. Even the *Birmingham News* in Oscar Adams' column speaks of [black] women as 'Mrs.' "[5]

As early as 1942, Nolen had advised Hill that a number of prominent Alabamians, including Governor Dixon, Representatives Sam Hobbs and George Grant, and Hamner Cobbs, a Greensboro newspaper editor, had expressed forebodings that the war would effect changes in southern racial mores. Among their concerns, Nolen reported, were that the government had trained more skilled blacks than industry could absorb, that blacks rejected by local draft boards might refuse to perform manual labor as civilians, that black servicemen stationed at Camp Rucker might engage in sexual relations with white women of the nearby countryside, and that blacks wasted valuable rubber by driving the secondhand cars rejected by white buyers. *Birmingham Age-Herald* columnist John Temple Graves II, his New Deal loyalty eroding but not yet entirely vanished, also warned Hill: "You can't imagine the talk that's going the rounds here now on the Negro question, the prominent people who are saying we are all going to have to get our guns out again. This is an issue, once thoroughly raised, on

which anybody can beat anybody politically in the South, as you know, and
the anti-New Deal crowd evidently see in it an excellent chance to arouse
the masses against the New Deal in the South. And it is." Bay Minette's
young and politically ambitious mayor, Jimmy Faulkner, noted one interesting aspect: "It is a funny thing to me that the only ones that see the negro
[*sic*] bogey are those that are already against Roosevelt." From Cullman,
James E. Folsom reported: "The [race] thing had our right thinking people
worried." From Montgomery, the friendly journalist Frederick Thompson
echoed Graves's prediction: "The racial issue, tragically precipitated by
inter-administration forces, is burning like a bale of cotton at the core.
Sooner or later it will flame."[6]

But who was to lead the assault against Hill? Political speculation
focused upon two Birmingham prospects, both members of the gentry,
prominent corporation lawyers, and leading spokesmen for business and
industrial interests. The more widely known, Frank Dixon, as governor
from 1939 to 1943, had led the outcry against further federal incursion in
matters hitherto unregulated or handled at the state level. Dixon had
emphasized economy and efficiency in state government and instituted a
state civil service system that forbade nonelective state, county, or city
employees to campaign for political candidates. In 1940 he had headed
Alabama's anti-Roosevelt forces. Now Dixon warned that further extension of federal power would bring about a restructuring of southern race
relations. Columnist Graves, reporting that Dixon might run for the Senate, confided to Hill: "Frank is about to turn into a counterpart of his uncle,
Tom Dixon, author of *The Clansman*, etc., and look upon himself as
annointed [*sic*] to save Alabama and the South from the Negro."[7]

Another potential challenger was James A. Simpson, the popular president pro tem of the Alabama Senate. As Dixon's protégé, Simpson had
advocated the state civil service system, old-age pensions, a teacher retirement act, and other manifestations of progressive government during his
twelve years in the state legislature. But Simpson's record also showed that
he had been less than enthusiastic about taxes on big corporations, appropriations for education, free school textbooks, and rural electrification. A
big man, likable, and dedicated to fighting the growth of centralized
federal government, Simpson had won the accolade of most valuable
legislator in 1939 and 1943 from reporters who followed the intricacies of
legislative activity. He had been unanimously elected to preside over the
state Senate where his leadership abilities had been closely observed by his
ambitious young page, George C. Wallace. But Simpson would be no

match for Hill in political sophistication, statewide recognition and connections, or platform charisma. His only hope of achieving a long-coveted seat in the United States Senate would lie in a renewed appeal to racism.[8]

Dixon and Simpson voiced similar views and represented the same political faction, but a rift developed between them in 1943 as to which would challenge Hill. By December this question had been resolved within the close confines of the anti-New Deal coalition. Although Simpson confided to his friend Clarence Allgood, "I'm not going to run unless they make me," he eventually agreed to embark upon the seemingly impossible task of eliminating Hill from the Senate, perhaps in hope of building sufficient support to challenge John Bankhead Jr. in 1946.[9]

To Robert Frazer, then on the faraway Italian front, Hill relayed the news that "James A. Simpson, fair-haired spokesman of the big mules, has announced against me." An astute grassroots political observer in Alabama thought that Simpson should have waited to make his move until the end of the war. "I don't think he can beat Lister Hill," this Birmingham druggist told a Simpson campaign worker. "He picked a tough horse to ride." Another pharmacist concurred: "Hill has all these old WPA's for him and all of these Government employees. I don't think anyone can beat Roosvelt [sic]." Nonetheless Jonathan Daniels, then an administrative assistant to FDR, sensed that Simpson's entry "really disturbed" Hill. Daniels promised to use his access to Roosevelt to give his friend all the help he could muster.[10]

Announcing his candidacy in the friendly confines of Mobile, never a Hill stronghold, Simpson called for a halt to the "wave of socialism and bureaucracy" and, in muted reference to race, urged that Alabama be allowed to handle racial matters without outside interference. Initially Hill sought to hew to the high road of national interest. Speaking to a labor audience in Bessemer, he advocated unconditional Axis surrender, an international organization dedicated to preserving the peace, and the retention of Alabama's wartime industries and airfields as the base of postwar prosperity. Referring only obliquely to his opposition, Hill warned against those who gave "lip service" to their commander in chief but sought "to cut the ground out from under him on the home front."[11]

As this election year opened, Alabama's Democratic Executive Committee confronted a move to bar those who had supported Republican presidential nominee Wendell Willkie in 1940 from becoming candidates in the Democratic primary of 1944. Such action would echo the precedent set by this committee in 1929 when it had barred Democratic supporters of

Herbert Hoover from becoming candidates in its next primary. Thereby the most conspicuous 1928 bolter, Tom Heflin, had been punished by being stripped of the Democratic label and left to run as an independent, doomed to lose his cherished Senate seat to the Democratic nominee, John Bankhead Jr. Thus, too, Alabama's political and economic leaders had reaffirmed their determination that no rebellious white element, like the Populists of the 1890s, should again achieve formal party status. Observing the expulsion of Heflin, Alabamians had been dramatically reminded of their leadership's insistence that they continue to settle their rivalries and differences within the all-white, one-party system that had prevailed since the mass disfranchisement of black voters in 1901.

But "Willkiecrats" were not punished in 1944 as had been the "Hoovercrats" in 1929. Klansmen and drys, who elected Bibb Graves and Hugo Black in 1926 and bolted for Hoover in 1928, had posed a threat to the status quo. But Democratic supporters of Willkie in 1940 represented the Alabama *establishment's* long-standing hostility to social and economic reforms imposed from Washington. The chairman of the state Democratic Executive Committee, Gessner T. McCorvey, a prominent Mobile lawyer and son of Hill's old college mentor, Professor Thomas Chalmers McCorvey, successfully led the move to defeat those who proposed barring this new-style party bolter. McCorvey used a familiar argument: "harsh regulations" might produce a second "white man's party" and expose Alabama again to the "grave danger of the rival political parties fighting for the Negro vote." Since only twenty-eight hundred Alabama blacks had been admitted to the franchise by 1944, McCorvey's warning was primarily rhetorical. In reality, his strong stand in favor of welcoming the strays of 1940 back into the Democratic fold ensured that neither Simpson's candidacy nor the party regularity of those who planned to vote for him would be questioned.[12]

With the Democratic primary rules in place, Alabama's major newspapers proceeded to choose sides. Predictably the *Huntsville Times, Decatur Daily,* and *Florence Times* viewed Hill's reelection as essential to protect TVA and ensure continuing prosperity for their region. After being wined and dined by Amelie Hill Laslie, editors of the *Montgomery Advertiser* and the *Alabama Journal* dutifully rallied to the support of their hometown candidate. (Privately Grover Hall Jr., then serving overseas, described Simpson to Roy Nolen as "a ventilator of back-to-nature economic doctrines.") To no one's surprise, Simpson was the choice of Ed Field, editor of the *Selma Times-Journal*, which frequently echoed the views of the

Black Belt–Birmingham political coalition. Nor was it unexpected that Editor Horace Hall of the *Dothan Eagle*, the dominant Wiregrass paper (whose business manager, Harry Hall, was Simpson's state campaign manager) should support the challenger. The *Gadsden Times* and *Tuscaloosa News*, their joint owners divided in attitude toward the candidates, chose to remain neutral. Frederick Thompson's sale of the *Mobile Register* to new interests in 1932 had left that port city bereft of a strong journalistic voice for progressive goals. Ralph Chandler, editor of the *Mobile Press* founded in 1929 by banking and corporate interests to oppose Thompson, concurred with Simpson's local campaign manager, Francis Inge, that Hill must be defeated. But this time Harry Ayers, owner of the *Anniston Star*, chose to favor the powerful incumbent over a potential newcomer to the Senate. After the election, Nolen commented sourly to Hill: "Harry has one h— of a time with himself, forever trying to adjust, re-adjust, adapt or re-adapt himself to every little wind."[13]

Such endorsements came as no surprise to perceptive Alabamians but the decision of the state's largest newspapers, the home-owned *Birmingham News* and *Age-Herald*, to back Hill angered Simpson and had a major impact upon voters in populous Jefferson County. Victor Hanson, an imposing and autocratic figure who owned the *News* and the *Age-Herald*, mingled socially with "big mules" and had long relied on his personal friend, Simpson, to represent his newspaper's legal interests. But when Hanson, partly influenced by his editors, decided to back a powerful and influential senator who could arrange important favors from Washington and whose reelection seemed a virtual certainty, he and his attorney had a bitter parting of the ways. Sundering his legal tie to the *News* and *Age-Herald*, Simpson, in political ads, accused his former employer of seeking to become a "political dictator" and labeled the wealthy Hanson "the biggest mule in Alabama." An infuriated Hanson ordered his editors to make an all-out effort to reelect Hill. He sent his chief editorial writer, McClellan ("Ted") Van der Veer, to Washington to compose six lengthy articles extolling Hill's leadership qualities. Numerous other pro-Hill editorials followed. The Hanson papers and John Temple Graves II, who now claimed "the New Deal is dealt" and opposed "any more federalism," moved toward a parting of the ways. In 1946 Graves's widely read column would begin to appear in the *Birmingham Post*.[14]

As had many newspaper owners and editors, other Alabama organizations and influential individuals made their choices for senator with economic considerations or political favor in mind. Most industrialists chafed over federal measures such as FEPC, price ceilings, wage-and-hour regulations, unemployment compensation, and increased taxes, all of which they considered unnecessary burdens on manufacturing. Officials of Associated Industries of Alabama, the Alabama and Birmingham Chambers of Commerce, the Farm Bureau, Extension Service, Alabama Power Company, United States Steel, and owners of textile plants, timberlands, sawmills, and papermills strongly favored Simpson. The majority of Birmingham's industrial and business leaders opposed Hill, including such prominent men as corporation lawyer Forney Johnston, textile executive Hugh Comer (whose brother, Donald, was one of Hill's few supporters among the corporate elite in 1944), insurance executive J. Frank Rushton Jr., realtor Sidney Smyer, soft-drink bottler James Lee, automobile dealers Don Drennen and Reese Adamson, industrialist Herbert Stockham, construction company owner W. R. J. Dunn, and utility executive Thomas W. Martin. Commenting on some of Hill's opponents, one supporter remarked that, if Simpson were elected, representatives of eastern corporate interests in Alabama could report to their national boards: "We can't elect a Republican down here but we have sent a man up there that will fight Roosevelt in anything he attempts to do."[15]

In Montgomery, Hill's opponents included his cousin, T. B. Hill Jr., a prominent attorney, and Marion Rushton, son of Hill's first political opponent, Ray Rushton. In Mobile, as Clarence Allgood later recalled, "we couldn't hardly get anyone to speak to us but Joe Lyons and a few of his friends." His loyal uncle advised Hill that most Mobile physicians backed Simpson in response to that candidate's charges that Hill favored "socialized medicine."[16]

But Hill's support, if not as economically powerful, was broader than that of Simpson. His most solid area of support was the Tennessee Valley, its voters pleased that Hill had led the opposition to Tennessee Senator Kenneth McKellar's effort to hamstring TVA by requiring that agency to come to Congress for authority to spend its surplus funds and for confirmation of its employees. (In December 1944, Hill would again take a leading role in defending TVA from fresh attack by opponents of public power. With John Bankhead voting on the opposite side, Hill helped to defeat an attempt to require that power produced at government projects be sold at the dam to private utilities which could then resell to customers at whatever rate they chose. On this aspect of public versus private power, Hill had almost totally reversed his viewpoint since 1932.)[17]

Hill's following also included the Alabama Education Association,

composed of teachers grateful for his long-standing efforts to raise their
salaries and improve their working conditions through federal aid; members of the Alabama Federation of Labor, the Congress of Industrial Organizations (CIO), Teamsters, United Mine Workers (UMW), Brotherhood
of Railroad Trainmen, and other labor groups, all rallying behind a
Rooseveltian, plus numerous federal employees of TVA, the Rural Electrification Administration (REA), the Farm Security Administration, and
military bases. Presidents of a number of county Farm Bureau affiliates
dared to differ with their leaders. Many cotton mill workers in Sylacauga
and Alexander City refused to follow the political lead of employers like
Hugh Comer and Benjamin C. Russell. M. E. Lazenby, editor of the
Alabama Christian Advocate and Dr. L. L. Gwaltney, editor of the *Alabama Baptist*, as well as other diehard drys finally forgave Hill for having
supported the wet Al Smith in 1928. "You worked for Smith. I voted for
Hoover," Lazenby wrote Hill. "I don't know which of us ought to be the
most ashamed. Perhaps both of us are willing to let the subject drop." After
all, Simpson as a state legislator had helped to defeat their most cherished
cause, a popular referendum on prohibition.[18]

Ed Reid, executive director of the Alabama League of Municipalities,
successfully rallied many mayors, probate judges, and other local officials
behind Hill. Progressive politicians like former lieutenant governors Albert Carmichael and Handy Ellis and Gadsden attorney Albert Rains also
joined the Hill forces. Birmingham's popular mayor, W. Cooper Green,
hoping that Hill would support him for the next Senate vacancy, came out
for him in the crucial, final weeks of the campaign. Surprisingly, so did the
senator's old opponent, Tom Heflin, grateful for Hill's sympathetic efforts
to restore him in some minor capacity to the federal payroll. But by far the
most influential politician to declare for Hill was his colleague, John
Bankhead Jr., who sensed that the coalition of big business and agricultural interests wanted, not just one, but *two* new senators. Victor Hanson
had warned Bankhead that "Simpson and his poison squad of henchmen
are not sparing you." In publicly announcing his support for Hill, Bankhead stressed that the junior senator, too, had championed causes dear to
the average farmer such as cheap, abundant fertilizer and generous federal
loans on basic agricultural commodities.[19]

Hill also held an advantage over Simpson in organization. Roy Nolen
and Foots Clement had perfected their sophisticated statewide network of
support for use by Hill's state campaign manager, Gordon Madison. In
Montgomery, Richard Rives, a former campaign manager for both Hugo

Black and Bibb Graves, proved a canny political adviser. In Birmingham, Clarence Allgood, Evelyn Hicks, Chester Austin, Oren C. Smith, and Tom Beach planned the campaign that would culminate in Hill's victory in Simpson's home county.

To counter the wealthy interests behind Simpson, however, Hill would need ample funds as well as skilled organization. No longer was it possible for a generous father, aided by friends and other family members, to fund a senatorial campaign. The expensive Hill-Simpson race, Allgood later recalled, "blew the lid off politics in this state as far as money is concerned." After it was over, Hill would complain to close friends that more money was spent to defeat him than had been spent in any previous Alabama campaign. He learned from Nolen that certain banking interests and other business leaders in Montgomery had contributed ten thousand dollars to his opponent. But Hill believed that many times this amount had come from outside the state.[20]

Hill, too, had generous supporters. Organized labor, the Reynolds Metals Company and other national manufacturers who wanted to stand in well with a member of the Senate Military Affairs Committee, and other major supporters prepared to contribute. Roosevelt himself hinted to Bernard Baruch how much he valued both Hill and Claude Pepper; the president believed that Baruch thereupon sent money to these candidates. Other affluent sources of campaign funding were Rufus Lackey, head of Brown Service Funeral Home in Birmingham, and his Montgomery associate, Sam Durden. When he needed campaign funds, Clarence Allgood remembered, "all I had to do was to call Rufus or Sam and we got it." Lackey, a behind-the-scenes political boss, had been a major financial backer of Bibb Graves and had contributed heavily to the campaigns of many state legislators. Now he evidently saw advantages in helping an important United States senator.[21]

For the first two months of the campaign, Hill adopted the posture that, as Democratic whip and a member of important Senate committees, his presence in Washington was essential to the war effort. More faithful to FDR at this point than majority leader Barkley, Hill voted against the two-billion-dollar-plus tax bill that Roosevelt had vetoed as "wholly ineffective" to meet the nation's financial needs in wartime. Explaining this stand to voters back home, Hill said he felt that the bill "placed too much tax burden on those with medium and small incomes and too little burden on those with large incomes and huge war profits." Barkley, his own political future foremost in mind, seized this opportunity to demonstrate his independence from Roosevelt by denouncing the veto message and dramatically offering to resign as Democratic leader. But Hill cast one of only fourteen votes to sustain Roosevelt's veto. ("First Avenue and Twentieth Street to the contrary notwithstanding," Nolen rejoiced.) Using statistics supplied by his friend Jonathan Daniels, Hill also emphasized that he had helped to create sixty thousand federal jobs, mostly war-related, in Alabama and that he was already making plans to retain these facilities permanently. In an effort to deflect Simpson, Hill added that he was standing guard on behalf of states' rights and against a federal anti-poll-tax law, FEPC, and "all efforts to force social equality upon our people."[22]

Back home, Simpson attempted to persuade the mass of Alabama voters that it was in their best interest to expel Hill from the Senate because of his association with a growing federal bureaucracy. He sent form letters to Alabama doctors, including Dr. Hill, warning that the Senate faced a pending bill to "socialize" medicine. This letter enraged Hill's father. "I have just received . . . this communication from the microcephalic idiot," he grouched to his son. Simpson's approach did attract some physicians, fearful that Congress might enact the pending national health insurance program. But based on past experience, the vast majority of the Alabama electorate waited for candidates to offer them stronger meat in exchange for votes.[23]

Members of Simpson's inner circle debated whether to play the trump card of racism. Initially the candidate himself proved reluctant. "I abhor the thought of riding the race issue into the U.S. Senate," Simpson told his campaign manager, Harry Hall, "but it looks like if I am going to get there it is the only way I can." Although Hall and supporters in north Alabama advised that to raise such a divisive issue during wartime might produce a backlash, Simpson eventually yielded to the fire-eaters. Hall suspected that Ed Field had been instrumental in the decision to employ this issue. Allgood recalled that Sidney Smyer had organized a Jefferson County meeting that "turned into a KKK rally." Crafty old Tom Heflin, himself a past master at exploiting prejudice, believed that the Simpson forces got their notion of using the race issue from observing the success of their Georgia neighbor, the "Wild Man from Sugar Creek," Eugene Talmadge.[24]

Early in 1944 the only aspects of the racial subject ripe for exploitation were the familiar issues of FEPC, abolition of the poll tax, and the then remote possibility that federal financial aid might lead to school integration. Foes of the poll tax, Virginia Durr loud among them, struggled to bring that matter to a Senate vote, but the Roosevelt administration, reluctant to endanger the reelection of Hill and Pepper, did not mount a vigorous effort in its behalf. Not until after the May Democratic primaries in the South did the Senate face a vote to limit debate on the poll tax and thus curb a southern filibuster. Supporters of cloture failed to muster the necessary two-thirds majority.[25]

Alabama school superintendent Elbert Norton, rising to Hill's defense on the issue of federal aid to education, assured teachers and parents that the state would control the spending of such funds. To defuse the FEPC issue, Hill and Bankhead voted with other southern senators in late March to deny appropriations to that agency. "[FEPC] has done harm and should be abolished," Hill declared in a press release. At the White House, Daniels urged his boss to postpone any comments favorable to FEPC lest he aid the foes of Hill and Pepper.[26]

But on 3 April 1944, the Simpson forces received from an unexpected quarter the fresh ammunition they needed. Reversing its previous stand, the United States Supreme Court sounded the death knell of the white primary. In *Smith v. Allwright*, the court ruled 8 to 1 that the Democratic party in Texas could no longer bar black voters from its primary because such action was equivalent to discrimination by the state itself and therefore forbidden by the Fifteenth Amendment. Hugo Black had voted with the majority.

Although the *Smith* decision applied only to Texas (Justice Owen J. Roberts, the lone dissenter, compared this and similar decisions to "a restricted railroad ticket, good for this day and train only"), southern Democrats who had barred blacks from the hitherto "private" confines of their party clearly saw it as an omen of drastic political change in their own states. Alabama Democrats immediately put their minds to work to devise other artificial barriers against black voting. Meantime Simpson's forces made political capital out of this threat to Alabama's white primary. "Jim's friends are all over town today screaming about the Supreme Court decision," Allgood reported glumly to Nolen. Publicly Simpson described the ruling as "the gravest threat to white supremacy since Reconstruction."[27]

No matter how initially reluctant he may have been to employ prejudice as a weapon in his campaign, Simpson permitted his supporters to escalate its usage. *Alabama*, a magazine published by Associated Industries of Alabama, and the *Southern Watchman*, Hamner Cobbs's weekly newspaper widely distributed by Simpson supporters during the campaign, published the most strident attacks on Hill. *Alabama* reminded its readers that Hill had been on the committee to escort the black president of Liberia,

Edwin Barclay, to the Senate floor in 1943, an occasion on which most southern senators had chosen to be absent from their seats. This anti-New Deal organ also published photographs of blacks and whites taking the postal-clerk examination in an unsegregated Birmingham courtroom. In his newspaper, Cobbs warned that federal aid to education would lead to "mongrelization" and published photographs of a racially mixed classroom and of Mrs. Roosevelt with blacks.[28]

The *Montgomery Advertiser* reported that Simpson forces had revived the old issue of Hill's religion. In Birmingham, Allgood also heard rumors that Simpson workers were whispering that Hill was "a Jew, a Catholic, and a crook." Even before this campaign had started in earnest, William Hill had reported to his nephew that one bitter foe in Mobile had tried "to make capital out of the fact that Sister [Lillian Hill Rucker] belonged to the Catholic Church and that you also had Jew blood in you—that you was [*sic*] not what you claimed to be." With this matter always in the back of his mind, Hill instructed Nolen to include in campaign advertisements only a "very brief summary" of his family history, along with the statement that "my family has been in Alabama for over a hundred years."[29]

Eventually the zealous Simpson followers made a critical mistake by carrying their efforts to foment prejudice too far. Through a Simpson press release, newspapers were informed that black men supervised white women workers in the Wilcox County Farm Security office. When this report of work conditions in the sensitive Black Belt turned out to be incorrect, the *Birmingham News* and other Hill supporters charged that Simpson had used false information to court votes. Hill, jumping at an opportunity to take the offensive, deplored the "cry nigger" campaign of his opponent and declared that Simpson had "waved a lighted match over the powder keg of race relations and class hatred."[30]

But now Hill, at the urging of John Bankhead Jr., Joseph Lyons, and many others, also employed prejudicial appeals. He assured industrial workers in Bessemer that he not only favored segregation in schools but also on buses. He implied that Simpson, a native of Tennessee, would be less trustworthy in matters of race than one who had been born in Alabama. His aides dug up the fact that Simpson in 1927 had cast in the Alabama House the sole vote against an amendment that struck from the Alabama Code a loophole that had made it possible for mulattoes to be classified as whites after the fifth generation. Those who wrote Hill's advertisements jumped on this old issue. Under the heading, "The Truth about Simpson and the Negro Question," one Hill advertisement stated: "It was Jim Simpson who voted against a bill to define a negro [*sic*] as a person with any negro blood, even a drop." Another ad, headed "Simpson Brands Himself a Hypocrite," advised voters that "Lister Hill not only believes in white supremacy—he votes for it." Hill assured an audience in Gadsden that, had he been in the Alabama legislature in 1927, he would have voted "for white supremacy."[31]

As the campaign drew to a close, the *Birmingham News*, intensifying its demand for Hill's reelection, declared in a front-page editorial that Simpson had raised the race issue to "make political capital" but that it had "backfired disastrously." Nonetheless Simpson supporters refused to be deterred from their course. In a full-page ad in the *Montgomery Advertiser* only a week before the primary, Simpson asked: "Can Alabama Afford to Hush-Hush the Race Issue? Shall we face this vital question now or shall we make a Munich of it?"[32]

When the votes were counted, Hill had received 55.5 percent, a substantial but less than overwhelming victory. He carried forty-three of Alabama's sixty-seven counties, including Simpson's home county, Jefferson; his own home county of Montgomery; most of the Black Belt; all but two counties in the Wiregrass; most of his old congressional district; and nine counties in the Tennessee Valley (see Appendix, Map 3). The *Decatur Daily* boasted: "Without the [Tennessee] valley factor, it was anybody's race." Editor Barrett Shelton speculated that north Alabama had taken a lesson from the Black Belt in the value of political unity. "Has the time arrived," Shelton asked, "when the great area north of Jefferson County has decided to assert its real strength in state and national politics?"[33]

As expected, Hill's major bases of support had also consisted of teachers, organized labor, federal jobholders, state and county officials, and the great majority of those who bothered to obtain absentee ballots. About half of Alabama farmers disobeyed the political orders of their leaders in the Farm Bureau and Extension Service, preferring to take Bankhead's recommendation and also appreciative of the benefits of rural electricity and government loans. But in Hill's opinion, the farm vote had not been decisive. "In spite of John's splendid statement," Hill told Nolen, "it was the city folks who did the job . . . the machinery that [Bankhead] ought to have controlled did not function." Nolen's analysis bore this out. In Jefferson County, characterized by Nolen as "the lodging place for overseers of absenteeism," Hill had carried 185 boxes and tied 4, out of a total of 250 boxes. Largely due to Frank Boykin's influence, Mobile had been the only major urban area to go for Simpson.[34]

But despite Hill's record, his well-organized campaign, and the big groups aligned behind him, almost half of Alabama's voters had declared their preference for a new senator. Thousands of Republicans had crossed party lines to vote against Hill, joined by disgruntled Democrats who planned to vote Republican that fall. Simpson had also triumphed in lumber-area boxes, textile-mill villages, and a portion of the coal fields (including Bankhead's home county, Walker), and carried half of the farmers. Nolen believed that Simpson's slightly over 100,000 votes had been made up of 75,000 Republicans ("regular and 'Big Mule' ") plus another one-fourth composed of citizens whose votes had been obtained "under the severest coercion" from their bosses.[35]

For isolated, sparsely educated, and economically insecure white Alabamians, racism had frequently offered a welcome diversion from misery as well as a rare source of pride. But race had failed to ignite the majority of the Alabama electorate against Hill, the New Deal, and Roosevelt. Why had not this form of demagoguery, a proven device for masking economic concerns and rousing voters, prevailed in 1944? Much of the credit belonged to Hill himself. Simpson and his supporters found it difficult to pin the label of an advocate of "social equality" on one who had spoken and voted against FEPC and against federal laws to outlaw lynchings and poll taxes and who fervently proclaimed his dedication to continued segregation of schools and buses. Despite the *Smith* decision, the eventual breakdown of their legally segregated way of life seemed a remote possibility to the majority of Alabama voters. Editors of the Hanson newspapers sensed that most voters believed that Simpson had exaggerated this danger and thus had threatened wartime unity. After the campaign, Frank Dixon remained convinced that it had been necessary to bring in and play up the race issue, which, he correctly predicted, would be raised in many an Alabama political contest to come. But Simpson confessed to Harry Hall that he had made a mistake in allowing race to be injected as early as 1944.[36]

Nonetheless, Simpson had given Hill a bad scare. When the war ended and when Roosevelt, like Bibb Graves, passed from the scene, anti-New Dealers expected to be in a much stronger position to oppose those who advocated federal laws that further threatened their economic and political preeminence. But in 1944 Roosevelt was still very much in charge. Delighted with the twin victories of Hill and Claude Pepper but cautious lest he again appear to meddle in southern politics, the president delegated to his press secretary, Stephen Early, the pleasure of informing both New

Deal stalwarts "how much the results have rejoiced [FDR]." Many of Hill's Senate friends also sent congratulations. "Alabama knows a good man," wired Harry Truman, who had little inkling in the early spring of 1944 of what his own future held.[37]

But the campaign also left a substantial residue of bitterness on both sides. Privately Frank Dixon confided to Grover Hall Jr. that Hill's twenty-five thousand majority could be attributed to the fact that probate judges, county officeholders, and federal "teat-suckers" had access to automobiles and scarce gasoline. "You can't win a political campaign, anymore than you can win a war, without gasoline," Dixon grumbled. But Dixon laid an even larger share of the blame for Simpson's defeat on Victor Hanson. The Birmingham publisher, Dixon wrote Hall, "is riding to the usual fall which comes to those in this country who turn vicious in their use of power."[38]

Hill, too, nurtured ill feelings. He confided to George Norris, who had himself suffered the bitter taste of defeat in 1942, that he had been attacked by "selfish interests [which] follow the same pattern as the big industrialists of Germany used when they put Adolf Hitler and his Nazis in control of the German government." Sympathetic White House intimates Stephen Early, Jonathan Daniels, Sam Rosenman, and Paul Porter urged Hill to tell his side of this political saga on the Senate floor. Cautioned by Nolen to "rest on your laurels," Hill resisted this temptation. But privately he told his version of the 1944 Alabama Democratic primary to leading Senate Democrats, warning that this had been "merely the first battle in the war against a fourth term for FDR." Still smarting years later from the memory of the Simpson campaign, Hill sometimes refused to receive those spokesmen for Associated Industries and the Alabama State Chamber of Commerce who, he believed, had called him "a pinko and a wild-eyed liberal" in 1944. But, as his friend Jesse Hearin had predicted, Hill also felt politically stronger for having prevailed in what he felt had been a "mean, nasty, treacherous and tough campaign." His victory over a major opponent, backed by powerful forces in Alabama and outside the state, added to Hill's aura of invincibility and helped to discourage other formidable opponents for eighteen years.[39]

"The poll tax must go"

At the same time they approved a fourth term for Roosevelt by a slightly lower majority than that of 1940, Alabamians formally ratified the results of their Democratic senatorial primary. Hill easily won reelection over a little-known Republican nominee and a candidate still waving the hopeless banner of prohibition. Much to Nolen's joy, Hill had outpolled even "the Champ" [FDR]. Before this election, Hill had taken care to warn Roosevelt against permitting the Justice Department to institute criminal proceedings in connection with the barring of black voters from Alabama's Democratic primary. Such action, Hill told his friend Jonathan Daniels, might escalate "impotent rumblings against the New Deal into actual revolt at the polls." Attorney General Francis Biddle, already doubtful of the prospect for winning such suits before Alabama juries, drew back.[40]

Hill had chosen not to seek a delegate's seat at the Democratic convention while running for reelection, but he had attended the convention and dutifully nominated John Bankhead Jr. for the vice presidency. As he had in three previous national elections, he then stumped nationally for "the South's proven friend" against a new spokesman for "the ancient enemy." If Republicans should succeed in putting Thomas E. Dewey in the White House, Hill feared that Dewey would take foreign-policy advice from John Foster Dulles, "an attorney for cartels, monopolists, tariff barons and German-American Bundists," and that the Senate Foreign Relations Committee would be headed by Hiram Johnson, "an unreconstructed isolationist, one of the last of the cabal that defeated the League of Nations." Don't worry that the fourth term would set a new precedent, Hill urged members of the Carolina Political Union. After all, George Washington, too, had served his country for sixteen years, first as commander in chief, then as president in the aftermath of war.[41]

Another Democratic victory and his own fresh mandate made Hill uncharacteristically bold. Having been reelected as senator and majority whip and chosen one of three new Democrats on the powerful Senate Foreign Relations Committee, was he not sufficiently entrenched to take a chance or two? Be more independent of FDR, Hugo Black's old law partner, Crampton Harris, urged. Harris believed that Americans were slowly turning away from their long dependence on Roosevelt. When they looked for a new leader, Harris wondered if Lister Hill might not catch their fancy. But to be a national figure, Hill realized, a Southerner must somehow dissociate himself from suffrage restrictions and other overtly racist policies. Reflecting on the fact that he had beaten Simpson by only twenty-five thousand votes, Hill must also have been struck anew by his need for an expanded electorate in Alabama.[42]

With his home base and perhaps his national image in mind, Hill seized an opportunity in February 1945 to speak out at last against the poll tax. Alarmed Alabama Democrats were considering how best to respond to the *Smith* decision when their legislature met in May. Frank Dixon suggested to Gessner McCorvey that "the best lawyers on the State [Democratic] Executive Committee" be asked to devise a plan to avoid mass registration of blacks in their party's ranks. McCorvey agreed that Alabama should tighten its registration process, including retention of the cumulative poll tax as a "lawful method of getting rid of a large number of people who would not cast an intelligent ballot even if they were given the right to vote."[43]

Shortly after McCorvey announced this plan of action, Hill flatly announced that "the poll tax must go." Taking heart from the Georgia legislature's repeal of that state's poll tax, he called on Alabama legislators to follow suit. Hill was not so rash as to advocate federal action and took care to assure white Alabamians that removal of this tax would not, by itself, enfranchise blacks. After all, he pointed out, county registrars, enforcing state laws, decided who was fit to vote in Alabama. But now that Georgia had removed its barrier, Hill characterized Alabama's poll tax, which cumulated each year for voters from the ages of twenty-one to forty-five, as "the most burdensome, restrictive, indefensible, and undemocratic" of all. In effect, it disfranchised hundreds of thousands of white Alabamians. Some foes of repeal, Hill hinted in his statement, preferred a limited electorate so that they could more easily control the state. Jim Simpson objected that Hill should thus impugn the motives of those who differed with him.[44]

Atticus Mullin observed in the *Montgomery Advertiser* that it took "plenty of political nerve and courage" for Hill to speak, even cautiously, against the poll tax. "There are people in Alabama who will hold it against him as long as they live," Mullin predicted. Like Hill, the columnist described these critics as "the same people . . . who always oppose anything that means progress, either in government or human welfare." Claribel McCann, Dr. Hill's longtime friend and associate, informed the senator that the pastor of Montgomery's First Methodist Church had compared his action in "upsetting the applecart of tradition" to that of Jesus Christ. Noting Hill's stand, the liberal *New Republic* lauded him as "one of the real moral leaders of the New South." But the Alabama legislature would be in no mood that May to follow such leadership. In a hot session, members were to vote down proposals to repeal the poll tax altogether or to eliminate its cumulative provisions. Opponents of repeal would enact

McCorvey's plan, to become known as the Boswell amendment, making access to the ballot box even more difficult.[45]

"Not since Abraham Lincoln fell"

To homefolk in Alabama, Hill also must have appeared rash as he led fierce Senate fights in early 1945 to confirm his longtime friends and frequent dinner guests, Henry Wallace and Aubrey Williams, to become, respectively, secretary of commerce and head of the Rural Electrification Administration. Both nominations had been widely attacked in the anti-Roosevelt press as evidence that the president was again "swinging to the left." Opening what was to be a bitter battle over confirmation of the former vice president, Hill denounced Wallace's opponents, including most Republicans and the majority of southern Democrats, for indulging in "malignance and hysteria." With an eye to his home base, Hill stressed that Wallace would help the South fight inequitable freight rates. Eventually Roosevelt won the Wallace fight, whereupon administration foes turned with fresh zeal to strike down Aubrey Williams.[46]

In sticking up for Williams, Hill exposed himself to the risk of even greater fury from home. This fellow Alabamian, who had emerged as a major proponent of the New Deal's left wing while deputy administrator of WPA and head of the National Youth Administration, had attracted the ire of right-wing elements like the *Chicago Tribune* and Congressman Hamilton Fish of New York, who had once characterized Williams as "the pinkest of the pink." Now many southern Democrats, including Kenneth McKellar, Tom Connally, Richard Russell, and Theodore Bilbo, charged Williams with being a Communist sympathizer, a religious backslider, and an advocate of blacks and whites using the same toilet facilities. When Bilbo broached the toilet matter, Williams candidly admitted that sharing such a facility might be the inevitable consequence of equal-employment opportunities. At this, William Fulbright and John Bankhead Jr. balked. Originally a nominal supporter of confirmation, Bankhead took this opportunity to bow out, angrily informing the nominee: "This is too much, Mr. Williams!"[47]

But Hill assured the Senate that Williams "has been all his life a humanitarian." Along with fellow southerners Claude Pepper and Allen Ellender, he stuck by the nominee to the bitter end. Jesse Hearin, always sensitive to groundswells in Alabama, cautioned Hill not to risk his own career "for a fire brand and a red flag." But Hill refused to be deterred. The issue, he wrote Hearin, was bigger than a fight over Williams; it was an effort to slap the administration. Striking back at Williams's opponents, Hill and George Aiken claimed that powerful business interests, fearful of losing their monopoly on REA construction materials, were working behind the scenes to defeat Williams. After Williams's nomination had been rejected by a substantial Senate majority, the pragmatic Hill advised his stubbornly forthright friend that, had he been more equivocal on the subject of toilets, he might have been narrowly confirmed.[48]

Engrossed in their fight for his nominees, Roosevelt's staunch followers had little time for concern about their leader's mortality. News of the president's sudden death on 12 April 1945 stunned Hill. He had lost his chief political mentor, the towering figure who had so vividly impressed and shaped him as a young congressman, this native aristocrat who had demonstrated to him that a privileged American who achieved high political office could use that power in behalf of the needs and aspirations of the less privileged. As Roosevelt's funeral cortege passed the Senate Office Building, Hill wrote Nolen: "I'm sure you know how heavy my heart is." In his formal expression of sorrow, he declared: "Not since Abraham Lincoln fell has this nation suffered such a tragedy. . . . [Roosevelt] fought for human rights, human progress, and human welfare. He fought for a fairer and a better opportunity for all the people."[49]

Less than a month later, Hill and Nolen debated whether Hill should pay a final tribute to Roosevelt in Alabama's capitol. But with the nation then concentrated on the surrender of Germany and Governor Chauncey Sparks's administration cool toward the New Deal legacy, the timing did not seem right. Resignedly, Hill wrote his political manager: "My tribute has already been paid. I paid it while [FDR] was living in my support of him, his leadership, his principals [sic] and his programs. Twice the people of Alabama elected me to the Senate as a Franklin Roosevelt Senator. In the past twelve years I have not made a single speech of any consequence in Alabama that I did not pay tribute to him and his leadership. In the days to come I shall again and again proclaim him in Askalon and tell of him on the streets of Gath."[50]

Although he was to serve under four more presidents, to Hill these successors would seem puny compared with FDR. Carl Elliott, one of his Alabama congressional colleagues, remembered that, even years after Roosevelt's death, Hill would shed a tear when he talked about his Chief.[51]

The Transition

1 9 4 5 – 1 9 4 6

"Just a bunch of political refugees"

President Harry S Truman. In the first shock of transition, Americans had a hard time associating this title, borne so long and majestically by Franklin Roosevelt, with one who seemed just a plain, everyday fellow. Most quickly rallied behind this underdog who obviously was doing his damndest to handle a tough new job. But intimates of Roosevelt found it almost inconceivable that Truman cronies like Edwin Pauley, John Snyder, Harry Vaughan, George Allen, and Leslie Biffle now stood at a president's elbow instead of ordained New Dealers such as Henry Wallace, Claude Pepper, Hugo Black, William O. Douglas, Thomas Corcoran, and Lister Hill.

Corcoran, in one of his late evening telephone conversations (with the Federal Bureau of Investigation—FBI—listening in to see what this famed political operative might be plotting), told Hill that he had been to parties of the old guard and seen "a bunch of guys that had the world in their hands last year, and now they're just a bunch of political refugees . . . a helpless bunch of sheep." Try though he did, Corcoran could not manipulate Washington appointments as he had in the heyday of the New Deal. Observing the almost wholesale shift of cabinet posts, ambassadorships, board appointments, federal judgeships, and other seats of power from New Dealers to persons for whom the Roosevelt crowd had little regard, Corcoran scornfully decried the new president as another Ulysses S. Grant, "loyal, honest, and dumb as hell." In an even more pessimistic moment, he predicted: "This experience is going to prove institutionally that democracy can't do it; that unless it has an uncommon man in the Presidency, it won't work." To hearten Corcoran, Hill invoked his father's old rallying cry: "Chin up, tail over the dashboard!"[1]

During Truman's first tentative months in the presidency, Hill found his old Senate colleague approachable, even desirous of his help. Fighting McKellar and other enemies of David Lilienthal, Hill and Bankhead persuaded Truman to reappoint Lilienthal to another nine-year term as TVA chairman. When Stimson at last retired from the War Department in September 1945, Truman offered this post to Hill. But to preside over a peacetime military establishment would offer little challenge compared to the role of a Senate leader in shaping the peace and bringing about domestic reforms. Hill preferred to stump the country on behalf of world cooperation and the new United Nations. He had other unfinished business: federal aid to education, unification of the armed forces, programs to bring hospitals, libraries, and telephones to rural Americans. During Barkley's lengthy illness and while that Kentuckian led the long probe into Pearl Harbor, Hill occupied the heady position of acting majority leader. Much to the disappointment of Jim Simpson and his friends, Hill quietly said No to Truman's offer.[2]

But could Hill continue to function effectively under this new and increasingly confident president? How was he to retain his Senate seat while pressing for passage of Truman's policies, which, now that war had ended in both Europe and Japan, included bold new proposals on civil rights and national health? True, the new president wanted to carry on such New Deal policies as price and rent controls, unemployment benefits and the minimum wage, and favored a postwar program of major construction projects financed partly by the federal government. But by the fall of 1945, Truman was also urging that FEPC be made permanent and that Social Security be expanded to include health insurance for all Americans.[3]

On one policy of the early Truman administration, however, Hill found himself eager to side with the president. Throughout his long service on the House and Senate Military Affairs committees, he had urged unification of the armed forces. Squabbles and rivalry between service branches, Hill felt, had caused the British to lose Crete and contributed to American unpreparedness at Pearl Harbor. At the beginning of the war, he had been prominent among those imploring Roosevelt to coordinate his military chiefs. Now Hill believed that consolidation of the Army and Navy into a single department would heighten American capabilities for the atomic age.[4]

In 1945, Hill introduced a bill to create a single Department of Armed

Forces, a concept also supported by his old friend Josephus Daniels, once secretary of the Navy himself, as well as by Generals George Marshall, Douglas MacArthur, and Dwight Eisenhower. But the Navy's brass, fearful that the Army would dominate any such arrangement, vigorously opposed Hill's bill. "I was at dinner with [Navy Secretary James V.] Jim Forrestal last night," Corcoran reported to Hill early the following morning, "and he plaintively said to me: 'Does Lister Hill forget that I'm a friend of his?' "[5]

By December 1945, this cause had gained a powerful supporter. "The Big Boss himself is going to shoot for it [in] the next few days," Hill reported exultantly to Corcoran. Truman favored unification of the armed services based on his experiences as a senatorial investigator of costly, sometimes fraudulent, wartime contracts. As Hill had anticipated, the president sent a special message to Congress recommending that the three branches be consolidated under a Department of National Defense headed by a civilian secretary, aided by a chief of staff and three undersecretaries for ground, sea, and air forces. Hill and two other Senate co-sponsors of the administration's proposal pressed the Senate to adopt this plan. But Forrestal and other Navy leaders objected so long and vehemently to the idea of a single chief of staff that Truman eventually decided to delete this position. Other compromises followed.[6]

As eventually agreed to in June 1947, the unification plan made no provision for a Department of Defense and gave the secretary of defense little authority other than that of coordinator. Shrewdly Truman named Forrestal as the nation's first defense secretary, thereby allowing the program's most ardent opponent to experience its shortcomings firsthand. Hill expressed dissatisfaction with the outcome of this initial skirmish. After the plan had been in effect for a year, he observed that service rivalries continued and military expenses had escalated. Hill suspected the branches of spending more money to fight one another than to build a unified defense and vowed to "raise Cain" until real unification took place. But when that process finally got underway in 1949, Hill had decided to concentrate his energies on other matters.[7]

"We must preserve the freedom of the individual doctor"

At the same time that he cooperated with Truman on the issue of unification, Hill differed with the president over a postwar approach to national health. Prior to Roosevelt's death, Hill and a nominal Republican co-sponsor, Senator Harold Burton of Ohio, had introduced a major plan to construct new hospitals throughout the nation with particular emphasis on rural facilities. This proposal reposed quietly in the Senate Committee on Education and Labor until Truman announced in September 1945 that he planned to recommend a program to ensure that all Americans had the right to adequate medical care.[8]

To achieve this goal, Truman proposed comprehensive, prepaid medical insurance for all Americans, hospital expansion, increased support of public, maternal, and child health services, and federal aid to medical research and education. Under the plan, all employed persons and their dependents would be covered by a tax of 4 percent on the first $3,600 of wages and salaries. Since recipients would be free to choose their own doctors and hospitals, Truman insisted that the plan would *not* be social-ized medicine wherein "all doctors work as employees of the government." But the prospect of compulsory health insurance triggered cries of alarm from the National Physicians Committee and the American Medical Asso-ciation (AMA).[9]

In many respects, Truman's proposal resembled the Wagner-Murray-Dingell bill introduced in 1943 and frequently cited by Simpson supporters in the Alabama senatorial campaign of 1944 to create the impression that Hill favored socialized medicine. As one of Truman's senior advisers recalled, the president realized that his health-insurance proposal would not pass but "wanted to scare these doctors and make them do something" about medical care for the poor. If so, Truman partially achieved this objective. The Hill-Burton bill, supported by "Mr. Republican" himself, Senator Robert Taft of Ohio, suddenly emerged from committee to com-pete for Senate approval with the more comprehensive plan proposed by Truman.[10]

Over a fifteen-year period of economic depression and war, the United States had fallen far behind in hospital upkeep and construction. Forty percent of the nation's counties had no hospital facilities whatever. The South, still predominantly rural, particularly lagged in this regard. Else-where numerous hospitals had suffered fiscal neglect, obsolescence, or severe overcrowding.[11]

Meantime, labor-union membership, protected by the Wagner Act and stimulated by the needs of war, had vastly increased in numbers, strength, and militancy. During World War II, unions had bargained successfully for health-care benefits, thereby making thousands more Americans eligible for hospital care. Organized labor, led by the CIO, pressed Truman and Congress to set up a postwar program of national health insurance. Hastily the American Medical Association, other health-care organizations, the vast majority of physicians, Senator Taft, and powerful business interests joined forces to attack such a program as "totalitarian" and "socialistic." As Truman had foreseen, this aspect of his health program was doomed from the start. Some concession seemed imperative, however, to curb labor's postwar unrest.[12]

As an alternative to Truman's plan, the American Hospital Association (AHA) proposed a three-pronged approach: expansion of privately financed health insurance, public care for the indigent, and a vast hospital construction program to provide better care and stimulate the economy as had New Deal projects in the 1930s. The bipartisan Hill-Burton bill, embodying the hospital expansion aspect of the AHA program, was to sail through both houses of Congress. Organized medicine, important foundations, and major business interests favored it. Even labor, foreseeing a large number of construction jobs and more hospital beds for union members who had won private insurance benefits through collective bargaining, agreed to go along.[13]

In the spring of 1946, while Congress debated the Hill-Burton bill, Dr. L. L. Hill Jr., who had pioneered an unexplored aspect of heart surgery, founded his own hospital, donated his services liberally to the poor, earned the gratitude and affection of thousands of patients, and prospered by reason of hard work and constant study, died in Montgomery after a lingering illness. The doctor had retired in 1937. He believed that no physician should practice after reaching seventy because "he cannot trust his reactions after that age." But retirement bored Dr. Hill. "I had just about as well be dead as not to practice," he fumed. He passed his days reading, corresponding with fellow physicians, riding around Montgomery to inspect his properties or to have his head shaved at the barbershop, telling and retelling long stories, and quoting Robert Ingersoll to his grandchildren. Miss McCann nursed his ailments but, for companionship and the latest Montgomery gossip, Dr. Hill turned more and more to his wife. Both had always shared a passionate concern for their elder son and followed every detail of his career. But Dr. Hill, increasingly alienated by Roosevelt's policies, complained that Lister tried to "padlock" his lips. Never one to keep his opinions to himself, the doctor declared, in loud stage whispers, that Grover Cleveland had been "the last Democratic President"; Woodrow Wilson "a leftist" who had introduced all kinds of "socialism"; and, as for Roosevelt, the less said the better. At least he and Lister had agreed on the necessity for American intervention in World War II. The doctor's younger son, Luther Lyons Hill, had resigned from the Army in 1923, much to his father's displeasure. But in World War II, Luther returned to the military, eventually becoming a brigadier general; through Luther's career, the doctor realized his dream of martial glory. When Dr. Hill died, his two sons, two daughters, and wife stood by his bedside. His funeral was held at his home; the doctor had been true to Ingersoll to the end. Lilly Lyons Hill would survive her husband by little more than a year; her funeral would take place at St. Peter's Catholic Church and she would be remembered by the *Montgomery Advertiser* as a "faithful member" of that congregation.[14]

In selecting a Democratic Senate sponsor for their program, the American Hospital Association and the American Medical Association could not have made a more fitting choice than the son of this physician who epitomized the traditional, highly personal, and individualistic American medical practitioner. Lister Hill would be unlikely to advocate a radical alteration in the delivery of medical care. Furthermore, he was a seasoned legislator, persuasive advocate, majority whip, and served on the Senate Committee on Education and Labor that oversaw health-related matters.

Hill-Burton, signed by Truman in August, had been carefully crafted by the hospital industry to limit the federal government's role primarily to that of financial backer. The law provided for a three-million-dollar survey of state needs to be followed by a five-year program authorizing seventy-five million dollars per year for hospital construction. This sum was to be allocated, not by the federal government, but according to a formula devised by Taft based on population and per-capita income, thus favoring poorer rural and southern states. The Federal Hospital Council, dominated by health and medical authorities, philanthropists, and rural politicians, was to oversee the distribution of federal funds. Hill-Burton also explicitly barred federal officials from any say-so in hospital policy, thereby reinforcing the strong hand of the medical profession over internal matters.[15]

During Senate debate on Hill-Burton, William Langer of North Dakota proposed an amendment to forbid racial or religious discrimination in hospitals receiving Hill-Burton funds. Opposing this amendment, Hill declared that administrative rules for hospitals were best left to states. By a voice vote, the Senate rejected Langer's proposal. As finally approved, the bill permitted hospitals receiving federal aid to segregate patients and doctors according to the "separate but equal" formula. Hundreds of Hill-

Burton hospitals in the South separated black and white doctors and patients. Not until 1963 would the federal court issue a ruling requiring desegregation of Hill-Burton facilities.[16]

Senate advocates of national health insurance, notably Robert Wagner, had also objected that the Hill-Burton bill ignored the needs of low-income patients. To counter such objections, its sponsors conceded that all hospitals receiving Hill-Burton funds should furnish a "reasonable" volume of free care for those unable to pay. But neither the surgeon general nor individual states provided any guidelines for administering this provision. The concept of free care for the poor was almost completely ignored until health-rights advocates rediscovered the Hill-Burton legislation in the early 1970s.[17]

The first hospital project approved for federal aid under Hill-Burton was an 87-bed general hospital in Langdale, Alabama, where 40,000 people had previously been served by two small hospitals with a total of 50 beds. Dedicating this facility, Hill complimented the cotton-mill workers of this region, who had signed up for a voluntary, prepaid health insurance plan, for helping to provide medical care for themselves "without compulsion or reliance upon a socialized system." Alabama was to become a leader among states taking advantage of Hill-Burton funding. By 1968, Hill-Burton facilities had been built in 65 of the state's 67 counties, primarily in rural areas.[18]

As Hill-Burton legislation was extended and amended, new hospitals blossomed throughout the nation's predominantly poorer, rural areas. Between 1947 and 1975, when this program began to wind down, the federal government disbursed $4.2 billion in construction funds, matched by an estimated $11 billion from state and local coffers. Overall, the program assisted in financing almost one-third of all hospital projects in the nation, with the federal government contributing about 10 percent of the annual cost of all hospital construction. Reviewing Hill-Burton years after its enactment, Hill recalled proudly that he had insisted on the concepts of federal "seed money" and "joint tithing" in keeping with the biblical injunction, "where your treasure is, there will your heart be also."[19]

In areas that previously had no medical facilities, Americans welcomed the reassuring presence of a hospital or clinic. By 1968, when Hill retired from the Senate, the program had helped to finance 9,200 new hospitals, nursing homes, outpatient clinics, rehabilitation facilities, and public health units, providing a total of 416,000 new beds. Millions of grateful citizens, to whom Lister Hill was an unfamiliar name, realized that a law known as Hill-Burton had brought medical facilities to their communities. Hill-Burton's chief achievements were to raise the number of hospital beds in low-income states nearer to the level attained by high-income states and, by providing hospital facilities in rural areas, attract more physicians to practice outside of urban areas.[20]

But with advances in medical treatment and changing needs, such as the demand for long-term and ambulatory facilities, certain shortcomings of the Hill-Burton approach became apparent. The poorest communities proved unable to come up with matching funds, thereby concentrating most new hospitals in middle-income areas. The poor in central cities received little or no benefit from a program that emphasized rural needs. In later years, critics would contend that Hill-Burton eventually helped to create an oversupply of hospital beds. Advocates of broader federal responsibility for the health of Americans contended that the act, by emphasizing the roles of state officials and the medical profession, had excluded labor, consumer, and popular interests from its decision-making process and thereby reinforced private control of health care delivery.[21]

In 1949, when Truman would again propose that national health insurance be a mandatory part of the Social Security program, Hill was to counter with a voluntary health insurance plan administered, like Hill-Burton, by states and local officials. To Nolen, Hill confided: "May be able to work out a proposition to provide medical care and hospitalization for all who need it, with the support of the doctors, the medical associations, etc." Under Hill's proposal, those unable to pay would receive government-supported membership in private health insurance programs; those of limited income would pay part of their hospital and medical costs. Thus, in Hill's view, poor Americans would preserve their "independence" and "sense of individual responsibility" while the nation preserved "the tried and tested practices of American medicine." While assuring physicians that he strongly believed "we must preserve the freedom of the individual doctor," Hill warned that the traditional free enterprise system of American medicine could not be defended simply by denouncing socialized medicine. He urged the medical profession to rally behind a "better solution . . . than socialized medicine offers." But neither the AMA nor the backers of Truman's plan wanted to follow this middle road.[22]

As originally conceived, Hill-Burton, the most widely known legislation sponsored by Lister Hill during his forty-five years in Congress, represented an essentially conservative approach to national health needs. It had been crafted by the hospital and medical establishment and guided through the Senate by Taft to deflect labor's demand for national health insurance by limiting the government's role in health care to that of subsidizing voluntary nonprofit hospitals. Two decades were to pass after enactment of the Hill-Burton program before one aspect of Truman's more radical approach, Medicare for the aged, would be written into law. Ironically, however, a large number of Alabama doctors, because they opposed Hill's *economic* philosophy, would fight his reelection in 1950, 1956, and 1962, even though he had played a crucial role in defending the sovereignty of their profession.[23]

"I am taking no part in the governor's race"

In the aftershock of war, new political leaders emerged, not only on the national scene, but in Hill's home state as well. To the surprise of Hill and fellow progressives and the consternation of right-wing Alabama Democrats, a "wild card," seemingly out of nowhere, seized their party's nomination for governor in the spring of 1946. Accompanied by a rollicking hillbilly band, passing a "suds bucket" to collect the meager offerings of voters in overalls or feed-sack dresses, waving his cornshuck mop as a symbol of clean politics, a towering, thirty-seven-year-old war veteran, James E. ("Big Jim") Folsom, put together a coalition of small farmers, organized labor, returning GIs, and a smattering of liberal idealists like Gould Beech and Aubrey Williams. Backed by this combination, Folsom vanquished four candidates of more traditional stripe—two mild progressives, Lieutenant Governor Handy Ellis, once Bibb Graves's floor leader, and Public Service Commissioner Gordon Persons; and representing the anti-New Deal wing of the party, Commissioner of Agriculture and Industries Joe Poole, who had been Governor Dixon's Senate floor leader, and Calhoun County probate judge, Elbert Boozer, a former Anniston business executive.[24]

In the runoff between Folsom and Ellis, Hill maintained his public posture of aloofness from gubernatorial elections. Recalling that Roosevelt's biggest political failure had been his attempted purge of New Deal opponents, Hill reminded Nolen: "People simply do not want a man in high public office to attempt to tell them whom they shall elect to another public office." Disclaiming rumors that he would come out openly for Folsom, he wired the *Montgomery Advertiser*: "I am taking no part in the governor's race." But the fact that Richard Rives and Roy Nolen, two of Hill's closest advisers, actively supported Folsom in the runoff caused political observers to suspect that the senator had lent Folsom at least tactical support.[25]

Roy Nolen had long since alerted Hill that, "ridiculous and laughable" as it might seem, Folsom appeared to be attracting a lot of attention "across-the-creek." But what would happen once Folsom took office, Hill asked Nolen. "Who is going to run the show?" the senator wondered. "Are you willing to undertake the job? If not, is Bill Feagin young enough and capable enough to do the job?" He had long since realized, Hill added, that "it is better to leave power in the hands of the enemy than it is to take that power if you cannot meet the responsibility which the power imposes." To observe the Folsom phenomenon and "witness it from the inside," Nolen quietly assisted Folsom's campaign.[26]

Folsom's unexpected victory projected a more radical element onto Alabama's political battlefield where, since the 1930s, only New Dealers and defenders of the status quo had warred. Cherishing a Jacksonian faith in rule by the popular majority, he had pledged to institute such reforms as free textbooks, a $600 annual increase in the pay of Alabama schoolteachers who then drew average salaries of $1,800 per year, a nine-month school term, state old-age pensions for farmers, paved farm-to-market roads, improved health facilities, and other expanded state services. Obviously Folsom's "People's Program," if enacted, would lead to heavier taxes on corporate and landed wealth. But what alarmed Alabama's agricultural and industrial establishment even more about the unconventional and independent Folsom was his expressed determination to bring about a political revolution in Alabama by attacking two bulwarks of minority strength: the cumulative poll tax, a major factor in severely limiting Alabama's electorate, and a legislature so apportioned in favor of propertied interests in Black Belt counties that one-third of the state's population could elect a majority in both legislative houses.[27]

How had this upstart, who had lost three previous races for political office, pulled off such a coup? Reporting to Hill, Jesse Hearin ascribed Folsom's victory to postwar resentment of special interest cliques, such as the Farm Bureau and Extension Service, and of political domination by a relative few. Frank Dixon confided in a friend his puzzlement at the Farm Bureau's loss of influence over rural Alabamians. Richard Rives informed Hill that Folsom represented "a revolt against machines and the 'ins' all over the state." Other political analysts noted that Folsom had succeeded in conveying the message that he, better than his rivals, understood the needs of average "fokes."[28]

Deeply conservative in his personal behavior, Hill viewed the Folsom phenomenon with mixed emotions. When he was with those whom he trusted, he sometimes poked fun at Folsom's political antics and personal style. Hill, too, was a master stump speaker but he addressed the voters from above, as befitted a paternalistic leader from a different and higher background than that of his audience. By contrast, Folsom identified himself as a man of the people, a friend or neighbor to those who lived near the "branchheads" and the forks of the creeks. Observing these two disparate stylists at a Democratic rally in 1948, a political commentator noted that Hill seemed somewhat ill at ease on the same platform with Folsom and his band, the Strawberry Pickers, busily sawing out a tune called "Roly Poly." To this observer, "tall, bald, and pale" Hill, gazing at the backs of the band members' new green and white shirts, seemed to be "pondering how it all happened . . . and finding the answer elusive."[29]

Although he would continue to regard Folsom warily and to hold him at arm's length, Hill evidently decided that he had no choice but to cooperate with the future governor. He played host to Folsom when the nominee visited Washington in August 1946, to be presented to Truman, Democratic national chairman, Robert Hannegan, and other national Democratic dignitaries. Harry Truman evidently did not inspire Folsom's awe or enthusiasm. If he had escorted Folsom to meet Truman's predecessor, Hill thought, "Jim would have almost knocked the reporters down with a Franklin D. Roosevelt human rights statement." But Hill found this big country fellow, who had risen so suddenly to the governorship of his state, at least philosophically congenial. As Gould Beech put it years later, Hill and Folsom, although separated by a "social distance," had common enemies. Hill sensed that Folsom would fight "the forces of greed and reaction" but had doubts as to whether such a tyro could handle these opponents. Nolen concurred. "Just between you and me, Lister," the postmaster reported on the eve of Folsom's inauguration, "Jim Folsom and his coterie did not look too good to take over the helm of state." As Folsom launched a term that was to prove the truth of this hunch, Nolen lamented the new governor's lack of "character," relaying the gossip that "[Folsom] publicly laps up champagne almost like an Iowa hog at the mash trough." Such a reputation, Nolen predicted to Hill, would kill Folsom's chances to enact his programs.[30]

"Brother Sparkman is running and has no money"

Even before Folsom took office in January 1947, he and Hill had found themselves on the same side in two major campaigns. Less than two months after the gubernatorial primary, Alabama faced the choice of a new United States senator to replace John Bankhead Jr., who died in the summer of 1946. Bankhead's death had not been unexpected. During the senator's final illness, political machines had begun to stir. Jim Simpson had been seriously considering a race against Bankhead even before 1944. Perhaps the Hill forces should help elect Simpson, one strategist suggested, so he would no longer pose a threat to Hill. But the senator firmly rejected this idea. For several years, Hill had been talking up his protégé, John Sparkman of Huntsville, to voters in other parts of Alabama.[31]

In announcing his candidacy, Sparkman, at Nolen's behest, had laid bare his simple background. Like many others born on tenant farms, he had grown up in a household without electricity. The Sparkmans kept their milk cans deep in their well. His mother scrubbed the family clothes over a tub and washboard and pressed them, even on the hottest summer days, with a "sad iron" heated on top of a wood-burning stove. "Is there any wonder," Sparkman asked, "that I have been an ardent supporter of [rural electrification]?" Because Sparkman had attended a one-room, one-teacher school, in session three or four months a year "[if] we were lucky," he was to become an enthusiastic congressional backer of federal aid to education "without federal control." Following this speech, Nolen told Hill that it had hurt Sparkman's pride—and that of his wife—to make such public revelation of his plain origins. But Nolen deemed it essential that voters know "about one really from the grass roots, as John is."[32]

Sparkman's father had borrowed seventy-five dollars against his next cotton crop to launch his son into higher education. At the University of Alabama, John had risen at 4 A.M. each day to roll cinders and fire boilers in the school power plant for $5.25 a week. Like Lister Hill before him, he had been elected president of the student body. Smart as well as hard working and personable, Sparkman earned a Phi Beta Kappa key in addition to his A.B., M.A., and law degrees. By 1946 he was a veteran of five terms in the House and had been chosen as Democratic whip. Although he would have little difficulty carrying his own Eighth District and the rest of the Tennessee Valley, Sparkman had no statewide machine and no campaign funds. Clarence Allgood and John Horne, who had been a campus kingmaker at Tuscaloosa, busied themselves contacting every Pi Kappa

Alpha in Alabama to plead: "Brother Sparkman is running and has no money." Foots Clement and Nolen lent Sparkman the essential assistance of the skilled Hill organization. They also helped raise money for Sparkman's radio speeches and newspaper ads and for leaflets to be placed in rural mailboxes.[33]

After Bankhead's funeral, Hill, hitherto publicly aloof from the campaigns of fellow Alabama politicians, openly placed his considerable influence behind Sparkman. To Jesse Hearin, Hill described Sparkman as one who "serves all the people and cannot be influenced or controlled by any selfish interest." Courting another supporter, Hill emphasized: "[Sparkman] and I work perfectly together." This in itself was enough to win over many Alabamians. "When your friends once knew of your preference," responded a Montgomery doctor, "victory was assured." But when Hill announced he would cast an absentee ballot for Sparkman, the *Alabama Journal* objected that, by thus flaunting his favoritism, Hill made it clear that he sought to control *two* votes in the Senate.[34]

As it turned out, Sparkman, although endorsed by Alabama's most potent politicians, Hill and Folsom, and supported by organized labor, veterans, county officeholders, teachers, residents of the Tennessee Valley, and other Hill stalwarts, needed every vote he could get. On 30 July 1946, he prevailed without a runoff over his leading opponents, Simpson and Frank Boykin, a Mobile congressman with strong ties to business and lumber interests in Alabama's First District, by a margin of only 230 votes. Nolen rejoiced to Mrs. Albert Thomas of Auburn, a fellow Democratic leader: "Thanks to fate . . . Alabama now has for the first time two United States Senators and a Governor who, individually or collectively, owe nothing to First Avenue and 20th Street, or to the 'Black Belt.' " John D. Hill, aware of who had been chief strategist of Sparkman's victory, complimented Nolen on "a masterful job."[35]

The new Democratic senatorial nominee, frank to recognize his debt to Hill, instructed members of his staff that their first priority would be to cooperate with the senior senator without whose aid he probably could not have been elected. John Horne, who became Sparkman's administrative assistant in 1947, clearly understood that his boss had been "anointed" by Lister Hill. Although their offices would not always work in harmony, Hill and Sparkman were to close ranks when politically expedient.[36]

Cordial to one another on the surface, the two Alabama senators were never close personal friends. Although for a time they lived only a few blocks apart in Washington, a social gap separated a member of the

Alabama gentry from one who had risen out of hard-scrabble, farm ante-
cedents. Hill and his political coterie, convinced that they had put Sparkman in the Senate, felt that their protégé never displayed sufficient grati-
tude. But although he may not have shown this to Hill's satisfaction,
Sparkman did remember who had been his chief benefactor in the 1946
Democratic primary. Almost forty years after that election, he was asked to
account for the fact that Alabama had sent Democratic loyalists to the
Senate in the 1940s when other southern states elected senators with strong
Republican leanings like Harry Byrd, Carter Glass, W. Lee O'Daniel, and
"Cotton Ed" Smith. Sparkman replied succinctly: "Due to the leadership of
Lister Hill."[37]

Sparkman's elevation to the Senate strengthened a remarkably progressive congressional delegation for a Deep South state. By the late 1940s,
north Alabama voters had sent to the House Bob Jones, Carl Elliott, and
Kenneth Roberts, all groomed in the New Deal tradition by Foots Clement,
as well as Albert Rains, who represented labor's viewpoint in the Gadsden
industrial district. This delegation also included four south Alabama representatives who generally opposed social change or innovation. But no
matter what their philosophical orientation, the majority of these politically astute Alabamians were highly regarded on Capitol Hill. Bob Jones
and Carl Elliott, in particular, were to hold influential committee assignments. In several informal polls, fellow House members rated the Alabama delegation the best in that body.[38]

"I am opposed to the Boswell amendment"

Although the successful Folsom and Sparkman campaigns represented
defeats for big farmers and "big mules," that coalition rebounded in the fall
of 1946. Rather than focusing on an individual, this test of strength came
on a matter of political strategy and was decided by an emotional appeal
to racism. At issue was the Boswell amendment, designed by Gessner
McCorvey and strongly supported by Frank Dixon, to limit the Alabama
electorate to those whom they perceived, because of birth, education, or
financial position, to have a genuine stake in society. This proposed
amendment to the state constitution would eliminate a 1901 loophole
whereby the right to vote had been extended to those presumably solid
citizens who owned forty acres of land or personal property assessed at
three hundred dollars. To continue to use this method of qualifying in the

1940s, McCorvey argued, would permit anybody to vote who owned "some junky automobile."[39]

But the heart of this amendment was its "understanding" clause. Now that the Supreme Court had overturned the white primary, those who wished to restrict the suffrage would have to rely heavily on the cumulative poll tax and on local registrars endowed with arbitrary authority to judge potential voters, not on literacy alone but on a new voting prerequisite— their ability to "understand" any article of the United States Constitution.[40]

Its backers felt it imperative to pass the Boswell amendment before Folsom could assume office and begin to push in earnest for poll-tax repeal and a constitutional convention to reapportion the legislature on a one-man, one-vote basis, thereby loosening the purse strings of state and local government. McCorvey frankly told members of the Alabama legislature that a cumulative poll tax was a legitimate method of barring from suffrage "a very large number of people who would not cast an intelligent ballot even if they were given the right to vote." Unless admission to the polls were rigorously guarded, Dixon feared that his political allies might never again elect a United States senator or governor and might be ousted as well from their stronghold in a malapportioned legislature.[41]

Representatives of big agriculture joined major corporate and industrial interests to push for this new barrier. But the majority of Alabama's overwhelmingly white electorate, which had just chosen a professed Jacksonian as governor, could scarcely be exhorted to approve the principle of suffrage restricted to the propertied, educated, and wellborn. This intention must be cloaked in the ancient regalia of white supremacy. Dixon, leading speechmaker for the Boswell amendment, vividly pictured the potential effects of its rejection: racially mixed schools and juries, black officeholders in city and county governments, and a strong black minority in the state legislature. Such an outcome, Dixon warned, would mean Reconstruction reborn.[42]

Masses of white Alabama voters might be lured by this argument once again, but more sophisticated political observers understood that the Boswell amendment would allow registrars not only to discriminate against qualified blacks but also against whites who happened to be poor farmers, union members, or Republicans. Richard Rives, then a gradualist on the matter of black rights, warned that, if the amendment should pass, the majority of Alabamians might never regain control of their political affairs because the electorate would be permanently limited to those already registered or deemed acceptable by the registrars. "The chains we forge to shackle qualified Negroes," Rives told a Montgomery audience, "can be used to keep the white voters of Alabama from walking to the polls." Responding to this charge, Horace Wilkinson of Birmingham, a former president of the Alabama Bar Association, avowed racist, and a leader in the 1928 bolt against Al Smith, declared candidly: "This is a small price to pay, if it has to be paid, to keep this inferior, unreliable, irresponsible, easily corrupted [black] race from destroying the highest civilization known to man."[43]

Hill did not take to the stump in the Boswell dispute as did Dixon. To give his opponents any excuse to claim that he favored black suffrage would be a grave political risk. But two months before the special election, Hill publicly allied himself with Folsom, Sparkman, the CIO, the National Association for the Advancement of Colored People (NAACP), Republicans, and the *Birmingham News* in opposition to the amendment. In his press release announcing "I am opposed to the Boswell amendment," Hill, like Rives, focused on the threat to *white* voting rights. The amendment was intended to serve greedy, special interests, he charged, and "would be a backward step toward those wicked old days when only men with title, wealth, or rank could vote." On another occasion, Hill put it even more bluntly: the amendment was designed to prohibit voting "by those whom the Big Mules do not approve."[44]

But abstract appeals to democratic principles and outcries against arbitrary power failed to move the majority of Alabama voters as did impassioned rhetoric recalling the dark days of Reconstruction or as did warnings against racial intermarriage and mongrelization. With the war ended, it no longer seemed somewhat unpatriotic to engage in such divisive talk. With no central personality like Franklin Roosevelt, Bibb Graves, or Lister Hill to galvanize them and force them to concentrate on their economic and political shortcomings, the majority of Alabama voters fell once more into a trap baited with race. In nineteen counties in which there was no real chance of black political domination, voters supported the amendment as did many rank-and-file labor-union members in industrial areas. But unlike the state legislature, which had approved the amendment almost unanimously, the total popular vote divided almost equally. Black Belt counties, where blacks made up 40 percent or more of the population, and wealthy suburbs around Birmingham helped to provide a 53.7 percent victory for the Boswellites.[45]

As Rives had foreseen, passage of this restrictive measure virtually invited federal intervention. Three years later, a three-judge federal district court, composed of Alabama natives, ruled the Boswell amendment an unconstitutional violation of the Fifteenth Amendment. By declining to reconsider this decision, the Supreme Court indicated its agreement. But the amendment's passage in 1946, through the use of an old political ploy, gave clear warning to Hill, Folsom, Sparkman, and their supporters of what lay ahead should Truman continue to press for civil rights.[46]

"I'm having trouble gettin' [Truman] down there at the big house"

When Truman's proposal for a permanent FEPC had come before Congress in early 1946, Hill, although Democratic whip, joined the southern filibuster against what he called "this new force act." After Southerners lambasted the agency for three weeks and an attempt at cloture failed, Truman gave up this fight. With its funds cut off, the wartime FEPC expired at the end of June. The concept of a permanent FEPC was doomed.[47]

After the filibuster, Hill's relations with the White House, never cozy as in the Roosevelt days, deteriorated. In April, he complained to Corcoran: "I'm having trouble gettin' him [Truman] down there at the big house." The White House telephone number is National 1414, Corcoran jokingly reminded his friend; call up and tell them that you are the Senate whip and you need to talk to Truman face to face. Hill laughed. "I'm Joe Stalin right now," he responded.[48]

Hill continued to function as whip and, in Barkley's absence, as majority leader, keeping a watchful eye on the Senate floor, striding purposefully through the Capitol corridors, a lean and decorous figure in his customary blue double-breasted suit and horn-rimmed glasses. Meantime Truman increasingly committed himself on civil rights matters. In August the president promised to back a new antilynching bill. In December he established the President's Committee on Civil Rights, charging its members to study and report on all aspects of that explosive topic. Confiding in his staff member Paul Duncan, Hill pondered the "contradiction, the conflict of interest" between the mood of his Alabama constituents, who had just approved the Boswell amendment in the hope that it would prevent black voting, and the actions of his party's leader. "I can't go in there and be the president's man with this kind of legislation," Hill told Duncan.[49]

Late in December 1946, Hill surprised friends and supporters by announcing that he would relinquish the duties of Democratic whip. Publicly

he attributed his decision to the fact that Republicans were to take over
control of Congress in January 1947, diminishing his status to that of
assistant leader of the minority. But Hill, the political realist, foresaw an
inescapable clash between Truman and his party's southern wing. By
resigning as Democratic whip, he placed retention of his Senate seat above
all other considerations. Hereafter Hill would attempt to restrict his sphere
of influence to subjects as far removed as possible from the forthcoming
struggle over the rights of blacks.[50]

By choosing this course of action, Hill also ended his close partnership
with Alben Barkley, who had become his friend and mentor during their
five years of collaboration. Scott Lucas, a moderate and easygoing Mid-
westerner acceptable both to Truman and to most southern senators, was to
become his party's new whip. Astute politician though he was, Hill could
not have foreseen that two years later Barkley would become Truman's
vice president, thereby vacating the key Senate post of Democratic leader.
Who would have been better equipped to succeed Barkley as leader than
one who had been his chief assistant for six years during a momentous war
and its aftermath?[51]

With blacks and many others astir over civil rights, Hill now knew that a
political figure from the Deep South had little or no chance at the Presidency. But he had allowed himself to dream of occupying the powerful
position of Democratic leader in the Senate. In turning away from the post
of whip, he began his retreat from the Democratic party's national leadership ranks. Talk of Hill as his party's leader in the Senate revived after
Illinois voters rejected Lucas in 1950. But Hill, even though he had a
fresh, six-year mandate, refused to essay this risk. Sensing a power
vacuum, a brash and aggressive newcomer, who had entered the Senate in
1949, seized the post of Democratic leader in 1953. Lyndon Johnson, a
natural risk-taker less fettered by his Texas constituents on matters of race,
thereby took a long stride toward the White House.[52]

The Democratic Loyalist

I   9   4   8   –   I   9   5   0

"I . . . will as always mark my cross under our rooster"

As another presidential election year opened, Harry Truman found himself between the legendary Scylla and Charybdis. To prevail over the likely Republican nominee, Thomas E. Dewey, and the threat of a third party led by Henry A. Wallace, whom Truman had fired as commerce secretary after a dispute over foreign policy, the president knew he would have to court black voters. Yet by strongly advocating civil rights measures, Truman realized he would give anti-New Deal southern Democrats a potent weapon with which to oppose his nomination and election.

His strong sense of history and genuine desire to do right also propelled Truman toward a stand on civil rights much bolder than any proposed by Roosevelt. In February 1948, the president asked Congress to abolish the poll tax, make lynching a federal crime, prohibit segregation on interstate trains and buses, curtail job discrimination, establish a permanent FEPC, and set up a civil rights division within the Justice Department. Black leaders hailed this as "the greatest freedom document since the Emancipation Proclamation." But the white South erupted in angry revolt.[1]

Twenty-one southern senators, Lister Hill among them, vowed to fight Truman's program. From Montgomery, the representative of a little-heeded Alabama element protested Hill's stand. E. D. Nixon, president of the Alabama Conference of NAACP branches, advised his senator: "Negroes of the South are greatly alarmed by your opposition. . . ." But Hill evidently saw nothing to gain by replying to Nixon. Southern governors, led by South Carolina's Strom Thurmond, termed the proposals an insult to their region. Southern donors canceled an estimated half-million dollars in contributions to the Democratic National Committee. Within a few weeks

Truman's standing in polls of southern voters dropped more than twenty points.[2]

The prospect of the federal government again seeking to bring about sweeping changes in their racial mores incensed average white southerners, always prey to their emotions on this flammable subject. The vast majority of their leaders also ardently believed that an orderly society in the South could be preserved only through continued segregation and white dominance. In 1942, Frank Dixon, in a widely reported speech to the Southern Society of New York, had voiced the fears of many of his fellow patricians: "Either white men control [blacks] or no white man can live [in the South] unless he is willing to abandon all of that personal and racial pride which has made the Anglo-Saxon great." Even after the zenith of Hitlerism, Dixon had confided to Grover Hall Jr.: "The Huns have wrecked the theories of the master race with which we were contented so long. . . . But I buy dogs of a certain breed to fight, and I know the sons of Man-O'-War are going to win races. . . . I prefer to keep my faith."[3]

Race relations was only one of the areas into which the federal government had intruded. While Franklin Roosevelt had occupied the White House, southern defenders of the status quo had felt their autonomy in matters affecting labor and the economy increasingly threatened by New Deal measures. Most of these men believed it imperative that the tide toward centralization of governmental powers be reversed in order that, as Dixon expressed it, "the dead weight of Washington bureaucracy and destructive taxation [can] be removed from the backs of American business."[4]

In 1936, when the Democratic convention abolished its century-old "two-thirds rule," the South had lost its veto power over that party's presidential nominee. Helpless to control this selection, representatives of dominant economic interests in the region had been seeking a way out of their historic alliance with a party whose policies imperiled their hegemony. Truman, with his civil rights proposals, presented them with a time-tested emotional issue by which they hoped to regain control of their party machinery within Alabama and, perhaps, spark nationwide enthusiasm for their fight against governmental activism.

Before Truman sent his civil rights message to Congress, Hill had publicly proclaimed his support for the president as 1948 Democratic nominee. But in the face of this turn of events, could he continue to back Truman and keep Alabama loyal to the national Democratic party? At first Hill sought to maintain this delicate balance, although flanked on one side by his longtime political enemies and on the other by the unpredictable Folsom, whose coterie now included Aubrey Williams and Gould Beech. Williams, as publisher, and Beech, as editor, directed the *Southern Farmer*, a journal financed by Marshall Field, the wealthy Chicago publisher, to advance the cause of small farmers. Occasionally Hill heard from his old friend Aubrey, but their political paths had diverged. Nolen advised Hill to steer clear of both factions: "The reactionary group would isolate us from national party affairs. The [Folsom] group would isolate us from international . . . and national affairs too. . . . real true Alabama Democrats want no part in either kind of isolation."[5]

Complicating Alabama politics still further, Folsom had broken away from his fragile coalition with Hill and Sparkman. The governor had surprised almost everyone by announcing in late January 1948 that he wished to be a presidential candidate or at least a favorite son. Folsom differed with his state's two senators and Truman on foreign policy matters. An admirer of Henry Wallace, he opposed Truman's toughening stand toward the Soviets and preferred to spend American tax money on domestic needs rather than to support what he considered reactionary regimes abroad.[6]

But Folsom also had political motives. Why should a man of his broad popularity among rank-and-file Alabamians play second fiddle to Hill and Sparkman in the national councils of the Democratic party? If he could elect his choice, Phillip Hamm, to replace Sparkman in 1948 and later take over Hill's seat himself, Folsom could dominate his state much as Huey Long had once controlled Louisiana. "The Big Boy on Goat Hill is very seriously considering running against you in 1950," Alabama House Speaker William M. Beck warned Hill. Clarence Allgood reported: "The big money boys are thrilled to death over a split . . . between you and Folsom."[7]

At first Hill tried to evade any formal role as delegate-at-large to the 1948 Democratic convention. Canny advisers like Foots Clement, Tom Beach, Clarence Allgood, Clarence Mullins, Charles Dobbins, and Leon McCord warned him not to "get mixed up in all the politics in Alabama." Hill, too, doubted that he could champion Truman in Alabama "with the Folsom crowd cutting on the one side and the Big Mules, their satellites and hirelings driving their knives in on the other side." Only Nolen advised him to enter the fray, arguing that, by publicly demonstrating his strength, Hill could scare off a strong opponent in 1950. To challenge his friend, Nolen argued that, without Roosevelt's coattails to cling to, Democrats "are now called upon to sweat out their own existence." Eventually Nolen's view prevailed.[8]

Entering his name in the race for delegate-at-large, Hill pledged to continue fighting the threat of federal laws to end poll taxes, lynching, and segregation. But he also reiterated his intent to back Truman, emphasizing his support of the president's foreign policy to contain the spread of Soviet influence to Greece and Turkey and to rebuild Europe's economy through the Marshall Plan. He opposed isolation, Hill declared pointedly, not only in foreign policy but also in domestic matters and Democratic party affairs. Unless Alabama Democrats had a third alternative in their May primary, they would be forced to choose, as Hill viewed it, between "[Henry] Wallace fellow travellers on the one hand and reactionary bolters on the other."[9]

Hill's entry into the delegate race elicited predictable reactions. While the *Birmingham News* still backed him, the *Birmingham Post* warned against "supine acceptance of the Second Reconstruction" and the *Mobile Press* scoffed: "It would take a master of double talk to oppose the anti-segregation program and continue to support Harry Truman." Many of Hill's friends applauded. "Fight it out now instead of at a later date," counseled Jesse Hearin. Bill Beck praised Hill for opposing "the reactionary element in Alabama [that] is trying to wreck the Democratic party." But many feared that the senator had taken too grave a risk. Testing the political wind, Clarence Allgood reported a widespread feeling that Hill had made an uncharacteristic political blunder in offering himself as a Truman delegate. "I have talked with people from all groups and I have found not one who will say he is for Truman," reported the worried Allgood. Richard Rives warned: "[Alabamians] are thinking with their feelings, not their intellects. They need a scapegoat and Truman is it." Another correspondent expressed it bluntly: "People . . . are mad as the very devil with Truman." Talk of Hill as "all washed up" circulated in the corridors of Alabama's capitol.[10]

Hill soon realized he must change course. Sparkman, his own reelection uppermost in mind, had already renounced Truman, leaving Hill virtually isolated as a presidential loyalist. To Rives, who had urged him to stick to his guns, Hill explained: "When John Sparkman issued his statement, it did not seem possible for us to be separated." Gradually Hill put out word that he would support some candidate other than Truman. He would seek to convince northern Democrats, he assured one voter, "how impossible Truman is and just how necessary it is to get rid of him."[11]

Hill may even have convinced himself that Truman's renomination would seriously threaten party and national unity. To *New Republic* editor Michael Straight, who also had called on Truman to step aside, Hill expressed hope that his party could find some "man for the hour." Six weeks before the Alabama primary, Hill concluded that Dwight Eisenhower might be such a man. If the former Allied commander in chief could be drafted, Hill announced that he would be willing to place Ike's name in nomination, as he had that of FDR in 1940. His new stance had the desired effect. As one correspondent put it: "Had you followed Mr. Truman, I could not have followed you."[12]

Even though he abandoned the president, Hill still sought to prevent a potential walkout of Alabama's convention delegates. The State Democratic Executive Committee, controlled by Black Belt interests and representatives of big business, had called on all candidates for delegate and alternate to pledge that they would bolt if Democrats adopted any of the Truman civil rights proposals. Before Gessner McCorvey had become its chairman in 1939, this committee had traditionally remained neutral in intraparty contests. Now McCorvey planned to use committee funds to promote walkout candidates.[13]

"Don't bolt the party!" Hill countered in a statewide radio address. Carry on the fight against civil rights within the Democratic family, he pleaded, rather than split the party and help elect Dewey. Hill needed a base to which he could retreat in the eventuality of Truman's nomination. An appeal to party loyalty was to be that base. Horace Wilkinson, among the most prominent of the bolters, demanded to know what Hill would do if Democrats should nominate Truman or anyone who advocated civil rights. "I am an Alabama Democrat," Hill responded firmly, "and will as always mark my cross under our rooster." (The Alabama Democratic party emblem was a rooster with the words "White Supremacy for the Right" emblazoned above its head.)[14]

After a quarter of a century in politics, Hill was well aware of the real nature of this newest dispute. The battle between bolters and Democratic loyalists constituted yet another chapter in the ongoing struggle between the forces of big business and large agricultural organizations versus organized labor and smaller entrepreneurs, most of whom lived in north Alabama, the home of small farmers, TVA, and relatively few blacks. At issue were economic theories as well as party control in Alabama. By his civil rights proposals, Truman had indeed provided opponents of centralized power and the "welfare state" with a golden opportunity to seize the political reins from the now divided forces of Folsom, Hill, and Sparkman.

If this donnybrook should cost Democrats a national election, Frank

Dixon believed that such a result would be worthwhile "if by so doing we can restore, within the national Democratic party, the bargaining power that we lost with the abolition of the two-thirds rule." But if southern opponents of the New Deal should fail to regain their power in national Democratic councils, Dixon feared that they would have no recourse except to join the Republican party. To affiliate in 1948 with a party still vividly associated in Alabama with the Civil War and Reconstruction would mean political powerlessness and isolation. To move in this direction would also bring an end to the one-party system within whose intimate bounds Alabamians had struck political bargains since 1901. Dixon knew that some opposition vehicle other than Republicanism must be found.[15]

With Roy Nolen ill, Foots Clement took charge of the awesome Hill political machine. From Washington, the senator himself kept up a barrage of telephone calls to key Alabamians, pleading the cause of party loyalty. Addressing the state CIO convention, Hill reminded labor that the Republican-controlled Eightieth Congress had passed the Taft-Hartley Act, "which I voted against and fought all the way." Venturing into the depths of the Wiregrass, a lion's den of anti-Trumanism, he revived his famed "Call the Roll" speech, calling many in his audience by name and exhorting them to remember all the economic benefits they had reaped during the Roosevelt and Truman administrations.[16]

On 4 May 1948, Alabama Democrats chose fourteen convention delegates pledged to walk out if a civil rights plank were adopted and twelve who opposed such action. Paradoxically Lister Hill had run 18,500 votes ahead of the next highest vote getter, former Governor Chauncey Sparks, a professed loyalist. ("Glory be to God and the Democratic Party!" Jesse Hearin cheered.) Two walkout delegates, Handy Ellis and Eugene ("Bull") Connor ran third and fourth. As Birmingham police commissioner, Connor had just come to national attention and delighted many Alabamians by tossing Idaho Senator Glen Taylor in jail for attempting to enter a meeting in that city through the "colored" entrance.[17]

Hill had registered a personal triumph, but Folsom and Democratic Executive Committee Chairman McCorvey had taken a licking by failing to win delegate slots. The governor had run last in the runoff for delegates. Almost every candidate endorsed by Folsom had suffered defeat, including Phillip Hamm who had been soundly trounced by Sparkman. Folsom's dramatic drop in popularity resulted from several factors. He had been unable to rouse voters with his attacks on foreign aid, internationalism, and "fancy panters in our State Department." He had been embarrassed by

charges that some of his subordinates had abused the patronage or misman-
aged state government. An even more grievous embarrassment had been
the public revelation in March that Folsom had fathered an illegitimate
child shortly before his 1946 election. Without denying that this child was
his son, Folsom tried to ignore the paternity suit. But many Alabama
voters evidently felt that "Kissin' Jim" had now carried his unconventional
conduct too far.[18]

Folsom and his protégés were not the only losers in this Democratic
family fight. Harry Truman had failed to win a single Alabama presidential
elector. While party loyalists had concentrated their energies on the delegate race, the Dixon-McCorvey-Wilkinson wing of the party had fielded a
slate of presidential elector candidates who claimed the right to vote for
someone else if Truman or anyone who favored civil rights became the
Democratic nominee. These "unpledged" candidates had won all eleven of
the state's electoral posts. As a result Alabama was to be the only state in
November 1948 on whose ballot the national Democratic nominees were
not represented. No Alabama resident would be able to vote for Truman.
But what appeared to be a substantial victory for the bolters was to backfire
and contribute to the downfall of their splinter movement.[19]

More than 160,000 Alabama Democrats, confused by conflicting demands that they bolt or remain loyal to their party, had recognized on their
lengthy primary ballot at least one familiar name that they evidently
trusted. Many who may not have understood the issues in this struggle had
nonetheless been willing for Lister Hill to represent them at the Democratic convention in Philadelphia. Hill's long career in public service had
been untainted by any hint of scandal or any charges of malfeasance such
as those that had surfaced during Folsom's brief tenure in office. Many of
his constituents gratefully remembered Hill's efforts to improve the quality
of their lives. Too, Foots Clement had again worked his political magic.
But it was the ailing older magician, Roy Nolen, who had given Hill the
courage to embark on this possibly perilous course. As early as 1947,
Nolen had alerted Hill that the Alabama electorate would be about 100,000
voters larger by 1950. With old Roosevelt-haters accounting for around
100,000 out of a total of 350,000 to 375,000 voters, Nolen felt that Hill
needed to appeal to nearly all the remainder. "I am a firm believer in
winning elections between campaigns," the postmaster had counseled.
After his 1948 victory, Hill wrote Roy: "Once again, your judgement
proved sound and right." As a result of this campaign, Hill assured both of
these key advisers: "1950 is far brighter today than it was sixty days ago."[20]

"Where's Lister?"

By the time Democrats convened in July, Hill had abandoned hope that Eisenhower might emerge as nominee. He and numerous other prominent politicians had attempted without success to persuade the popular general to accept a Democratic draft. But Eisenhower refused to consider this option, thereby eliminating the only potential nominee behind whose candidacy Alabama Democrats could have united.[21]

By custom, the person who led the primary ticket headed Alabama's delegation to the Democratic convention. But now Handy Ellis, who had run against Folsom in 1946, challenged Hill for the chairmanship. Ellis had a problem, however—one of his fellow walkout delegates was too ill to attend. This man's alternate was a young and relatively inexperienced state legislator of progressive inclination who had been elected as a loyalist. If George C. Wallace were seated, the delegation would be tied 13 to 13. In case of a tie, the rules specified that the chairmanship should go to the governor. But in the event that the governor were not a delegate, the senior senator was entitled to assume the chair.[22]

Behind the scenes, Frank Dixon and Marion Rushton, Alabama's national Democratic committeeman and chairman of the Alabama States' Rights Committee, devised a plan to block Hill's election. Presiding at a session to organize the delegation, Rushton ruled that George Wallace could not take the place of the ailing delegate until *after* a chairman had been elected. Ellis was then elected by a vote of 13 to 12.[23]

Fired by the oratory of Mayor Hubert Humphrey of Minneapolis, Democrats adopted a strong civil rights plank. Thereupon Ellis, climaxing an address to the delegates, announced dramatically: "We are carrying out our pledge to the people of Alabama. We bid you good-bye!" As had the fiery Alabama secessionist William Lowndes Yancey in 1860, Ellis led twelve Alabama bolters, joined this time only by twenty-two Mississippians, out of the Democratic convention. With George Wallace formally seated, the remaining Alabama delegates elected Hill as chairman. To protect themselves from further criticism back home, 263 southerners, including the Alabama loyalists, had made the symbolic and obviously futile gesture of backing Senator Richard Russell of Georgia for the presidential nomination. Hill, who had mounted the Democratic rostrum in 1940 to nominate the unbeatable Roosevelt, now felt compelled to place in nomination the name of his southern colleague and publicly to advocate Russell's hopeless cause.[24]

Yet by leading the loyalist effort, Hill had helped to prevent bolters from completely dominating the Alabama Democratic party. By remaining in the hall with his fellow loyalists, he had seen to it that his state had not totally isolated itself from the national Democratic conclave. In refusing to desert his party, he had also protected his congressional seniority and hard-earned committee posts. But when he returned to Alabama, Hill would face further tests of his political agility.

His opponents moved rapidly. They hoped to create a stalemate in the electoral college and thereby move the choice of a president into the House of Representatives where southern members might bargain more effectively. To achieve this and other objectives, they summoned like-minded Southern leaders and an excitable crowd of onlookers to Birmingham's Municipal Auditorium to create a States' Rights party (quickly nicknamed the "Dixiecrats"). At the start of this assemblage, "Bull" Connor, a one-time baseball announcer, used his booming voice to call those who had bolted the Democratic convention to the rostrum for a heroes' welcome. The crowd was pointedly reminded that Hill was not among these heroes. "Where's Lister?" someone called out. Others quickly took up this chant. Harry Truman was not the only political leader whom the Dixiecrats hoped to consign to oblivion.[25]

Frank Dixon had been one of the primary instigators of this convention, but Dixon declined to head the ticket. Strategists then agreed upon a team of governors, Strom Thurmond of South Carolina and Fielding Wright of Mississippi. Whether the States' Rights party was an actual third party or a revolt within the Democratic party remained unclear. As McCorvey saw it, "we just choose not to affiliate with the national party this year."[26]

But Alabama's presidential electors now had southern candidates to whom they could give their votes. Alabama voters could support Thurmond and Wright while technically casting their ballots under the Democratic rooster. Anyone who failed to support the electors, duly chosen in a Democratic primary, risked being barred from that party's next primary. McCorvey realized that Hill, Sparks, and the Alabama attorney general, Albert A. Carmichael, were far too experienced to fall into this old trap but he hoped that less politically astute loyalists, like Folsom, might not foresee the consequences of failing to vote for the Democratic electors.[27]

Folsom sought legal means of forcing these electors to cast Alabama's votes for Truman. When these efforts failed, loyalists considered calling the legislature into special session to place Truman electors on the ballot. But realizing Folsom's weak hold on the legislature and fearing that such a move might result in defeat, Hill, Sparkman, and other loyalist leaders agreed to forgo this avenue, thus postponing a showdown on the issue of party loyalty. Folsom was not so pragmatic. As the governor persisted in his protests, an annoyed Horace Wilkinson retorted: "You are a disgrace to the State. A buzzard holds his nose every time he flies over the Governor's office now."[28]

Although Hill and Sparkman announced that they would vote for the Democratic electors, they failed to stump for the Thurmond-Wright ticket. Frank Dixon charged that Hill was no true enemy of civil rights. But in sweltering Washington that August, Hill filibustered for seven hours against an administration bill to end poll taxes. To pass such a measure, he told the Senate, would "rape" the U.S. Constitution and open the door to other intrusions into states' rights. Commenting on this performance, Grover Hall Jr., by then editor of the *Montgomery Advertiser*, defended Hill from Dixon's attack: "We don't care a hoot below what Dixon, McCorvey *et al* do to make the most of Hill's Dixiecrat malingering . . . on the floor of the United States Senate. . . . he struck the blows that count."[29]

In response to the many moderate Democrats who asked him what to do on election day, Hill made it clear that only electors pledged to Dewey, Thurmond, or Henry Wallace would appear on the Alabama ballot. Patiently he reiterated his intention to honor his oath as a Democratic candidate by voting under the rooster. When Hill did make a public address that fall, he reminded Alabamians that states' rights was "only part of the story." It had been the *federal* government, he reminded a Labor Day audience in Birmingham, that had outlawed child labor and sweatshops, endorsed collective bargaining, mandated minimum wages, limited work hours, eliminated freight-rate differentials, and provided funds for the GI Bill of Rights, old-age pensions, rural electricity, TVA, hospitals, and waterways. "Above all rights," Hill exhorted these union members, "stands the right of the people to live in . . . human dignity."[30]

But many of these very federal measures had been opposed by States' Rights leaders. Birmingham-Southern College economist E. Q. Hawk suspected that Hill's opponents intended to use civil rights as a battle cry "to crystallize prejudice against all social legislation." The *Opelika Daily News* agreed that those now agitating the civil rights issue had found "a natural smoke screen" to conceal other motives such as unseating Hill. Ralph McGill, editor of the *Atlanta Constitution*, contended that the Dixiecrat movement "had nothing to do with states' rights." McGill pictured

Alabama States' Rights leaders as working from their "spiritual and ancestral home" of Birmingham in a "brazen attempt to hold onto the state machinery and use it in a blackmail job [against the national Democratic party]." Their success in stymieing would-be Truman voters in Alabama was, in McGill's view, "one of the most totalitarian assaults on the American system of voting we have seen in our entire political history." Hill and Sparkman, the Atlanta editor wrote, "are staking their political fortunes in this fight."[31]

On election night, Henrietta and Lister Hill gave a small dinner party at their Washington home. Around the table were trusted Alabama friends like Hugo Black and Douglass Cater. Conversation focused on the expected Republican victory and on Alabama's first defection from the Democratic presidential lists since Reconstruction. (Gessner McCorvey would relish the memory of this latter victory for many years. "It almost killed my friends Lister Hill and John Sparkman when they were unable to deliver Alabama's eleven electoral votes to the National Democratic party in 1948," McCorvey recalled.)[32]

But after the last returns of the 1948 national election had been counted, a triumphant Harry Truman gleefully poked fun at those who had predicted his political demise. The hopes of States' Righters that they could stalemate the election process had been reduced to ashes. Dixiecrats had won 39 electoral votes instead of the 127 "Solid South" votes that might have thrown the election into the House where they had hoped to bargain Strom Thurmond into the presidency. Their only votes had come from Alabama, Mississippi, Louisiana, and Arkansas where States' Rights electors had also been listed as official representatives of the Democratic party. American politics had again demonstrated its unpredictability as well as the vitality of its two-party system.[33]

Although he had not been a candidate for office that November, Lister Hill had emerged victorious. Having managed to stand by his party, Hill would not be persona non grata at the White House. Truman, a political realist himself, understood that his former colleague in the Senate had found it necessary to declare against him. Just to make certain of this, one of Hill's friends assured presidential adviser John R. Steelman that Hill had been no Dixiecrat but that "self protection and expediency forced his silence in this campaign." From Texas, a newly elected United States senator noted how skillfully Hill had maneuvered through dangerous political shoals in 1948. "I am going to do my best to emulate you. You have taught me much by precept and example," Lyndon Johnson wrote Hill.[34]

Hill's Alabama political fortunes had also risen since the start of this election year. He was to benefit from the frustration felt by many Alabamians who had wanted to vote for Truman. S. A. Lynne, a Decatur attorney, predicted to Hill: "Frank Dixon was hoping to be in a position to offer for the Senate and this gets rid of him. . . . I am hopeful now that you will have no opposition." Another correspondent advised his senator: "People of Alabama who were denied their right to vote the straight Democratic ticket are expecting you to lead us out of this muddle."[35]

"Had we had a telephone we could have called a doctor"

At least the warring factions were to have a hiatus before renewing their battle for political control of Alabama. Hill hoped to remain in Washington during most of 1949. With Democrats back in control of Congress, he expected to find the climate on Capitol Hill more hospitable toward his long-cherished concepts of federal financial aid to public education and to telephone service for rural Americans. Somewhat wistfully, Hill observed the election of Scott Lucas to succeed Vice President Barkley as majority leader. Now that he was president in his own right, Truman even more vigorously demanded passage of his entire civil rights program. Not even so adroit a politician as Lister Hill could have championed this cause while fighting administration foes back home.[36]

It seemed more productive that Hill now exercise his seniority to obtain an important committee post. Congress, attempting to streamline itself in 1947, had limited each senator to two committees. Reluctantly Hill had surrendered his post on the Foreign Relations Committee, choosing to remain on Armed Services and on Labor and Public Welfare (formerly the Education and Labor Committee). With the Democrats' return to power, he now had a chance to become a member of the powerful Appropriations Committee. It caused Hill further pain to end his years of service on congressional committees that oversaw military matters. But other postwar concerns appeared more compelling. An opportunity to serve on the Senate committee that handled all appropriations was too valuable to miss. His choice of the committees on Appropriations and on Labor and Public Welfare was to put Hill in a crucial position to achieve many of his legislative goals.[37]

But Senate seniority exacted its burden as well as its rewards. Hill described the Appropriations Committee to Nolen as "the hardest working committee in the Senate," with Labor and Public Welfare "not far behind." Because of his six subcommittee assignments in his new appropriations post, Hill would oversee funding for the armed services, agriculture, labor and public health, TVA, the departments of State, Justice, and Commerce, and the District of Columbia. In addition to these awesome responsibilities, he still strove for unification of the armed forces, federal aid to education, repeal of Taft-Hartley, and construction of more public power transmission lines. Hill described the congressional session of 1949 to Nolen as "the hardest one I have ever known."[38]

Federal aid to education had been Hill's earliest legislative goal. At the start of his professional career, he had pushed this idea that had been impressed upon him by his father and by his experience as the young chairman of the Montgomery school board. Always this concept had fallen victim to the argument that acceptance of federal money would threaten local control over education, leading to a lowering of standards and, in southern public schools, to racial integration. Even educators disagreed among themselves on the advisability of federal aid.

Opening Senate debate on a new version of this measure in April 1949, Hill argued that the educational system of the United States, like its hospitals, had suffered from an attrition of teachers and underfunding while national attention had been obsessed by World War II. Hill particularly wanted fellow senators to realize that 100,000 teachers a year were leaving that profession because minimum teaching salaries in three-fourths of the states were still below two thousand dollars a year. "The public school teacher is the vanishing American," Hill told the Senate. His program would upgrade teacher salaries and help equalize educational opportunities between poor and rich states. Although Alabama and most other low-income states spent a larger proportion of their income on education than did wealthier states, the discrepancy of educational opportunity in America continued to widen. Southern states in particular, Hill pointed out, had more children to educate and less taxable wealth. But these arguments failed to persuade the Senate. It would require a dramatic turn of events in Cold War rivalry to convince Americans of the need for federal aid to education.[39]

But the timing appeared right for another measure that Hill had pushed for five years. He wanted the federal government to help bring telephones to rural Americans as it had helped to provide them with electricity through Franklin Roosevelt's Rural Electrification Administration. Although the majority of American farms had access to electric service by 1949, telephones remained a rarity in many rural communities. In the early 1900s, groups of farmers had gotten together to construct and finance telephone cooperatives. But the Bell companies had begun to take over more profitable territories following World War I. The number of rural telephones dropped from almost 2.5 million to 1.5 million between 1920 and 1940. Farmer-owned cooperatives lost subscribers because they had antiquated lines, inadequate equipment, and could not provide exchange or long distance service.[40]

Noting this plight, Hill and Representative W. R. Poage, a Texas Democrat, had introduced legislation in 1944 to authorize REA loans to help finance telephone service in rural areas. But when the American Telephone and Telegraph Company (AT&T) promised to remedy the situation as soon as possible, the Hill-Poage bill had been shelved. Like the power trust of the 1930s, AT&T lobbyists fought government intervention by declaring that service to rural areas was not feasible and promising that private industry would eventually fill this need.[41]

Meantime millions of rural Americans, midway into the twentieth century, had no access to Alexander Graham Bell's invaluable 1876 invention. In hundreds of postcards, letters, and telegrams, Alabama farm people implored their senior senator to help them get telephones so that they could quickly get in touch with doctors, veterinarians, mechanics, weather forecasters, friends, and relatives. In 1949 only 7 percent of Alabama farms had telephone service. Most of Hill's rural correspondents stressed their need of phones in time of illness. "I've had both of my babies without a doctor because it took so much time to get [one]," a woman wrote Hill from her home on remote Sand Mountain. Relatives of another young woman who had died from serious burns wrote: "Had we had a telephone we could have called a doctor and maybe saved a life." One resident of Brewton, who possessed the lone telephone for miles around, reported that his instrument worked only about one-third of the time.[42]

With Poage chairing the House Agriculture Subcommittee and Hill strategically positioned on the Senate Appropriations Committee, its sponsors succeeded in getting their bill passed in October 1949. Truman had promised to sign this measure as soon as it reached his desk. Hill had earmarked special funds in an appropriations bill so that REA could begin this program immediately.[43]

The Hill-Poage bill authorized REA to make low-interest, long-term loans to small, independent telephone companies for expansion and improvement of rural service. One year later, the first telephone under the

Rural Telephone Act went into service. By 1955 thousands of rural homes, churches, schools, and businesses, including twenty-five thousand new users in Alabama, boasted modern, efficient telephone service. The number of rural telephones in Hill's home state had increased more than one-third.[44]

Passage of the Rural Telephone Act further impressed Hill with the importance of his new post on the Appropriations Committee and the value of collaboration with a skilled colleague in the House. He was to use these instruments to attain even more far-reaching legislative goals.

"Those great Dixiecrat statesmen are all afraid of you"

As 1950 opened, Alabama politicians wondered who would have the temerity to oppose Hill's reelection. It was generally conceded that Jim Simpson would have little chance in a rerun of the 1944 race. States' Righters Marion Rushton, Frank Dixon, Handy Ellis, Roy F. Parker, of Attalla, and Tom Abernathy, editor of the *Talladega Daily Home*, hopeful that Hill's big victory in May 1948 had been due to his widely known name rather than his loyalist stand, were reported to be assessing their chances for the Senate. On lists of other prospective opponents appeared the names of Congressmen Frank Boykin, a States' Righter; Albert Rains, a loyalist; and former Congressman Joe Starnes, of Guntersville, defeated in 1944 by Rains. Rumor had it that three prominent Birmingham men—Frank P. Samford, a wealthy insurance executive; Mortimer Jordan, former state collector of internal revenue; and John Temple Graves II—were contemplating whether or not to make this challenge. Nolen suspected that Frank Dixon had been one of those encouraging the columnist to venture into politics. Luther Patrick, former Birmingham congressman, reported to Hill: "The Tories are frantically trying to find someone to oppose you."[45]

When no strong opponent took the plunge, Waights Taylor, of Livingston, assured Hill: "Those great Dixiecrat statesmen are all afraid of you." Nolen relayed the information from one of his informants that Alabama doctors "seemed to be grateful" for Hill's stand against "socialized medicine." All Alabamians with sense enough to be senator, this informant told Nolen, "know [Hill] can't be beat."[46]

But another political consideration may have accounted for this vacuum. Also at stake in the 1950 Democratic primary was control of the State Democratic Executive Committee (SDEC), made up of eight members from each of Alabama's nine congressional districts. Membership on the SDEC had never been generally regarded as a political plum. In a one-party system, this committee performed routine functions such as conducting spring primaries, setting qualifications for candidates, and deciding contested elections. Defenders of the status quo, aware of the committee's potential power, had always deemed it important to dominate this organization so as to be positioned, if necessary, to punish apostates like Tom Heflin. During the 1940s, Gessner McCorvey, a member since 1934, had inspired this committee to take its activist stands in favor of the Boswell amendment and in opposition to Truman's election.[47]

If a major figure were to challenge Hill, the senator would surely rush home to mount the political stump. Riding on Hill's coattails, a majority of loyalists might be elected to the SDEC. Why risk arousing Hill and thereby threatening their control of this committee? All things considered, States' Righters decided that the most realistic course of action would be to mount only token opposition to Hill.[48]

When the SDEC met in January 1950, Montgomery was already in the grip of political fever. Fifteen candidates had entered a free-for-all gubernatorial race to succeed Folsom. One hopeful, Gordon Persons, had already draped his banner over the balcony of the Exchange Hotel. But no candidate had filed against Hill. "If the boys are planning anything serious against you, they are waiting mighty late," publisher Charles Dobbins of the newly established *Montgomery Examiner* advised Hill.[49]

Even before this meeting had assembled, Chairman McCorvey threatened to bar from candidacy all "Trumancrats" who, like Folsom, could not swear that they had supported the entire 1948 ticket, including the Dixiecrat electors. But McCorvey's new threat had been met by almost unanimous opposition from the Alabama press. Newspapers of such disparate views as the *Birmingham News* and the *Selma Times-Journal* urged that Democratic differences be settled by the voters rather than by dictates from the committee.[50]

At their caucus just before this meeting, States' Righters evidently decided that it would be hopeless to attempt to bar those who had backed Truman. Foots Clement concluded that the Dixiecrats simply had no stomach for another all-out fight against the Hill organization. Richard Rives, eager to help Hill "once more win over the Alabama Bourbons," seemed somewhat disappointed when this confrontation did not take place. But Rives concluded that this decision removed a potentially "formidable obstacle" to Hill's reelection. "That committee," Rives wrote Hill, "has so much legal power that could be used against you and others with whom Gessner does not see eye to eye. . . ."[51]

On the final day for qualifying, however, Lawrence E. McNeil, a thirty-seven-year-old Bessemer realtor and insurance executive who had never before sought political office, announced for the Senate. The sudden appearance of this neophyte, unscarred by previous political battles, puzzled the Hill forces. McNeil claimed to be a States' Rights Democrat opposed to "Eastern radicals" and "the National Socialist Democratic Party." But who had encouraged him to undertake such a quixotic venture? Ben F. Ray thought perhaps McNeil had been so swayed by propaganda from the real-estate lobby that "like the little duck in the pond he just floated over the dam." William Mitch of Birmingham, president of District 20 of the United Mine Workers, believed that McNeil had been picked by the Dixiecrats to provide at least a semblance of opposition to Hill. Luther Patrick also suspected that Horace Wilkinson, Frank Dixon, and "Bull" Connor had inspired this young man to take on the role of giant killer. But no matter who may have instigated McNeil's candidacy, Hill's supporters urged the senator to ignore it. "Stay in Washington. We will take care of you," one friend assured him.[52]

Evidently Hill agreed that this would be his best tactic. McNeil tried his best to taunt his opponent to debate "big government, big spending, big taxes, and . . . government controls," but the senator had bigger fish to fry. Hill planned to concentrate his energies on winning control of the SDEC, thereby assuring that Alabama's eleven electoral votes would not be held hostage by States' Righters in 1952.[53]

"We are fighting desperately to bring Alabama back into the Democratic Party"

With Hill only lightly challenged and the grain yet to be separated from the chaff in the gubernatorial contest, political attention focused on an obscure race hitherto ignored by the mass of Alabama voters. Although States' Righters had found it hard to attract "name" candidates in north Alabama, slates of loyalist and States' Rights candidates for the SDEC appeared in every congressional district. This contest would become a test of the strength and ingenuity of two opposing strategists, Gessner McCorvey and Foots Clement.[54]

Arrayed against one another over the airwaves and on the stump were

Alabama's leading orators. Big guns for the loyalists were Hill, Sparkman, Folsom, and north Alabama Congressmen Rains, Elliott, and Jones. Lesser luminaries included former Governor Sparks, House Speaker Beck, Mayor Cooper Green of Birmingham, National Democratic Committee Secretary Dorothy Vredenburgh, even eighty-one-year-old Tom Heflin, the chief bolter of 1928. Tom Abernathy emerged as the most vigorous spokesman of the States' Righters, aided by gubernatorial candidate "Bull" Connor, Handy Ellis, Frank Dixon, Horace Wilkinson, John Temple Graves II, and Selma's Congressman Sam Hobbs. Each side had press support. The *Mobile Press-Register*, *Dothan Eagle*, *Southern Watchman*, and *Talladega Daily Home* advocated the States' Rights position. The *Birmingham News* and the *Age-Herald*, *Montgomery Advertiser*, *Huntsville Times*, *Tuscaloosa News*, and *Anniston Star* supported the cause of party loyalty. To counter the efforts of the Farm Bureau and Extension Service, Foots Clement enlisted the Young Democrats of Alabama, the American Federation of Labor (AFL), the CIO's Political Action Committee, the Alabama Joint Labor Council, and Ed Reid's potent Alabama League of Municipalities.[55]

Both sides appeared to be well financed. Textile magnate Donald Comer allowed several large States' Rights newspaper advertisements to be published over his name. Seeking financial support, McCorvey put cards on every desk in the eighteen-story Merchants National Bank Building of Mobile. Eddie Reid, commenting on this strategy, advised Hill: "Dixiecrats are actively campaigning in the 'tall buildings' and in the financially powerful institutions." To counter the resources of the business community, loyalists made use of the Hill and Sparkman war chests and, so Tom Abernathy suspected, that of their national party.[56]

Technically this may have been a brouhaha over whether representatives of Alabama Democrats should be bound to support the national nominee or free to bolt their party. But both sides knew that this issue would only bore and confuse the electorate. Alabamians expected simpler and more dramatic appeals for their votes. To satisfy this appetite, Hill charged States' Righters with being Republican wolves in Democratic clothing. "Keep on calling them Dixiecrats, and Republicans at heart," Nolen had advised. ". . . you will remember that the slogans 'Hoovercrats'–'Polly-wog'— stuck after much repetition." In response, Abernathy, McNeil, and other States' Righters stepped up their efforts to tar the "Trumanites" with the brush of "socialism."[57]

As in 1944, the anti-administration bloc turned to racist appeals to raise the gorges of plain, white Alabamians, set them to roaring and applauding, and lure them into their camp. To freshen the folk memory of black politicians during Reconstruction, Frank Dixon characterized this election as "the most important since Alabama had rid itself of carpetbaggers" in 1874. His cohorts were less circumspect. Tom Abernathy described Truman as the "white knight of the [NAACP] . . . pledged to deliver a mongrelized South to the bosses of Harlem." Horace Wilkinson swore that he would "rather die fighting for states' rights than live on Truman Boulevard in a nigger heaven." Hill and Sparkman responded vigorously. Only powerful, experienced senators, Hill argued, could defeat FEPC and other "so-called civil rights bills." Sparkman told a rally: "You haven't heard of any civil rights legislation enacted into law and it wasn't any Dixiecrats in Alabama that prevented it. . . ." Privately, the Hill faction suspected that big industrial interests, especially mineowners and the United States Steel Corporation, were encouraging a Klan revival. "The Alabama Klan is unquestionably . . . directed from tall buildings . . . most likely from *one certain tall building*," Albert Carmichael advised Hill.[58]

Inevitably a race that generated such exchanges and promised to have major political impact attracted national attention. Columnist Stewart Alsop speculated that this "apparently obscure" contest could have "a far-reaching effect on the whole national political future." An Associated Press analyst reported that administration sources regarded Alabama as a "test case" in their efforts to quench revolt within the Democratic party. Although the president had gone fishing off Key West, Hill and Sparkman let Truman know "we are fighting desperately to bring Alabama back into the Democratic Party."[59]

In their May 2 primary, Alabama Democrats seated 38 loyalists, 26 States' Righters, and 1 uncommitted member on the SDEC. In a runoff, loyalists picked up five additional seats and States' Righters captured two. Holding a majority of 43 seats to 28, Alabama loyalists prepared to assume control of their state's Democratic party machinery in 1951. Arthur Krock of the *New York Times* called this "a victory of national significance" for the Truman administration. William Boyle Jr., Democratic national chairman, found the outcome "extremely gratifying." In a letter to Hill, an obscure Alabama voter offered his own analysis: "It looks as if we will be abel [*sic*] to go to the polls and vote democratic [*sic*] in the next election if we want to."[60]

But had this been a clear-cut victory for the loyalists? Political observers, noting that States' Righters had polled 120,478 votes to the loyalists'

180,108, did not think so. In north Alabama, loyalists had swept all eight seats in the Fifth, Seventh, and Eighth Congressional districts represented by Rains, Jones, and Elliott. But States' Righters had captured all eight places in the Mobile-dominated First District and six of eight seats in Hill's onetime sinecure, the Second District. Results in other districts had been close. Analysts of county returns noted that Black Belt counties, with a high proportion of disfranchised black residents, had voted heavily in favor of States' Righters, while areas of labor union strength, such as Anniston and Tuscaloosa, had returned loyalist majorities.[61]

Although use of the race issue had again failed to attract a majority of Alabama voters, States' Righters had demonstrated vitality and a sizable following. The *Birmingham News* interpreted the election results to mean that this revolt would continue. The editor of the *Huntsville Times* made an even more prescient observation: "The Dixiecrat movement is washed up, unless something else comes along in the next few years to revive it."[62]

Loyalists had prevailed partly because many Alabamians still resented the fact that they had been unable to vote for Truman in 1948. Also this outcome demonstrated that most Alabama voters remained loyal to "the party of our forefathers" and of FDR. But the real key to this victory had been the leadership of Hill, Sparkman, Folsom, and the loyalist congressmen. States' Righters had no such array of major state officeholders in their ranks. Years later, Gessner McCorvey, still nursing his disaffection, would admit: "I give Lister and John primary credit for the successful fight they made in the election of National Loyalists rather than real Democrats as members of the State Democratic Executive Committee."[63]

Compared to the excitement generated by the committee race, other contests seemed anticlimactic. Gordon Persons, who publicly expressed guarded support for the loyalist cause, had defeated Folsom's cohort, Phillip Hamm, in a runoff for the governorship. As expected, Lister Hill, who won 67 percent of the total votes cast in the senatorial race, had consigned Lawrence McNeil back to political obscurity. Without deigning to campaign against McNeil, Hill had polled a larger majority of the total vote than he had against either Heflin or Simpson. He had carried sixty counties, losing only three in the Black Belt, one in the Wiregrass, and three in the timber regions and sand hills of southwest Alabama (see Appendix, Map 4).[64]

Again most citizens in the Wiregrass and the vast majority in the Tennessee Valley had proved their loyalty to Hill and to the still-fresh memory of Franklin Roosevelt. From Sheffield, a laboring man assured Hill: "As far as we north Alabama people and particularly we union labor members in all of Alabama are concerned, you and Senator Sparkman are as safe as Wilson Dam and the TVA." But Hill had also earned constituents' gratitude by his own legislative achievements. As Speaker Bill Beck, of mountainous De Kalb County, put it: "We appreciate all these good hospitals . . . and rural telephones." A Birmingham resident, worried that his rent might be raised, praised Hill's stands in behalf of continued rent controls and medium-priced housing. "We have no lobby to fight our battles for us," this man wrote. "We depend on our representatives like yourself and John Sparkman."[65]

Although the States' Rights movement suffered blows to its prestige in Alabama and other southern states in 1950, it partially accomplished its aim of linking southern progressives to the Truman administration's policies on race. Claude Pepper, taunted as a friend to "niggers" and "Commies," had lost his Florida Senate seat to George Smathers. North Carolina's newly appointed Senator Frank P. Graham, an advocate of social justice and a former chairman of the Southern Conference for Human Welfare, had fallen victim to the racist campaign of Willis D. Smith, who had passed out circulars with the simple message: "If you want your wife and daughter eating at the same table with Negroes, vote for Graham."[66]

The twin defeats of Pepper and Graham represented a severe setback for economic and political progressivism in the South. But the southern legislator who had exemplified this tradition longer than any other member then in Congress had withstood the States' Righters. Cheered by his victories, Hill forecast to a Washington reporter that States' Righters were getting weaker and "on the whole, liberalism in the South is marching on." But there were limits beyond which prudent southern liberals could not tread if they wished to retain their fighting positions. Now that the southern primaries were over, the administration resumed its purposely delayed struggle for civil rights measures. Taking the Senate floor to fight a permanent FEPC, Hill decried this proposal as unconstitutional and "of evil character."[67]

"Helmsman, mind your left rudder"

The year 1950 held one more political test for Hill, albeit not a major one. John G. Crommelin of Montgomery, a former career officer in the Naval Air Force, had announced in early spring that he intended to run against Hill in the November general election. This would mark the first challenge by a self-styled independent candidate to a Democratic senatorial nominee since Heflin, cast out of the Democratic party, had made his forlorn campaign against John Bankhead Jr. in 1930. Like the former secretary of the Navy, James V. Forrestal, Crommelin had been a bitter and outspoken foe of armed forces unification. As Hill had anticipated, service rivalries had intensified. Crommelin, chief instigator of the 1949 "Revolt of the Admirals," charged that the Army and Air Force sought to destroy naval aviation so as to reduce Navy influence in the military establishment. His comments on this issue, including his call for the removal of General Omar Bradley as chairman of the joint chiefs of staff, had provoked Pentagon higher-ups to discipline Crommelin by furloughing him on partial pay. Shortly thereafter, Crommelin had retired at the rank of rear admiral and returned to his native Montgomery.[68]

With Americans uneasy over the involvement of their men and resources in the Korean conflict, Crommelin evidently regarded military prepared- ness as a hot issue with which to promote his Senate candidacy. He also charged that Hill was an advocate of socialist policies, including socialized medicine. In Mobile, Crommelin forces distributed handbills with the message: "Defeat the Author of the Hill-Burton Socialized Medicine Bill. Doctors, this is your fight too." Roy Nolen, ill but still alert, advised Hill: "Crommelin is hobnobbing around with the same kind of folks who have always been against you." Hill, without responding directly to Crommelin, confined his campaign to speeches before civic and veterans' organiza- tions.[69]

Obviously hoping to attract the States' Rights dissidents, Crommelin described himself as "an independent Alabama Democrat." But at least publicly, Gessner McCorvey and Frank Dixon, conscious of the penalty for party irregularity, called on their followers to support the entire Democratic primary ticket. To encourage such public expressions, Ben Ray wrote McCorvey: "Folks respect and admire a good loser." Republicans, so Fred Taylor of the *Birmingham News* reported, had refrained from offering a nominal opponent in the November race so that members of their party would be free to vote for Crommelin. As election day neared, Hill's managers expressed concern that large numbers of loyalists, confident of Hill's reelection, might not bother to vote. "Don't take Crommelin too lightly," a union official warned Hill. "He is making a very aggressive campaign . . . is a real headline hunter . . . and has backing of the reactionary and Dixiecrat elements in Alabama."[70]

Although the total vote in November was less than half that of the May primary, enough of his supporters turned out to validate Hill's claim to a third Senate term. In his concession statement, Crommelin, although he had failed to receive a majority in a single county, strongly hinted that he would be heard from again in Alabama politics. "Helmsman, mind your left rudder," he cautioned Hill.[71]

Later that November, Roy Nolen, the major force in Hill's earlier victories, died following a two-year illness. Although Nolen had not been as active as usual in the donnybrooks of 1948 and 1950, he had kept his finger on the pulse of Alabama politics almost to the very end. Hill felt keenly the loss of this alter ego whom he called "Old Maestro" and who, he believed, had made such "a mighty and invaluable contribution to all that has come to pass." Since 1933, Nolen had devoted himself almost single-mindedly to what he described as "Lister's magnificently rising career." After passage of the Hatch Act of 1939, forbidding federal officeholders to participate in political campaigns, the postmaster had been more circumspect in his activities, signing many of his letters to Hill "Mr. X." In the bitter aftermath of the 1944 campaign, Nolen had been required to make affidavit that he had taken no part in politics that year. Evidently he felt no compunction in swearing that, although he frequently visited Hill's Montgomery office, "such visitations are of a personal nature and are not in any way connected with political campaign management." But without Nolen's astute advice and unstinting loyalty, Hill might well have foundered on the treacherous political shoals of the 1940s. Over and over, Hill had acknowledged this debt and effusively expressed his gratitude. In autographing a picture for Nolen many years before the postmaster's death, Hill had described their relationship more simply: "To Roy L. Nolen, friend, master strategist and comrade in the cause."[72]

Nolen's successor, Foots Clement, reflecting on the complex political struggle of May 1950, felt cautiously optimistic about future tests of strength such as the 1952 presidential election, Sparkman's reelection in 1954, and Hill's next campaign in 1956. "We have won the third round of our 15-round battle," Foots wrote Lister. "The Dixiecrats won the first and the Democrats won the last two and there are twelve to go."[73]

But Jesse Hearin sensed that the political struggle of 1950 had left a "residue of extreme bitterness" in Alabama. Hearin reported to his friend, Hugo Black, that hatred of Hill and Sparkman "by special interests and those who have grown rich since Roosevelt became president is the most intense thing I have witnessed in a long time." In particular, many of Hill's former neighbors and hometown social acquaintances were now hostile toward the man who had served them as congressman and senator for over a quarter of a century. "The bitterness in Montgomery toward Lister Hill is distressing," Hearin told Justice Black.[74]

With Hugo Black, right, *1940s*

On the boardwalk in Atlantic City, 1942. Left to right: *Justice Hugo Black, Senator Alben Barkley, and Henrietta and Lister Hill.*

At the 1948 Democratic National Convention, Hill, lower left,
*remains at the microphone as thirteen Alabama delegates
and all twenty-two Mississippi delegates walk out*

With Clarence Allgood, right, *after a fishing expedition, mid-1940s*

With Vice President Alben Barkley, left, *in the late 1940s*

At the *1952 Democratic National Convention in Chicago, whooping it up for Richard Russell of Georgia as his name is placed in nomination for the presidency.* Left to right: *Evelyn Hicks, John Sparkman, Hill, Herman Talmadge.*

Discussing a civil rights filibuster with Alabama's junior senator,
John Sparkman, right, 1954

*With Mississippi senator John Stennis, right, taking part in the dedication
of Jefferson Davis Memorial Park at Fort Monroe, Virginia, 1956*

CHAPTER 9

The Democratic Loyalist

I 9 5 I – I 9 5 4

"Ben, our purpose is to cut the balls off the Dixiecrat party"

At the height of the 1950 struggle over control of the Alabama Democratic party, Ronald Hood, one of the young journalists cultivated by Hill, wrote the senator: "The most disheartening thing about Southern politics is that at least as far back as [John C.] Calhoun, our best leaders have had to devote their energies to issues foolishly brought up, to the neglect of great national issues." Although he evoked the storied Calhoun, Hood's comment had been inspired by Hill's situation during the protracted tug-of-war between Democratic loyalists and party dissenters. To direct the fight against administration foes in his home state and ensure that Alabama's electoral votes not be cast for a splinter party in 1952 demanded constant vigilance and consumed much of Hill's time and abundant energy.[1]

Despite this distraction, Hill had pressed his fight for federal aid to education. In 1951 he led a controversial effort to acquire a new source of educational funds: royalties from the nation's undersea oil resources. The Supreme Court had ruled in 1947 and 1950 that submerged coastal lands *beyond* the low-tide mark belonged to the nation as a whole rather than to adjoining states such as California, Texas, and Louisiana. Hill urged that this potential wealth (then modestly estimated at forty billion dollars) be dedicated, temporarily, to defense expenses and thereafter to the nation's public schools. This proposal aroused cries of outrage from politicians in the affected states and from representatives of private oil interests. When not diverted by political enemies on his home front, Hill was to play a major role in the long and heated dispute over what was popularly misnamed tidelands oil.[2]

181

At the onset of 1951, Alabama loyalists solidified their control of the SDEC by deciding a contested election in the Third Congressional District in favor of their own candidates. Richard Rives had donated his legal services to represent these loyalist contenders before the SDEC. (Shortly thereafter, Rives was named to the Fifth Circuit of the United States Court of Appeals. Tutored in law by Wiley Hill and for many years his law partner, Dick Rives was, in Robert Frazer's words, "practically a Hill." The Rives and Hill families had known one another since they had owned adjoining plantations before the Civil War. Rives had a long history of political involvement on behalf of progressives such as Hill, Black, and Graves, all of whom valued this quiet but effective tactician, and had been considered a likely gubernatorial prospect himself in early 1942. Originally a gradualist on civil rights, he had been influenced to a more activist outlook by his Harvard-educated only son, who had died in 1949 as the result of an automobile accident. After Rives had recovered somewhat from his grief, retiring Fifth Circuit Judge Leon McCord hand-picked him as his successor. Hill, who considered Rives "a valiant leader for our cause," persuaded Sparkman to go along in submitting his name to Truman. Hugo Black quietly added his endorsement. Rives, in cooperation with Frank M. Johnson Jr., who was to be named a federal district judge by Eisenhower in 1955, was to bring about a revolution in the racial and political climate of Alabama by striking down segregation and discrimination in schools, parks, jury selection, higher education, voting, and legislative apportionment.)[3]

To tighten their hold on the SDEC, loyalists also deposed Gessner McCorvey from the post of chairman in January 1951. By tradition, Alabama governors indicated their choices for this strategic post. Gordon Persons let it be known that he favored Ben F. Ray, a Birmingham attorney. Although a loyalist by 1951, Ray had championed Alabama's most famous bolter, Tom Heflin, in 1928; thus, Persons hoped, the new chairman would be acceptable to both factions. After he was elected over Tom Abernathy, Ray issued a call for party unity. But rather than healing, the intraparty breach widened.[4]

During the summer of 1951, Alabama States' Righters took new heart as their favorite target, Harry Truman, slipped dramatically in national popularity. Truman's low standing in the polls reflected a national restiveness brought on by the stalemate in Korea, the president's dismissal of General MacArthur, the Alger Hiss affair, the "communist in government" allegations of Senator Joseph R. McCarthy, and the "mink coat" and "deep freeze" scandals involving top Democratic officials. Gleeful Republicans lumped all these problems under the label, "the mess in Washington."[5]

To take advantage of Truman's declining status, anti-administration forces in Alabama put on a new show of strength in September, summoning Farm Bureau officials, representatives of mineowners, and States' Rights party leaders such as McCorvey, Abernathy, and Wilkinson to a rally and strategy session in Selma. Sponsors of this get-together included Marion Rushton, Donald Comer, John Temple Graves II, and former Congressman Sam Hobbs. Senator Harry F. Byrd arrived from Virginia to exhort a crowd of three thousand (including many of Alabama's business, industrial, financial, and farm leaders): "Democrats of the South [must] not permit Trumanites to press down upon the brow of America the un-Democratic crown of waste, of socialism, and of dictation from Washington." In a more intimate session, party dissidents adopted a manifesto calling for renewed emphasis on state government, curbs on the federal courts and Congress, and limits on federal taxation.[6]

As the 1952 presidential election year opened, the SDEC met in Montgomery for another showdown on the issue of party loyalty. To oversee this important gathering, Hill, accompanied by Sparkman, Jones, Rains, and Elliott, arrived by plane from Washington. He and his fellow legislators, Hill told the press, had returned to Alabama "to be with our 1950 campaign friends." In a less public setting, Hill (not averse to the use of earthy language in the presence of trusted political allies) instructed Ray: "Ben, our purpose is to cut the balls off the Dixiecrat party. History is not going to record whether we do it with a scalpel or a knife."[7]

Toward this end, loyalists planned to require all candidates and voters in the forthcoming Democratic primary to swear that they had supported the ticket in the preceding election and would support all nominees chosen in the primary including (a new specification) those nominated for president and vice president at the national convention. Except for this additional phrase, this was the same pledge used by party regulars to drum Tom Heflin out of the party in 1930.[8]

States' Righters had considered using the "Heflin pledge" in 1950 to bar "Trumancrats" from the primaries. But in 1952 Gessner McCorvey objected strenuously. Reversing his 1950 stand, McCorvey argued that the primary should be open to "Democrats of all shades of thought" and urged the committee to adopt "the usual, customary and traditional oath." Sidney Smyer, a representative of the Birmingham district, told fellow SDEC members that Hill, Sparkman, and their "congressional henchmen" had devised this scheme "at the bidding of their masters who control the National Democratic Party." Speaking for the loyalists, Chairman Ray announced bluntly that he had no respect for those who claimed to be Democrats but voted Republican. "The best way to keep Republicans out [of the Democratic Party]," Ray told the SDEC, "is never let them get in."[9]

Controlling a majority of the committee, loyalists adopted the strengthened oath effectively barring States' Rights electors from the party ballot. Exultant over this victory, Hill's faction passed a resolution expressing gratitude to the Democratic party for the benefits gained in Alabama and the nation during the New Deal, including Social Security, public works, TVA, and higher wages. Sardonic States' Righters (voicing themes strikingly reminiscent of Republican oratory) tried to amend this motion to add mink coats, deep freezes, higher taxes, and a huge national debt.[10]

Stymied in the SDEC, the anti-Truman bloc took its cause to court. In the circuit court of Birmingham and the Alabama Supreme Court, Horace Wilkinson won a suit against the loyalty oath by arguing that, under the Twelfth Amendment, presidential electors had the right to vote for whomever they chose. Jubilant States' Righters prepared to place on the Democratic ballot a slate of electors opposed to the nomination of Truman or any other person favored by the president. Among their prospective candidates were Wilkinson, McCorvey, Frank Samford, Donald Comer, Wallace Malone, a prominent Dothan banker, and Walter Givhan, a Dallas County planter. Polling these potential electors, the *Montgomery Advertiser* reported that a majority had indicated that they might cast their electoral votes for the Republican presidential nominee.[11]

But the possibility that Alabamians might again be deprived of the right to vote for the Democratic presidential nominee ended in early April. Ben Ray had appealed the state court ruling to the United States Supreme Court. (If Ray should lose there, Wilkinson jibed, "[he] may appeal to Moscow.")[12] In a 5-to-2 decision (with Frankfurter ill and Hugo Black abstaining because two of Ray's lawyers had once served as his clerks), the high court ruled that candidates for presidential electors could be compelled to pledge their support for the national nominees of their party. "Where a state authorizes a party to choose its nominees for elector in a party primary and to fix qualifications . . . we see no federal constitutional objection to . . . this pledge," the Court majority declared. In dissent, Justices Robert Jackson and William O. Douglas argued that the pledge, in effect, disfranchised party members who refused to conform to the majority view.[13]

As Foots Clement expressed it, loyalists had won another round. Only one set of presidential electors, bound by oath to support the Democratic nominees, would appear on the Alabama Democratic primary ballot. Ray and Hill seized this opportunity to describe the Supreme Court decision as a victory for states' rights. But to a friend in north Alabama, Hill made a more practical observation: "We simply could not permit Republicans at heart to take the name, the prestige, and the machinery of our Democratic party."[14]

With the States' Rights movement stalemated, signs of nascent Republicanism appeared in Alabama. Tom Abernathy, despairing of the splinter-party tactic, resigned from the SDEC and went over to the Republican ranks. The *Montgomery Advertiser*, departing from Democratic fealty for the first time in its 124-year history, announced its intent to support Eisenhower. Winton M. Blount, a wealthy Montgomery contractor, organized an Alabama Citizens for Eisenhower movement in the old capital of the Confederacy.[15]

Hill's long record of success in thwarting their plans intensified the hostility of his foes. The *Mobile Press* and *Mobile Register* even refused to publish an account of Hill awarding prizes in a fishing competition. "You are constantly attacked by both the local daily papers," Joe Lyons wrote his nephew. Among the well-to-do of Montgomery, feelings ran especially high against a native son whom they considered to have, like Franklin Roosevelt, betrayed the interests of his own class. The old New Dealer, Jesse Hearin, who had retired to Montgomery, complained to Hill that he felt "a bit lonesome to talk with someone who does not resent living in the twentieth century." After attending a Rotary Club meeting, Hearin reported: "No one is eligible to speak aloud unless he can picture a true America only when TVA has been turned over to the power companies, rural electric lines torn down, and every humanitarian measure devised and practiced for twenty years be forgotten." Hearin also notified Hill that the senator had achieved a new distinction: some Alabamians now hated him more than they hated Hugo Black. Urging his friend to regard this as a compliment, Hearin wrote: "The greatest strength you have lies in the people who hate you."[16]

"The greatest disappointment Lister Hill ever had"

Although they had maneuvered their party securely within loyalist control, Hill and Sparkman, as candidates for delegates-at-large to the national convention, confronted another quandary. Neither had dared to favor Truman as the 1948 nominee. Hill, in announcing his candidacy for the 1952 delegation, stated that he opposed the renomination of this president whom the majority of white southerners found unacceptable. But having sworn to support the Democratic standard bearer, Hill and Sparkman appeared to have been hoisted with their own petard.

Truman's announcement in late March that he would not seek reelection resolved their dilemma. The president's decision also opened the way for a renewal of Hill's old friendship with Truman. No matter how often he may have denigrated Truman to Alabama voters, Hill admired his onetime Senate colleague. Yet he considered this plain-born Missourian to have emerged from a different class from that of FDR (and that of Lister Hill). "[Truman] was out of the soil of America," Hill once remarked.[17]

After Truman retired to Independence, Hill sometimes urged the former president to meet with his "night school" of liberal senators. At the end of World War II, Hill had taken it upon himself to assemble like-minded colleagues twice a month to discuss current issues at informal, off-the-record dinner meetings similar to those he had organized as a House member in the 1930s. Of these get-togethers, Hill wrote Truman: "Being fairly homogeneous in political outlook, we . . . discuss matters perhaps more frankly than would be the case in a larger group." Hill even enshrined an autographed picture of Truman on his office wall. Thanking Truman for this gift, he expressed his admiration for the president's boldness in opposing Soviet aggression. "But for Harry Truman," Hill wrote, "Joe Stalin would have the world by the tail with a down-hill push."[18]

In the Alabama primary that May, every Democratic voter received a ballot imprinted with the loyalty pledge. Some stayed away from the polls to avoid this pledge. But members of the Wilcox County Democratic Executive Committee announced that, being "free-born white men," they would vote as they saw fit in the primary and general election. Others refused to heed the pledge on the grounds that it was a moral obligation unenforceable in law. Chairman Ray responded sternly: "We submit the moral obligation is greater than the legal obligation."[19]

Despite these defectors, loyalists again won an overwhelming victory. Eleven presidential electors, pledged to support the nominee of the national party, were elected without opposition. In November they would cast Alabama's electoral votes for the Democratic presidential candidate. Twenty-five of Alabama's twenty-six convention delegates, including Hill and Sparkman, were also chosen in the primary. This predominantly loyalist delegation elected Hill as chairman. States' Righters, deprived of Truman as a foil and unable to place their own candidates on the ballot, appeared to be thoroughly whipped. Grover Hall Jr. commented, "[Dixiecrats] are orbiting to starboard in the wilderness."[20]

But winners in this political donnybrook also had problems to face. Hill and Sparkman must choose between several Democratic presidential hopefuls: fellow Southerners Estes Kefauver, Richard Russell, and Alben Barkley; New York's urbane Averell Harriman, or Illinois's reluctant Adlai Stevenson. Kefauver, Harriman, and Stevenson had advocated civil rights. Barkley, at seventy-four, was considered too old to be president. Weighing their options, Alabama's senators declared for Russell.[21]

Their decision dismayed Alabama labor leaders. Spokesmen for the UMW, CIO, and Railroad Brotherhoods protested that Russell had an antilabor record and could not possibly win the presidency. Chiding Hill for wasting his vote, another Alabama supporter commented: "The day Alabama can send a delegation to Congress or a political convention to bargain for something other than White Supremacy or States Rights will indeed be fine." But Ben Leader of Birmingham considered this a wise move. "[States' Righters] can't jump on someone for championing the cause of their own champion," he advised Hill.[22]

With the stench of nearby stockyards hovering in the air, Democrats convened that July in Chicago's steamy amphitheater. For the first time, television kept watch over the proceedings of a national political convention. In full view of the cameras, Democrats wrangled over a proposal by Kefauver and Harriman to require that all delegates sign a pledge of loyalty to the party nominees *before* being seated at the convention. Despite the shouted protests of Alabama's Lieutenant Governor James B. Allen, Hill signed the controversial pledge on behalf of his delegation. Other southern delegations were not so firmly controlled: South Carolina, Louisiana, and Virginia delegations refused to sign; Texas, Mississippi, Florida, and Georgia delegates (contending that a loyalty pledge was contrary to the laws and party rules of their states) signed only after this pledge had been watered down.[23]

Unseen by television cameras, Democrats wrangled over the thorny issue of civil rights. In platform committee hearings, John Sparkman played a major role in working out a compromise proposal. Talk of Alabama's junior senator as a possible vice presidential nominee began to circulate through the convention floor and hotel corridors. Why Sparkman rather than his senior colleague, who had sponsored Sparkman's election to the Senate, arranged for him to serve on powerful committees that dovetailed with Hill's own assignments, and masterminded the long struggle to keep Alabama loyal to the Democratic party?[24]

The *Congressional Quarterly* noted in 1952 that Hill and Sparkman disagreed on fewer issues than any senators from a single state. Even their rare disagreements came over minor issues. Political scientists, rating senators on legislative ability, integrity, and issues, ranked the Hill-Sparkman team fourth in the nation in senatorial caliber, outshone only by the teams from Massachusetts, New York, and Connecticut. ("Alabama ranks near the bottom on so many other counts but can take pride in its senators," the *Gadsden Times* rejoiced.)[25]

However, this relationship was more complicated than it appeared. Although they closed ranks when necessary, Alabama's senators did not trust one another implicitly. Hill confided to Jesse Hearin that, from the start, he had insisted that Sparkman support "the cause." But infighting often broke out between the senators and members of their staffs. Foots Clement spent many hours trying to keep Hill and Sparkman on the same track, especially after influential bankers began to take an interest in Sparkman and sought to separate these allies.[26]

Reflecting on their senatorial team in later years, several close observers of Alabama politics agreed that Hill had been the leader and the more statesmanlike of the two. Carl Elliott described Hill as the "mental leader" of the fight over control of the SDEC. Neil Davis commented that Hill, a scion of privilege, had not used his Senate position for personal gain but that Sparkman, the son of sharecroppers, aspired to become (as he did) a millionaire. Barney Weeks, the veteran Alabama lobbyist for the AFL-CIO, recalled that Hill "sincerely believed in some of the things we were fighting for; it was just a matter of keeping him informed about what kind of help we needed." When Hill's political power began to wane in 1962, Weeks observed that Sparkman sought to put some distance between himself and his colleague. After Hill left the Senate, Weeks found Sparkman much harder to influence. Summing up his impression of Alabama's senators, Weeks concluded: "John Sparkman looked good only because Lister Hill was there."[27]

Yet Sparkman, for a number of reasons, was tapped for the national limelight in 1952. He was younger than Hill; his southern inflection less pronounced. Coming from a deprived economic background, Sparkman seemed "more like the people" than the somewhat aloof Hill. Sparkman's political base in north Alabama contained fewer blacks and thus had fewer racial problems than Hill's home region deep in the Black Belt. Furthermore, Sparkman actively sought the nomination. His longtime administrative assistant, the former campus politician John Horne, organized a concerted drive to bring Sparkman to Adlai Stevenson's attention. Most important of all, Harry Truman, perhaps hoping that the affable Sparkman would offer a populist flavor to a ticket headed by a cool intellectual, spoke a good word for another fellow from simple origins.[28]

Masking his hurt at having been passed over in favor of his protégé, Hill placed Sparkman's name in nomination over national television. He made a Western campaign swing in behalf of the Stevenson-Sparkman ticket but, uncharacteristically, he also took a long vacation at Rehoboth Beach in the midst of a national election. Hill let on to friends that he did not envy Sparkman and would not have wanted to waste his time on a futile campaign to defeat the popular Eisenhower. But his political intimate, Foots Clement, reported to other loyalist leaders that "the greatest disappointment Lister Hill ever had" was the fact that he was not chosen as his party's vice presidential nominee in 1952.[29]

"It is *fashionable* to like Ike"

Even with Sparkman on the national ticket, Alabama Democrats expected that 1952 would bring the most powerful challenge to their hegemony since the epic struggle of 1928. But this would not be a grassroots revolt fired by anti-Catholicism, prohibition, and nativism. Ed Reid foresaw another battle between advocates and opponents of an increasing federal role in the economic sphere. "We shall face the stiffest opposition from the haters of progressive government . . . since the inception of the New Deal," Reid predicted to the old 1928 bolter Ben Ray.[30]

So as not to jeopardize their influence in state and local politics, some who had paraded under the rubric of the States' Rights party in 1948 set up organizations called "Jeffersonial Democrats," "Eisenhower Democrats," "Young Persons for Eisenhower," and "Women for Eisenhower." John C. Godbold, who had once practiced law with Richard Rives and who headed the statewide Stevenson-Sparkman campaign, scoffed at such labels as "a fraud, a farce, and a subterfuge." As Godbold saw it: "Republicans are trying to sell the voters on the proposition that somehow votes for Ike are not votes for the Republicans."[31]

To avoid any taint of Republicanism, old pols like Gessner McCorvey and Horace Wilkinson announced that they would not vote at all. Frank Dixon refused to say whom he planned to support. Bruce Henderson, hoping to win statewide political office, pledged nominal loyalty to the Democratic ticket. But other prominent States' Rights leaders and sympathizers, like Donald Comer, Edward A. O'Neal, Wallace Malone, and Tom Abernathy, openly backed Eisenhower. Loyalists suspected that many others planned to vote Republican when they reached the privacy of the polling booth. Old-line Taft Republicans (little suspecting that these Johnnys-come-lately would soon oust them from leadership of their party in Alabama) welcomed all potential converts.[32]

As the campaign entered its final weeks, Lister Hill recovered somewhat from his disappointment at having been passed over by his party's kingmakers. He admired Stevenson whose eloquence and air of authority reminded him of Woodrow Wilson. But lest Stevenson be tempted by offers of political bargains from Texas and California, Hill pressed the Democratic candidate to make it clear to the Texas governor, Allan Shivers, that he supported the Supreme Court's decision and would follow Truman's example in vetoing any effort to assign offshore oil royalties to adjoining states.[33]

Also Hill had no intention of letting personal pique interfere with his long struggle to keep Alabama in the national Democratic column. This renewed challenge stirred his blood and evoked his old-time oratorical fervor. Before a Democratic gathering in the ballroom of the Jefferson Davis Hotel in Montgomery, Hill, flailing his arms, pantomimed, mocked, and mimicked his enemies. As his audience roared approval, he jeered: "It is *fashionable* to like Ike. People who have made their financial position— and with government contracts . . . have heard that Mr. and Mrs. So-and-So are for Ike. So they say, 'We'll be for Ike and then perhaps Mr. and Mrs. So-and-So will at long last know that we, too, are nice people.' " Old-line Democrats, who had heard Hill speak many times, remarked that he was at his "toughest" that night.[34]

In November 1952, Alabama Democrats beat back a strong Republican challenge, but Eisenhower received more than one-third of the popular votes. As had those who ran under the States' Rights party banner in 1948, the Republican nominee made his strongest Alabama showing in the Black

Belt. For the first time since 1928, the Alabama GOP had made a major impact in presidential politics. Governor Persons attributed this outcome to Ike's magnetism, but the *Montgomery Advertiser* claimed that Alabamians were beginning to dispel the "black magic" of the Democratic label and exhorted "drinking drys" like Gessner McCorvey and Bruce Henderson to join the swelling Republican ranks. "This 'Democrats for Ike' foolishness has got to be abandoned," Grover Hall Jr. admonished. Looking ahead, Republicans and their allies wondered if the 1952 outcome offered hope that they might defeat Sparkman in 1954.[35]

"A crop failure for us Plantation Whigs"

At its January 1954 meeting, the SDEC denied its party label to potential candidates described by Chairman Ray as "those who 'rode the elephant to the polls' in November, 1952." Adopting an even more stringent pledge than that of two years earlier, the committee barred as Democratic candidates not only those who had voted Republican or independent tickets but (a new requirement) those who had refused or failed to vote for or "aid and support" the Stevenson-Sparkman ticket. In vain, Gessner McCorvey protested that he and other lifelong Alabama Democrats could not bring themselves to support Stevenson because of that candidate's "anti-Southern sentiments" on the matter of race. But the loyalist majority, led by Ray, Roy Mayhall, Robert W. Gwin, and Judge Frank Embry, rammed through the tougher oath outlawing all they deemed "traitors." At Ray's behest, some party clerks would later warn those signing the oath that they could be prosecuted if they swore falsely. McCorvey, complaining that he had been "Heflinized," did not seek reelection to the SDEC, thus ending his long tenure as the leading spokesman in the committee for those who had called themselves States' Rights Democrats.[36]

Races for governor and United States senator occupied center stage in the Democratic primary of May 1954, almost completely submerging interest in contests for the SDEC. Lister Hill, assuming the situation to be well in hand, remained in Washington, leaving the detail work of this campaign to Ray, Mayhall, and Clement. The senator advised constituents that he "strongly supported" Sparkman but would, as usual, keep hands off the governor's race (although rumor had it that Hill and Sparkman had sponsored Jimmy Faulkner in an effort to defeat Folsom).[37]

The two major Senate contenders, Sparkman and former Congressman

Laurie Battle of Birmingham, generally considered a tool of "big mules"
and the beneficiary of their generous campaign contributions, had differed
on almost every major issue that had come before them in Congress.
Battle, finding it hard to excite voters by opposing federal housing, TVA,
unions, foreign aid, the United Nations, and federal control of offshore oil,
fell back on the old issue of race, charging that Sparkman had run for vice
president on a platform advocating civil rights. But with a Republican in
the White House, federal responsibility for civil rights matters could no
longer be laid solely on the Democratic doorstep.[38]

A third Senate candidate, John Crommelin, also sought to unseat Sparkman, whom he called Hill's "tool" and "puppet." In a telegram to Eisenhower, Crommelin charged that Judge Rives had violated the Hatch Act by
supporting Hill and Sparkman. Crommelin urged the president not to
appoint any other "Sparkman-Hill-Clement minion" to the bench. Raising
the demagogic ante, he also alleged that Jews (whom he called by the
euphemism of "Eskimos") and Communists had conspired to undermine
America's strength. Observing the Alabama election, the *New York Times*
described Sparkman as fighting for his political life. If their enemies could
unseat the junior senator, the *Nation* predicted that their next target would
be Lister Hill, "the master strategist of Southern liberals."[39]

But on primary day, Alabama Democrats again exhibited their strong
loyalty to the national party and their support for progressive causes by
returning Folsom to the governor's chair and decisively reelecting Sparkman. Folsom carried 61 of Alabama's 67 counties and polled 50.9 percent
of the vote to triumph over six other candidates without a runoff. He and
Jimmy Faulkner, both loyal Democrats and progressives, received 75
percent of the total vote. James B. Allen ran a distant third. Bruce Henderson, the only avowed States' Rights candidate in the gubernatorial race,
received 8 percent of the total vote. Sparkman swept back into office with
heavy support from north Alabama, organized labor, and new black voters. The *Montgomery Advertiser* reported that Sparkman's almost 324,000
votes were the most ever cast for an Alabama political candidate.[40]

Commenting on the 1954 primary results, Neil Davis noted: "Since
1948, the voters have had opportunity three times to state their preference
and each time the majority have chosen the liberal Democratic side."
Grover Hall Jr., conceding that Fair Dealers and neo-Populists now dominated the governor's office, both Senate seats, and the SDEC, described
this election as "a crop failure for us Plantation Whigs" and noted that
opponents of this point of view "are defending a shrinking perimeter."[41]

With Franklin Roosevelt and the New Deal fading into history, what factors had influenced the majority of Alabamians to take such a different course from other Deep South states by voting for the champions of progressive government? With the issue of race muted and a Republican having succeeded Truman in the White House, States' Rights Democrats had lost their favorite issues. Thomas L. Stokes, columnist for the *Washington Evening Star*, wondered if appeals to racial prejudices could no longer "be exploited . . . to becloud economic benefits such as higher wages." But other factors had also influenced this outcome. The stringent new oath, engineered by Hill and the loyalists, had barred most States' Righters from seeking office. An even more potent factor was the increased size and changing nature of the Alabama electorate. In 1953, supporters of the Meek bill (primarily women's clubs and labor unions) had succeeded in their long fight to persuade the Alabama legislature to approve a referendum on lowering the cumulative feature of Alabama's poll tax.[42]

Familiar alignments had formed on this issue. Leading loyalists, such as Hill, Sparkman, Ray, and Folsom, spoke out for lowering the cumulative period. The great majority of Alabama newspapers backed this change. Even James B. Allen and Bruce Henderson, with ambitions to become governor uppermost in mind, yielded to the strong tide favoring this reform. Representatives of the old States' Rights element, such as Frank Dixon, Gessner McCorvey, and members of the Jefferson County Democratic Executive Committee, comprised the chief opposition and raised the old bugaboos of Communism and racial integration.[43]

But foes of the poll tax won this referendum by a comfortable margin. No longer would a registrant be required to pay $1.50 for each year dating back to his or her twenty-first birthday before being placed on the voter rolls. The Meek bill reduced the maximum cumulative period from twenty-four years ($36) to two years ($3). Alabama's Attorney General Si Garrett went even further by waiving poll taxes altogether for those over forty-five years of age.[44]

As a consequence of these changes, an estimated 200,000 new voters had registered by 1954. In the Senate race, almost 215,000 more votes were cast than in the Hill-McNeil contest of 1950. Whereas only 19 percent of all adults in Alabama had voted in 1950, almost one-third voted in 1954. Referring to these new voters, most of them white women and poor whites, Gessner McCorvey confided glumly to Frank Dixon that those who favored a restricted electorate could do little to stem this tide "even though they are of a type which has no business voting."[45]

Black voters, too, increased in number from 2,800 in 1944 to approximately 50,000 by 1954 (although ten counties, most of them in the Black Belt, still contained no black voters). Despite the discouraging fact that no black had held public office in Alabama since Reconstruction, nine black candidates appeared on the 1954 primary ballot, including Arthur Shores of Birmingham who unsuccessfully sought a seat in the state legislature. The overwhelming majority of these black voters favored Sparkman and the racially moderate Folsom. On primary day, the *New York Times* commended Alabama for "underscoring the changing pattern of race relations in the South."[46]

Most of these new voters joined the ranks of those who supported Folsom, Sparkman, and Hill. This growing majority favored Folsom's programs for improved schools, higher pay for teachers, old-age pensions, better health care, further industrialization, and (Folsom's pet project) reapportionment of the legislature. They also applauded Sparkman's loyalty to TVA, his support of public housing, veterans' benefits, and farm parity, and his vote against the Taft-Hartley law. Sparkman also profited, so the *Andalusia Star-News* noted, from his close relationship with Hill, "Alabama's most dominant political figure."[47]

But the "pattern of good humor in Alabama," as Grover Hall Jr. described this political climate, was about to be dispelled. On 17 May 1954, the United States Supreme Court unanimously held that racial segregration in public schools was unconstitutional. Fortunately for John Sparkman, the Court handed down this decision after the first Alabama primary. It also came too late to have much effect upon the 1 June Democratic runoff for positions on the SDEC.[48]

But *Brown v. Board* breathed new life into an issue used by many southern politicians since the late nineteenth century to arouse the gut emotions of whites, divide the ranks of the poor, and distract attention from economic and political concerns. During the Great Depression and World War II, Americans had focused on matters that seemed more immediate than that of racial injustice. Except for the plebiscite over the Boswell amendment, Alabama politicians who sought to raise the old issue of race to foster their own interests, like Jim Simpson and the States' Righters, had found that the time was not yet right.

Now the Court's momentous decision, foreshadowing a basic readjustment of American race relations, put a torch to this smoldering fire. In the conflagration that followed, Lister Hill would deem it essential—as Ronald Hood deplored—to devote an increasing share of his energies to the futile southern outcry against inevitable change.

The Senior Statesman

I 9 5 5 – I 9 5 6

"He wanted to pass laws. That was his heaven on earth."

In January 1955, Lister Hill would begin to make his own major contributions to "the cause." TVA had been George Norris's vision. The New Deal had been put together by Franklin Roosevelt and other innovative thinkers, Hugo Black having envisioned federal regulation of work hours long before Hill. The hospital industry and the medical establishment had crafted the Hill-Burton Act. Hill's efforts to achieve his long-sought goal of federal aid to education had been thwarted by the stratagem of racial objections. Because of this same obstacle, he had long since relinquished his dreams of the presidency or of becoming his party's leader in the Senate. Now that noisy, rough, and skilled operative, Lyndon Johnson, bossed Senate Democrats. When speaking to his staff, Hill always referred to Johnson as "the Majority Leader," seldom betraying his innermost thoughts about this man who held a position that—save for the politics of race—might have been his. But trusted associates heard Hill express his concealed bitterness. "He hated Johnson," one recalled.[1]

With the expert help of Roy Nolen and Foots Clement, Hill had led the successful—except in 1948—fight to keep Alabama loyal to the national Democratic party. He had been instrumental in making telephone service possible for millions of rural Americans. But up to this point in his congressional career, Hill had been more of a faithful and conscientious lieutenant than a strong-willed and powerful leader, able to bring about far-reaching changes for society's betterment.

By the age of sixty, Hill, ranking eighth in seniority, had become one of the Senate's most powerful members. After more than a quarter of a century in that body, he was unquestionably a member of its "inner club," one of the "old boys" along with other Southerners of long tenure like Richard Russell, Pat Harrison, Harry Byrd, Walter George, and Kenneth McKellar. With Democrats controlling the Senate even though a Republican occupied the White House, Southerners had returned to a position of tremendous power. One Senate staff member recalled how craftily these veteran legislators used this power, packing the most important agricultural committees with Southerners and trying to lump as many liberals as possible on one committee "so they would do the least harm." Hill and Russell served under Johnson on the Senate Democrats' "board of directors"; this policy committee mapped party strategy on important issues. When social legislation arose, these strategists turned to Hill. In the *New York Times*, William White reported: "[Hill] is able to appeal to Southerners for policies they would find suspect coming from another man."[2]

Recognizing Hill's seniority and knowing they could count on him to protect them on sensitive southern issues, these Democratic leaders agreed that he should chair the Labor and Public Welfare Committee on which he had served since 1938. Originally named the Committee on Education and Labor, this standing body of the Senate had been established at the end of the Civil War. During the early twentieth century, it had few functions other than to encourage vocational education, develop new bureaus dealing with women and children in the work force, and adopt a resolution favoring Mother's Day. But as enthusiasm for broad new social programs burst forth during the New Deal and thereafter, this committee's scope would grow to affect the lives of nearly every American.[3]

As chairman, Hill presided in an imposing, historic—but drafty— chamber in the Capitol, only a few seconds' walk from the Senate floor. The entire Senate had once met in this room in the era of such giants as Clay, Webster, and Calhoun. After a Senate wing was added to the Capitol in 1859, the Supreme Court held its sessions in this room until provided in 1935 with its own marble-columned building. As a young congressman, Hill had seen Chief Justices William Howard Taft and Charles Evans Hughes and Justice Harlan F. Stone at work here. Now Hill, at the start of the Eighty-fourth Congress, presided from this high dais, with crystal chandelier overhead and fireplace to one side, flanked on important occasions by all twelve members of his committee, ranging in political philosophy from Barry Goldwater on the right to Herbert Lehman, James Murray, Paul Douglas, and young John Kennedy on the left. Hill was to hold this chairmanship through the Ninetieth Congress of 1967–68; as its responsibilities exploded, the committee's staff was to grow from 14 to 114. By tradition, the chairman had his choice of which of its three major subcommittees he would lead; passing over education, with its thorny issues, and labor, relatively weak in the politics of his home state, Hill chose the Health Subcommittee.[4]

His committee staff, like his office staff, found Senator Hill more than demanding. "I never worked for a tougher boss . . . demanding isn't the word for it," recalled Stewart McClure, the chief clerk, who observed many senators at close range during twenty-four years on Capitol Hill. McClure found in his new boss the same human failings experienced by those who worked in Hill's office. To ascertain if staffers were performing effectively, the senator encouraged them to gossip to him about one another. McClure concluded that this was "one method of running an intelligence operation." When he wished assistance, Hill would telephone all three major staff members simultaneously. "Those phones would ring and we'd jump," McClure remembered. "Yes, sir!" the three would respond in unison.[5]

Their chairman scrutinized every speech or statement written for him by these subordinates, carefully removing the "one-liners" and occasionally inserting a bit of his own "broad, almost slapstick humor." He still took his work home in the evenings, especially bills or amendments he planned to sponsor, then grilled his staff until "he knew everything contained in a bill, every question that could possibly be asked and what the answers were." By these procedures, Hill demonstrated his pride in his own intellectual capacity and expertise. To be caught without knowing the answers would be "unthinkable."[6]

Fellow senators found Hill a courteous, diplomatic, but firm leader. On his desk, he kept a biographical directory; by frequently consulting this volume, he knew many details about his colleagues, often including their places and dates of birth, the names of their wives, and the dates they entered Congress. Before every committee meeting, he telephoned to find out how each stood on issues to arise, seek a consensus, and, if unsuccessful, to discover what pitfalls lay ahead. He persuaded Republicans, as he had Harold Burton, to allow their names to appear as co-sponsors of big health measures; even starch and rigid Styles Bridges of New Hampshire often succumbed to Hill's blandishments. Much to the disgust of his staff, Hill insisted on referring to these purportedly bipartisan measures as "team efforts." One close associate recalled: "he was a real vaseline artist . . . about the contributions of the minority."[7]

Hill took particular care to keep on good terms with that powerful opponent of social programs, Robert Taft. Filibustering for one of his causes, he attempted to flatter Taft by telling the Senate that he always turned to his Ohio colleague for advice in "difficult and abstruse" matters. "He is my lawyer," Hill fervently proclaimed. This struck a spark even from the cold and humorless Taft. "The senator from Alabama is supposed to speak from his desk," Taft rejoined. "It is not proper for him to approach me and pat me on the head."[8]

But unlike Lyndon Johnson, Hill never massaged the shoulders of his colleagues, told them salacious jokes, raised his voice, or swore in public. In dress and demeanor, he exemplified the gentleman in politics. Yet he allowed no senator—junior, senior, or his equal in rank—to challenge his prerogatives as chairman. "He didn't enjoy anybody trying to take his place, even partly," McClure recalled.[9]

At the same time that he took over this chairmanship, Hill also assumed the chairmanship of the Appropriations Subcommittee that oversaw these same areas. In choosing this subcommittee, he passed over the chance to head an appropriations subcommittee on military affairs or agriculture. Those who persuaded him to give up the opportunity to oversee funding of the military—his longtime interest—argued that in peacetime this position would offer little challenge; instead, he could become a national figure in the relatively noncontroversial area of basic research to improve the nation's health. Because of his dovetailing committee posts, Hill would have the rare opportunity to control the funding of programs that he had helped to create.[10]

Hill found his new responsibilities vastly preferable to the tedium of seeking favors for constituents. Now he was performing the *real* work of a senator. Even after thirty-two years in Congress, he stuck to his routine of working on Saturdays, although now he permitted himself to leave the Capitol that day to have lunch—and his one public Manhattan—at Wearley's, his favorite restaurant. Even then talk always focused on the business of the day. But this exhilarated Hill. "He loved what he was doing," McClure remembered. "He didn't want to go home, or go to Europe, or go back to politick. He wanted to pass laws. That was his heaven on earth."[11]

Hill needed some counterpoise to the never-ending struggles of Alabama politics. Also he needed new interests. Of his close family confidants in Montgomery, only the devoted Amelie remained. His favorite uncle, Will Hill, who had retired at eighty-four after eighteen years as Montgomery County probate judge, died in early 1955. Roy Nolen had passed from the scene. "So many of our friends gone," Hill commented wistfully to Judge Rives. "I sorely miss them all."[12]

Old New Dealers like Alben Barkley, Samuel Rosenman, Paul Douglas, Tommy Corcoran, Hugo Black, Thurman Arnold, and Claude Pepper no longer gathered to josh, tell old political stories, and sing in the backyard of the handsome suburban home that Dr. Hill had helped his son acquire. Clifford and Virginia Durr and Aubrey Williams had gone home to Alabama; Jonathan Daniels had returned to North Carolina to edit his father's newspaper. George Norris had died two years after his 1942 defeat; Harry Truman had retired to Missouri. Dwight Eisenhower sat in the Oval Office. As did most Americans, Hill liked Ike. "You couldn't know the man without liking him," he recalled later. But what a contrast between this cautious man from plain Kansas origins and that daring aristocrat Franklin Roosevelt! Hill's new challenges came at an opportune time in his life.[13]

"We do not intend to use Dixon-Yates power, and that's that"

Midway into Eisenhower's first term, Hill played a crucial role in two sharp conflicts between congressional Democrats and the Republican administration. One skirmish involved a planned incursion by private power interests into TVA territory; the other reflected opposing points of view on a policy affecting the health of millions of American children. Due in large measure to Hill, the administration would lose face in both battles and critics would charge Eisenhower with ignorance of his own policies.

Increasingly, Hill had assumed the role of chief congressional guardian of TVA, ever alert to threats posed by Willkie, McKellar, and less visible enemies of this multifaceted experiment. Early in the Truman administration, he suspected private utility interests of launching a massive propaganda campaign to discredit TVA and thereby block any similar development. At issue, Hill told the Senate, was whether rivers and watersheds should be developed "democratically in the public interest . . . or turned over to those who would exploit them for their own profit."[14]

But this struggle seemed to be endless. Although Eisenhower had promised in his campaign not to interfere with TVA, the president now used the private power companies' favorite phrase, "creeping socialism," to describe that agency. In 1954, Eisenhower proposed an atomic energy policy excluding TVA and other public power organizations from any share in the promise of electric energy produced from the atom. Such unlikely filibus-

terers as Lehman, Wayne Morse, and Hubert Humphrey joined Hill, the
chief strategist on this issue, to force Republicans to amend this bill to
admit participation by TVA.[15]

By 1955, Hill had come a long way from the cautious young congressman of the 1920s with his doubts about putting government in the power
business. His twenty-year study of TVA's budget and operating methods
would help Hill play a crucial role in the battle royal over what was
popularly called the "Dixon-Yates" contract. Edgar Dixon, president of
Middle South Utilities, Inc., and Eugene Yates, chairman of the board of
the Southern Company, proposed to construct a steam generating plant in
Arkansas, across the river from Memphis, to supply the growing power
needs of that city and, purportedly, to supply extra power for the Atomic
Energy Commission (AEC). Eisenhower had just denied TVA's request for
funds to build a similar plant and indicated his desire to cut TVA's power
commitments to the AEC in the name of helping to balance the national
budget. But the president approved this new contract even though all
power purchased by the AEC from its Arkansas plant was to be resold to
TVA and used in the Memphis area, thereby allowing private interests to
make a 9 to 11 percent annual return on their investment.[16]

By agreeing to allow the AEC to serve in this "broker" role and denying
TVA's bid to produce power for Memphis at a cheaper rate, the Eisenhower
administration demonstrated that, at whatever cost to consumers, it preferred private power to public power. The controversial Dixon-Yates contract made its way through the attorney general's office, the Joint Committee on Atomic Energy, and the Securities and Exchange Commission
toward final approval. But in February 1955, Hill, in a dramatic speech on
the Senate floor, charged that a member of the banking firm that had
arranged financing for Dixon-Yates had, at the same time, acted as a
consultant on TVA for the Bureau of the Budget. Adolph Wenzell vigorously denied that his governmental role had been other than that of an
unpaid financial adviser. But by raising the question of a conflict of
interest, Hill delayed the final awarding of the contract. Meantime, the city
of Memphis rescued the Eisenhower administration from its political embarrassment by voting to build a municipal power-generating plant. "We do
not intend to use Dixon-Yates power, and that's that!" a city official said.[17]

Eventually, Eisenhower canceled the controversial Dixon-Yates contract
rather than risk further criticism during his reelection campaign. Pushing
his momentary advantage, Hill persuaded the Senate to increase TVA's
annual appropriation by almost one million dollars, most of this sum to be

used to investigate the feasibility of more multipurpose dams, more fertilizer research, and added farm demonstration programs. Referring to
Dixon-Yates and Eisenhower's other efforts to hamstring public power, Hill
charged during the presidential campaign of 1956: "TVA has no worse
enemy than the Eisenhower administration."[18]

"We don't believe in a pauper's oath"

His stunning revelation on Dixon-Yates whetted Hill's appetite for further
jousting with representatives of "the ancient enemy." Another opportunity
soon presented itself. For almost a year, Hill and others interested in health
had been aware of the testing of a vaccine against the dread disease
poliomyelitis, the leading crippler of American children. Announcement
of the success of the Salk vaccine in April 1955 electrified the nation;
people honked their horns, blew factory whistles, gave thanks, and hugged
their children. Oveta Culp Hobby, Eisenhower's secretary of health, education, and welfare, promptly licensed six drug companies to put this supposed miracle drug on the market.

The following day, Secretary Hobby appeared before Hill's committee to
testify on pending health and medical legislation. Hill urged the secretary
to assure Americans that the Salk vaccine would be distributed equitably in
all parts of the country and to children of all income levels. Hobby appeared to believe that this could be accomplished by the simple expedient
of children being taken to their doctors. Hill acknowledged this viewpoint
with his customary courtesy but inwardly, so one close associate recalled,
"he was just wild!" Appealing to Eisenhower, Hill suggested that the
president call a White House conference to work out a voluntary plan "to
make certain that every child needing the vaccine will get it." Eisenhower
called this conference but its results were not disclosed for almost a
month.[19]

General confusion followed in the wake of the Salk discovery. Fears
arose that the vaccine would be distributed in a "grey market." Production
and distribution were temporarily halted when several children who had
been inoculated developed polio. Vaccine produced by one laboratory was
removed from circulation. Meantime, Hill, Lehman, Representative Albert Rains of Gadsden, and other Democrats introduced bills to give
Eisenhower "standby controls" in case, when Congress was not in session,
the president needed to take over distribution of the vaccine to ensure that

it would be made available to high-risk groups ahead of adults. Speaking for herself and Eisenhower, Hobby resisted the idea that any national controls might be needed. But even the rock-ribbed Republican *New York Herald-Tribune* warned Hobby to see to it that pregnant women and young children got the first shots.[20]

Eventually Hobby revealed the administration's proposal to spend twenty-eight million dollars to vaccinate poor children. Initially Hill supported this request. But he warned those who testified in behalf of the administration plan: "We're not going to pass [this bill] with the clause in it that says you've got to be financially needy if you're going to get the vaccine. . . . We don't believe in a pauper's oath."[21]

By midsummer, with the peak polio season looming ahead, Hill had decided that the administration's plan was "gravely defective" in providing vaccine for only eleven million of the nation's fifty-one million children. To line up schoolchildren and divide them publicly "into objects of charity" or those able to pay would convert "a boon to all humanity . . . into an instrumentality of humiliation." Speaking for all Democrats on his committee, he proposed a countermeasure to provide free vaccinations to all children whose parents desired it. Even though her department already had a policy of making vaccines against diptheria, smallpox, whooping cough, and tetanus freely available to the poor, Hobby protested that this new step would lead to "socialized medicine by the back door." To put the label of "socialized medicine" on a program under which the government paid private laboratories for the vaccine and recompensed private doctors to give inoculations, the *Washington Post* responded, "is to render that much abused term even more ridiculous than it has already become."[22]

Hobby's inept appearance on the witness stand, her efforts to pass the buck for the confusion to her subordinate, Dr. Leonard A. Scheele, head of the Public Health Service, and her Scrooge-like image as one insensitive to the poor hastened her departure from the cabinet. Rumors spread that she would soon resign to care for her ailing husband; old Washington hands suspected that such rumors sometimes represented a broad hint from the White House. Drew Pearson reported that Eisenhower and his embattled secretary had had a heated discussion on the mishandling of the Salk program. In June, Hobby handed in her resignation and returned to Texas.[23]

In 1956, Hill's committee successfully proposed a bill to provide free vaccine against all the major children's diseases. "No problem then," Stewart McClure recalled. "[Eisenhower] didn't want that fight again!"

Recalling Hill's opposition to Hobby's policies, the committee's chief clerk concluded with satisfaction: "We burned her." Hill remembered their differences more tactfully: "That gentle lady from Texas . . . didn't do anything to stand up."[24]

Another Senate Democrat, ambitious Estes Kefauver of Tennessee, followed up both the Hobby and the Dixon-Yates fights with highly publicized Senate investigations that would help him win nomination for the vice presidency.[25] But Hill, facing his own reelection in 1956, had no further desire for the empty honor of second place on a ticket to challenge the popular Eisenhower.

"People want to be . . . judged by a judge . . . of their own blood and bones"

Aggressive Democrat though he was, Hill failed to fight a decision by Eisenhower that was to have momentous impact on Alabama. Apparently he acceded in Eisenhower's nomination in 1955 of Frank M. Johnson Jr. to become United States district court judge for the middle district of Alabama. Thereby Hill passed over the opportunity to endorse a rival candidate, his first cousin, Thomas Bowen Hill, former president of the state bar association.[26]

During the 1940s and 1950s, the Hill brothers and their descendants had drifted apart politically. The faction once led by Will and Wiley Hill lost its grip on Montgomery politics in 1952. Hugh Sparrow of the *Birmingham News* reported Montgomery to be abuzz with talk of the "crack up" of the Hill machine when its candidates failed to win a local election that summer. Relations between Senator Hill and his cousin, T. B. Hill, had been strained for over a decade. T. B. Hill had supported Simpson in 1944, favored the States' Rights movement, and thereafter drifted toward Republicanism. By 1952, he had proclaimed himself an "Eisenhower Democrat."[27]

Many in Montgomery, heart of the middle district, backed the candidacy of T. B. Hill. As one put it: "People want to be . . . judged by a . . . judge of their own blood and bones." Others urged the president to name either T. B. Hill or some other candidate "wedded openly to the Southern way of life." But more was at issue here than a nominee's birthplace or avowed dedication to the status quo. In essence, this was a Republican family squabble between old-line party faithfuls and Johnnys-come-lately like

T. B. Hill. The GOP hoped to win over more dissident Democrats, but Alabamians who had been Republicans for generations were not eager to share their patronage with these new converts. Claude Vardaman of Birmingham, chairman of the Alabama Republican Executive Committee, recommended that Eisenhower appoint Johnson, a federal district attorney for north Alabama whose family had been Republicans since the Civil War. The *Montgomery Advertiser* protested against "importing" a man from north Alabama, a region defined by many in that city as "anything just north of Montgomery."[28]

As a matter of courtesy, even presidents of an opposite party consulted United States senators before making key appointments within their states. "I am not going to comment on any of the candidates," Hill responded when asked if he would prefer his cousin or other Montgomery contenders. Democratic loyalists Hill and Sparkman opposed the appointment of turn-coat Democrats to federal office. Drew Pearson, reporting that both senators would okay Johnson, commented that Hill "definitely" did not favor his cousin.[29]

During Eisenhower's recovery from a heart attack in mid-1955, the appointment hung fire, reviving the hopes of those who favored a south Alabamian over one from north Alabama whose racial views were little known but whose economic leanings were suspect because he had once been close to a leading Folsomite, George C. Wallace. But eventually Vardaman prevailed. Johnson, nominated in October, would become the nation's youngest federal judge. Within five months, Judge Johnson would join Judge Rives to rule in favor of blacks who challenged the constitutionality of segregated seating on Montgomery buses. In the years that followed, Johnson and Rives, Hill's earlier choice for the U.S. Court of Appeals for the Fifth District, would issue other rulings that consigned Alabama's racial segregation laws to history.[30]

"We have to have big-scale research on heart, cancer, and stroke"

Two dedicated, energetic, and wealthy women persuaded Hill to interest himself in the federal role in medical research. Mary Lasker, who had inherited an estimated eighty million dollars from her husband, the advertising genius Albert Lasker, and Florence Mahoney, divorced from Daniel Mahoney of the Cox newspaper chain, had met Hill when they first sought federal support of health research in the mid-1940s.

At this time both women primarily depended upon Claude Pepper to champion this cause before Congress. Seeking another powerful senator to carry on after Pepper's defeat in 1950, they eventually chose Hill. At a dinner party in her elegant Georgetown home, Mahoney urged Hill in late 1954 to assume the chair of the appropriations Subcommittee on Health. The persuasive Lasker added: "We have to have big-scale research on heart, cancer, and stroke. That's defense of the U.S. every day. The Department of Defense only defends us when we are attacked." Lasker and Mahoney focused on Hill at a timely moment: they replaced others, like Bob La Follette Jr., George Norris, and Roy Nolen, who had once inspired and needled him to translate his ingrained sense of responsibility into concrete accomplishments.[31]

Prior to 1930, the federal government had involved itself in medical research in only a limited fashion, primarily during health crises. Between 1930 and 1950, a national policy began to take shape; basic research into cancer, heart, mental health, and dental diseases had been authorized by the mid-1940s. After 1955, Lasker and Mahoney teamed with Hill, Representative John Fogarty of Rhode Island, and a group of activist physicians to bring about federal funding of medical research on an unprecedented scale. Within a decade, the annual appropriation of the National Institutes of Health (NIH) would balloon from $70 million to $1.5 billion. By means of grants to reseachers at medical centers throughout the nation, NIH by 1967 would directly support over 40 percent of biomedical research in the United States.[32]

"Washington's Noble Conspirators," as the journalist Elizabeth Drew called proponents of this program, found themselves up against the Eisenhower administration's desire to cut the budget, including NIH funding. Ike's close adviser, Sherman Adams, and Treasury Secretary George Humphrey particularly opposed spending federal money for medical research. "Why didn't you come to see me when Roosevelt was President?" Hill asked Mahoney and Lasker. "We could have gotten anything from him." Years later, Hill recalled: "Most of what we did in health we had to push it ourselves. We had no leadership from [Eisenhower]."[33]

Marion Folsom, Hobby's successor as health, education, and welfare secretary, proved to be the health lobby's friend in this administration. Hill remembered that "[Folsom] was as forward as you could be in the Eisenhower cabinet," persuading the president, after his heart attack, to approve an increase of thirty million dollars in the medical research budget. Senator Margaret Chase Smith of Maine also urged fellow Republicans to step up funding in this area. "Except for the leadership of Senator Hill," Smith told

Secretary Folsom, "we wouldn't be doing what we are doing." But when Democrats regained the White House, the health lobby still encountered presidential opposition.[34]

With the help of her "stable" of medical allies, Lasker orchestrated many committee hearings over which Hill presided. "If you gave Hill an idea that he liked, he took it instantly," she recalled years later. Lasker rounded up "stars" of the medical profession like Dr. Sidney Farber of Harvard, Dr. Michael De Bakey, the famed Houston heart surgeon, and Dr. Howard Rusk, who had pioneered vocational rehabilitation in his New York City clinic, and coached these physicians to speak in lay language (such as "heart attack") rather than arcane medical terminology. "Hill loved to have a witness whom he could call 'Doctor,'" Stewart McClure remembered. But when Florence Mahoney brought in one medical expert who described every known method of birth control, an embarrassed Hill scolded her: "Don't you ever do that to me again!"[35]

These "evangelistic pizazz" doctors made headlines and appeared on the nightly television news; the committee voted to fund their proposals, and future Democratic administrations at least proved more amenable than Eisenhower. Essential to the success of this teamwork was House concurrence. Irish Catholic John Fogarty, a onetime bricklayer, presided over the House appropriations subcommittee dealing with health, education, and welfare (HEW). Initially Fogarty displayed little interest in medical research but, prodded by Lasker and Mahoney, he developed such a sincere commitment to this cause that he later refused to abandon his post to run for the Senate. In background and personality, Fogarty and Hill could scarcely have been more dissimilar, but their commitment to a common goal transcended this social and regional gap.[36]

As Mahoney had promised, Hill found that medical research attracted few, if any, real enemies. Major illnesses such as heart disease, stroke, and cancer made no distinctions as to party, religion, class, or powerful position, Presidents Eisenhower and Johnson both suffering heart attacks while in office. Opening hearings on NIH appropriations in 1960, Hill reminded his colleagues that five senators, including Taft and Arthur Vandenberg, had died of cancer in recent years. Lasker believed that NIH researchers should concentrate on applied research to develop cures for these killer diseases—such as the artificial heart, anticoagulant drugs, and cancer chemotherapy—rather than devote themselves solely to basic research. Her viewpoint, although disputed by many at NIH, helped to win votes in Congress by reminding lawmakers of their own mortality.[37]

With his courtly manner, medical background, and detailed grasp of each measure, Hill swayed Republicans and Democrats alike. Republican Charles Potter of Michigan found it "thrilling" to work under such a "real professional in these health programs" as Hill. Democrat Paul Douglas of Illinois, frustrated that he could not persuade the Senate to fund one of his own projects, openly expressed his admiration of Hill's skill as a proselytizer: "[Hill] is so persuasive, so charming, so quietly indispensable, and so personally self-effacing that we want to give him everything possible." But even the sympathetic Douglas commented that NIH had "money running out of their ears, money they do not always know what to do with."[38]

With a national research program generously funded, Hill broached the idea of international cooperation in medical research. Disease and disability, he told the Senate, are the common enemies of all humans; techniques to fight these ravages should be shared without regard to national boundaries. An obscure laboratory in Poland, Thailand, or Ecuador, he postulated, might produce a discovery with great implications for scientists in Washington, Paris, or London. Dr. Rusk also emphasized the importance of shortening the time between scientific achievements in the laboratory and their application at a patient's bedside. Hill's bill to authorize fifty million dollars annually to support exchange of research information, under a new National Institute for International Medical Research, was to win congressional approval in 1959. Dr. Milton Eisenhower indicated the Eisenhower administration's support, thereby clearing the path for what Hill hoped would be "a moral equivalent for war."[39]

"In recognition of distinguished service to libraries"

As a young congressman representing a predominantly poor, isolated agricultural district, Hill had sought to improve the lives of rural Americans. He had wangled additional postal routes to bring the Sears Roebuck catalog and other mail to their doors, supported the concept of rural electrification, and helped to establish REA cooperatives. He had pushed for cheaper fertilizer and low-interest government loans. During his second term in the Senate, he had led movements to bring telephone and hospital service to remote sections. In 1956, after almost a decade of effort, Hill finally succeeded in persuading Congress to allot federal funds for rural libraries.

As World War II wound down, Hill had put forth his first suggestion that

the federal government help provide books to relieve boredom and isolation in rural America and promote the Jeffersonian ideal of an educated
citizenry. Why not send out millions of volumes from army libraries, he
proposed, using surplus army ambulances as bookmobiles? Some books
reached rural areas under this concept but even the army, with its generous
supplies, could not make up for the lack of reading materials in rural areas.
With Representative Emily Taft Douglas of Illinois as co-sponsor, Hill
proposed in 1946 that the federal government allocate $25,000 a year to
help set up additional public libraries.[40]

Many members of Congress who had grown up in rural surroundings,
like House Speaker Sam Rayburn of Texas, favored this proposal. But
powerful Robert Taft insisted that constitutional responsibility for libraries
rested with states and communities. Although Hill found a Republican
supporter in George Aiken of Vermont, Taft's arguments prevailed. In
1950, the Senate approved this measure but the House voted it down. Even
young Representative John Kennedy, accustomed to New England's rich
library resources, questioned the wisdom of spending federal dollars for a
rural library program.[41]

One of Hill's most effective qualities, a Senate staff member noted, was
his extraordinary patience. After the Labor and Public Welfare Committee
approved one minor health measure, the chairman had announced: "Gen-
tlemen, that completes twelve years of work on my part. Now all we have
to do is get it through the House." Hill exhibited similar persistence in
support of rural libraries. In 1951, aided by Aiken and Paul Douglas, he
introduced a new bill, altered to meet some of Taft's objections. To press
his cause, Hill testified before a House subcommittee that thirty-three
million Americans had no library services whatever, while another thirty-
five million had wholly inadequate facilities. In his home state, with only
1.5 million public library books for three million residents, almost one-
third of Alabama citizens had no access to libraries. Using Taft's concept
of state responsibility, Alabama allocated a mere thirty-four cents per
capita for library services.[42]

Librarians, too, mounted a major offensive in behalf of this measure. In
the House, another Alabamian, Carl Elliott, elected in 1948, became a
major champion of this cause. Fortunately the library bill did not immediately run afoul of the political obstacles that had obstructed many an
education bill—the issues of religion and race. Public libraries, even if
racially segregated, served all students, whether they attended public or
parochial schools. Hill and his co-sponsors, anticipating states' rights

objections, had provided that states should control all federal money for library development.[43]

In June 1956, Congress and Eisenhower approved the Library Services Act authorizing 7.5 million dollars annually (later cut by Eisenhower and his supporters to two million dollars) to develop library services in rural areas. Jubilant librarians, recognizing Hill as the original sponsor of this measure and its consistent supporter, declared him an honorary member of the American Library Association "in recognition of distinguished service to libraries." Five years after passage of this act, a hundred rural counties had been aided to develop libraries, six million books purchased, and state and local funding increased by over 50 percent. As in the Hill-Burton bill, "seed money" again reaped an abundant harvest.[44]

In 1961, Hill, Elliott, and John Fogarty, with crucial tactical help from Speaker Rayburn, would lead a successful drive to extend this act for five years. Once converted, President Kennedy proved an enthusiast, recommending not only 7.5 million dollars annually but extending this principle to include urban areas and construction. As the Senate debated this bill on the fateful afternoon of 22 November 1963, the stunning news of the president's assassination burst upon that chamber. When members resumed their duties four days later, their first act was to approve the late president's proposal; House passage quickly followed. One partisan commented: "The [library] bill passed really as a memorial tribute to President Kennedy. . . . every library built or renovated since that time has been a partial Presidential library. . . ."[45]

While a senator, John Kennedy had linked his name with that of Hill on another library matter. The old Army medical library, located in an ancient, red-brick Washington building without an elevator, toilet facilities, or adequate lighting, had fallen on hard times. Years passed in which this library did not purchase a single book; the job of director usually went to a senior Army medical officer on his final tour of duty. Since the end of World War II, several commissions had debated what to do about this situation; at hearings before his committee, Hill listened to various proposals including a bid to move that facility to Chicago.[46]

In 1956, the Hill-Kennedy bill, authorizing a new building to house the library, passed Congress. Dr. Frank B. Rogers, who was to become the new library's first director, remembered Hill's close involvement in all details of this project. But as for Kennedy, Dr. Rogers recalled: "I had the feeling he was there in name only." Hill remembered later that Eisenhower "didn't recommend [the library] or support it a damn bit but he did sign it."

Its board decided to locate this new facility on an old golf course next to the National Institutes of Health in Bethesda. Construction would begin in 1959; the Army's holdings were to be moved to this modern building in 1962. One skyscraper wing of this new National Library of Medicine was to be named the Lister Hill National Center for Biomedical Communications.[47]

Defending TVA (while embarrassing the Eisenhower administration), winning the battles for free vaccine for children and for aid to rural libraries, funding a vast federal endeavor to find cures for killer diseases, helping to launch a modern medical research library—these were heady and positive achievements, the rewards of seniority, the proper concerns of a United States senator. But 1956 would pose other challenges to Hill's political ingenuity. He could not continue to serve "the cause" unless he won reelection. To do so would plunge Hill once again into the morass of racial politics.

CHAPTER 11

The Politics of Race

1 9 5 6 — 1 9 5 7

"I . . . will do all in my power to maintain segregation"

Prior to 1956, race had been a muted theme in Alabama politics compared to the bugaboo of Catholicism in the 1920s, the economic woes of the 1930s, and the threat of Hitlerism in the first half of the 1940s. During his 1944 campaign against Hill, Simpson had tried futilely to ignite the racial fuse. States' Righters, clamoring against Truman's civil rights proposals, had managed only one big political victory: the 1946 referendum on the Boswell amendment. Ritualistically, Hill, too, had sounded racial themes in his efforts to keep Alabama in the Democratic column in 1928, prevail over Simpson, and help stalemate Truman's efforts to end the poll tax and establish a permanent FEPC.

Except for a few minor incidents, the atmosphere in Montgomery had been calm in the months following the first *Brown* decision in 1954. Even after Senator James Eastland of Mississippi summoned Virginia Durr and Aubrey Williams before his Internal Security Subcommittee to answer charges of subversion, many of their Montgomery acquaintances regarded such accusations as "silly." Nonetheless, Clifford Durr's law practice dwindled and advertisers dropped their patronage of Williams's *Southern Farmer*. Privately Hill sought Lyndon Johnson's help in calming Eastland's investigative zeal. But Hill also deemed it prudent to maintain his distance between himself and these old friends. "I don't blame you one whit," the understanding Williams wrote. "The only thing that gets me down . . . is not ever seeing you and having some happy moments together such as we used to."[1]

Hill would also find it increasingly awkward to keep up his close ties with Justice Black. When Hill issued conventional expressions of "shock" and "dismay" over the first *Brown* decision, Grover Hall Jr. had scoffed: "Black is one of [Hill's] most intimate friends. They spend much time together plumbing Aristotle's *Politics* and speculating on the future glories of populism. . . . the senator must have shrewdly observed whether Justice Black was still taking his briefcase home . . . and other signs that the baby was coming." After all, the editor added, the timing of the *Brown* opinion "had a lot of bearing on the outcome of the Sparkman-Battle race." But friends remembered later that "a little coolness" began to creep into this relationship as Black "took the heat" from fellow Southerners while Hill stoutly defended segregation. Hill's daughter, Henrietta, vividly recalled that her father had ordered that Black's picture be removed from its place of prominence in their home.[2]

The second *Brown* decision of 1955, with its cloudy directive that public schools be integrated with "all deliberate speed," also failed to provoke gut reactions in rank-and-file white Alabamians. These combustible people would exhibit a rising sense of alarm, however, in the wake of simpler, more readily comprehended actions—a black congressman having a social cocktail with the governor of Alabama, a black woman refusing to move to the back of the bus, a black student seeking to enter the hitherto whites-only University of Alabama. The first two events in this trilogy took place in Hill's hometown late in 1955; the third at his alma mater in Tuscaloosa in February 1956.

In November 1955, Folsom, who had been overwhelmingly reelected to a second term one year earlier, invited a visiting black congressman, Adam Clayton Powell of New York, to sit down with him for a Scotch and soda in the governor's mansion, thereby committing what most white Alabamians regarded as an unpardonable breach of the racial mores. Largely due to this incident and to his subsequent moderate expressions on racial issues, Folsom was never to regain his hold over the majority of Alabama's white voters.[3]

Less than a month later, Rosa Parks, a black seamstress, refused a Montgomery bus driver's order to yield her seat to a white passenger. Her arrest inspired a court suit, challenging the constitutionality of segregated public transportation, and a year-long bus boycott by Montgomery blacks. This open demonstration of long-concealed black resentment provoked a violent response: a bomb damaged the home of Dr. Martin Luther King Jr., a young minister just emerging as the major public spokesman for the boycott. In rural areas near Montgomery, the Citizens' Council, organized to foster grassroots white intransigency, spread in a few months from five to seventeen Black Belt counties.[4]

As 1956 opened, the overwhelming majority of Alabama legislators, invoking an ancient and generally discredited doctrine, formally declared the *Brown* decision "null, void and of no effect" in their state. Folsom, digging his political grave ever deeper, commented: "Just a bunch of hogwash." But Hill, composing his response on a Senate memo pad, put the best face he could on this futile action: "Interposition was first suggested and exercised by Kentucky and Virginia under the leadership of Thomas Jefferson and James Madison and since then interposition has been used a number of times. The Legislature of Alabama had a good precedent for its action which was entirely constitutional and legal. I support the State of Alabama and its interposition." A few weeks later, Sam Engelhardt of Tuskegee, leader of the Citizens' Council movement in Alabama, was able to display fifteen thousand members and sympathizers at a Montgomery rally where Eastland denounced Communism, integration, and civil rights.[5]

When Autherine Lucy attempted unsuccessfully to become the first black student at the University of Alabama that February, Hill and Sparkman adopted a hands-off position: this crisis belonged to Folsom and the university Board of Trustees. But there would be no escape hatch when Strom Thurmond and Harry Byrd devised what was to be termed the "Southern Manifesto," criticizing the *Brown* decision and urging its reversal. One hundred southern senators and representatives, including the entire Alabama congressional delegation, signed this political document intended primarily for southern consumption. Among Southerners in the Senate only Kefauver, Albert Gore, and Lyndon Johnson felt secure—or ambitious—enough to ignore this declaration. The *Washington Post* found it regrettable that progressive southerners like Hill, Sparkman, and Fulbright had deemed it necessary to sign a proposal seeking "to nullify a decision of the Supreme Court." But northern Democrats like Herbert Lehman and Paul Douglas, realizing that these colleagues might be replaced by extreme reactionaries on political and economic issues, tempered their comments on the "Manifesto."[6]

To Engelhardt, who congratulated him on this stand, Hill responded: "I . . . will do all in my power to maintain segregation." Yet not every white Alabamian applauded. "Your name on such a document," Jo Richardson wrote, "is a great blow to the hopes of many fair-minded Southerners, white as well as black. . . . I can only conclude that you have become a victim of political expediency." Hoping to appease this former supporter, Hill responded that he had acted to protect two fundamental rights: to choose one's associates and to determine the educational destinies of one's children. Had Hill attempted to defend the preeminence of these rights to Justice Black during one of their philosophical discussions, the evening might well have ended in a rousing argument.[7]

"Hill runs scared even when he is not running"

When Congress convened in January 1956, Hill found himself one of its nine senior members. Only six House members and two senators, Walter George of Georgia and Carl Hayden of Arizona, both in their late seventies, had served in Congress longer than he. Only seven members had been in the Senate more years than Hill. His immense experience, geniality, and long record of commitment to improving the human condition caused many Democratic colleagues to look to Hill for leadership in long-range planning. As a young House member in the heady days of the New Deal, Hill had been the leading spirit in gathering fellow progressives for informal meetings to plot their future course. In the early 1950s, he had revived these dinners. The "Lister Hill Club," a group of some twenty-five progressive Democrats including Paul Douglas, Bill Fulbright, John F. Kennedy, Hubert Humphrey, and Mike Mansfield, met at the Occidental Restaurant at their leader's invitation. Occasionally an "alumnus" like Frank Graham or seventy-eight-year-old Herbert Lehman, who had retired from the Senate at the end of 1956, rejoined these gatherings.[8]

On Hill's sixty-first birthday in late December 1955, the *Montgomery Advertiser* had judged him to be as lean, vigorous, and wary as ever. Grover Hall Jr. observed that, although some Alabamians wished their senator "would choke," it appeared obvious from Hill's lack of a prominent opponent that "many more wish him well." Only a "crank or merely nominal candidate," Hall predicted, would think of challenging such a powerful incumbent. But even though Hill appeared to be "about as close to unassailable politically as they come," this shrewd commentator perceived that "Hill runs scared even when he is not running." Never, Hall forecast, would Hill allow himself to get in a plight like that of Walter George, who was about to be dumped by his state's power structure on grounds that George had become more interested in national and international matters than in promoting the affairs of Georgia in the nation's capital.[9]

Months before the May 1956 Democratic primary, his traditional foes had begun to discuss who might have a chance to unseat Hill when he sought reelection to his fourth Senate term. Names like Frank Samford and Laurie Battle had been bruited about but no major opponent appeared ready to take on this task. Ed Dannelly of the *Andalusia Star-News* advised the senator that he had "the most powerful hold on the Alabama constituency of any man in my lifetime." Neil Davis of the *Lee County Bulletin* attributed this seeming invincibility to widespread appreciation for Hill's many years of effort to improve schools, farms, pay, working conditions, and health.[10]

But even one in such wide political favor could stumble fatally should he commit a racial faux pas as had the well-meaning but maladroit Folsom. Hill had always accepted this basic reality of political survival in Alabama. Never had he indicated—except perhaps in his earlier conversations with Justice Black—that he was anything but a staunch advocate of the racial status quo. Since his first days in the Senate, he had vigorously opposed every threat of federal interference in matters affecting race. Because he had so carefully protected this flank, Hill had escaped having his career foreshortened like that of gentle Frank Graham or his status diminished like that of outspoken Claude Pepper. Now he had no intention of sacrificing his hard-earned Senate power by emulating the hapless Folsom or the idealistic but politically impotent Durrs and Aubrey Williams.

Members of Alabama's House delegation, some of whom aspired to the Senate, had long sought to catch Hill in a vulnerable position on race. Expressing their general realism, one concluded: "Civil rights would be the last issue on which I would challenge Hill." Only a political tyro would essay such an apparently hopeless task.[11]

Running against Hill as an independent in 1950, John Crommelin had failed to carry a single county. In the 1954 Democratic primary, he had won only 3.5 percent of the total anti-Sparkman vote. Undeterred, Crommelin decided in the winter of 1956 to make a third try for the Senate. "That sore thumb John Crommelin has bobbed up again," Harry Ayers advised Hill. Billy Partlow of Tuscaloosa commented wryly: "First time I ever heard of a Republican running in a Democratic primary." The *Opelika Daily News* expressed consternation: "Throw [Hill] out now because a former naval officer wants to vent his spleen? Unthinkable!"[12]

Seeking organized support, Crommelin made common cause with Asa ("Ace") Earl Carter, executive secretary of the North Alabama Citizens' Council. "The mountain people . . . the real redneck . . . is our strength," Carter had proclaimed. But in actuality Carter found more support in the union and working-class elements around Birmingham than among isolated and independent-minded farmers of the north Alabama hill country. Unlike Engelhardt, who sought to enlist middle-class respectables, including Jews and Catholics, in a movement focused solely against black civil rights, Carter barred Jews from joining his councils, threatened to put federal judges in jail, and called for Folsom's impeachment. Although Engelhardt condemned Carter as a "fascist," Carter's assumption of this label would seriously diminish the council's reputation for respectable protest. More than a decade later, Engelhardt was to comment bitterly: "Ace . . . killed the Council dead."[13]

In early 1956, however, Crommelin perceived Carter as a natural ally. The admiral, a frequent speaker at Carter rallies, boasted that he would "make Lister Hill join the Citizens' Council or tell us why he won't." Crommelin also sought to persuade these listeners that Hill had introduced the resolution to abolish the two-thirds rule at the 1936 Democratic convention and that, by sponsoring the Hill-Burton program, federal aid to education, and the tidelands oil bill, Hill sought to break down segregation in hospitals and schools. These allegations paled, however, in comparison to Crommelin's most extravagant claim: Hill, he said, planned to use the mental health research program as a means of committing his political enemies to a mental hospital in Alaska. Reporting this to Hill's office, Clarence Allgood asked: "How crazy can you get?"[14]

Meantime the more moderate Montgomery County Citizens' Council demanded that all candidates for statewide office respond to a list of racially loaded questions such as: "Do you here and now say to the negro [sic] that you do not want his vote?" By 1956, fifty-three thousand blacks, comprising only 6 percent of Alabama's total registered voters, had managed to surmount the standardized literacy test that had replaced the Boswell amendment, the cumulative poll tax, and other barriers to exercise of the ballot. Although black voters were relatively few in number, their leaders quietly put out word as to which candidates they preferred. Like the more extreme whites, black voters sensed that Hill's words and actions in behalf of segregation were pro forma political expressions. Far better that they trust a member of the white gentry, who had demonstrated his concern for the poor and underprivileged even while mouthing racial shibboleths, than desist from voting and thereby help Crommelin's cause.[15]

Folsom, running for Democratic national committeeman in hope of recouping his political fortunes, refused to answer the Citizens' Council questionnaire. Hill ignored the specific questions but—more canny than Folsom—he wrote across this questionnaire: "I shall continue to fight as I have fought through the years for the maintenance of segregation and the Southern customs, traditions and way of life."[16]

At first Hill sought to ignore Crommelin as he had Lawrence McNeil in 1950. But Crommelin's fantasies, spread by printed circulars, seemed to demand some form of denial. Hill's campaign office pointed out that the senator had not attended the 1936 Democratic convention and that the Hill-Burton bill specifically called for racial segregation in hospitals. But aside from this formal denial, Hill did not deign to campaign against Crommelin. Through advertisements and press releases, he reminded voters once again of his support for New Deal measures, national defense, international cooperation for peace, rural hospitals and telephones, TVA, free polio vaccine, and health research, and his opposition to Dixon-Yates, discriminatory freight rates, FEPC, and attempts by Congress to abolish the poll tax, outlaw lynching, and curb the filibuster.[17]

With no lively gubernatorial race to entertain them and with Hill's reelection a virtual certainty, most white voters appeared indifferent as to who would represent Alabama in the highest councils of the national Democratic party and at its national convention. Those who did turn out proved once again the power of racial rhetoric. Charles W. McKay Jr., the head of Talladega's Citizens' Council but a virtual unknown in statewide politics, handed Folsom the worst defeat of his career. McKay, who had scorchingly decried the governor's inactivity on the bus boycott and the Autherine Lucy matter and had branded Folsom as "host of the whiskey-drinking Negro Congressman from Harlem," won 232,000 votes to only 79,000 for Folsom and 44,000 for a third candidate. The governor carried only five north Alabama counties. With one exception, Folsom's entire slate went down to defeat. The *Alabama Journal* rejoiced over the "death knell of Folsomism" and the demise of the "Hill-Sparkman-Folsom dreibund."[18]

Other candidates, more widely known than McKay, also benefited from the politics of race. Laurie Battle, resoundingly defeated by Sparkman two years earlier, led the ticket for delegate at large to the national Democratic convention, polling twenty-five thousand votes more than Adlai Stevenson's former running mate. "Bull" Connor, who made a poor showing in the gubernatorial race of 1950, also earned a delegate slot in this statewide race. Circuit Judge George Wallace, who had criticized Folsom as "soft" on segregation, won a delegate seat from his congressional district, inspiring Rex Thomas, Alabama political analyst for the Associated Press, to forecast that Wallace would henceforth be a potent political factor. Alabama's delegation to the national Democratic convention was to be heavily weighted with Citizens' Council members, supporters, and other strong advocates of segregation.[19]

But at the same time that they made these choices based primarily on racist appeals, Alabamians gave Lister Hill 68 percent of their votes, the biggest percentage he had ever won in a senatorial race.[20] By remaining in Washington, Hill maintained his distance from the Citizens' Council and finessed the matter of whether he would speak at its rallies. Crommelin had failed in his boast to "make Lister Hill join the Citizens' Council." But he frightened Hill into intensifying his fulminations against even the slightest threat to the citadel of segregation.

Some observers found Crommelin's total vote surprisingly high. But this figure would have come as no shock to the astute Roy Nolen, who had long ago estimated Alabama's hard-core opponents of national Democratic policies at around 100,000. Simpson had received 101,000 votes in 1944. In 1950, the virtually unknown McNeil had attracted 112,000 anti-Hill votes. Now Crommelin had brought this number to 115,000, carrying four Black Belt counties and one other rural county, and coming within 500 votes of winning Mobile County (see Appendix, Map 5). But Crommelin's percentage of the total vote had been slightly lower than that of McNeil. Despite the surmise by some observers that the Citizens' Council had lured many rank-and-file union members away from their traditional allegiance, the *Andalusia Star-News* characterized Crommelin's total as "the usual vote that can be classified as anti-Hill, regardless of who is the Senator's opposition."[21]

At least a national election would provide some respite from political infighting in Alabama. In Chicago, southern Democrats bargained to support the nomination of Adlai Stevenson in exchange for a watered-down plank on civil rights in their party's platform. With the Republican party courting black support more strongly than that of the white South, dissident Democrats in Alabama found themselves bereft of their favorite issue and of their best argument for a political alternative. Stevenson carried Alabama in November by a 56.5 percent majority. Without Sparkman as his running mate, the Democratic nominee polled almost 10 percent fewer votes in Alabama than four years earlier. No Republican took on the apparently hopeless task of defeating Hill.[22]

Meantime the court case sparked by Rosa Parks's arrest made its way toward a significant finale. Clifford Durr quietly assisted Fred Gray, the Montgomery attorney who served as counsel for the NAACP in the case of

Browder v. Gayle. Shortly after Gray had instigated this case, a local draft board reclassified him from deferred status to 1-A, indicating eligibility for immediate service. When General Lewis Hershey, head of the national draft board, overruled the Montgomery unit, Hill deemed it expedient to call for a congressional investigation of Hershey's action.[23]

As this flap died down, Gray pressed his case before a three-judge panel composed of Richard Rives, Frank Johnson, and Seybourn H. Lynne. With Lynne dissenting, Rives and Johnson ruled that segregation on public buses violated the equal-protection and due-process clauses of the Fourteenth Amendment. In December 1956—following the national election—the Supreme Court affirmed this majority opinion. Ending their long boycott, blacks boarded Montgomery buses to sit wherever they chose.

His natural caution had again ensured Hill's political survival. Now his instincts—honed over more than three decades—told him that passions over the issue of race were to become even more heated. Already Folsom had fallen victim to his moderation and impulsivity over racial issues. Only because Sparkman had been the 1950 vice presidential nominee had he been able to wrest the chairmanship of Alabama's Democratic convention delegation—and its consequent power—away from Laurie Battle. As the fight over civil rights intensified, it was to provide the ideal smokescreen for further efforts by those who had sought so long and unsuccessfully to unseat Hill. "Running scared" even though he had a fresh, six-year mandate, Hill would seek to armor himself even more strongly against further challenges from the right.

"They won concessions by being the fine men they are"

During a presidential election year, concerted efforts to pass civil rights bills had been shelved by tacit consent of both major parties. Democrats, as proof of their commitment, had approved the administration's moderate proposal in mid-1956 but delayed forwarding this measure to the Senate until the closing days of that session, too late to set off a long and heated filibuster. Wary Lyndon Johnson, anticipating the transmittal of this House bill, had stationed Hill as presiding officer of that chamber. The House messenger appeared at the door of an almost deserted Senate during an hour when most members were at lunch. Hill—fully realizing its import—looked over the chamber, saw no senator who might object, and quickly interrupted Mike Mansfield so as to receive the message. "Without objec-

tion," Hill committed the controversial measure to the "Eastland grave-
yard" of the Senate Judiciary Committee. Here it would rest until the start
of a new Congress. As 1957 opened, Hill told the *Montgomery Advertiser*
that "the toughest fight ever" over civil rights loomed ahead.[24]

This struggle began with parliamentary maneuvers. Civil rights advocates, determined not to be caught napping when another House-approved
bill reached the Senate, enlisted enough Democrats to bring this measure
directly to the floor, thereby circumventing Eastland. Next they sought to
limit the traditional right of filibustering. Majority leader Johnson won this
second skirmish but, fearing that the southern bloc might eventually lose
its cherished weapon, Johnson devised a new strategy. Southerners would
not filibuster lest they lose this right altogether. Instead, they would seek to
weaken the administration's bill while reserving the filibuster for use
against tougher measures sure to come. Hill, like most Southerners, followed Johnson's lead.[25]

As his contribution to this strategy, Hill focused on one controversial
aspect of the program proposed by Attorney General Herbert Brownell Jr.:
a provision empowering the attorney general to bring injunctions charging
criminal violations of civil rights. For fear that southern juries would not
convict, such trials were to take place without juries. The AFL-CIO,
evidently having forgotten the days when its leaders fought for jury trials
for those charged by injunction in labor disputes, now supported the
concept that alleged violators of civil rights should be deprived of this
traditional right.[26]

In a major speech, Hill assailed the dangers of "government by injunction." Recalling that he had for thirty-four years endeavored to work for
"forward-looking policies and programs that meant progress" such as
Social Security, the Fair Labor Standards Act, the Wagner Act, and the act
creating the National Institutes of Health, Hill deplored a return to the
"judicial tyranny" that existed before the Norris-LaGuardia Act of 1932
had guaranteed jury trials to those charged with violating "yellow dog"
contracts. To bolster his argument, he quoted labor's old hero Samuel
Gompers, Justice Felix Frankfurter, the 1928 platforms of both major
parties, and a recent editorial in the *New York Times* questioning the
wisdom of this provision.[27]

But Hill's most effective work in behalf of jury trials took place behind
the scenes. Labor was not wholly united on this issue. To further widen this
split, Hill persuaded John L. Lewis, still smarting from the five-million-
dollar fine he had incurred for defying a federal judge's injunction, and the

traditionally segregationist Railroad Brotherhoods to pressure wavering senators to vote for a jury trial amendment. As finally approved, the Civil Rights Act of 1957 contained a compromise. Trials might take place with or without juries except in case of a fine of more than three hundred dollars or a jail term in excess of forty-five days; those so penalized might demand a jury trial. Hill deemed it "ridiculous" that the question of a jury trial could be decided by a one-cent difference in the amount of the fine or a one-minute difference in the length of a jail term. "If a man is a little bad, he has no right to a jury trial," he pointed out, "whereas if he is very bad, he shall have that right."[28]

But in Alabama, the jury trial fight had a significant side effect: by allowing *any* citizen over twenty-one to serve on a federal jury, it set women, heretofore barred from jury service altogether, along the road to attaining this basic and long-sought duty of citizenship.[29]

In their zeal, civil rights advocates had left themselves vulnerable to a charge of violating one basic constitutional right while trying to guarantee another. Hill, always in search of constitutional arguments with which to combat civil rights measures, must have been delighted at the opportunity to defend such a hallowed cause as jury trial and to point out labor's inconsistency. Furthermore, as columnist Doris Fleeson noted, no senator wanted to cause colleagues like Hill, Russell, and John Stennis to lose face. "They won concessions," she concluded, "by being the fine men they are." Only five southern senators voted for the eventual Civil Rights Act of 1957: Kefauver and Albert Gore of Tennessee, Johnson and newly elected Ralph Yarborough of Texas, and Smathers. Instead of obstructing this mild yet historic measure, Johnson had helped clear the way for its passage, thus transforming himself from a regional politician to a national figure and potential presidential candidate.[30]

If Hill ever doubted that his own longevity in the Senate was worth its price in struggle, compromise, and occasional alliance with southern reactionaries, he must have been reassured by other events during the summer of 1957. In the face of an economy drive led by Johnson and House Speaker Sam Rayburn, the Senate approved Hill's request for five million dollars to bolster rural libraries and thirty-two million dollars more than Eisenhower had requested for medical research into potential cures for cancer, arthritis, heart disease, neurological problems, and mental illness. In August, Hill, Sparkman, Gore, and other champions of TVA beat back further efforts by the Eisenhower administration and private power interests to (as Hill put it) "kill" TVA by putting its finances under the Budget

Bureau, giving the secretary of the treasury a veto over its activities, and appointing an opponent of TVA to its board.[31]

During floor debate over increased medical research funds, sixteen of Hill's colleagues, ranging in political philosophy from Eastland and Stennis of Mississippi and Arizona's Goldwater, on the right, to Morse and Neuberger of Oregon and Pastore of Rhode Island, on the left, had risen spontaneously to pay tribute to the sponsor of this measure. Pastore and Neuberger praised Hill's humanitarianism and his "enduring monument" of health research; Eastland asserted that no member in the history of the Senate had sponsored more "constructive legislation" than Lister Hill.[32]

"A Bombay snake charmer could learn some lessons from [Hill]"

After this major struggle over the Civil Rights Act of 1957, Hill uncharacteristically took a vacation. He and his wife—at their own expense, he later let it be known—went to a meeting in London and thence for a pleasure trip on the Continent. While Hill had been abroad in 1937, Roosevelt had nominated Hugo Black for the Supreme Court. Even more momentous events transpired when the Hills took this European sojourn. On 24 September 1957, Eisenhower dispatched federal troops to ensure the integration of Little Rock's Central High School; a few days later, the Russians stunned the world by launching Sputnik, an artificial Earth satellite. "You have missed a lot of fireworks," Clarence Allgood wrote Hill. Sparkman, on a tour of Asia, sent home statements condemning the president's Little Rock action, surprising a *Montgomery Advertiser* editor who had doubted that Sparkman "would even be audacious enough to endorse the Ten Commandments without waiting for Hill."[33]

Upon his return, Hill, describing Eisenhower as having "invaded the soil of a sister state with armed troops," joined the southern chorus of condemnation. But beneath this seeming outrage, he must have felt relieved. Now that the president had taken such drastic action, "Eisenhower Democrats" in Alabama would find it more difficult to foster Republicanism. As one Thomasville Democrat put it: "I certainly hope that our milk-and-water Alabamians who voted for Eisenhower are ashamed of themselves now."[34]

Addressing a major rally of Alabama Democrats in December, Hill spent fifty-one minutes—keeping his audience up late at night—excoriating Eisenhower's "incompetent and derelict administration," stressing the futility of another "splinter party" effort, and extolling the Democratic party as "our buckler and our shield . . . the means of our deliverance from economic exploitation by the North and East." To desert the Democrats, he warned, would strip the South of its major chairmanships in Congress. His weary listeners included a greatly subdued Jim Folsom and several of those who hoped to succeed the governor in 1959, including Jimmy Faulkner of Bay Minette, widely rumored to be the choice of the "machine" masterminded by Hill, Sparkman, Foots Clement, and the state Democratic chairman, Roy Mayhall.[35]

To celebrate the holidays and another birthday, Hill returned to Montgomery. Bob Ingram, a longtime political reporter, found the senator jaunty, relaxed, and willing to answer almost any question. No, Hill said, he had not attended the recent wedding of Hugo Black to his second wife. Yes, the South could solve its racial problems if it could convince citizens in other areas that federal pressure to integrate would soon fall upon *them*; Americans would then demand repeal of this new civil rights measure as they had prohibition. "A Bombay snake charmer could learn some lessons from the senator," Ingram marveled. But despite his good humor and professed optimism, Hill knew that civil rights supporters would not rest on their 1957 laurels; thus he was soon to face renewed demands for proof of his southern fealty.[36]

The Shifting Sands of Politics

I 9 5 8 – I 9 6 I

"The Scylla of race and the Charybdis of religion"

Sputnik caused a nationwide sense of crisis in the United States in the fall of 1957; many Americans compared the Russians' startling feat to the Japanese attack on Pearl Harbor. This achievement did more than damage American pride and prestige; it fueled fears that the Russians now led in the arms race as well as in space. Out of this national mood of panic and depression, which lasted for months, arose a widespread demand that the federal government do something to restore American technological preeminence and military strength.[1]

Hill had been in Berlin when the Russians announced the launching of Sputnik; thus he sensed the panicky reaction of western Europe before that of the United States. On his first day back at Capitol Hill, he found atop the messages piled on his desk a memorandum from Stewart McClure, chief clerk of the Labor and Public Welfare Committee, who had been quick to envision how his boss could use this crisis to achieve a goal that Hill had sought for almost four decades. Minutes later, Hill summoned his committee staff: "Got your memorandum, St'rt, let's see what we can do."[2]

Hill had been reared in a family in which education had been regarded as indispensable, at least for men. Dr. Hill and Professor Starke had reinforced this belief; furthermore, one who admired Thomas Jefferson could scarcely fail to consider education as the surest means of bringing about an enlightened citizenry. As the young chairman of the Montgomery Board of Education, Hill had observed firsthand the low salaries of teachers and the meagerly equipped schools of the South. In his first political campaign, he had adopted his father's suggestion that to propose federal funding for education would attract the votes of poor but ambitious white voters. When he reached the Senate, Hill had set out to make his mark—and advance "the cause"—by broadening the federal government's commitment to education.

But numerous opponents, starting with Ray Rushton in 1923, had fought this concept by raising the specter of centralized control or the more emotional issues of religion and integration. Despite many attempts, Hill had been unsuccessful in steering a federal aid to education bill between what he called "the Scylla of race and the Charybdis of religion."[3]

During his first term in the Senate, he and Elbert Thomas of Utah had proposed that the federal government commit $300 million annually to education, to be divided among states on the basis of school attendance and financial need. Marshall Field's newspaper, *PM*, noted that such a formula would be of particular benefit to southern blacks due to a provision that racial minorities should receive their pro-rata share of federal money. But even in the midst of an all-out war, the racial issue—plus opposition from richer states—had doomed this measure.[4]

In 1946, Hill's proposal that the federal government provide funds to help equalize hospital facilities over the nation had breezed through Congress. But his efforts to apply this same principle to help equalize educational opportunities failed even though Hill had persuaded "Mr. Republican" Robert Taft that federal aid would be economically justifiable as a means of overcoming illiteracy and upgrading job skills. Catholics, their schools barred from federal benefits, bitterly criticized the Hill-Taft-Thomas bill. Protestant denominations—particularly Southern Baptists—uttered cries of alarm at any potential breach in the wall between church and state. With help from Walter George, Hill managed to boost federal funds for the less controversial area of vocational education; otherwise his efforts in behalf of education bore no fruit.[5]

In debates over Hill-Burton, fears of federal control had been quickly laid to rest by assurances that states would handle the distribution of federal funds and that segregation would not be threatened. Clearly, health-related measures—if pushed by powerful figures and skilled lobbyists of the medical establishment—could be passed at a time when education bills remained stalemated.

In vain, Hill pointed out the inequity between children in predominantly rural and low-income states like Alabama and those in vastly richer states like New York. In the 1940s, Alabama ranked eighth among the forty-eight states in the percentage of its tax monies spent for public education; New York ranked forty-second. Yet in 1949, Alabama's almost 2.5 percent of total tax income dedicated to education yielded only $87 per year for each schoolchild; whereas New York, by committing only 1.5 percent of its funds for this purpose, raised $213 annually per child. Not only did southern states have less income with which to finance education, but the percentage of children to adults remained higher in the South than in other areas.[6]

Trying a new approach, Hill focused on offshore oil as a potentially rich source of nontax funds for national needs. Use of revenues from public lands to support education, he pointed out, had been sanctioned by the Founding Fathers. Now he proposed to extend this concept and that of the Morrill Act of 1862, which had granted public lands to states to establish colleges, to earmark revenues from offshore oil for the support of American education. To bypass the religious issue, Hill proposed that this money be placed in trust for later appropriation to schools.[7]

Roars of outrage from oil producers and politicians in Texas, Louisiana, and California, who regarded what they called "tidelands oil" as state property, drowned out the voices of educators, parents, and labor-union representatives who favored this proposal. Hill had no luck this time in winning over Taft; furthermore, Lyndon Johnson, attuned to Texas oil interests, added his powerful opposition. Even in Alabama, with its miniscule coastline, representatives of vested interests in oil revenues called Hill a "communist"; some suggested that his next step would be to nationalize coal and iron deposits. Although Sparkman followed Hill's lead, members of Alabama's House delegation, influenced by Sam Hobbs, who expressed his objections in constitutional terms, opposed their senators.[8]

Nonetheless, Hill doggedly pushed "oil-for-education" from 1951 to 1955. When Congress voted to uphold the claims of states to all oil within their historic three- or ten-mile coastal boundaries, he countered with a proposal to reserve for education the oil revenues from beyond this limit to the outer edge of the continental shelf—a distance of 150 miles at some points. Hill's perseverance paid off when the Senate passed his amendment, co-sponsored by a bipartisan group of thirty-four colleagues. The *Congressional Record* noted that during this debate a number of senators— including some who opposed this measure—again spoke warmly of Hill's leadership in behalf of education and health. But behind the closed doors of a congressional conference, House members, less susceptible to the blandishments of the senator from Alabama, joined Republican senators in agreeing to give the federal government paramount rights over lands beyond the traditional three- and ten-mile limits but refusing to earmark such oil revenues for education. There the idea of "oil-for-education" died. At least, Hill reflected privately, this fight may have helped to prevent the "grabbing of other great national resources" such as public lands and forests, mineral deposits, and public power projects.[9]

Perhaps the next best hope would lie in supporting Eisenhower's proposal for federal aid to school construction. Hill introduced his own costlier version of this concept. But again the threat of riders from civil rights advocates, plus opposition from Catholics whose schools had not been included in Hill's bill, stymied this approach. As racial tensions rose, prospects for federal aid to education fell. Early in 1957, Crampton Harris urged Hill not to put his name on any bill to improve education or hospitals. "You should be free to fight the riders," Harris advised, "without being stigmatized as the author of iniquitous (from the Alabama viewpoint) legislation." Drew Pearson described Hill as "worried sick" over the possibility of a rider by Adam Clayton Powell, adding: "The great senator is acquiring the title of 'Fence Sitter Hill' because of his skittishness over the school bill." Thus matters stood while the battle raged over the 1957 civil rights bill and the Russians prepared for their coup.[10]

"A matter of national survival"

Although Stewart McClure invented this bill's appealing title, he had not been alone in envisioning the possibility of passing a federal aid to education measure in the name of national defense. Eisenhower and high-ranking members of his administration also sensed this chance to put an education measure of their own devising on the books. So did Carl Elliott, who had represented coal miners and hard-scrabble farmers of northwest Alabama in Congress for almost ten years.[11]

Elliott's interest had arisen, not due to family or philosophical influences like those that had attracted Hill to this cause, but out of his own struggle for a formal education. Like Sparkman, Elliott had come from plain farm folk. When he had arrived at the age of sixteen on the Tuscaloosa campus of the University of Alabama, Elliott had only two dollars in his pocket. He had cut grass, fired furnaces, painted roofs, and swept floors to pay for his A.B. and law degrees; he also came under the influence of that political entrepreneur Foots Clement.[12]

From the day he arrived in Congress, Elliott had determined to make federally sponsored college scholarships his top priority. He introduced a

bill to this effect in every session. As chairman of a special subcommittee
of the House Education and Labor Committee, he conducted hearings on
the topic of student financial aid throughout the nation during the fall of
1957. When Graham Barden of North Carolina, chairman of the House
Education and Labor Committee, announced his opposition to federal aid
to education for any purpose, Elliott became floor manager for this cause;
thus a historic measure was to be guided through Congress by two Alabamians.[13]

With numerous aides and supporters, Hill and Elliott spent most of the
holiday season of 1957 in a suite of rooms in Birmingham's Tutwiler
Hotel, feverishly preparing their proposal. Abandoning the approach of
school construction, they focused on the more opportune idea of linking
scientific manpower needs and national security as a rationale for providing language laboratories, modern scientific equipment, scholarships and
loans for promising students, and training institutes for teachers. The Hill-
Elliott proposal was to affect all levels of public education from first grade
through doctoral studies.[14]

Meantime, HEW Secretary Marion B. Folsom and Assistant Secretary
Eliot Richardson obeyed Eisenhower's mild directive to "get something
new and in the public mood" but not too expensive or too broadly based.
Eisenhower preferred to center narrowly on science education rather than
to secure any extensive crash program. The administration bill would
prove more generous to schools; the Hill-Elliott bill would focus on individual students. Meantime, the education establishment stubbornly continued to push for a general aid measure. When Congress convened in
January 1958, its members faced these three approaches to the same
problem.[15]

Elliott's challenge—generally considered impossible—would be to get
the rambunctious House to approve any form of federal aid to education.
Hill's role—eminently suited to his talents—would be to reconcile his and
Elliott's ideas with the broad but unrealistic aspirations of the professional
educators, on the one hand, and, on the other, the president's profound
conviction that "God helps those who help themselves." Adopting a posture of brisk optimism, the Alabamians set about to win—if not everything—something.[16]

During seven weeks of hearings before his Labor and Public Welfare
Committee, Hill employed the technique that had worked so well in attracting support for health measures. He ordered his staff to round up star
witnesses such as Dr. Lee DuBridge, president of the California Institute

of Technology; Wernher von Braun, of the Army's ballistic missile agency at Huntsville; Dr. Edward Teller, "father of the H-Bomb," and Vice Admiral Hyman G. Rickover, "father of the nuclear sub." Each of these high-powered witnesses paid lip service to the idea of local responsibility while comparing American public education unfavorably with that of the Russians. Stewart McClure, who helped to arrange this testimony, remembered: "If anybody brought up the . . . dreadful spectre of socialism, we had Edward Teller and the Hydrogen Bomb to clobber them with."[17]

Other witnesses proved less tractable. Professional educators reiterated their plea for general aid; engineers and spokesmen for the Scientific Manpower Commission refused to go along with the argument that America lagged behind the Russians. Some senators, like the forthright Ralph Flanders of Vermont, also rejected this "false assumption." But Hill ignored those who would not play his game. Concluding his hearings, he stressed again that "the finest minds in the nation" had advised the Senate to act on education reform as "a matter of national survival."[18]

As spring and summer passed, delicate behind-the-scenes negotiations proceeded among Hill, Elliott, who was conducting hearings of his own, and Richardson, who was trying to keep Eisenhower in line. Both sides determined to resolve their differences in the interest of passing an education bill. In hope of avoiding riders, assurances were given to Adam Clayton Powell that the program would be antidiscriminatory; parochial schools were made eligible for federal loans to upgrade the teaching of science, math, and foreign languages.

But as Hill's hearings neared an end, Alexander Smith of New Jersey created a heated controversy by proposing that professors be required to take loyalty oaths before receiving any federal funds. Cries of indignation rose from the academic community. "We'll get rid of it later," Hill had whispered to an aide when Smith proposed this idea. But Jack Kennedy, too impatient to wait for careful maneuvering and with presidential hopes uppermost in mind, hastily moved that the committee strike Smith's proposal from the bill. "Stewart, this will be recommitted," Hill accurately prophesied to McClure. Eventually, Hill, Kennedy, and the outraged academics were to see the so-called "loyalty oath" included in the revised bill. But Kennedy had scored highly with a professoriate that had hitherto regarded him as a lightweight.[19]

In the heat of August, each chamber passed its version of what Hill and Elliott still insisted was a "defense-education bill." This concept had become increasingly harder to uphold as the crisis mood over Sputnik faded and the United States launched satellites of its own. In conference, Elliott and Richardson lost their cherished idea of federal scholarships for talented students. Eisenhower privately opposed this departure from individualism; furthermore, a congressional majority could not swallow the idea of scholarships paid for by the federal government. Instead, the government would offer only low-interest student loans.[20]

On August 22—after further encomiums for Hill's "fruitful" career and legislative acumen—the Senate approved the conference report. Strom Thurmond issued one final blast, predicting that the measure would be unfair to the South by withholding funds from segregated schools and colleges. In the House, Carl Elliott's patience and willingness to compromise bore fruit shortly thereafter. Thirty southern and border-state members, who had opposed the previous school construction bill, voted for federal aid to education under the guise of aiding national defense. Commenting on the bill's diehard opponents in both houses, *Time* called the new law a "sore defeat for hard-rock States'-righters."[21]

Although they lost the scholarship program and had been forced to compromise on other issues, Hill, Elliott, and Richardson won their bipartisan battle. In the name of the Cold War, the National Defense Education Act (NDEA) of 1958 committed the federal government to a program of massive assistance to states, local communities, and private institutions. By the end of its first year, the NDEA had funded 1,000 fellowships for graduate students at 23 universities, trained 2,100 guidance counselors at 50 summer institutes, supported 12 foreign-language institutes to teach 925 teachers, and set up student loan funds at 1,201 colleges. Under its aegis, HEW had spent almost $35 million to assist elementary and secondary schools in obtaining scientific equipment and training supervisors. But of greater future significance, the NDEA proved to be a "psychological breakthrough." For the first time since 1862, the federal government made a major commitment to improve the quality of education throughout the nation. Further commitments were to follow.[22]

Signing the bill in September, Eisenhower again stressed its emergency and temporary nature. Some critics still muttered that national security had been a deceptive rationale for launching such a huge federal program. But the three major architects of new Public Law 864—Richardson, Hill, and Elliott—expressed pleasure over their bipartisan success. The *New York Times* praised Elliott for having achieved the seemingly impossible in bringing about House approval. But the "long-haul credit," said the *Times*, belonged to Lister Hill, who had patiently but persistently pushed for federal aid to education during the quarter of a century that such legislation had been pending in Congress.[23]

Indeed the NDEA victory must have been sweet for Hill. By cloaking his objective in the garb of national defense, he had successfully navigated federal aid between "the Scylla of race and the Charybdis of religion." Such dissembling might shock men from other regions of the country, like Wyoming's sole House member, Keith Thomson, who had warned the House not to be deceived about the "emergency" nature of this legislation, or Wisconsin's self-righteous Senator William Proxmire who had called the bill "a moral flop."[24] But Hill had come out of *southern* politics with its tradition of concealing real objectives behind high-sounding labels—like "states' rights." If the end be worthy, why not use his opponents' favorite tactic?

"Nixon Republicans in disguise"

Hill had other satisfactions in 1958. Alabama doctors gave him their Gorgas Award, named for the pioneering physician who had helped him qualify for the Army in World War I. The Tennessee Valley Public Power Association, recognizing TVA's longest congressional champion, gave Hill its distinguished service award to mark the twenty-fifth anniversary of the TVA Act. Another major river development that Hill had pushed for years finally got underway. The Alabama Power Company—in "partnership" (as Eisenhower put it) with the federal government—undertook a $120 million, multipurpose program on the Coosa River, with the federal government agreeing to build locks on these private dams and construct supplemental dams to make the Coosa and Alabama rivers navigable from Rome, Georgia, to Mobile. In midsummer, Congress voted to extend all provisions of the Hill-Burton program until June 1964.[25]

But Hill also witnessed during 1958 the first hard evidence that the race issue was eroding his heretofore impregnable political base. In their Spring primary, Alabama Democrats set out to nominate a governor and to elect new members to the State Democratic Executive Committee. At issue in the committee race—as usual—was the pledge of loyalty to the Democratic ticket. Loyalist Democrats had readopted an oath preventing those who had voted for Eisenhower and Nixon in 1956 from becoming candidates in their primary and requiring that all candidates pledge to support the primary winners in the next general election.[26]

In his column, John Temple Graves II objected to "blind allegiance to a national ticket that could be [Walter] Reuther, Roy Wilkins, Kefauver, or the unconscionable [G. Mennen] Soapy Williams." Other antiloyalists argued that killing the oath would allow Alabama Democrats to become an independent political force, free to deal with either party. But Sparkman, recalling the 1948 Dixiecrat revolt as a "deadend street mistake," responded: "Politics doesn't work that way." The oath, as Sparkman described it, "only says 'if you vote Republican you cannot run on the Democratic ticket.' "[27]

State Democratic Chairman Roy Mayhall labeled opponents of the oath "Nixon Republicans in disguise" who had been "undercover" since Little Rock. Privately, Clarence Allgood warned Hill that "our dear friends Sid Smyer, Frank Dixon, John Temple Graves and others of their stripe are again making an earnest effort to take the Committee away from us." Allgood also alerted Hill to a more ominous turn of events: "the Union voters . . . are straying away from us."[28]

In the May primary and runoff, antiloyalists placed a majority of what the *Alabama Journal* triumphantly called "real Alabama Democrats" on the SDEC; these members would soon elect Sam Engelhardt, former executive secretary of the Citizens' Council, as SDEC chairman. In the governor's race, Jimmy Faulkner, reputed to be Hill's choice, failed to make the runoff, as did John Crommelin who had presented himself as the candidate most opposed to race "mongrelizing." Instead, John Patterson, the only candidate independent of Folsom or his influence, defeated George Wallace, who had also denounced the outgoing governor but, to his dismay, found himself "outsegged." Wallace's defeat may have forestalled other long-range plans. Some Hill supporters suspected that, in return for financial backing from Dixiecrats, Wallace had pledged to use the office of governor to fight the reelections of Sparkman and Hill.[29]

However, Wallace was not the only Alabama political figure to be judged in 1958 as insufficiently tough against civil rights. Testing the political winds in south Alabama, John Horne, Sparkman's administrative assistant, reported that some former supporters of Hill and Sparkman doubted—no matter what the record showed—that Alabama's senators had been "strong enough and outspoken enough for segregation and against the Negro." Once again, Horne reported, opponents had used the race issue as a "smokescreen" behind which they laid other plans. The *Anniston Star* forecast that the Dixiecrats' "real motive" was to defeat Hill and Sparkman; the *Birmingham Post-Herald*, a Dixiecrat sympathizer, also hinted that the primary results "may have portents for Hill and Sparkman." Obviously alarmed, Hill pledged to filibuster eighteen hours—or longer if necessary—against any civil rights bill introduced in the next Congress.[30]

"There is no Republican Party in Dixie. Little Rock finished it."

By 1959, Hill had begun to enjoy the rewards of seniority, power, and prestige. Presidents of more than twelve hundred of the nation's colleges, realizing that their institutions could obtain nine federal dollars for every one dollar they put up, had received the National Defense Education Act with enthusiasm. In May, the Senate overwhelmingly approved his proposal to appropriate fifty million dollars annually for international cooperation in medical research, popularly known as "Health for Peace." Only Republican leader Everett Dirksen, who called this "squandermania," had bothered to raise his voice against a bill co-sponsored by sixty-three senators and thus certain to pass.[31]

Recognizing Hill's leadership of medically related legislation, seven hundred national leaders of the medical profession, government, and science gave him their "Health-USA" award at a large Washington luncheon. Dr. Howard Rusk—evidently deeming it the ultimate tribute—told this audience that he subconsciously thought of Hill "as a doctor, as one of us." In the fall of that same year, Hill and John Fogarty became the first lay persons to receive—from the hands of Eleanor Roosevelt—the prestigious Albert Lasker Awards for "extraordinary public service to the nation's health." Reporting this honor, the New York Post noted that Hill was often described as one "who might have been President if born above the Mason-Dixon line."[32]

Those who gathered to honor Hill on such occasions regarded him as a benevolent fixture in the Senate, one who transcended petty concerns and favored broad humanitarian programs. Few such admirers even noticed that this practical politician felt compelled to defend the filibuster rule, to fight against extending the life of the Civil Rights Commission, and to denounce a proposed constitutional amendment to abolish the poll tax as "unwarranted, unnecessary, and unjustifiable."[33]

But shrewd Drew Pearson noted that, even as Hill received these plaudits, he appeared less enthusiastic about pushing further education or labor bills through his committee. The Washington Post displayed Pearson's

surmise under the headline "Lister's Liberalism Fading." Pearson attributed this to rumors that Hill and his brother, Luther, had inherited two
million dollars "some time ago." Asked by the *Birmingham News* to
comment on Pearson's column, Hill responded that Dr. Hill's estate had
been "far from $2 million" and intimated that his two sisters had also
shared in their father's will. Whatever the amount of his estate and who-
ever the heirs, Dr. Hill had died before his elder son had begun to shape
major social legislation. Pearson had correctly sensed Hill's growing sense
of unease and his increasing reluctance to be associated with controversial
legislation but, ignorant of Alabama politics, he had mistaken its cause.[34]

For twenty years—since his first election to the Senate over the already
discredited Tom Heflin—opponents had tried in vain to defeat Hill. Only
once had they been able to persuade a major politician to undertake this
task; even though using race as an issue, Jim Simpson had won only 44
percent of Alabama voters. Discouraged by this test of strength, other
seasoned politicians shied away from running against Hill. McNeil and
Crommelin attracted only the usual one-third of the Alabama electorate
willing to back anyone other than a powerful senator who strongly espoused such federal programs as rural electrification and telephone cooperatives, the wage and hour law, TVA, the Wagner Act, unemployment
compensation, and attempts to aid small farmers. These and other out-
growths of an increasing federal presence intruded into and profoundly
altered an economy over which Hill's opponents had once presided virtually unchallenged.

This opposition had changed little since 1938 when it had been comprised of the majority of Alabama's industrialists, business leaders, owners
of large timber and mineral lands, the Farm Bureau, the Alabama Power
Company, and lawyers and politicians who represented these interests.
Occasionally Hill and some element of this informal coalition made a
temporary truce, as when he and the Alabama Power Company worked
together to develop the Coosa-Alabama waterway. Some newly prosperous
Alabamians—many of them physicians—added their votes to the anti-Hill
camp.

But obviously Hill still retained the loyalty of that two-thirds of the
electorate to whom federal programs had brought higher wages, a shorter
work week, stronger unions, electricity, telephones, farm ownership, hospitals, improved schools, and college loans. North Alabama, steadily
growing in population and prosperity due to TVA, continued to be the chief
bastion of Hill supporters. To detach these Alabamians from their benefac-

tor posed an almost insoluble problem for Hill's opponents. The Hill "machine," under the smooth direction of Roy Nolen and Foots Clement, mobilized the organizational strength of teachers, federal employees, probate judges, municipal officials, and union members. New voters, primarily women and blacks, flocked to Hill's banner after Alabama's poll tax ceased to be cumulative.

During the presidencies of Roosevelt and Truman, his enemies had sought in vain to tar Hill with Democratic racial policies. After their third party effort had also proved a dismal failure, they had timidly ventured toward open Republicanism under the guise of "Eisenhower Democrats." But Eisenhower himself had stalemated this process. Frank Dixon—guiding spirit of the States' Rights movement and Hill's most persistent adversary—conceded the impossibility of winning an Alabama majority to Republicanism without the political weapon of race. "There is no Republican Party in Dixie," Dixon admitted. "Little Rock finished it so far as our people are concerned." Thus it would be necessary to try once again to wrest control of Alabama's Democratic party away from Hill and the loyalists.[35]

"A considerable tonic for the states' righters"

As another election year opened, both sides jockeyed for position. At stake would be John Sparkman's Senate seat and the presidency itself. Like Hill, Sparkman appeared unbeatable; only John Crommelin, pledging to stand up for "white Christian citizens," and a filling station operator essayed this hopeless task. Instead, party dissidents, attempting to repeat their 1948 coup of controlling Alabama's electoral votes, offered a slate of states' rights candidates to oppose loyalists for Alabama's presidential electors. Familiar names of those who had opposed Hill in the past, including Frank Dixon, Lawrence McNeil, Walter Givhan, Edmund Blair, Bruce Henderson, and Wallace Malone, appeared on the list of states' rights candidates.[36]

Dixon, intellectual leader of the antiloyalists, told audiences that, with Republicans pledged to destroy segregation, and northern Democrats "insistent on creating a race of mixed-blood mongrels to inhabit this fair Southern land of ours," the only hope for southern segregationists lay in the electoral college. If southern states could present a solid front of electors pledged only to "states rights and racial integrity," perhaps they could force the presidential election into the House of Representatives where they could bargain for concessions on civil rights and for a president more to their liking than such Democratic front-runners as John Kennedy, Lyndon Johnson, Stuart Symington, and Hubert Humphrey. Or perhaps, so some loyalists suspected, those who called themselves states' righters meant to deliver Alabama's electoral votes to the Republican party.[37]

Except for Governor John Patterson, an ardent Kennedy supporter, antiloyalists had the stump almost to themselves. Sparkman, concerned with his own reelection, stayed clear of intraparty squabbles. Hill chose to take a major role in leading a team of Senate filibusterers against civil rights proposals and the anti-poll-tax amendment; when Hill's turn came to speak all night or to lead a twenty-four-hour marathon, Henrietta put extra wheat germ in her husband's breakfast cereal. Not even Hill, with his energy and commitment, could serve on both fronts at once. Despite pleas from Harry Ayers and other loyalists that he come home to lead their cause, Hill confined himself to a single television speech, press releases warning that federal funds would dry up if Alabamians left the Democratic party, and an occasional jab like "I have not forgotten the Republican bayonets at Little Rock."[38]

As expected, Sparkman won overwhelmingly. His 83 percent majority topped Hill's 1956 high of 68 percent. But in the race for presidential electors, on which antiloyalists had concentrated, Alabama Democrats divided almost evenly: six states' righters, including Dixon, Malone, Henderson, and Blair, and five loyalists were to cast the state's ballots for the presidency. The Dothan Eagle jubilantly declared this a "considerable tonic for the states' righters." Foots Clement confided to Hill that he had underestimated opposition strength and that the loyalist cause had suffered due to "certain prospective nominees" at the Democratic convention. If Kennedy were the nominee, Foots predicted, "a familiar chant in Alabama will be 'I'd rather vote for a Negro than for a Catholic.' " Sentiment of this kind, the campaign manager noted, was especially pronounced in Hill's stronghold of north Alabama.[39]

As an ambitious young congressman in 1928, Hill—raising the issue of race against Herbert Hoover—had been the busiest Alabama speechmaker for the Democratic party's Catholic nominee. But when his party nominated another Catholic three decades later, Hill maintained a comparatively low profile. He, Sparkman, and Alabama's loyalist congressmen, the Andalusia Star-News noted, had been "conspicuous in their absence" from the 1960 Democratic convention. James Free, Washington correspondent for the *Birmingham News*, speculated that the convention could have been a "political booby trap" had Hill and Sparkman been forced to choose a presidential nominee from four fellow senators. Eugene Patterson of the *Atlanta Constitution* offered a slightly different interpretation: Johnson, the powerful majority leader, had advised Russell, Talmadge, Hill, and Sparkman to stay home lest they be politically damaged by supporting him.[40]

Once Democrats cast their die, Hill pledged to work for the Kennedy-Johnson ticket against the "ancient enemy." As an easygoing Senate neophyte in 1952, Kennedy had been assigned to Hill's Labor and Public Welfare Committee and given the obscure job of chairing its Railroad Retirement Subcommittee. Kennedy had hated this subcommittee but he later turned down Hill's offer that he head a Special Subcommittee on Aging. "Senator Kennedy will *never* be interested in the problems of the aging," his aide, Ted Sorensen, frostily informed Hill's emissaries.[41]

Eventually Kennedy had taken the chair of the Labor Subcommittee, an assignment that Hill himself had always carefully avoided. Their names had appeared jointly on a bill to establish a National Library of Medicine; however, Kennedy's role had been merely titular. No matter what private reservations the conscientious chairman may have had regarding this prima donna who often simply handed him his proxy, Hill had been his usual cordial self in dealing with Kennedy. On the surface at least, their relationship appeared friendly.[42]

By the fall of 1960, Kennedy—scanning the nation for presidential supporters—exhibited a sudden interest in health care for the elderly. The Massachusetts senator became one of the chief proponents of a bill to expand Social Security by providing medical and hospitalization benefits as the *right* of every aged citizen. But the Senate's chief authority on medical issues took a different tack. Hill favored—and Congress eventually agreed to—a middle road backed by the AMA. Under the Kerr-Mills plan, medical care for the elderly would be based on need; furthermore, states would be primarily responsible for this program, thus avoiding any suspicion of "socialized medicine." The sliding-scale formula of federal support, based on that in the Hill-Burton bill, would favor relatively low-income states; this federal money would be paid directly to physicians and hospitals.[43]

Declaring that Kennedy and the "Northern Democratic bloc" had tried to move "too far and too fast" toward a huge new federal program, Hill's longtime supporter, the *Birmingham News*, applauded its senator's stand.

Under new leadership and now owned by the Newhouse chain, the *News*—
once Alabama's most widely circulated supporter of progressive government—was gradually moving to the right. Evading a choice between
states' rights and loyalist electors, the *News* left this matter to the voters.
Not so the *Montgomery Advertiser*. "Old Grandma," as Hill's hometown
newspaper liked to be known, flatly urged its readers to disregard their
"jolly, elegant senior senator . . . the chief Democrat in Alabama" and
vote the Nixon-Lodge ticket.[44]

Revival of the Catholic issue heartened Alabama Republicans and
would-be Republicans. Here was another lure by which they might wrest
their state's electoral votes away from traditional Democratic allegiance.
Invited to respond to attacks on Kennedy by militant Baptists and Methodists, Hill told the *Tuscaloosa News* that Kennedy's voting record in Congress had been "the same as mine—absolutely for separation of church and
state."[45]

To hold Alabama in line, Democrats sent in big guns: Sam Rayburn,
Russell Long, George Smathers, even Harry Truman, the only Democratic
presidential nominee to fail to win Alabama's electoral vote since Reconstruction. Introducing Truman to a friendly Decatur audience, Hill "to the
delight of the crowd [threatened] to steal some of the thunder from Truman" by castigating Republicans for their persistent opposition to TVA. As
the campaign neared its end, Lister and Henrietta Hill rode with vice
presidential nominee Lyndon Johnson on his whistle-stop train tour of
Alabama. But compared to 1928, when he had held a safe congressional
seat, Hill seemed to be merely going through the motions of party fealty.[46]

Despite Kennedy's religious affiliation and his last-minute telephone
call to the wife of Martin Luther King Jr., Democrats won 58.6 percent of
the total Alabama vote in November. But when the electoral college met,
Alabama's six antiloyalist presidential electors voted for Virginia's Senator
Harry Byrd. Only eight Mississippi electors joined this second futile protest.[47]

Another omen troubled Foots Clement and Hill as they contemplated a
senatorial campaign only two years hence: 41.7 percent of those who cast
their ballots in Alabama had voted for the Republican ticket of Nixon and
Lodge. Little Rock notwithstanding, in presidential politics "the ancient
enemy" had more than doubled its Alabama supporters since the heated
campaign against Harry Truman in 1948.[48] Catholicism had been a factor—but not the major factor—in the minds of most of these new converts.

The changing of the guard in January 1961 must have reminded Lister

Hill of 1933 when another Democrat had taken over the White House after years of Republican dominance. Now it was not he but the new president who was young, ambitious, and full of plans for the future. In the first flush of victory, the Senate's bloc of liberal Democrats spoke glowingly of reforms they planned to institute. With Lyndon Johnson moving to the vice presidency, Montana's Mike Mansfield would assume the post of majority leader. Hill's name was among those mentioned as assistant leader.[49] But for an elder statesman to resume a post he had relinquished a decade earlier would be unseemly; for one seeking reelection in Alabama to serve the Kennedy administration in any guise would be unthinkable.

Nonetheless it was like old times to see a Democrat sitting in the Oval Office. Visiting this president who had been a freshman senator only ten years earlier, Hill remarked that he had been invited to Eisenhower's office alone only once in eight years; even on that occasion he and Ike had been chaperoned by Sherman Adams.[50] Now the chairman of the Senate's Labor and Public Welfare Committee could discuss future health and medical legislation with a former junior member of that committee, free of the presence of a watchful chief of staff. Still, Hill did not feel as comfortable with this young Democratic president as he had with Franklin Roosevelt or his old Senate friend Harry Truman.

But a Democratic administration also meant patronage and looser control of the purse strings. At Hill's instigation, Kennedy promoted Dr. Luther Leonidas Terry, of Red Level, Alabama—a namesake of Dr. Hill—from an administrative post at NIH to surgeon general of the Public Health Service. The first Kennedy budget included $375,000 to complete plans for development of the Coosa-Alabama waterway; Eisenhower, who had vigorously opposed funds for this program, evidently wanted to be a "partner" in name only.[51]

Again Hill had opportunities to shape the federal bench. His faithful Jefferson County political watchdog, Clarence Allgood, was appointed a federal district judge for north Alabama. In 1963, Allgood was to uphold the Birmingham school board's action expelling or suspending more than one thousand black schoolchildren arrested while demonstrating for civil rights; this opinion would quickly be overruled by Fifth Circuit Judge Elbert Tuttle.[52]

Hill also suggested Walter Pettus Gewin, Foots Clement's law partner, for the U.S. Fifth Circuit Court of Appeals. Originally this Fifth Circuit judgeship had been promised to Foots. But when he found that he was terminally ill, Foots expressed the wish that this appointment go to his law partner. Initially perceived as a segregationist, Gewin would gradually become sensitive to the injustice of racial discrimination. In 1964, he would write a landmark decision against segregation in public amusement parks; by the 1970s, Gewin would join the court majority in deciding important school cases in favor of black plaintiffs.[53]

The death of Foots Clement in September 1961 deprived Hill of a second indispensable Alabama mentor; this loss would have a nearly disastrous effect on Hill's campaign for a fifth Senate term. Many times in the months ahead Hill was to lament: "I sure wish Foots were here!"[54]

The Strongest Challenge

1 9 6 2

"I wish you would tell me how in the h— Lister Hill don't ever have any opposition"

After the death of Foots Clement, Hill thought of retiring. How could he continue to dominate Alabama politics from faraway Washington with no Nolen or Clement in the watchtower, the loyal Allgood now on the bench, and Ed Reid often sounding more like a critic than a friend? Henrietta Hill had begun to show the first symptoms of Parkinson's disease, a progressive nervous disorder for which medical research had thus far failed to find a cure. Hill realized that, at the age of sixty-seven and after almost forty years in Congress, he had reached the zenith of his power and influence; he had long ago resigned himself to the fact that he would never be majority leader, vice president, or president. But leaders of organized medicine had only begun to express their gratitude for his vigorous sponsorship of federal funding for research; librarians and educators continued to praise his legislative achievements. To remain in his beloved Senate, sponsor more beneficial laws, and receive further tributes proved irresistible, especially when no major opponent loomed on the horizon. In January 1962, Hill announced that he would run on his record.[1]

But even if the political way seemed clear, the cautious Hill deemed it essential to reaffirm his southern loyalty. By 1962, only Alabama and four other southern states retained the poll tax as a prerequisite to voting. That spring, Hill—using the ploy of states' rights for his own purposes—vociferously expressed his opposition to the anti-poll-tax amendment and to abolishing literacy tests for voters who had sixth-grade educations or higher. Only *states*, Hill insisted, had the right to determine the qualifications of voters; abolition of the literacy test, he scoffed, was a "Bobby Kennedy foundling" left on the doorstep of Congress.[2]

On the Senate floor, majority leader Mansfield described Hill and Stennis as the chief obstacles against these proposals. But Mansfield sounded only mildly reproving. Was he actually trying to *help* his southern colleagues? The *Atlanta Journal*, Richard Rovere of the *New Yorker*, and even some Alabama newspapers suspected that this filibuster was "phony," a mere "tribal ritual" to appease the voters back home. To give away this game did not help matters, especially when Martin Luther King Jr. described Hill in the *Alabama Journal* as "forced to adopt segregationist stands by his constituents."[3]

This time Hill's token opposition consisted of the persistent Crommelin and Donald G. Hallmark, a politically unknown, young Montgomery engineer and local Citizens' Council leader. The *Montgomery Advertiser* candidly described Hallmark as "well-meaning but misplaced" and Crommelin as simply "misplaced." Remaining in Washington and not deigning to campaign, Hill won his largest endorsement as a senator; three of every four voters cast their ballots for his reelection and he carried every county but Crommelin's home county of Elmore (see Appendix, Map 6).[4]

But the Democratic primary of 1962 spelled the end of political power for Jim Folsom. Campaigning for governor against four strong opponents, including George Wallace and "Bull" Connor, Folsom had plaintively asked Ed Leigh McMillan, Hill's sole supporter among Alabama's wealthy lumbermen: "I wish you would tell me how in the h— Lister Hill don't ever have any opposition and every time I am a candidate the opposition gets better?" To counteract Wallace and Connor, Folsom belatedly employed racism. Even so, he narrowly failed to make the runoff in which George Wallace—determined never to be "outsegged" again—defeated Ryan De Graffenreid, who had been labeled "soft" on this crucial issue.[5]

Thus, sixteen years after he had burst on the Alabama political scene, Folsom was finished. His previous moderation on the subject of race, the rankling memory of his social drink with Adam Clayton Powell, his disastrous last-minute appeal on television—when he appeared too drunk to remember the names of his children—and his general ineptitude in the art of governance consigned Folsom to "Buck's Pocket," that remote mountain fastness reputed to be the symbolic refuge of Alabama's political losers. "Big Jim" would enter his name in other races but his candidacy would be perceived as pathetic.

During his two terms as governor and despite his overwhelming popularity, Folsom had not achieved a single one of his major objectives: reapportionment, elimination or reduction of the poll tax, increased financial support for the aged, substantial improvement in public education. He had possessed the political mystique to lead the revolution that he sought to bring about in Alabama. But as Hill and Roy Nolen had feared from the start, Folsom had been too unsophisticated and undisciplined, too trusting of his subordinates, and—worst flaw of all—too impatient.[6]

In 1962, a new and powerful figure moved to the front of Alabama's political stage. Wallace's timing, although he had not planned it this way, proved to be perfect. Martin Luther King Jr. and other black leaders were pressing their cause; John and Robert Kennedy were becoming increasingly identified with this movement. Now this scenario was to have its third, vital element: a cocky and verbal opponent capable of attracting national attention.

Wallace, like Sparkman and Folsom, had risen from plain Alabama origins; he had patterned his campaigns after Folsom's folksy and entertaining style. Like Hill in his youth, Wallace was an instinctive politician who could enter a crowd of fifty to one hundred citizens and emerge a few minutes later fully aware of its consensus. Several years earlier, Foots had alerted Hill to this new political force and sought to ensure that the veteran senator and this young upstart would not become adversaries.

Unlike the pragmatic Foots, Carl Elliott had feared Wallace and urged Hill to lead a coalition to head him off. However, Hill had no intention of risking his own career by taking on Wallace. After all, this new governor was a fellow Democrat who had once shown progressive inclinations and who helped restore Roy Mayhall to the helm of the State Democratic Executive Committee after loyalist members won a narrow majority in the May primary. Already Wallace had exhibited his remarkable ability to influence Alabama's emotional white electorate. Hill might need the help of this governor-nominate in fighting representatives of the "ancient"— and more dangerous—enemy.[7]

Thus as Wallace prepared to assume the office of governor, he and Hill appeared friendly, at least on the surface. But Hill never trusted Wallace. Who knew what this new governor sought to accomplish, what secret supporters he might have, or what office he might seek next?

"We are meeting our foes under their true flag"

As Hill had noted in 1952, Republicanism was becoming fashionable in the silk-stocking suburbs of Montgomery, Birmingham, and Mobile. While the popular Eisenhower held sway, many who had chafed for three decades over federal activism in economic matters openly abandoned the Democratic label. Republican migrants from the North swelled these GOP ranks. Little Rock had briefly retarded Republican growth, but since 1961 a Democratic president had been forced to cope with the increasingly militant civil rights movement. Here was a chance for Republicans to add to their ranks a much larger southern white constituency—Alabama's heretofore faithful New Deal Democrats and their more prosperous sons and daughters.

The tools for this task were at hand: in May 1962, "Freedom Riders," seeking to integrate interstate transportation, were met by angry crowds of Klansmen and other plain whites in the bus terminals of Anniston, Birmingham, and Montgomery. In Congress, the poll-tax and literacy tests appeared in peril. In Mississippi, James Meredith persisted in his legal efforts to become the first black student at "Ole Miss." Speaking for the Supreme Court, Hugo Black had aroused a torrent of outrage by his opinion in *Engel v. Vitale* outlawing the reading of an official prayer in the New York public schools. In open invitation to disgruntled Democrats, the Republican state chairman, Claude Vardaman, had declared: "Under Ike it was respectable to be a Republican; under Kennedy it is an honor."[8]

Borrowing "Dixie" as their theme song, "exuberant and well-dressed" Republicans filled Birmingham's Municipal Auditorium in June. "Young Turks" ousted old-guard fixtures like Vardaman and elected their own leader, John Grenier, a thirty-year-old lawyer from New Orleans. Having gained party control, these restless, tough-minded young urbanites sought electoral victories. Knowing they could not beat Wallace at his own game, they decided against a gubernatorial contest; instead, they would oppose local Democrats in a number of counties, seek three seats in the House, and—most important of all—try to oust Hill from the Senate.[9]

James Douglas Martin, a former Democrat chosen by the Grenier forces to challenge Hill, was as unknown and untried as Lawrence McNeil or Donald Hallmark. Born in Birmingham's blue-collar suburb of Tarrant, a hotbed of Klan activity during the 1920s, Martin had risen in the Army to the rank of major, graduated from night law school, and become a successful oil distributor in Gadsden and president of the Associated Industries of

Alabama. At forty-four, handsome, personable, and married to a former "Miss Alabama," Martin made an attractive and energetic candidate. Unlike McNeil or Hallmark, he would not be a symbol of halfhearted, token resistance to the national Democratic party but the focal point of this new and fervent Republicanism. As one faithful Democrat marveled: "We are in a rather unique position in Alabama in that we are meeting our foes under their true flag."[10]

Having selected a promising candidate, Grenier set out to transform the lethargic old GOP into a modern vote-getting machine. Republican offices sprang up over Alabama. Party leaders were assigned a quota of votes for each congressional district. Thousands of converts boldly adorned their cars with the "Vote Republican" bumper stickers passed out at football games and county fairs; Martin's handsome countenance smiled from billboards, newspaper ads, and slickly produced television spots; "Elect Martin" banners draped the streets of many suburbs and small towns. For those Democrats who might find the Republican label politically or financially embarrassing, Grenier and his advisers concocted an appealing disguise—"Rebels for Martin"—that attracted Donald Hallmark, among others.[11]

Zealous women, outnumbering male workers 20 to 1, contributed hundreds of hours to staff local Republican headquarters or booths at county fairs, play hostess at fund-raising coffees, and accompany their candidate as "Maids for Martin," dressed in red, white, and blue, wearing white sailor hats, handing out literature, waving Confederate flags, snake dancing, and singing—to the tune of "The Old Gray Mare"—"Ole Lister Hill Ain't What He Used to Be." Texas Republicans had first mined this rich source of free campaign labor. Many a middle-class housewife—including numbers of doctors' wives—found this new pastime much more fun than her usual, decorous pursuits of church circle, bridge game, or literary club. Women Democrats, many of them wage-earners as well as wives and mothers, could not match their Republican counterparts in fervor, funds, or free time.[12]

Having begun to solicit campaign contributions in July, Republicans proved far more effective fund-raisers than the tardily organized Democrats. Local committees and "Rebels for Martin" brought in hundreds of small donations but these enthusiasts alone could not raise sufficient money for numerous billboards and newspaper advertisements, thousands of bumper stickers, several statewide mailings, and the costs of Martin's busy speaking schedule. Democrats charged—and Republicans denied—

that Martin received $300,000 from the Republican National Committee as well as sizable donations from out-of-state oil and gas interests. Barney Weeks, president of the Alabama Labor Council, suspected that the national office of the American Medical Association also contributed substantially to the fight against Hill. Martin himself boasted that he had received voluntary donations from some members of the State Democratic Executive Committee, a claim heatedly challenged by Chairman Mayhall. Under the disclosure rules of that era, no records of out-of-state contributions were kept; Martin's known expenses totaled around $100,000.[13]

Hill, once so proud that he had incurred no campaign debts to big contributors other than his father, soon realized he would have to lose his cherished "virginity" on this score. Sam Durden, his longtime Montgomery friend, took on the belated task of raising a campaign war chest. But old friends and family members could not match the Republican outlay. Eventually Hill accepted $10,000 from Mary Lasker, $1,000 from his old New Deal buddy Tom Corcoran, and—so one insider said—$10,000 from Rufus Lackey. In the campaign's final hours, Cronin received an envelope marked "Here's George's [Wallace] contribution." In all, Hill's known expenditures totaled less than half those of Martin.[14]

Although Martin had more money to spend, Hill received the backing of the majority of the state's major dailies: the *Birmingham News*, *Anniston Star*, *Tuscaloosa News*, and a solid array of Tennessee Valley newspapers, including the *Huntsville Times*, *Florence Times*, *Decatur Daily*, and Muscle Shoals *Valley Voice*. Outside of north Alabama, the senator's press supporters included Auburn's *Lee County Bulletin*, the *Andalusia Star-News*, and the *Lafayette Sun*. Martin's backers included the *Dothan Eagle*, *Mobile Press-Register*, *Centreville Press*, *Clarke County Democrat* and Hamner Cobbs's weekly *Southern Watchman*. Hill's hometown newspaper, the *Montgomery Advertiser*, made no endorsement; Will Hill Tankersley reported to his cousin that the *Advertiser* would only "grudgingly" print anything favorable to Hill or his family.[15]

Despite the heat and humidity of July, Martin adapted zestfully to the panoply, fireworks, fish fries, barbecues, and country music of the campaign trail. Although at first he may have considered his quest a mere formality, Hill's challenger began to believe he might be elected. His growing conviction, coupled with his natural gift for oratory and apparent sincerity, attracted ever larger crowds. Martin's advisers scheduled most of his rallies in the Wiregrass and Black Belt; at the height of the campaign, the Republican candidate even held forth from the hallowed spot at Alabama's capitol where Jefferson Davis had taken his oath as president of the Confederacy. Both candidates, observers noted, seemed ill at ease about their national parties. Martin's billboards and ads bore no party label; instead, the Republican candidate stressed his loyalty to Alabama, the South, and the Confederacy. Hill attempted the difficult task of making this a contest between Democrats and Republicans without mentioning the current Democratic president.[16]

Martin learned quickly that catchy slogans could rouse unsophisticated and sparsely educated white Alabamians to pray, stomp, and cheer. In years past, Hill had brought many an audience to its feet with scornful allusions to "Hoovercrats," "Willkiecrats," and "the ancient enemy," or dramatic appeals to the icons of the Confederacy, the "party of our forefathers," and "white supremacy." Now it was his turn to receive verbal jousts. "Listless Lister," Martin jibed, "Alabama's Jacob Javits . . . the waterboy for the Bobby-and-Jack touch football team." Jimmy Lawson, closely attuned to rural Alabamians, reported to Hill: "Every conceivable type of Kennedy story including little Bobby and his wife's habit of jumping into swimming pools fully clothed was laid at your door." (The scornful manner in which many now referred to the president as "Jack" and the attorney general as "Bobby-sox" reminded one Democrat of those white Alabamians who—objecting to her racial attitudes—had called Mrs. Franklin Roosevelt "old Eleanor.")[17]

Like Hill and Wallace, Martin knew that his listeners, lacking the patience or predilection for complexity, expected politicians to express issues in simple, graphic word pictures. Seeking their support for an end to federal controls in agriculture, the Republican candidate told his listeners: "You can't plant corn to feed your chickens without permission from a bureaucrat." To evoke their religious fervor, he declared: "Our children [can't] join in a simple prayer without bringing forth a solemn edict by the Supreme Court." To arouse them against taxes, government spending, and the rising national debt, Martin pronounced: "Socialism no longer creeps, it gallops." Hill—so Martin implied—was responsible, literally or by association, for all these matters of which he complained.[18]

While Martin played on the emotions and prejudices of rural folk, his supporters worked to encourage more silk-stocking urbanites to defect from the Democratic party. Many in the Mobile area—a friend reported to Hill—had criticized the senator's appointments to the federal bench, particularly those of Judges Rives and Gewin; another disappointed voter wrote: "these men appear to have been 'brainwashed' by their appointment." Calls for the impeachment of Chief Justice Earl Warren, Justice Black, and other members of the Supreme Court also flooded Hill's office. Reiterating his belief in separation of church and state, Hill responded: "I do not think . . . recitation of non-denominational prayers in our schools violates this principle." Following *Engel v. Vitale*, Hill informed many constituents that he had offered a bill to provide that the Constitution "not be construed to prohibit the recitation of such prayers." Small wonder that he and Hugo Black no longer spent their evenings together.[19]

Civic and country clubs proved particularly fertile fields for Republican recruitment. At a civic club luncheon in Birmingham, Jim Simpson predicted to E. L. Holland Jr., a *Birmingham News* editorial writer, that Martin would use Black's prayer decision as proof that Hill had done nothing to curb the Supreme Court. At the Montgomery Kiwanis Club, a speaker, quoting the Americans for Constitutional Government, attacked the "radical voting records" of Hill and Sparkman. Marie Stokes Jemison, one of Hill's Birmingham supporters, described "groups of what I would term hysterical women whose reading is limited and few of whom attend lectures . . ." handing out pink, anti-Hill flyers at the Birmingham Country Club.[20]

Opposition from such quarters was nothing new to Hill. But the Senate's widely acclaimed champion of medical and health matters also began to receive word that Alabama physicians and their wives were moving into the Republican camp. Two Tuscaloosa doctors reported that "a determined effort" was underway to turn members of their profession against Hill; an attorney in Mobile noted that doctors, nurses, pharmacists, and grateful patients (particularly women)—modern counterparts of the same forces that had first elected Hill to Congress—were planning to vote for Martin; others telephoned Hill's office to report that members of women's auxiliaries of the Alabama Medical Association were conducting a door-to-door campaign against Hill. Informing Hill of this growing opposition, one perplexed friend confessed: "Why, I do not know." But another friend attributed the increase of Republicanism among doctors to "concern over more federal controls and [over] a growing tendency toward socialism."[21]

Many of these physicians had received their medical training after World War I under the G.I. Bill on which Hill's name had appeared as a cosponsor; many practiced in the almost two hundred hospitals and health facilities constructed in Alabama under the Hill-Burton program; others had received federal research grants from the National Institutes of Health into whose coffers Hill had steered millions of federal dollars. Furthermore, most members of Alabama's close-knit medical fraternity knew that Hill was the son of a distinguished doctor and that many of his family members, including his cousin, Dr. Champ Lyons, and his brothers-in-law, Dr. E. W. Rucker and Dr. Carney Laslie, were highly regarded fellow members of their profession.

When Harry Truman had first advocated compulsory national health insurance for all Americans in 1945, Hill had steadfastly insisted that "we must preserve the freedom of the individual doctor"; the Hill-Burton program had been conceived to head off Truman's more sweeping proposal. When Truman had again proposed compulsory health insurance in 1949, Hill had countered with a bill calling for a voluntary program to be administered by the states. In 1960, Hill and Sparkman had voted against a Kennedy-backed bill, extending medical benefits for all Social Security retirees sixty-eight and over, in favor of the Kerr-Mills bill to help provide medical care only for elderly citizens who could not pass a means test. In the summer of 1962, Hill played a crucial role in rounding up four or five votes to defeat a new Kennedy administration proposal for medical care for the aged.[22]

Many constituents, including leaders of organized labor and groups of older citizens, disapproved of Hill's stand against Medicare, as it became known; as one disappointed voter put it: "After your support of the hospitals, was hoping you would be for old folks medical care." Advisers warned Hill that this vote would "cost him dearly" in Jefferson County and other urban centers. But Hill sought to counteract persistent Republican claims that he favored "socialized medicine" with its implication of desegregated hospitals and waiting rooms; also he appeared to have genuine concern over the possibility of government interference with the private practice of medicine. At first, his vote appeared to have had the desired political effect. "You really tore the local Republicans in the fat when you voted against 'medicare,'" a Mobile friend rejoiced.[23]

Over the long run, however, Hill's opposition to Medicare did not alter the drift of doctors toward Republicanism. Administrators of larger medical installations and numerous older doctors assured him of their appreciation for past favors and their continued support. But substantial numbers of younger physicians—many of whom had benefited directly from Hill's legislative achievements—aligned themselves behind Martin.

The defection of so many members of his father's profession hurt and angered Hill. But doctors, even if bolstered by wives, patients, and other supporters, lacked sufficient strength to sway a statewide election. Republicans needed some issue of wider appeal with which to entice droves of Alabama voters away from traditional Democratic loyalty. Unintentionally, John Kennedy, James Meredith, and Governor Ross Barnett of Mississippi would provide this new and volatile scenario.

In late September, Hugo Black, the Supreme Court justice responsible for matters involving the Fifth Circuit, upheld that court's order directing the University of Mississippi to admit Meredith. Governor Barnett defied this and subsequent federal court directives; full-scale rioting broke out on the Oxford campus, and emotional hysteria gripped large numbers of Mississippians. Despite Kennedy's unwillingness to emulate Eisenhower's tactic of sending federal troops to the South, the president eventually felt compelled to order forty-four hundred federal marshals and national guardsmen to restore order, enforce federal authority, and ensure Meredith's admission.[24]

When Martin immediately offered "to stand by [Barnett's] side," Ted Sorensen informed Kennedy: "the Republicans are taking the straight Ross Barnett line." Alabama's entire congressional delegation also hastened to assure Mississippi's intransigent governor of its support ("Mississippi's fight is Alabama's fight") and went through the ritual of asking Kennedy to remove the troops. (As one Washington correspondent commented, "that sort of thing is done among political friends without anyone getting sore.") Repeatedly Hill and the Democrats reminded the voters of Little Rock— but to no avail.[25]

In Alabama, thousands reacted with fury to this dramatic sequence of events in Mississippi. These emotional whites, seeking a scapegoat upon whom to vent their anger and egged on by Martin and the Republicans, focused on their senior senator.

"Call the roll! Call the roll!"

Barrett Shelton, Hill's longtime supporter, had candidly admitted in his Fourth of July editorial that "sleeping Democrats who traditionally take the November general election for granted" had their work cut out for them in facing a combination of new residents along with "Republicans who call themselves Democrats, Ku Klux and other 'nigger-haters.'" Noting that Alabama's traditionally Democratic farm vote had also declined substantially, the Decatur editor concluded: "I am not going to fool myself that we are facing the Republican party of twenty years ago."[26]

Ralph Silver, hired to direct Hill's advertising campaign, also confessed his amazement at the sight of "life long Democrats calmly [saying] they are going to vote for Martin." Astute Ed Reid conceded "Hill is in serious trouble." Alarmed supporters, noting that Martin had even made forays into the Tennessee Valley, pleaded with the senator to "come to Alabama and make some speeches as soon as possible."[27]

To Hill, it seemed incomprehensible that a little-known *Republican* actually posed a serious threat. Engrossed in his Senate duties and beguiled by his admirers into thinking himself an unassailable national figure, he stubbornly resisted the pleas of his staff and supporters that he come home to campaign. Over the years Hill had gradually lost his zest for strenuous campaigning. Judge Virgil Pittman, of Gadsden, co-chairman of the Democratic Campaign Committee, remembered later: "He would not come! He just wouldn't do it! . . . We tried to frighten him. And we still couldn't get him down here!" But in October, with the Senate adjourned and most of his white constituents in a frenzy over the integration of "Ole Miss," Hill finally and reluctantly returned to Alabama to face the most serious challenge of his forty years in politics. Election day was less than three weeks away.[28]

When Hill and his administrative assistant, Don Cronin, reached Montgomery, they found the Hill machine, so efficient and powerful in the days of Roy Nolen and Foots Clement, almost dismantled due to lack of usage and the deaths of its leaders. Relatively few of those who had comprised Hill's 1920s network of friends, kin, and neighbors remained. Only rarely did a grateful constituent recall that Dr. Hill had operated on a wife or mother. An increasing number of correspondents reminded Hill that he had been their *parents'* political favorite; the prominent Birmingham merchant Isadore Pizitz remembered: "You were dearly loved by my father."[29]

Another appreciative voter in Lafayette regretted "that so many of our people have such short memories." But certain memories seemed to persist. A Birmingham supporter alerted Hill that she had been told that "you had joined the Catholic Church." Ralph Silver confided to Cronin that he would be careful to avoid any hint that Hill had Jewish ancestry because "[that] makes the KKK see red."[30]

Others warned Hill that Republicans intended to make his age an issue. Fourth-graders reminded the senator that they had studied about him in their Alabama history books; the *Piedmont Journal*, although supporting his reelection, referred to Hill as "venerable." Hearing talk about the need for a younger man in the Senate, a Birmingham friend retorted: "the old coon dog knows where the coons stay." To complaints that many younger voters had never seen Hill, the editor of the Muscle Shoals *Valley Voice* responded: "Look around you. You can easily see his accomplishments." But even John C. Persons, chairman of the board of Birmingham's powerful and conservative First National Bank, solemnly advised Hill that "men of your generation and mine are becoming less effective" due to the new crop of younger voters.[31]

Frantically Cronin began to telephone old friends within the ranks of probate judges, sheriffs, mayors, labor officials, physicians, teachers, and editors. But a one-man telephone campaign would be no match for Grenier's efficiently organized and highly enthusiastic Republicans. Seeking allies, Hill and Cronin turned to Alabama's loyalist Democrats: Ed Reid, assisted by Virgil Pittman and Evelyn Hicks Shannon, would direct a statewide Democratic campaign to reelect Hill and to assure that no Republican challenger would oust one of the state's eight remaining congressmen. But Cronin remembered later that "Eddie never became a junior Foots"; ill health also hampered Reid's effectiveness.[32]

In theory the idea of "one for all and all for one" seemed feasible, but in actuality it turned out to be cumbersome and unfocused. The congressmen were not used to campaigning as a statewide team, nor did they feel seriously threatened by three Republican opponents. To coordinate their appearances at Democratic rallies posed a major logistical problem for Shannon. Not until the campaign's closing days did several of Hill's House colleagues—notably Elliott and Rains—really put their shoulders to the wheel for him.[33]

Shannon struggled to get Sparkman and Wallace to appear at these rallies. Sparkman, a lackluster orator compared with Hill and Wallace, limited his role mostly to smiling for group photographs at the few campaign functions he attended. The governor-nominate, a sure crowd pleaser when his own political fortunes were at stake, also proved hard to corral. In later years, Wallace would claim that he had played a substantial role in Hill's narrow 1962 victory. But although Wallace appeared at a number of early rallies and urged support for *Alabama* Democrats, he dropped from sight in the final weeks of the campaign perhaps because—so Carl Elliott alerted Hill—Wallace's harsh attacks on the federal government and calls upon audiences to "stand up for Alabama" seemed to echo and reinforce Martin's themes. Some observers suspected the incoming governor of having hedged his bet by permitting some of his supporters to work for Martin. If Hill should lose, Wallace may have thought that he could easily beat Martin in a 1968 Senate race. But whatever his inner thoughts and however tongue-in-cheek his support, Wallace at least publicly proclaimed himself a Hill supporter.[34]

Eastland and Russell came to Alabama to testify to Hill's southern fealty; Harry Truman offered to help. But Hill realized that he had to rely on himself. No congressman, fellow senator, or future governor—and certainly not the president of the United States—could or would save him from political humiliation and possible defeat. His campaign skills rusty due to long absence from the stump, Hill—iron-willed as ever—forced himself to tour Alabama's back roads, eat barbecue, and seek to arouse bored high school students by praising their bands, telling jokes about billy goats, excoriating Republicans, and exhorting these puzzled youngsters with his favorite 1937 battle cry: "Let him answer to his name; call the roll! call the roll!"[35]

Regaining his old oratorical rhythm, Hill ceased to "talk down" to his listeners and began to shake their hands and remember their names. He constantly reminded them that he—and the Democratic party—had fought to make their rivers navigable, end discriminatory freight rates, defend TVA from its enemies, and bring military installations, libraries, telephones, and hospitals to their isolated communities. In late October, Hill began to sound racist themes that evoked yells and whistles from his listeners. He had killed ten "integration" bills in his committee, he told a crowd of coal miners and poor farmers in Jasper; Republicans, he warned, had elected a "Negro" legislator in Georgia. Although Sparkman and four congressmen shared the podium in Jasper, Hill—a reporter noted—had been "the star of the show."[36]

Reluctantly Hill also conceded that he must reach out for wider support via television. He had ignored a surprising suggestion from the *Birmingham News* that the senatorial contenders debate one another; no point in giving the lesser-known Martin such an opportunity. But prodded by his advisers, Hill made several statewide television appeals, trying to put aside memories of his disastrous nominating speech for Franklin Roosevelt and to forget his sensitivity about being bald. (One former aide, Paul Duncan, hoping to help Hill get over this latter fixation, often asked: "Senator, have you ever heard of a man named Eisenhower?") But Hill remained ill at ease when deprived of the familiar sight and predictable reactions of a live audience; furthermore, the camera exaggerated his age and nervousness. "It looked bad when the senator's hand shook so badly when holding . . . the Republican platform," Julian Butler reported to Cronin. Seeing Hill on television, Stewart McClure found it hard to believe that this obviously miserable man with a squeaking voice was the commanding, self-assured chairman of the Senate's Labor and Public Welfare Committee.[37]

"All of a sudden, Kennedy isn't such a dirty word . . . anymore"

As November neared, many wondered whether the racial confrontation at "Ole Miss" would prove a crucial factor in bringing about the election of Alabama's first Republican senator since Reconstruction. With the exception of George Wallace, embattled Democrats had been hard put to dissociate themselves from the president and attorney general who had ordered this show of federal force less than seventy-five miles from Alabama's border. The Rebels of Mississippi might be traditional foes of Alabama's Crimson Tide, but even fierce football rivalry could not evoke the emotions aroused by the prospect of integration. Seeking votes in poor and sparsely populated southwest Alabama, Hill was shocked by the racial hostility emanating from a crowd of white papermill workers. Was any emotional appeal—even *patriotism*—more compelling than this?[38]

From the start, Martin had criticized Kennedy and Hill—for "wasteful foreign aid bills," failing to meet the "challenge of Communism," and for "silence, indecision and inaction" in the face of the Russian buildup of military weapons in Cuba. In late September, Hill had voted for a Senate resolution expressing American determination to fight, if necessary, to prevent Cuba from falling into the Russian sphere. But thereafter he avoided this topic, obviously more comfortable with old themes like Herbert Hoover and the "Republican depression." Martin, however, seemed determined not to let this subject die. "Bobby Kennedy, the Department of Justice, in fact the whole administration, is fiddling in Mississippi while Cuba burns!" Martin railed.[39]

On 22 October, John Kennedy, announcing to the nation his quarantine of military shipments to Cuba and his demand for withdrawal of Soviet missiles, heightened a crisis that gripped and terrified the entire civilized world. For six nerve-wracking days, Americans confronted the actual possibility of nuclear war. On 28 October, the president reported that the Soviet bases had been dismantled. Compared to a confrontation of this magnitude, the fight over integration of "Ole Miss" seemed like child's play.

The day after Kennedy's radio address, Cronin reported to a Sparkman aide that "things are beginning to pick up due to Cuba." Virgil Pittman and others urged voters not to "swap good Democratic horses in the middle of the stream." Praising Kennedy's strong stand, Hill pronounced: "The Communists respect one thing—that is strength;" Martin, reluctant to lose one of his main issues, accused Kennedy of "belated" action. The *Birmingham News*, eager to push this sudden turn of events in Hill's favor, noted: "All of a sudden, Kennedy isn't such a dirty word in Alabama anymore."[40]

Four days after Kennedy's welcome announcement that the Russians had complied with American demands, Alabama voters went to the polls. Drew Pearson had predicted that the Hill-Martin contest would be "the most significant Senate race in the nation." If Hill should lose, Pearson postulated that most southern Democratic members of Congress would desert Kennedy; all southern states—except Georgia and North Carolina—would go Republican in 1964, and the breakup of the Solid South would have begun.[41]

Hill, Cronin, and a few close friends awaited the outcome in the senator's Montgomery home. When early returns from Birmingham, Mobile, Montgomery, south Alabama, and the Wiregrass showed Martin ahead, national television networks began to focus on this unexpected trend in Alabama. The tense little group at Hill's home became increasingly disconsolate, especially at the news that Montgomery County had gone Republican. But late in the evening, as returns from the Tennessee Valley trickled in, the Martin tide began to recede. Just after midnight, Hill finally took the lead by a margin so thin that Martin refused to concede for two days. In mid-November when all ballots had been counted, it would be clear that Republicans, by attracting almost half of the votes, had made their best showing in an Alabama senatorial race. Hill had won his fifth term in the Senate by a margin of a little over 1 percent.[42]

Harry Truman "held [his] breath about Alabama" on election night; he was "sorry as I can be," Truman wrote his former Senate colleague "that the people in Alabama do not appreciate one of the great Senators of the United States." Kennedy, concerned over the implications of these Republican campaigns in the Deep South for his own political future, had also watched the Alabama returns with special interest. In a postscript to the formal White House letter of congratulations, Kennedy's special assistant Larry O'Brien noted: "You gave us a scare last night."[43]

"They had reacted to the cry of 'wolf' once too often"

How had a virtually unknown Republican come so close to defeating an incumbent hitherto considered invincible? Obviously Republicans had caught their opponents napping, their party had been smoothly organized and well financed, and Martin had proved an aggressive and attractive candidate. No doubt Democrats had a deep schism within their party or that their candidate at first had been loath to campaign, appeared out of touch with the mood of his constituents, and had neglected to keep up his own political fences. But what other factors accounted for this precipitous decline in Hill's political fortunes?

Studying the voting pattern, observers noted that Hill's base had shrunk from statewide proportions (he had won 66 of 67 counties in the recent Democratic primary and 62 counties in the 1956 primary) to 37 counties, most of them in the Tennessee Valley and the hill country. The senator had lost decisively in his home county of Montgomery. He had also lost nine neighboring counties in the Black Belt, most of his old congressional district, and almost the entire Wiregrass (see Appendix, Map 7). Wallace Malone, with no TVA in his area, appeared to have succeeded in what one of Hill's friends described as "his aim [of making the Wiregrass] a strong Republican fortress."[44]

Hill's neighbors—and many former friends—had deserted him. His son L. Lister, then beginning to practice law in Montgomery, had been shocked and hurt by the hostility of most members of Montgomery's establishment toward his father. "Much as we love Lister," gloated the *Alabama Journal*, "his political views are anathema in this part of the state." Yet until 1952 the Black Belt and much of neighboring south Alabama had been faithful to the Democratic party, even when asked to swallow the bitter pill of its Catholic presidential candidate in 1928. At the opposite end of Alabama, Bob Jones's Eighth Congressional District in the Tennessee Valley—also Sparkman's home base—had given Hill a majority of more than 19,000 votes.[45]

Representatives of north and south Alabama exchanged barbs over this: the *Alabama Journal* described Hill as "TVA's representative in the U.S. Senate"; not wholly in jest, two north Alabama state legislators proposed that both Hill and Alabama's capital move "from the Republican stronghold of Montgomery," adding: "We will be proud and happy to have Lister Hill as an adopted son of the Tennessee valley instead of Montgomery county where he has been repudiated."[46]

Historically, north Alabama had been a center of considerable Republicanism, reflecting support by these hill country farmers for that party's nineteenth-century crusade against slavery and their resentment of lowland Democrats who controlled Alabama's government and had forced the hills into a civil war for which nonslaveowners had little or no enthusiasm. As late as the 1920s, Republicanism attracted substantial minorities in north Alabama. During tests of strength over state and local matters where the Democratic party predominated, most north Alabamians—especially after the advent of TVA—mobilized behind progressive politicians like Hill, Sparkman, Folsom, Rains, Elliott, Jones, and Roberts. But given an opportunity to rally to their old Republican flag in 1962, voters in twenty-five of twenty-nine north Alabama counties returned substantial majorities for the Democratic senatorial candidate. Hill himself believed: "North Alabama saved me."[47]

On the surface, it appeared that many voters in north and south Alabama had swapped political *views* in the course of a century. But the real change had taken place in the national focus of the two parties: the twentieth-century Republican party, having gradually withdrawn from its protective posture toward blacks, primarily represented the interests of the financially comfortable and the well-to-do; the Democratic party, having fallen heir to most black voters, now represented the aspirations of those who sought a larger share of privilege and power. Those north Alabama Republicans and south Alabama Democrats who deserted their traditional allegiances in 1962 had merely decided to vote their old convictions under a different party label.

In choosing a senator, the majority of white voters in the Tennessee Valley—Democrats as well as Republicans—had placed *economic* considerations—especially the safeguarding of TVA—ahead of their inherent racism. "About everything good we have up here either was initiated or assisted by Senator Hill," the editor of the *Florence Times* explained. Those who voted for Martin because they perceived him to be more virulent on the subject of race feared the effects of integration on their personal lives and the lives of their children. After the furor over "Ole Miss" died down, a few of these less affluent Alabamians—so one overly optimistic observer reported—"[began] to see through the fog . . . and realize that they had reacted to the cry of 'wolf' once too often."[48]

The majority of white voters in the Black Belt, where the electorate was more disproportionately female than in other sections of the state, also sensed that civil rights for blacks would bring about revolutionary changes in their societal mores. Even some members of the United Daughters of the Confederacy were reported to have marked their ballots for a Republican.[49] But many of these traditional Democrats—men in particular—realized that more was involved here than an end to segregation ordinances: fundamental changes in the racial status quo would also diminish their political and economic power.

Scanning the vote pattern for further clues, political analysts noted that more than one-third of those who had taken part in the Democratic gubernatorial primary in May failed to vote at all in the November general election. Some guessed that Alabama voters simply were not accustomed to two-party contests. But Sparkman accurately attributed this smaller turnout to Democrats who refused to vote for their party because of Oxford yet could not bring themselves to vote Republican. After all, Sparkman noted, Martin—with all his hoopla—had won only thirty thousand more votes than a little-known Republican, Julian Elgin, who had been Sparkman's nominal opponent in 1960.[50]

In addition to his white supporters in north Alabama, another bloc of voters claimed credit for Hill's narrow margin of victory. Blacks, although comprising only 7 percent of Alabama's registered voters in 1960, apparently gave the majority of their votes to the Democratic nominee. A Mobile black claimed that over 80 percent of the estimated ten thousand black voters in that city backed Hill; since the senator had won by less than seven thousand votes, Alex L. Herman concluded: "you can see what we did for him." W. C. Patton, leader of a black registration drive in Birmingham, advised Hill that he owed his reelection to "the solidified vote of the Negro," adding: "we shall expect more from you . . . in every respect than has been ours to receive in the past." Other prominent black leaders in Birmingham, such as Arthur D. Shores and A. G. Gaston, also backed Hill. Macon County, the only Black Belt county in which black voters outnumbered whites, gave Hill a 75 percent majority.[51]

If he gained in black support, Hill appeared to have lost some of his followers in organized labor. Leaders like Barney Weeks remained loyal but even Weeks conceded "some defections" on the part of rank-and-file members, primarily due to anger over "Ole Miss." Martin had carried Jefferson County, a mélange of well-to-do and working-class voters, sweeping Mountain Brook and even posting slight majorities in its labor districts. But having lost to Martin in his own home county, Hill returned the favor; largely due to vigorous support by labor and Albert Rains, he won 57 percent of the vote in Martin's home county of Etowah. Judge

Walter Gewin concluded: "The senator [Hill] was the easiest and only single target at which they could shoot." Jimmy Lawson wrote Hill: "No one else could have survived the type of attack made on you."[52]

Carl Elliott, reflecting on the Hill-Martin campaign more than a decade later, remembered another, almost forgotten group of voters who had helped to save Hill. "The old-line, anti-Hoover Depression Democrats voted for Lister," Elliott recalled. "That was their last gasp. They can't ever do it again."[53]

To Hill, the defection of numerous Alabama doctors was the unkindest cut of all. At the risk of losing many votes from labor and senior citizens, he had yielded to organized medicine's demand that he oppose Medicare; nonetheless, rumors circulated in Mobile that he planned to vote for a Medicare bill after he won reelection. In many physicians, the term "socialized medicine" aroused emotions as strong as those evoked in many union members by scare words like "racial mongrelization." Hill had given no Alabama voter—black or white—the slightest reason to claim that he favored either Medicare or civil rights. Nonetheless, he had been deserted by many beneficiaries of two major causes he had championed—improved facilities and more research funds for doctors and better conditions for working people.[54]

Reflecting on the Alabama senatorial election, some southern Republican leaders considered it unfortunate that their party should have campaigned—even in Alabama—largely on appeals to racism. They described Martin's campaign as "more anti-Kennedy for the wrong reasons than pro-Republican" and found it embarrassing that Klan members and representatives of other racist organizations should now be "whooping it up" for the Grand Old Party of black liberation. Southern Republicans deceived themselves, some of their leaders confided to Ralph McGill, if they believed that "racist votes" cast for Republicans in South Carolina and Alabama would later support a presidential nominee strongly committed to civil rights, like Nelson Rockefeller or George Romney.[55]

Loyalist Democrats, seeking some comfort other than their narrow escape from defeat in the Senate race, noted that Alabama Republicans had failed to win a single House seat. Also this surge of Republicanism might have the positive effect of jolting some Alabama Democrats into the realization that they must forget factional differences and unite to fight this new challenger. But—as one Democratic leader, Robert Vance, reflected—if growing Republicanism meant the end of the Dixiecrat movement, this short-run gain could presage long-range trouble.[56]

*With Governor "Big Jim" Folsom, center, and Congressman Carl Elliott, right,
at a meeting in Washington, 1958*

*With Congressman Carl Elliott, right, reviewing their
National Defense Education bill, 1958*

Receiving the Albert Lasker Award from Eleanor Roosevelt, 1959

*With President Kennedy, center, and Congressman John Fogarty, right,
at the signing of a health measure in the Oval Office, early 1960s*

At the tenth anniversary ceremony of the National Institute of
Arthritis and Metabolic Diseases, 1961

Greeting a potential supporter during the 1962 senatorial campaign

With President Johnson at the signing of a health measure, 1965

CHAPTER 14

The Last Term

1 9 6 3 – 1 9 6 9

"We went through the torments of hell holding office in Washington in the 1960s"

Hill never got over his feelings of hurt and disillusionment resulting from his near defeat. His staff members, his allies in the health field, and even a White House aide noticed that, when he returned to Washington, the senator seemed shaken and uncharacteristically bitter that he had been rejected by those he had sought so strenuously to help. Had he not seen to it that his hometown gained handsome federal buildings, regional and federal offices, two major military installations, and modern hospitals and clinics? One faithful friend, expressing the opinion that Montgomery would "blow away" if deprived of the things that Hill had secured for it, suggested that "the hottest place in hell" be reserved for those citizens who had turned their backs on such a benefactor.[1]

Furthermore, had he not been honored—time after time—for his legislative achievements to foster medical facilities, professional training, and research into basic health problems? Old-time medical practitioners such as his father—Hill bitterly complained to a White House aide—had been replaced by what the *New England Journal of Medicine* called "merchants of medicine." Reporting the senator's angry mood to his White House superiors, Mike Manatos assumed that Hill wanted to "get even" and henceforth might be more receptive to Medicare.[2]

Perhaps to lift Hill's spirits, a number of senators took note of his twenty-fifth anniversary in the Senate and his membership in the "self-perpetuating oligarchy" that quietly ran that body, rising on the floor to pay tribute to Hill's role in TVA, Hill-Burton, and the National Defense Education Act and laud him as their leading statesman for health. President

266

Kennedy sent greetings; even the Alabama House of Representatives passed a resolution recognizing a long tenure that many of its members had doubtless voted to end in 1962.[3]

To check on southern discontent and talk face to face with George Wallace about the civil rights demonstrations in Birmingham, John Kennedy toured northern Alabama in May. Thirty years after Hill had given President-elect Franklin Roosevelt a firsthand look at poverty in the Tennessee Valley, Hill proudly showed Kennedy the transformation wrought by TVA. This bustling industrial and recreational area impressed Kennedy as "an eloquent rebuttal to those who saw nothing but evil in this public power project." Early in his presidency, Kennedy appeared hesitant about putting southern senators on the spot by launching a civil rights struggle. "If we drive Sparkman, Hill and other moderate southerners to the wall with a lot of civil rights demands that can't pass anyway," he asked Ted Sorensen, "then what happens to the Negro on minimum wages, housing and the rest?" But when he did decide to offer a civil rights bill, the president confided to intimates his wish that some southern Senator— perhaps Hill, Fulbright, or his friend George Smathers—would break with the predominant sentiment of his region and vote for a civil rights bill.[4]

Hill, Sparkman, and north Alabama House members were to find the 1960s a political nightmare. As crisis followed crisis—Wallace's "stand in the schoolhouse door" at Tuscaloosa, the Birmingham church bombing in which four black girls died, the Selma demonstrations and the march to Montgomery, the murders of three white civil rights activists—they faced an increasing outcry from their constituents that they abandon the national Democratic party. Militant Republicanism attracted many of Alabama's former Democrats; Republican strategists waited hopefully for the slightest hint that these incumbents might be "soft" on civil rights so they could be replaced by opponents of TVA and of federal assistance to health, education, housing, and small business. Meantime thousands of other Alabamians succumbed to the siren calls of a powerful governor consumed by his own various and shifting ambitions. As Bob Jones recalled: "We went through the torments of hell holding office in Washington in the 1960s."[5]

During the momentous autumn of 1963, anti-Kennedy mail from Alabama flooded Hill's office and those of his congressional colleagues; Erskine Smith, a Democratic leader in Birmingham, suspected that this massive outpouring of "Hate-Kennedy" sentiment had been fomented by Republicans, making use of racist appeals to build sentiment in favor of Barry Goldwater for president and against Hill, Sparkman, and the north

Alabama House members. The state Democratic chairman, Roy Mayhall, was appalled by the "great degree of hatred, intolerance, and disrespect" that prevailed in Alabama toward this president prior to and immediately following his assassination; many white Alabamians (even schoolchildren) cheered the news of Kennedy's death. But now southern foes of the national Democratic party found themselves facing a different president who understood southern politics and knew how to get laws passed in the face of emotional onslaughts from his own region.[6]

"You are going to meet George Wallace and the Republicans down the road"

No matter what may have been his private thoughts concerning Lyndon Johnson, Hill felt closer to the White House than he had during the brief era of the New Frontier. In some ways, the beginning of Johnson's presidency reminded many old-timers of the early days of the New Deal; even one of FDR's old Brain Trusters, Ben Cohen, reappeared at LBJ's elbow. Most reassuring of all, Johnson possessed much of Franklin Roosevelt's shrewdness and determination to change society for the better. Unlike Kennedy, this new president seemed receptive to advice from former Senate associates; Hill and other longtime southern Democrats would no longer suffer the indignity of being perceived as anachronisms by brash, young newcomers to White House power.[7]

Furthermore, the pragmatic Johnson did not suffer from any illusion that Hill would sacrifice his power on the altar of civil rights, only to find himself succeeded by a Republican or Democratic opponent of the programs for which he had fought so hard. Knowing that Johnson understood, Hill dutifully took on the chore of captain of one of the three teams organized to filibuster against the president's far-reaching proposal to end segregation in public accommodations.

Although he felt more comfortable with the new regime in Washington, Hill's relationship with Alabama's governor showed open signs of strain. Under pressure from Wallace, the State Democratic Executive Committee abandoned its insistence upon electors pledged to support the national party ticket. Instead, the committee majority acceded to Wallace's demand that it back an independent slate free to cast Alabama's ten electoral votes for whomever it chose, perhaps for Wallace himself. Barrett Shelton was among many who suspected that Wallace and the Republicans, although theoretical enemies, shared two common goals: to deny Lyndon Johnson Alabama's electoral votes and eventually to sweep Hill and Sparkman out of the Senate. "If you two senators lose this test of strength," Shelton warned Hill, "you are going to meet George Wallace and the Republicans down the road."[8]

But how could he lead a fight back home, Hill protested, when he must be on the Senate floor from 10 A.M. to 10 P.M. every third day of a six-day week? Being a team captain, he told Shelton, was a "much, much greater" task than simply serving in the ranks of filibusterers. He must keep debate going, try to spread speaking assignments equally, serve as "back-up" man to relieve his teammates by asking questions, as well as deliver his own lengthy speeches. Opening Senate debate against the administration's public accommodations bill, Hill, quoting Blackstone, James Madison, and William Pitt the Elder, warned against the dangers of lawmaking under pressure of open civil disobedience, of using the commerce clause to invade the rights of states and private individuals, and of conferring undue powers on the executive branch of government. Commending Hill for the "honor" and "dignity" of this speech, the *Birmingham News* editorialized: "This . . . is how men should fight."[9]

Enmeshed in this ritual from March through most of June, Hill could only issue statements urging Alabamians to support electors pledged to the national nominee lest they find themselves—as in 1948—unable to vote for the Democratic presidential candidate. Sparkman followed suit. As Shelton had predicted, this open split between Alabama's senators and the state's immensely popular governor was to deepen in the months ahead.[10]

Members of the House delegation, facing another at-large race in the May Democratic primary and fearful of running on a ticket in November with Johnson and a vice presidential nominee such as Robert Kennedy or Hubert Humphrey, kept prudently silent on this matter. This second at-large race resulted from the Wallace-dominated legislature's failure to enact a redistricting bill. Democratic candidates were required to run in their old districts in May, face runoffs if necessary, then run at large in June, with the top eight to face Republican nominees in November. Albert Rains—seeing the handwriting on the wall—announced that he would not seek reelection, thus, in effect, giving Jim Martin a clear road to take over his congressional seat.[11]

As primary day neared, those Democrats who had the most to lose or gain in this struggle appeared occupied with more pressing concerns— Wallace courting support in Wisconsin and Indiana for his presidential ambitions, Hill and Sparkman bogged down in another filibuster, and the congressmen (so the *Florence Times* put it) "tongue-tied by political expediency." Nonetheless, in their May primary Alabama Democrats (and many crossover Republicans) gave Wallace and his unpledged electors a stunning victory.[12]

Hastily, all eight congressmen, by offering Wallace their support in Maryland, sought to climb on the governor's bandwagon by appearing with him at a Maryland rally. Hill declined to attend. Carl Elliott, in particular, made this expedient gesture too late. In the Democratic statewide runoff, Wallace strategists omitted Elliott's name from thousands of pamphlets listing the governor's eight-man slate of congressional nominees; Republicans, invading this primary, and Black Belt Democrats also failed to mark Elliott's name. When he did not place among the top eight contenders in this race, one of Congress's two major champions of federal aid to education and libraries lost his seat in the House and his post on its powerful Rules Committee.[13]

For loyalist Democrats, worse was yet to come. In the presidential election, almost 70 percent of Alabama voters chose Goldwater over Johnson. With Wallace's unpledged electors on the ballot, Alabama was the only state in which voters had no clear-cut choice between Republican and Democratic presidential nominees. But even had such a choice been available, Neil Davis conceded that his state probably would have gone Republican anyway. Clifford Fulford, who had led the drive for pledged electors in Birmingham, concluded: "Alabama is a one-issue state led by a one-issue Governor and about all most seem to know or care about is that Barry Goldwater voted against the Civil Rights Bill."[14]

Furthermore, three Democratic House members—George Grant of Montgomery, George Huddleston Jr. of Birmingham, and Kenneth Roberts of Anniston—lost to Republican challengers; now a Republican was to hold Hill's old House seat in the Second District. Jim Martin coasted into the post vacated by Rains; another Republican, Jack Edwards, took over Frank Boykin's old Mobile sinecure. Only three Democrats—Armistead Selden, a cautious loyalist; George Andrews, usually a dissenter from his party's national policies; and Bob Jones, the sole remaining progressive— survived the Republican landslide.[15]

When the dust of this contest had settled, some of the ninety-four local Democratic officeholders who had also lost their jobs to Republicans expressed bitterness that the enormously popular titular head of Alabama's Democratic party had made no move to save them. Close political observers noted that Wallace and Martin—theoretically the leaders of opposite parties within Alabama—had never publicly criticized one another. Many remembered that Republicans had not fielded a candidate against Wallace in 1962 and that, during Hill's campaign for reelection, Wallace had sounded more like Martin than Martin himself. After surveying the state, *Birmingham News* analysts reported the consensus of political observers that Wallace and Martin stood for many of the same concepts and shared many financial backers. Perhaps—so a number of those interviewed told these reporters—the two had at least a tacit mutual-assistance pact. But whatever understanding Wallace may have had with the Republicans, political realists conceded that this governor—by escalating the issue of race to fever pitch—had displaced Hill and Sparkman as boss of the divided and disharmonious Alabama Democrats. "Where to now?" Neil Davis wondered.[16]

"Senator Hill will blow his stack"

At least 1965 would offer a brief but welcome respite from election-year politics. With Lyndon Johnson eager to create his Great Society, Hill no longer encountered an austere or hostile attitude from the White House toward health appropriations and programs. To champion Johnson's grandiose plans, Louisiana's Russell Long took up the responsibilities of Democratic whip. Asked to comment on the fact that another Deep South senator had assumed this politically risky post, Hill responded simply that "he hoped and believed that regional bars to Senate leadership are gone for good."[17]

But with national television focused on Martin Luther King's drive for voting rights in Alabama's Black Belt, Hill saw no escape for himself from regional conformity. Although he knew it was hopeless to oppose Johnson's dramatic plea for a voting-rights bill, he took an even stronger role in the southern opposition, even in the face of a national outpouring of support for King's marchers and their cause. If Congress should give in to every group demonstrating in the streets, he asked the Senate, "where will this road lead us and where can the line ever be drawn again?" For Congress to pass a bill abolishing poll taxes in state as well as federal elections, he argued, would invade a right clearly reserved to states; such action would only be constitutional if—as in 1964—the Constitution itself were amended. But even as he delivered his familiar arguments, Hill knew that—after their franchise had been enforced by the federal government—Alabama's new black voters would have little choice except to support him.[18]

Determined to champion causes of his own, Hill devoted himself more strenuously than ever to his legislative interests. Even the president noted that the chairman of the Senate's Committee on Labor and Public Welfare had become increasingly autocratic, independent of White House influence, and jealous of his prerogatives. "Senator Hill will blow his stack" if the administration should block his demand for an extra fifty million dollars for Hill-Burton, Jack Valenti once warned Johnson. When Hill was confined to Bethesda Hospital for several days with a badly broken wrist, Mike Manatos reported to the president that the "sensitive" senator would resent any suggestion that someone else handle legislation pending before his committee. Perturbed by a rumor that the president, looking for an appropriations bill to veto, had focused on the sums allotted for labor and HEW, Manatos warned Johnson that Hill was "the last individual" he should risk offending in this manner. "When you sign the bill for heart, cancer, and stroke," another White House aide cautioned the president, "be sure to mention Hill, its sole sponsor in the Senate."[19]

As befitted a senior lawmaker, Hill now spent most of his days on the Senate floor or in committee meetings, leaving Cronin to run his office and deal with the everyday concerns of voters back home. Over the years, Hill had found it increasingly irritating to expend his valuable time and energy arranging minor favors for constituents. Now he enjoyed release from this and other mundane chores, appearing only mildly interested in details that he had once insisted on supervising. Vaguely surprised when he noticed a new person on his office staff, Hill inquired of Cronin: "Who's that girl in the red dress?" Now that he was no longer their relentless taskmaster, his staff found their boss more human and took pride in working for such an important and powerful senator. "I will always remember you as . . . *my* senator and a very great man!" declared one departing staff member who had "found that working on Saturdays was my only downfall."[20]

With a sympathetic Democrat in the Oval Office, the majority of his Senate colleagues bowing to his leadership on matters of health, and Fogarty taking a similar role in the House, Hill won approval—almost at will—of the legislation he favored. He convinced the Senate to commit federal funds for regional programs to bring the latest advances in medicine to victims of heart disease, cancer, and stroke; help construct regional medical libraries and community facilities for health research, care of the mentally retarded, and treatment of the mentally ill; to enact stronger controls over drug abuse; foster vocational rehabilitation of the disabled and handicapped; and train medical librarians, health professionals, such as dental hygienists, physical therapists, and technologists, and teachers for the deaf, blind, and handicapped.

Under Johnson's strong hand, Congress finally overrode the American Medical Association's long-standing objection to federally underwritten health insurance for any group of Americans. The fact that many Alabama doctors had failed in 1962 to show their appreciation for Hill's dedication to their profession and for his previous opposition to Medicare still rankled. In the summer of 1965, Hill and Sparkman reversed themselves, voting in favor of Medicare, to provide hospital insurance for elderly recipients of Social Security; and Medicaid, to provide federal funding for state programs of medical care for the poor. Within a few weeks, the AMA came to the pragmatic conclusion that—having failed to beat these programs—it would join their advisory councils and reap their benefits. Medicare—as Hill later told an interviewer—had transformed millions of older Americans from charity patients to "paying customers."[21]

In other aspects of his fiefdom, Hill found that he could not always rule unchallenged. Despite his protestations, Hill-Burton had been amended to conform with a federal court decision barring segregation in hospitals receiving funds under this act.[22] Furthermore, Hill, Fogarty, and the health lobbyists found themselves increasingly on the defensive as Eisenhower, Kennedy, and even Johnson questioned whether Congress should continue to add an additional one hundred or two hundred million dollars each year to administration budgets for federal medical research.

Eisenhower had been the first chief executive to suggest that the government could be pushing medical research so fast that it might encourage "waste and boondoggle" in NIH and its network of university researchers. Gracious—and cagey—as ever, Hill agreed to a suggestion by his Republican colleague Leverett Saltonstall that an independent committee evaluate whether or not these research funds were being efficiently used. Packed with longtime advocates of this cause, like Sidney Farber, Michael De Bakey, and General David Sarnoff, the committee not only concluded that NIH funds had been spent "with remarkable efficiency" but recommended a $264 million increase in the president's next budget for medical research. By now, the federal government's annual investment in NIH was approaching one billion dollars.[23]

When his turn came to submit presidential budgets, Kennedy persuaded his fellow Democratic Irishman from New England, Fogarty, not to raise the administration's ante. But the adamant Hill refused to tolerate interference in his authority over appropriations from this former junior senator. With Hill marshaling his friends and supporters, William Proxmire failed in his annual efforts to reduce NIH appropriations. Any senator who voted against such increases, Proxmire complained, risked being pictured as "the fast friend of cancer, the buddy of heart disease."[24]

Eventually a special House committee investigated the question of whether there might be waste in NIH's administration of such a huge budget. Although the Fountain committee found little specific to criticize, its inquiry proved the first effective wedge into the domination of NIH appropriations by Congress. After Kennedy's assassination, Johnson created a second special committee to study "whether the American people are getting their money's worth" from NIH's approximately billion-dollar budget. The Woolridge committee concluded that NIH spent its budget "wisely and well in the public interest," suggesting only that it strengthen its organization and procedures. Thereafter, even Johnson sought to embrace the cause of medical research; Proxmire, finding it hopeless to fight this president as well as two major congressional proponents, temporarily abandoned his crusade.[25]

Hill also had the satisfaction of seeing the life and scope of some of his major achievements extended. In 1964, Hill-Burton had been expanded to fund construction of rehabilitation and diagnostic facilities as well as nursing homes; in 1966, major figures in the field of health gathered to observe the twentieth anniversary of this program that, through its formula for local-state-federal cost sharing, had brought about the construction of nearly ten thousand general and mental hospitals, tuberculosis sanitoriums, public health centers, nursing homes, and other specialized facilities.

In 1966, the Library Services Act was extended an additional five years and expanded to bring reading materials to prisoners, hospital patients, orphans, the aged, handicapped, and mentally ill. With fifty-two co-sponsors from both parties, Hill's measure whizzed through the Senate in less than five minutes. The House followed suit, with sponsors lauding this act as a model of federal grant legislation, preserving local and state responsibility while stimulating increased financial support for libraries.[26]

Backed by Kennedy and Johnson, the National Defense Education Act had also been extended and expanded to provide for construction of higher education facilities and enlargement of its graduate fellowship program. With the 1964 Civil Rights Act having outlawed discrimination in any program receiving federal assistance and with sentiment growing for aid to parochial schools, Hill found himself again confronting "the Scylla of race and the Charybdis of religion." Accordingly, the White House noted, Hill would not be one of the co-sponsors of a bill renewing the path-breaking legislation that he had fostered in 1958 under the umbrella of national security.[27]

By 1964, HEW had spent more than one billion dollars under the authority of NDEA, including financial assistance to more than 8,500 graduate students, 600,000 undergraduates, 42,000 vocational students, and 17,000 teachers of foreign languages. Moving away from national security preoccupations, Congress agreed to assist students in history, civics, geography, English, and reading, in addition to science, math, language, and engineering. Under Johnson's Great Society concept, the rationale for NDEA shifted from beating the Russians to abolishing poverty.[28]

On opening day of the Ninetieth Congress in January 1967, John Fogarty unexpectedly died of a heart attack; the loss of Fogarty would mark the beginning of the end of the powerful coalition that had funded medical research almost at will. After more than a decade, the cause of sustaining medical research as a major national priority had lost steam; those most intimately involved had fallen to fighting among themselves as to priorities and methods. With the costs of war in Southeast Asia escalating, domestic programs were bound to suffer. In 1968, Hill would once again lead the Senate in raising the proposed appropriations for the National Institutes of Health above the amounts proposed by the House or the Budget Bureau. But this was to be the last time that Hill would persuade his colleagues to follow his lead in this particular area; skeptical about its results, Congress eventually cut NIH funding. An era of unparalleled government generosity in funding basic medical research had ended.[29]

"Knowing when to quit"

At the close of December 1967—the day after Lister Hill's seventy-third birthday—the *Washington Post* observed in an editorial: "In public life, knowing when to quit is an essential ingredient of greatness and perhaps even of continued public esteem." Congratulating Senator Frank Carlson of Kansas on his decision to retire at the end of his present term, the *Post* noted that at least fifteen senators were seventy or older; with the work of

Congress so taxing, the *Post* questioned the capability of those members to carry such burdens into their late seventies or early eighties. Staying on, the editorial warned, might lead to political defeat, bitterness, and loss of prestige.[30]

For more than a year, Alabamians had speculated whether their senior senator would seek a sixth term. Hill would start his thirty-first year in the Senate in January; only Richard Russell, Louisiana's Allen Ellender, and Arizona's Carl Hayden had served longer in that body. Hill's health was good—better, in fact, than it had been immediately following the wearing filibusters of 1964 and 1965.[31]

Whether Hill chose to run or not, a number of political hopefuls had already hinted their interest in his seat. These possible candidates ranged from the unrealistic (Dallas County sheriff, Jim Clark), to the previously defeated (Folsom, Elliott, Jimmy Faulkner), to the less widely known (State Senator E. W. Skidmore, and the former state agriculture commissioner A. W. Todd), to the strongest potential challengers (state Attorney General MacDonald Gallion, Congressman Armistead Selden, Lieutenant Governor Albert Brewer, Jim Martin, former Lieutenant Governor James B. Allen, or even George Wallace himself). Joking over the size of this field, the *Foley Onlooker* compared it to the 1968 Alabama football squad.[32]

But with the filing date for Alabama's 1968 Democratic primary less than four months away, Hill remained silent. By this time in 1965, John Sparkman—frightened by his colleague's close call in 1962—had been vigorously promoting his own reelection for almost a year, spending weekends in Alabama, mending fences, and making contacts with new backers from the field of business. Some of these converts to Sparkman's cause had discovered that their junior senator could be vastly more helpful than Alabama's freshman Republican congressmen, especially since Sparkman chaired a housing subcommittee as well as the Select Committee on Small Business. Others feared that, if Sparkman were defeated, the Senate Committee on Banking and Currency might be headed either by Paul Douglas of Illinois or William Proxmire—both of whom they considered hostile to their interests. Some still smarted at the recollection that Douglas's wife had marched at Selma. Alarmed by both these prospects, national leaders of the business community passed word to their cohorts in Alabama: "Keep Sparkman." Shortly after the primary, Jimmy Lawson concluded: "These things elected Sparkman."[33]

Alabama politics had taken other unexpected turns in 1966. Ryan De Graffenried, considered the most likely challenger to the Wallace regime, died in an airplane crash in February. Wallace, barred from succeeding himself as governor, startled many old political pros by successfully masterminding the nomination of his wife, Lurleen. Jim Martin had made the mistake of announcing his candidacy for governor before Wallace played his hand; even after the stunning victory of the governor's wife in the Democratic primary, Martin pursued this hapless cause. In November, he won only 31 percent of the total vote; as one analyst later explained, "it was hard for a rich man's segregationist to beat a poor man's segregationist." By opposing Lurleen Wallace at the polls, Martin also destroyed whatever tacit cooperation prevailed between the governor and the Republicans. If Martin should again oppose Hill—so a political writer for the *Birmingham News* believed—"[he] could not expect to get in 1968 the kind of tacit and indirect support he got from Wallace in 1962."[34]

Rumors of a split between Martin and his 1962 campaign manager, John Grenier, spread after Grenier announced that he would take on the supposedly possible task of unseating Sparkman. Martin and Grenier had fallen out—so gossip had it—over their respective political assignments, especially after it became obvious that Alabama voters would follow their governor's advice to elect his wife. The *Andalusia Star-News*, although not a Martin supporter, sympathized with the congressman's hard luck in "[being] forced by his best friends to tackle the magic Wallace name at the polls." But Grenier, too, encountered formidable opposition in Sparkman and his new business backers. Opposed only by Crommelin and a little-known candidate from Huntsville with the politically familiar name of Frank (E.) Dixon, Sparkman had won 57 percent of Alabama's voters in the May primary, a far cry from his 1960 landslide of 83 percent but certainly a more comfortable victory than that of Lister Hill four years earlier. In the November election, Sparkman polled 60 percent of the vote.[35]

By the end of 1967, the field of those interested in challenging Hill had narrowed considerably. Wallace, obsessed with his presidential ambitions, no longer loomed as a possible Senate contender. The governor would be busy carrying his third-party bid to the nation by denouncing Lyndon Johnson, the Supreme Court, and Congress. With the regular Alabama Democratic machinery pledged to Wallace's candidacy, John Harper, Jefferson County Democratic chairman, proposed putting together a coalition of loyalists, blacks, and young voters pledged to Johnson. Thus Hill would find himself embroiled once more in an old conflict between party dissenters and loyalists; only now there were *new* players in this game.[36]

But even if Wallace had no interest in the 1968 Senate race, his loyal

lieutenant governor, Jim Allen, who had abstained from challenging Lurleen Wallace in 1966, would likely carry the governor's colors against Hill.
Awaiting the winner of Democratic infighting would probably be another
contest with Jim Martin. "You need to get back home," Barrett Shelton had
implored Hill months earlier. "You need for people to see you and to know
you. You need to start your campaign."[37]

"I beg to say that I will not be a candidate"

As he struggled to make up his mind, Hill often asked Cronin: "Can I
win?" To which that realistic aide responded: "Yes, but it will take a
herculean effort!" We would need to put together an organization, Cronin
explained, and to travel, as had Sparkman, seven days a week. After forty-
four years in Congress, the strain of all those working Saturdays and
Sundays and long filibusters had begun to tell on Hill. "I'm not as young as
I used to be," he confessed to this aide who had assumed the role of trusted
adviser once borne by Roy Nolen and Foots Clement. What's more, his
administrative assistant advised, the senator would have to update his
political style to prevail over Allen with his powerful Wallace backing.
Last but certainly not least, to engage in two grueling campaigns would
mean scrapping his beloved health legislation for at least six months. As he
watched Hill absorb all this, Cronin saw weariness in his boss's face and
body. "He was ready to get out," Cronin remembered.[38]

At 7:30 A.M. on Saturday, 20 January 1968, Hill telephoned Jim Free,
Washington correspondent for his longtime press supporter, the *Birmingham News*. He had heard that Alabama was astir over rumors about his
political future, Hill told Free, and he wished to settle this question.
Straining to keep his emotions under control, Hill read Free a brief statement. As of the following January, he stated, he would be seventy-four
years old and would have served in Congress forty-six years. He thanked
his friends and supporters. In a phrase both archaic and graceful, he
announced: "I beg to say that I will not be a candidate for reelection." Then
Hill went to his office, as he had almost every Saturday morning that
Congress had been in session since 1923.[39]

Hill's announcement saddened his friends and surprised his enemies.
Barney Weeks tried desperately to persuade Hill to change his mind. No,
Hill said, he had prepared his statement and called the press. "Alabama
without . . . Lister Hill in Congress hardly [seemed] possible" to the

Birmingham News. Neil Davis, responding to Wallace Malone's recent charge that Hill had "not stood up for Alabama . . . when the South was being castigated and tortured," told his readers that the senator had devoted four decades to improving the health, education, and economy of his state and nation. "Stand up for Alabama?" Davis asked. "Something other than fiery speechifying is involved."[40]

Perceiving Hill as no longer a threat to the established order of things, some old foes conceded that certain aspects of his service had been valuable. The *Montgomery Advertiser*, recalling the 1962 election but choosing not to mention that it had failed to support Hill, reflected that thousands of Alabamians had been "in such high dudgeon that they were willing to sacrifice Hill . . . who had done more for them and all Americans than any man the state has ever sent to Washington." Only a fearless candidate, the *Advertiser* added, would now seek to convince Alabama voters that they should have remained diseased, poor, and undereducated in order to protect states' rights. The *Alabama Journal* admitted that Hill had accomplished his missions of bringing electricity to remote farms, hospitals to isolated communities, and ensuring a more respectable living for many Alabamians. Unfortunately for Hill, the *Journal* added, the label of a "government-action man [becomes a handicap] when abundance creates a passion for the status quo." Hamner Cobbs admitted that he found Hill "much more acceptable than in the past, and . . . [I] have begun to recognize his great value to the country." Even Hill's most consistent foe, the *Mobile Register*, referred to his "distinguished, vital service to health."[41]

Outside Alabama, comments were blunter. The *Winston-Salem Journal* regretted that Alabama, having once sent to Washington "one of the brightest, most influential congressional delegations," was now dominated by Wallace "whose own populism is merely a sausage skin for his racist ambitions." Hill's name would grace historic legislation, this North Carolina editor predicted, "when George Wallace is reduced to a pathetic footnote in history." The *Greensboro* (N.C.) *Daily News* regretted that "the Alabama of George Wallace could not produce another Lister Hill and, if somehow one appeared, the state would not elect him."[42]

The *New York Times*, describing Hill as one of a dwindling band of white Southerners "trapped by the racial history of their region . . . who dared to be progressive on every issue except civil rights," declared that he had "done more for the health of Americans in modern times than any man outside the medical profession." Lyndon Johnson, soon to follow Hill's example in deciding not to run again, wrote: "It is hard to believe that you are truly leaving the Senate."[43]

Hill's decision set off political maneuvering in Alabama. Wallace still insisted he had no interest in the Senate. Barney Weeks sought to persuade Howell Heflin, nephew of Hill's first Senate opponent, to run for Hill's place. When Heflin declined, the labor leader concluded sadly: "We were left with nobody." Crommelin once again entered the lists; Folsom made a pathetic attempt to recapture some of his old popularity. Hill let it be known that he favored Selden, but the senator discovered that—unlike George Wallace—he could not transfer his popularity to another candidate. In the Democratic runoff of 1968, Allen narrowly defeated Selden. With Martin refusing to run "for personal reasons," Allen won an easy victory over a lesser-known Republican candidate.[44]

Only Hill knew what had prompted him to retire. The fact that five of his Senate colleagues also decided not to offer for reelection may have had some bearing. His wife's deteriorating health had surely been a major factor. Stewart McClure theorized that Hill knew he had "done his great work" and that—considering the public mood and the war in Vietnam—he could not hope to accomplish much more. The *Montgomery Advertiser* guessed that, although passions over the racial issue had cooled since 1962, the certainty of vigorous opposition from Jim Allen—or the possibility that Wallace might change his mind and run for the Senate—had caused Hill to decide against another long, hard fight for reelection. Bob Jones did not believe that Hill could have been beaten in 1968—but Hill had never been one to gamble. Perhaps above all, he had been influenced by the *Washington Post*'s warning—with its echo of his father's and Professor Starke's old adages—that a wise elder statesman should not suffer the fate of Norris and Walter George (and later Fulbright) but should end his career a winner.[45]

His announcement caught many of his colleagues and friends in the health lobby by surprise. "I was absolutely stunned," Mary Lasker remembered. When she and Florence Mahoney lost Hill as well as their House champion, Fogarty, medical research—so one writer put it—"[passed] into a condition of political orphanage." Members of Hill's Committee on Labor and Public Welfare formally expressed their "profound admiration" for their retiring chairman's "matchless record." If senators had to select only five members who had rendered "the greatest service to the people" in the entire history of that body, Ralph Yarborough told the Senate that

"Lister Hill would have to be on that list." Jacob Javits described his committee colleague as having "literally fought like a tiger . . . until some reasonable semblance of what he was seeking was effectuated." As a consequence of Wayne Morse's defeat in 1968, Yarborough would succeed Hill as chairman. Stewart McClure, who considered the Texan "one of the most disorganized" of senators, was appalled. "My God," the chief clerk thought to himself, "this man is going to fill the shoes left by Lister Hill? Never, never, never."[46]

During Hill's final months in the Senate, numerous organizations in the fields of health, education, and librarianship hastened to thank him for his work on their behalf. The American College of Cardiology, Association of American Medical Colleges, American College of Surgeons, National Heart Institute, American Library Association, National Education Association, and Alabama's major health associations (hoping to erase the bitter taste of 1962) all added to the plaques adorning Hill's office walls. But Hill's largest and most enduring monument would be a skyscraper addition to the National Library of Medicine that he had rescued from obsolescence. Both houses of Congress readily agreed to Sparkman's resolution that the new library annex to be built on the campus of the National Institutes of Health be named the Lister Hill Center for Biomedical Communications.

Although Hill had supported a broad spectrum of health legislation, he had always been careful to foster and expand his first major effort—the Hill-Burton hospital construction program. Hospital leaders feared that Hill-Burton would die when its sponsor retired and its legislation expired in 1969. Earlier Hill, concerned about the need for modernization of urban hospitals, had unsuccessfully proposed a bill to extend his program another five years. In midsummer of his last year in the Senate, he managed to tack onto another health measure a rider extending Hill-Burton construction grants for one additional year. As the *Medical World News* commented: "For a man about to retire, and in the face of Administration opposition, it was considered a significant legislative triumph. But it was also his last."[47]

In September 1968, the Department of Health, Education, and Welfare observed the tenth anniversary of the National Defense Education Act with a special ceremony. Congress had just approved a new Higher Education Act authorizing further enlargement of the student-loan and graduate-fellowship programs. HEW Secretary Wilbur Cohen felt that it would be "unthinkable" to observe this anniversary without the presence of Hill and

Carl Elliott. The department gave both men its Distinguished Public Service Award, after which Hill reminisced about the Sputnik crisis and the
genesis of this measure.[48]

On Tuesday, 19 November 1968, Hill went to his Senate office for the
last time. There was no fanfare. Aware that an era had ended, Tommy
Corcoran and Ben Cohen, his old friends from New Deal days, paid a brief
call. Hill bade his staff good-bye; he did not plan to return in January 1969
for the last few days of his term. The following day he went to New York to
receive a special Lasker Foundation Award on the same stage with two of
America's Nobel Prize winners for medical research.[49]

Then Lister Hill went home to Montgomery.

CHAPTER 15

The Homecoming

1 9 6 9 – 1 9 8 4

"Isn't it a hell of a thing when you . . . have to retire?"

What a wrenching experience it must have been for Hill to leave the Senate. At seventy-four, he felt almost as vigorous and energetic as ever. But with no laws to create, no coalitions to put together, not even any more jousts with the "ancient enemy," how was he to pass the time? Like his father, Hill had made work his paramount concern, his only hobby. He never even considered following Hugo Black's advice that he find more time to relax and that he take up some sport like tennis or golf. As he grew older, Hill occasionally wondered if he had made a mistake by worrying so much and failing to get "the pleasure out of life that [I] should have." Now his wife's illness made even the temporary diversion of travel impossible. Ever self-disciplined, Hill never complained that this circumstance virtually imprisoned him in Montgomery. But he hated retirement. Obviously already dreading this prospect, he had told an interviewer in 1967: "Isn't it a hell of a thing when you get to an age when you have to retire? I think we ought to pass a law against that!"[1]

On weekdays, Hill often made the hour-long walk from his unpretentious bungalow at 1618 Gilmer Avenue to his office in the imposing, marble post office building he had wangled for his hometown in the depths of the Great Depression. He still received a fair amount of mail; many Alabamians, in the habit of directing their appeals to him, wrote to request help with a pension, getting a son out of the service, or finding a job with a federal agency. Hill had once found these small requests bothersome; now they at least gave him something to do, if only to refer these correspondents to someone else.[2]

283

In the first years of his retirement, Hill sometimes wrote former colleagues in the Senate to suggest a piece of legislation or a cause he thought they should pursue. But with the passing of the years, he came to realize how remote he was from Washington and how little remained of his once-powerful influence. At least it was comforting to know someone else who must have had this same feeling. Hill wrote Harry Truman to congratulate the former president on his eighty-eighth birthday. "You truly stand with George Washington, Andrew Jackson—and the greatest!" he told Truman feelingly. How long ago it must have seemed that he and Truman had taken opposite paths on the issue of civil rights. After he had finished with the mail, Hill killed another hour or so by having lunch and greeting old friends at the Elite Restaurant. Some days he walked home.[3]

But as time passed, even the most isolated rural Alabamians realized that Hill no longer represented them in Washington. The mail dwindled to a trickle, no longer deserving the effort of a walk downtown. As had Dr. Hill, the senator spent much of his time in a book-lined study, reading late into the night, then rising early to get the *Advertiser* and try to find out what was going on in Washington. He wrote a paper about his father's famous heart operation. He enjoyed visits from his twin, Amelie, and from his daughter, son, in-laws, and grandchildren.

Hill also renewed his old friendship with Richard Rives, who had been his closest Montgomery confidant after the death of Roy Nolen. Montgomery's elite had welcomed Hill home with surface politeness; behind his back, many (women in particular) decried him for having been—like Franklin Roosevelt—a traitor to his class. But Rives had been proud of having as a friend "one who has done so much . . . to help average men and women enjoy a more abundant life." During the height of the racial troubles, Hill and Rives felt it prudent to meet secretly, if at all. Now their retirements made such caution unnecessary. It was good to have a kindred spirit in Montgomery with whom one could talk freely.[4]

But Hill and Hugo Black never mended the break brought about by the different demands of the 1950s and 1960s upon one who held a lifetime post in the nation's highest court and another subject to the whims and passions of the electorate. In April 1967, Henrietta and Lister Hill had attended a White House party given by President and Mrs. Johnson to honor Black's thirty years of service on the Supreme Court. Afterward, the justice's wife, Elizabeth, noted in her diary that this marked "the first time Lister has come around Hugo in almost ten years." It may also have been their last meeting.[5] Their paths, once so similar, had diverged. Black, free to express whatever views he chose, was to become a hero to civil libertarians who readily forgave his former expedient alliance with the Klan. Hill—who had considered the Supreme Court of the 1930s too conservative for its times—believed that by the late 1960s "the pendulum has swung too far in the other direction."[6] There could be no further meeting of their minds.

Occasionally an Alabama organization representing one of his interests—like the Rural Electric Cooperatives, the League of Women Voters, the American Legion, or an institution connected with health or education—presented Hill with another citation, plaque, or honorary degree. In Alabama, the largest and most fitting memorial to bear his name would be the Lister Hill Library, housing a health-related collection for students and faculty of the Medical Center of the University of Alabama at Birmingham, a major beneficiary of Hill's legislation and his skill in acquiring grants and appropriations. With obvious pleasure, Hill watched as this building was dedicated to him in October 1971.

In Montgomery, Hill would be memorialized on a smaller and more unobtrusive scale. His name would appear on a plaque in a downtown plaza named for him; after his death, his daughter and son would arrange for a bust of their father to be placed on the grounds of Alabama's historic, old capitol.

But although most Alabamians did not realize this, their state was filled with memorials to Hill's forty-five years in Congress. In rural counties, every hospital but two had been constructed with the help of Hill-Burton funds. In Alabama alone, this act resulted in almost three hundred additional health facilities, containing nearly ten thousand beds; each county in Alabama now had a public health center. In the nation as a whole, over nine thousand general and mental hospitals, rehabilitation facilities, crippled children's clinics, sanitoriums, nursing homes, and other health facilities—more than half of them located in towns of less than five thousand—had been completed with the help of Hill-Burton funds, adding almost half a million beds for patients.[7]

From the passage of the Library Services Act in 1956 until Hill's retirement in 1968, the number of books in Alabama's public libraries had almost doubled; almost every county had some form of free public library service. The modest goal of one public library book for each of Alabama's citizens was in sight. Nationally, the legislation originally sponsored by

Hill and Elliott had a snowballing effect in new library buildings for colleges, universities, schools, and communities; books and nonprint materials where they had never existed before.[8]

In rural Alabama, the electricity and telephone service for which Hill had fought were commonplace, even in the still sparsely populated Second Congressional District. Because of the aluminum plant at Listerhill, the Marshall Space Center at Huntsville, and the numerous military bases Hill had obtained for his state, thousands of Alabamians—most of them descendants of tenants and sharecroppers—now had skilled, well-paying jobs or businesses of their own. Unskilled workers, many of them blacks, had the protection of a minimum wage, the central issue of the Alabama senatorial campaign of 1937. Social Security, Medicare, and Medicaid assisted the elderly of both races; federal college loans helped their descendants to rise in status. By 1968, three billion dollars had been spent nationally under the Hill-Elliott NDEA to support 15,000 graduate fellows, make loans to 1.5 million undergraduates, train 122,000 teachers and 44,000 guidance counselors, establish 106 foreign-language and area-studies centers, and fund almost half a million projects in modernized teaching techniques.[9]

In the spring of 1980, the Lister Hill National Center for Biomedical Communications was completed in Bethesda, Maryland. One floor had been set aside for the Fogarty International Center. At eighty-five, Hill, although confined to a wheelchair, attended this dedication and heard his work extolled. The National Library of Medicine, so outdated when he had rescued it from decrepitude in 1956, had become the world's largest medical research library; the wing named for Hill housed a network of computers geared to using modern technology to keep health-care professionals around the world informed about the latest developments in medicine.

The tall tower bearing Hill's name overlooks the campus of the National Institutes of Health, elevated through the efforts of Hill, Fogarty, and the health lobby from an obscure governmental enterprise in the early 1950s to a medical research empire that by 1968 supported sixty-seven thousand senior research investigators, helped to train more than thirty-five thousand specialists in basic science and clinical areas, and sustained academic science programs and research projects in more than two thousand universities and medical schools. Between 1950 and 1968, these widespread and generously financed efforts conquered or brought closer to control the diseases of tuberculosis, pneumonia, poliomyelitis, malaria, mumps, diptheria, and German measles, and made major advances in the treatment of mental illness, heart disease, cancer, hypertension, rheumatoid arthritis, juvenile diabetes, vascular diseases, hepatitis, sickle cell anemia, Parkinson's disease, venereal disease, kidney disease, dental disease, blindness, and inborn errors of metabolism.[10]

Other buildings in Washington and New York City symbolize causes that Hill had pioneered: the Pentagon, headquarters for a unified national defense, and the United Nations building in New York City, where representatives of many countries and cultures struggle to resolve their differences.

When he was eighty-eight years old, Hill attended the fiftieth anniversary of another major national enterprise he had helped to create. George Norris had first envisioned the experiment in multipurpose river development that was to become the Tennessee Valley Authority. Franklin Roosevelt had possessed the power and boldness to bring Norris's vision to a reality. Hill, not yet forty years old in 1933 and not inclined by nature to derring-do, had gone along with Norris and Roosevelt. But as he watched TVA begin to transform northern Alabama and parts of neighboring states from predominant poverty and rurality to prosperity and industrialization, Hill had forgotten his initial doubts about putting the government in the power business. Even before Roosevelt and Norris had passed from the scene, Hill had become TVA's most vigilant, ardent, and powerful defender. By 1983, TVA had lost its reform image but it remained the New Deal's most visible accomplishment.

Despite the threat of stormy weather, Hill boarded the small plane provided by Governor George Wallace to take him to this ceremony. Citizens of the Tennessee Valley—who had helped elect him to five terms in the Senate and to give him his narrow margin of victory in 1962—had ample reasons other than sentimental to rise and clap that day for Lister Hill. In the course of their transition from poverty to middle-class status, many in this region turned away from the national party that had sponsored this benefaction. But now they greeted the old co-sponsor of TVA with genuine warmth. In his brief response, Hill joked that he hoped to be around for TVA's one hundredth birthday.

Lister Hill, surrounded by his family, died of pneumonia on 20 December 1984, a few days short of what would have been his ninetieth birthday. Around two hundred, including Governor George Wallace in his wheelchair, United States Senator Howell Heflin, and some of the judges named to the federal bench through Hill's influence, attended his simple funeral in a Montgomery cemetery. Military pallbearers bore the flag-draped casket of this veteran of World War I, former chairman of the House Military Affairs Committee, and former member of the Senate Armed Services Committee. An honor guard fired a twenty-one-gun salute. An Episcopal rector, assisted by a curate and a Catholic priest, read passages from Scripture. A bugler sounded taps.

C O D A

In retirement, Hill had spent hours in his bedroom, arranging envelopes stuffed with more than eighty pieces of major legislation he had sponsored. "I'm trying to get things together," he explained to one of his rare visitors from the press.[1] What did he hope the contents of these envelopes might reveal? That he had fulfilled Sir Joseph Lister's wish for his namesake to lead a life of "health, goodness, and usefulness"? That he had been successful enough to appease the demanding ghosts of old Luther Leonidas and Dr. L. L. Hill? That he, like George Norris, had dedicated himself to bettering the human condition? That his accomplishments would justify—to the shades of a Lilly Hill or a Frank Graham—his concessions to political reality?

Perhaps Hill, ever the Puritan, was accounting to himself. What had been the fruits of having managed to remain in Congress forty-five years, five months, and four days—longer than all but seven members in the history of that body? Of having always preferred caution to risk, been ever willing to compromise rather than lose his objective altogether, and of having—so one colleague put it—"harnessed himself with patience so as to bring a law before that body in its proper season"?[2]

What had been the rewards of having carefully guarded his personal reputation in matters of women and finances? Of having managed to get along with colleagues of different parties and disparate views? Of having held his staff to his own rigid standards? And, above all, of having made work his paramount concern—above pleasure, self-indulgence, even family?

Half a century after his own graduation from Starke School, Hill (addressing a class of boys who would attain manhood during the rebellious decade of the 1960s) had extolled Professor Starke's motto "Work Wins" and praised his old headmaster's insistence upon the "homely virtues of . . . truth and honesty, of courage and forthrightness, of humility and love of your fellow man."[3] Now, at the end of his career, Hill fingered the envelopes that symbolized his lifelong commitment to work and to the "homely virtues" as he had interpreted them.

Despite his Catholic upbringing and his professions of Methodism as an adult, Hill—like his father—had never wholeheartedly embraced conventional forms of religion. Like Jefferson, he judged himself and others primarily in terms of contributions to society. Expressing to Jesse Hearin his opinion of a powerful figure in Alabama's economy, Hill had once written: "What a pity a man who exercises so much economic power cannot have a bigger soul and a broader vision."[4]

George Norris exemplified to Hill the ideal public servant. From Norris and Franklin Roosevelt, Hill had learned that—when states could not or would not effect laws for the betterment of society—the power of the federal government could be brought into play. He had made himself a master of the process of creating laws that employed this strong, central power to open wider vistas of knowledge, alleviate physical pain and suffering, and add to the longevity, security, and dignity of the human condition. Long after Hill's retirement and death, the principle of federal aid to health research and education would continue to benefit countless Americans.

During Hill's first term in the Senate, Norris—exerting his influence upon this promising young legislator—had inscribed a gift of his picture: "To Senator Hill, with the hope that he will continue his never-ending fight for human liberty and higher and better civilization." Had he fulfilled his mentor's wish, Hill may have wondered as he rearranged the envelopes containing laws he had sponsored. On this score, those who knew Hill best—his Senate colleagues and his staff—had little doubt. Men who rarely concurred on other topics, like John Stennis and Mark Hatfield, agreed that Hill had led a "wonderful, productive life" and called him the nation's "Statesman for Health." Mary Lasker and Florence Mahoney remembered how handsomely Hill had credited others with achievements that had been primarily his own. Wayne Morse concluded that Hill had turned the once minor post of chairman of the Senate's Labor and Public Welfare Committee into "the greatest instrument for human progress in our legislative history."[5]

Even those who chafed under his stern discipline, like Mike Gorman, Don Cronin, and Stewart McClure, proved willing to overlook what a hard taskmaster Hill had been and to remember him as a "decent figure in politics," a "beautiful man," and, in McClure's estimate, "the greatest single legislator of this century, in terms of volume . . . impact . . . breadth of interest . . . and skill in creating laws."[6]

But in order to make his contributions, Hill had to attain and retain public office. His electoral victories exacted their price from one always subject to the whims and passions of a sparsely educated, racially divided, and easily manipulated citizenry and constantly opposed by powerful defenders of the status quo. His politic defection from the Catholic church, thereby grievously wounding Lilly Hill, and the concealment of his partially Jewish heritage had been Hill's initial concessions to political reality. But with the passage of time, these matters had faded into the realms of gossip and memory.

However, the third coin in the price of power for Lister Hill—his stand against civil rights—cast a lasting shadow over his long record of public service. In his home state, many on both sides of the philosophical spectrum faulted Hill for choosing the course of political survival. Virginia Durr, whose husband, Clifford, hàd sacrificed his promising career for principle but whose more pragmatic brother-in-law, Hugo Black, had once made a crucial bargain with the Klan, succinctly expressed the attitude of both sets of critics: "The reactionaries didn't think Lister was enough of a racist and the liberals thought he was too much of one. So he got caught in the crossfire."[7]

Many plain whites felt cheated that their senator managed to fight civil rights without invoking, as did Eastland and George Wallace, the harsh, gut-wrenching rhetoric of bigotry. But as he had grown older, Hill's sense of himself as a dignified, elder statesman, his pride in the United States Senate—and perhaps the memory of his own ties to persecuted minorities—had made him increasingly uncomfortable in using the language of bigotry, even to win Alabama audiences. To have survived as a non-demagogue amid the latent prejudice unleashed in 1962 by Wallace and the Martin campaign, was—even Gould Beech conceded—"an achievement in itself."[8] But most Alabamians—conditioned to expect their political leaders to be heroes, villains, or martyrs—found it hard to admire one who sought a middle course.

In his own mind, Hill resolved any doubts that may have nagged him on this question. When Neil Davis once criticized another politician who had failed to stand for principle, Hill had responded impatiently: "Look, what do you want? Do you want him to stick his neck out and get beat, or stay here and get something done?"[9]

For Hill, it was as simple as that. Had not his idol, Franklin Roosevelt, taken a similar, pragmatic attitude toward this issue in the interest of what he considered more pressing concerns? Had not friends like Barney Weeks implored Hill not to sacrifice his other objectives on the altar of civil rights? Indeed, had not blacks themselves shared the benefits of all the *other* causes Hill had championed? Had not some of those whom he had recommended for the federal bench—like Richard Rives and his successor, John Godbold; Walter Gewin, and the Republican Frank Johnson—employed the power of their secure positions to assist the cause of civil rights? Shrewd politicians like Carl Elliott, Bob Jones, and Albert Rains recognized Hill's "indirect" contributions to black Americans. Even the recklessly idealistic Gould Beech, long after the emotional tumult of the 1950s and 1960s had died down, wondered aloud whether political suicide—like that of "saintly" individuals such as Frank Graham—served any good purpose.[10]

Almost a decade after his retirement, Hill finally made his first public admission that his stand against civil rights had been dictated by expediency. "I had to do that to get elected. We all did," he told an interviewer. He was heartened, he added, that southern politicians no longer had to "yell 'nigger' " to get elected. But Hill appeared reluctant to dwell on this aspect of his long career, shutting off this line of questioning with the words, "That is past now."[11]

The historian, always seeking to label and categorize, is hard pressed to find a classification for Hill. The terms "Puritan" and "Victorian," although appropriate for one of Hill's background and proclivities, belong to eras long past and apply more to personality than to politics. Like the majority of "southern progressives," Hill had approached the task of effecting change paternalistically and within the cultural context of his region. He had endorsed the progressive goals of education, prohibition, and economic progress but, pragmatic from the beginning, opposed the constitutional amendment that brought about woman's suffrage and never fought lynching or other forms of racial injustice. But Hill had begun his career as this reform spirit began to lose strength and unity. To label Hill a southern progressive or a New Dealer would identify him too narrowly; many of his major accomplishments had come to fruition after the first four decades of the twentieth century.[12]

After World War II, his political enemies in Alabama sought to brand Hill as "liberal," a badge of honor for a number of open-minded Southerners during the heyday of FDR but, by the late 1940s, an increasingly unpopular term presumed to connote approval of federal interference in economic and political affairs, especially the sensitive area of race relations. (At the same time that they turned "liberal" into a label of pejoration,

Hill's opponents shed the appellation of "reactionary" that had been applied to them in the 1930s and preempted the more dignified and moderate-sounding term, "conservative.")

Real Senate liberals like Herbert Lehman, Hubert Humphrey, Paul Douglas, and Jacob Javits, had they taken this business of labels seriously, might have questioned whether Lister Hill—so personally conservative in manner, dress, language, Puritan ethics, and condescending attitude toward women (to an office secretary or the wife of a federal judge, "Hello, little girl!"), so publicly opposed to national health insurance, Medicare, and every civil rights measure to come before Congress—properly belonged in the company of those who consistently supported reform and individual dignity and freedom.

When they sensed that the word "liberal" failed to evoke sufficient animosity, opponents like Lawrence McNeil, John Crommelin, and Jim Martin sought to link Hill with those in the East and North whom they suspected of fostering a socialist form of government in the United States. But although citing his support for TVA and for government assistance to rural programs for electricity, telephone service, hospitals, schools, and libraries as grounds for this charge, his enemies never succeeded in convincing the majority of Alabama voters that Hill deserved the scare appellation of "socialist."

National leaders in the field of medicine appreciated the fact that Hill had been a constant foe of socialization of their profession, always seeking to strengthen and protect private practice by means of modern hospitals, more and better-trained physicians, and a stepped-up research attack on disease.[13] Hill himself took pride that, in programs like Hill-Burton and the Library Act, he had held fast to the biblical injunction "where your treasure is, there will your heart be also" by insisting that local sources, including private donors, should match federal "seed money."

Always more interested in results than abstract philosophy, Hill called himself a "Jefferson-Jackson Democrat." Ever cautious, he deemed it best to avoid the ideological identification of a "liberal"; when he wished to indicate his point of view, he always spoke vaguely of supporting "the cause."

Nonetheless, others frequently labeled Hill a "liberal." The Americans for Democratic Action (ADA), studying the Senate's 1961 voting record, announced that, among southern senators, only nationally ambitious Estes Kefauver had cast more "liberal" votes than Sparkman and Hill. During this same session, other southern senators, like Thurmond, Byrd, Willis

Robertson of Virginia, John McClellan of Arkansas, and Spessard Holland of Florida, had cast no "liberal" votes, the ADA reported, whereas Russell and Herman Talmadge of Georgia, and Smathers of Florida had cast a mere handful. Only Olin Johnston of South Carolina had come close to the "liberal" score posted by Hill and Sparkman. Furthermore, the ADA noted, Rains, Elliott, and Jones of Alabama's House delegation had also scored high on the "liberal" test.[14]

Journalist Douglas Kiker pondered how to explain the difference in political viewpoint between these Alabama legislators and the majority of senators and representatives from neighboring states. Was Georgia, for example, really more "conservative" than Alabama? Kiker had seen too many "fly-specked" pictures of FDR hanging on the walls of country stores in Georgia to believe this could be true. If Southerners were as adamantly opposed to "liberal" programs as they had been pictured, Kiker wondered why they had not defeated men like Hill, Sparkman, Rains, Elliott, and Jones.[15]

After all, the majority of whites in *every* southern state had regarded Franklin Roosevelt as a savior, hailed the New Deal programs that helped them rise out of poverty and despair, and rallied enthusiastically around their country's banner in World War II. Every southern state contained elements that had used race and states' rights as smokescreens behind which they sought to preserve the status quo. TVA had directly benefited not only Alabama but also Tennessee, Kentucky, Georgia, and Mississippi. Mountain folk of Republican heritage inhabited parts of Georgia, the Carolinas, Kentucky, and Tennessee, as well as Alabama.

How, then, account for numerous observations, beginning in the 1940s, that Alabama was the most liberal state in the South, trapped between the reactionary regimes that then ran Mississippi and Georgia? For the fact that its voters, in election after election, had chosen Hill, Sparkman, Rains, Elliott, Jones, Roberts and even middle-of-the-roaders like Selden and George Huddleston Jr. to represent them in Congress? Sparkman, asked in his old age to respond to this question, had given the unhesitating answer: "Due to the leadership of Lister Hill."[16]

From the late 1930s until the late 1950s, Hill (aided by his machine, his press supporters, and his Alabama congressional colleagues) had outmaneuvered forces that often prevailed in neighboring states where no such gifted leader arose to champion the cause of the less privileged. Until white Alabamians allowed themselves in the late 1950s and 1960s to be totally enthralled by the siren calls of racial discord, Hill had represented what he believed to be their best interests and their aspiration (expressed through their Populist fervor in the 1890s, their alliance with the Klan in the 1920s, and their choice of governors like Bibb Graves, Jim Folsom, and George Wallace) to improve the conditions and opportunities of their lives and the lives of their descendants.

Within the limits imposed upon him by those whom he sought to aid, Lister Hill served the cause.

APPENDIX

MAP I. *Alabama's Second Congressional District, 1923*

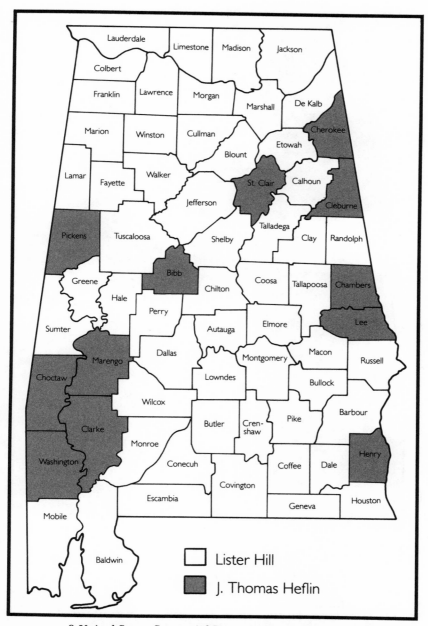

MAP 2. *1938 United States Senatorial Race, Special Democratic Primary,*
4 January 1938

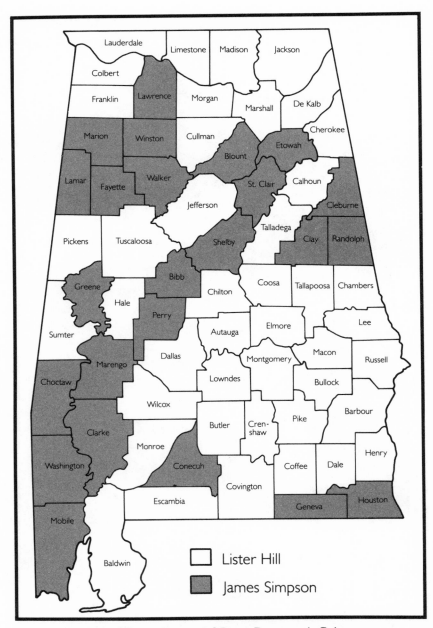

MAP 3. *1944 United States Senatorial Race, Democratic Primary,*
2 May 1944

MAP 4. *1950 United States Senatorial Race, Democratic Primary,*
2 May 1950

MAP 5. *1956 United States Senatorial Race, Democratic Primary, 1 May 1956*

MAP 6. *1962 United States Senatorial Race, Democratic Primary, 1 May 1962.*

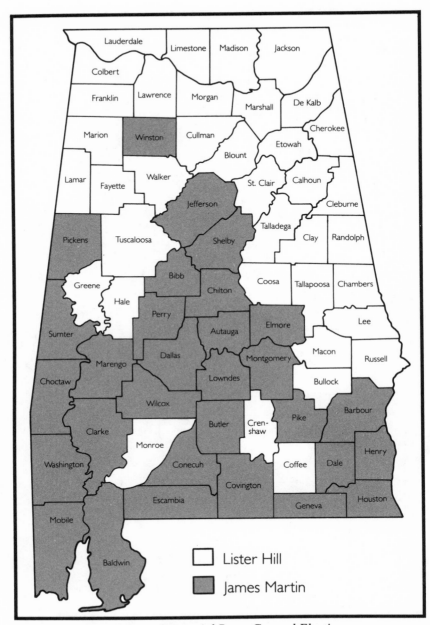

N O T E S

A C K N O W L E D G M E N T S

1. Lister Hill to Roy Nolen, 25 May 1944, Lister Hill Papers, Special Collections, Gorgas Library, University of Alabama, Tuscaloosa.
2. *Montgomery Advertiser*, 23 January 1968.

C H A P T E R I

1. Interview with Amelie Hill Laslie (henceforth, Laslie interview), Montgomery, 27 June 1983.
2. Laslie interview.
3. Lister Hill, "My Father: Dr. Luther Leonidas Hill," *Alabama Review* 24 (1971): 133–43.
4. Correspondence between Luther Lyons Hill Jr. and Lister Hill, Lister Hill Papers, Gorgas Library, University of Alabama, Tuscaloosa. Interview with Luther Lyons Hill Jr. (henceforth, Luther Lyons Hill Jr. interview), Des Moines, Ia., 27 August 1984.
5. Luther Lyons Hill Jr., "A Family Record" (unpublished manuscript in possession of L. L. Hill Jr., Des Moines, Ia.), p. 306.
6. "Lister Steps Down from the Hill," *Medical World News*, 1 November 1968, pp. 56–58.
7. Laslie interview.
8. [Luther Leonidas Hill], *Sermons, Addresses and Papers of Rev. Luther Leonidas Hill, Published for Private Circulation by His Children* (New York: Fleming H. Revell, 1919), pp. 276–89.
9. Membership in the Methodist Protestant church never matched that of its parent denomination. As late as 1880, the Methodist Episcopal church members outnumbered those in the Methodist Protestant church 8 to 1. In 1939, the Alabama Methodist Protestant church and the Alabama Methodist Episcopal church united with the Alabama and North Alabama Conferences of the newly organized Methodist church. William Warren Sweet, *Methodism in American History*, rev. ed. (Nashville: Abingdon Press, 1953), pp. 144–83.
10. Hill, "Family Record," p. 307.

11. A. B. Moore, *History of Alabama and Her People*, 2 vols. (Chicago and New York: American Historical Society, 1927), 2:8.

12. Hill, "Family Record," p. 306.

13. [Luther Leonidas Hill], *Sermons*, p. 18.

14. When Douglas was nominated for president by the Democratic convention of 1860, the Alabama delegation walked out to help form the southern wing of the Democratic party. In that election, only about one-seventh of Alabama voters, concentrated mostly in four north Alabama counties and Mobile, supported Douglas.

15. Hill, "Family Record," pp. 323–24.

16. Hill, "Family Record," pp. 325–26; [Luther Leonidas Hill], *Sermons*, p. 18. For references to Charles Buckley, see Sarah Woolfolk Wiggins, *The Scalawag in Alabama Politics, 1865–1881* (University: University of Alabama Press, 1977); Walter L. Fleming, *Civil War and Reconstruction in Alabama* (New York: Macmillan, 1905); and John Witherspoon DuBose and James K. Greer, eds., *Alabama's Tragic Decade: Ten Years of Alabama, 1865–1874* (Birmingham: Webb Book Company, 1940).

17. Luther Lyons Hill Jr. interview. Hill, "Family Record," pp. 323–24.

18. [Luther Leonidas Hill], *Sermons*, p. 21.

19. [Luther Leonidas Hill], *Sermons*, pp. 249–64.

20. Interview with Henrietta Hill Hubbard (henceforth, Hubbard interview), Montgomery, 27 May 1983. Hill, "Family Record," pp. 322–23.

21. Laslie interview.

22. [Luther Leonidas Hill], *Sermons*, p. 21.

23. Interview with Senator Hill's son, Luther Lister Hill (henceforth, Luther Lister Hill interview), Montgomery, 27 May 1983. *Alabama Journal*, 7 August 1948.

24. Hill, "Family Record," pp. 268–69.

25. Hill, "Family Record," pp. 268, 285.

26. Wayne Flynt, *Montgomery: An Illustrated History* (Windsor Hills, Calif.: Windsor Publications, 1980), p. 76; Moore, *History of Alabama*, 2:9. See also Dewey W. Grantham, *Southern Progressivism: The Reconciliation of Progress and Tradition* (Knoxville: University of Tennessee Press, 1983).

27. Hill, "Family Record," pp. 269–70.

28. Hill, "Family Record," pp. 278–79, 284–85.

29. C. M. Stanley, "Family Tree of the Hills of Montgomery," *Montgomery Advertiser* (n.d.), Hill Papers; Hill, "Family Record," p. 270.

30. Thomas W. Bradford to Lister Hill, 22 May 1950, Hill Papers. Interviews with Neil Davis (henceforth, Davis interview), Auburn, 19 March 1983; John C. Godbold (henceforth, Godbold interview), Montgomery, 12 April 1983; and Virginia Foster Durr (henceforth, Durr interview), Montgomery, 22 July 1983.

31. *Montgomery Advertiser*, 22 March 1955.

32. *Montgomery Independent*, 10 February 1965.

33. Leonard Dinnerstein and Mary Dale Polsson, eds., *Jews in the South* (Baton Rouge: Louisiana State University Press, 1973), pp. 3, 95.

34. Charles Summersell, *Alabama History for Schools* (Montgomery: Viewpoint Publications, 1975), p. 297.

35. General Landesarchiv Karlsruhe to Luther L. Hill Jr., 10 April 1979, copy in Horsler File, Pensacola Historical Society, Pensacola, Fla. Bela's brother, Samuel Weil, and her sister, Caroline, with her husband Louis Marx, also came to America. Samuel Weil became a prominent lawyer in Atlanta.

36. According to the 1880 census, Escambia County, Woolsey, Fla., District 18, p. 311, Bela's son, Henry Horsler, stated that both of his parents were born in Bavaria.

37. Circuit Court Case 992, *Horsler v. LeBlanc*, 1846, Historical Documents Section, Escambia County Courthouse, Pensacola, Fla.

38. Circuit Court Case 992, *The State of Florida v. Gabril LeBlanc and Catherine LeBlanc*, Historical Documents Section, Escambia County Courthouse, Pensacola, Fla.

39. Leo Wellhouse to Luther Lyons Hill Jr., 25 June 1976; Luther Lyons Hill Jr. to Leo Wellhouse, 11 October 1978, Horsler File, Pensacola Historical Society, Pensacola, Fla.

40. Minute Books A–D, 3 November 1845. Box no. 85–PL, Department of Archives and Manuscripts, Judicial Building, Pensacola, Fla.

41. Marriage record of Barbet Horsler and William Stine [a misspelling], 27 December 1849, St. Michael's Catholic Church, Pensacola, Fla. A civil ceremony denoting the marriage of James M. Langley and Barbet Stein, 17 June 1852, is recorded in Marriage Book C, p. 70, Escambia County Courthouse, Pensacola, Fla.

42. Court Cases 1853–1382; 1853–1385A; 1853–1400; 1853–1401, Historical Documents Section, Escambia County Courthouse, Pensacola, Fla.

43. Civil War letters of Mark Lyons to Amelia Horsler, 1862–63; typed copies in Horsler File, Pensacola Historical Society, Pensacola, Fla.

44. Baptismal records of St. John the Evangelist Church, Warrington, Fla., show an adult baptism on 9 February 1872, of a Miriam Barbara Langley, described as a Jew from Baden, Germany. At that time Barbet was evidently known as Barbara.

45. Court Cases 1869–4144; 1869–4163; 1871–5645; 1871–4495; 1873–4842; 1875–5072; 1875–5229; 1876–5645, Escambia County Courthouse, Pensacola, Fla.

46. Will of Barbet Langley, Probate Records, Escambia County Courthouse, Pensacola, Fla., 1902–0–797, 0–655, copy in Horsler File, Pensacola Historical Society. *Pensacola Daily News*, 26 March 1900.

47. Luther Lyons Hill Jr. interview.

48. Interview with Mark Lyons Jr. (henceforth, Mark Lyons Jr. interview), Mobile, 28 May 1983.

49. Civil War letters of Mark Lyons to Amelia Horsler.

50. Marriage record of Mark Lyons and Amelia Horsler, 19 May 1863, in the Catholic Church, Greenville, Alabama, recorded at St. Michael's Catholic Church, Pensacola, Fla. Civil War letters of Mark Lyons to Amelia Horsler.

51. Gould Beech to the author, 8 June 1983.

52. Because he had parted from Catholicism over his refusal to acknowledge the infallibility of the pope, Mark Lyons's funeral service was conducted by fellow members of the Order of Masons. Interview with Reba (Mrs. Herbert) Lyons (henceforth, Reba Lyons interview), Mobile, 29 May 1983. Mark Lyons Jr. interview. *Mobile Press-Register*, 5 January 1887, 13 July 1888.

53. Mark Lyons Jr. and Reba Lyons interviews. Moore, *History of Alabama*, 2:781.

54. Luther Lyons Hill Jr. interview.

55. References to family concern are contained in a letter from the Rev. Luther Leonidas Hill to Amelia Lyons, reprinted in [Luther Leonidas Hill], *Sermons*, pp. 268–72.

56. *Mobile Press-Register*, 13 July 1888.

57. Hill, "Family Record," pp. 266–67.

58. Hill, "Family Record," pp. 286, 301–2. Durr and Reba Lyons interviews.

59. Early records of St. Peter's Church, Montgomery. Flynt, *Montgomery*, p. 58. Grantham, *Southern Progressivism*, p. 20.

60. Durr interview. Hill, "Family Record," p. 266.

61. Hill, "Family Record," p. 266.

62. Hill, "Family Record," p. 270. St. Peter's School, according to church records, had a student body of around fifty at the turn of the century.

63. Luther Lyons Hill Jr. interview.

64. Interview with Senator Lister Hill conducted January–June 1967 by Harlan B. Phillips, Ph.D., Modern Manuscripts Section, History of Medicine Division, National Library of Medicine, Bethesda, Md. (henceforth, Phillips interview). Copy in possession of author.

65. Luther Lyons Hill Jr. interview.

66. Laslie interview.

67. Interview with former Representative Albert Rains (henceforth, Rains interview), Gadsden, 6 May 1983. Jonathan Daniels, *Frontier on the Potomac* (New York: Macmillan, 1946), p. 62.

68. Reba Lyons, Laslie, and Luther Lyons Hill Jr. interviews.

69. [Luther Leonidas Hill], *Sermons*, p. 17.

70. Hill, "Family Record," p. 241.

71. Hill, "Family Record," pp. 241–42.

72. Hill, "Family Record," pp. 243–45.

73. Dr. L. L. Hill to Dr. B. J. Baldwin, 29 November 1922. Copy in Dr. L. L. Hill Papers, Reynolds Historical Collection, Lister Hill Library, University of Alabama at Birmingham.

74. Hill, "Family Record," pp. 246–47.

75. Lister Hill, "Health in America: A Personal Perspective," in U.S. Department of Health, Education, and Welfare, *Health in America: 1776–1976* (Washington, D.C.: DHEW Pub. No. (HRA) 76–616, 1976), p. 6.

76. Lister Hill, "Health in America," pp. 6–7.

77. Hill, "Family Record," p. 250.

78. Lister Hill, "Health in America," p. 7; "Dinner honoring Dr. L. L. Hill on the 51st anniversary of his entrance into the medical profession," undated program, Montgomery County Medical Society, Lister Hill Clipping File, Alabama Department of Archives and History, Montgomery. Hill, "Family Record," p. 254.

79. Interview with Lister Hill, in *Washington Star*, 1 December 1968.

80. Program of dinner honoring Dr. L. L. Hill, Lister Hill Clipping File, Alabama Department of Archives and History. Dr. Robert S. Hill also studied at the University of Virginia and took advanced courses in gynecology under leading European specialists. Thomas McAdory Owen, *History of Alabama and Dictionary of Alabama Biography*, 6 vols. (Chicago: S. J. Clarke Company, 1921), 4:812.

81. Phillips interview. Numerous other accounts of this incident exist, among them Robert Barkdoll, "Lister Hill: Statesman for Health," *Today's Health*, June 1962, p. 79; Walling Keith, "Senate Won over Surgery," *Birmingham News*, 9 November 1966.

82. Davis interview. Interview with Don Cronin (henceforth, Cronin interview), Washington, D.C., 5 May 1979.

83. Hill, "Family Record," pp. 271–73.

84. Phillips interview. Lister Hill, "Health in America," p. 7; Martin M. Cummings, M.D., "Senator Lister Hill: Statesman for Health and Patron of Medical Libraries," *Alabama Journal of the Medical Science* 9 (January 1972): 4. Hill, "Family Record," pp. 281–82.

85. Lister Hill, "Health in America," p. 7.

86. Numerous accounts of this historic operation exist, among them Lister Hill, "Health in America," p. 7; *Birmingham News*, 17 June 1952; George A. O'Connell, Anniston, Ala., to Lister Hill, 25 April 1940, Hill Papers; Lister Hill, "My Father: Dr. Luther Leonidas Hill," *Alabama Review* 24 (1971): 133–43. Ironically, Henry Myrick was to die years later as a result of another stab wound.

87. Dr. Howard L. Holley to the author, 26 July 1983.

88. Phillips interview.

89. Press Release, 1937 Campaign Correspondence, Hill Papers; Lister Hill to Barrett Shelton, Decatur, 28 March 1942, Hill Papers; *Mobile Press-Register*, 8 May 1949.

90. Durr interview. Phillips interview. Lister Hill to Catesby ap R Jones, 27 May 1932, Hill Papers.

91. Phillips interview. William C. Rudulph to Lister Hill, 26 February 1950; Lister Hill to William C. Rudulph, 11 March 1950, Hill Papers.

92. Phillips interview. Lister Hill to Gus Baldwin, 20 October 1928; Lister Hill to Artemus Callaway, 15 September 1941, Hill Papers; Barkdoll, "Lister Hill," p. 79.

93. Evidently the planners of Montgomery were unaware of the correct spelling of Captain Thomas Macdonough's name. Phillips interview. Hill, "Family Record," pp. 238, 320.

94. *Montgomery Advertiser*, 1 November 1930.

95. [Luther Leonidas Hill], *Sermons*, p. 45. Marion Elias Lazenby, *History of Methodism in Alabama and West Florida: Being an Account of the Amazing March of Methodism through Alabama and West Florida* (North Alabama Conference and Alabama-West Florida Conference of the Methodist Church, 1960), pp. 314–15, 785. Homer Hill, Birmingham, to Representative Lister Hill, 10 February 1927; Lister Hill to Homer Hill, 24 November 1927, Hill Papers. Congressman Hill, who prided himself on answering his mail promptly, did not reply to Homer Hill for nine months. Eventually he wrote a cordial letter, inviting the waiter to call upon his father and his uncles if he were in Montgomery and containing a politician's typical promise to look up Homer Hill when he came to Birmingham.

96. Hill, "Family Record," pp. 240, 282, 342–43.

97. Hill, "Family Record," pp. 282–83.

98. Hill, "Family Record," p. 282. Text of undated (sometime in 1928) radio speech by Dr. Hill in Dr. L. L. Hill Papers.

99. Luther Lyons Hill Jr. interview.

100. Phillips interview.

101. Lister Hill to William C. Rudulph, Montgomery, 11 March 1950, Hill Papers.

102. Homer Hill to Lister Hill, 24 November 1927, Hill Papers.

103. Interview with Gould Beech (henceforth, Beech interview), Magnolia Springs, Ala., 24 March 1978.

104. Phillips interview.

105. Lister Hill to Gessner McCorvey, 31 May 1952 (written but not sent), Hill Papers. Thomas Chalmers McCorvey, *Alabama Historical Sketches* (Charlottesville: University of Virginia Press, 1960), pp. 208–22. Owen, *History of Alabama*, 4:1100.

106. Lister Hill to Dr. Chilton Thorington, Montgomery, 31 May 1928, Hill Papers.

107. Cronin interview.

108. Lee N. Allen, "The Woman Suffrage Movement in Alabama, 1910–1920," *Alabama Review* 11 (1958): 96.

109. Selma Allman to Lister Hill, 1 April 1948, Hill Papers.

110. Phillips interview. Lister Hill to Marian Hornberger, 29 April 1929, Hill Papers.

111. Phillips interview. U.S. Congress, *Congressional Directory*, 68th Cong., 1st Sess., December 1923, pp. 3–4. Press Release, 1937 Campaign Correspondence, Hill Papers.

112. Davis interview. Interviews with Paul Duncan (henceforth, Duncan interview), Magnolia Springs, Ala., 24 March 1978 and former Representative Bob Jones (henceforth, Jones interview), Scottsboro, Ala., 16 June 1983.

CHAPTER 2

1. Flynt, *Montgomery*, p. 45; *Alabama Journal*, 21 March 1955.

2. J. Mills Thornton III, "Challenge and Response in the Montgomery Bus Boycott

of 1955–1956," *Alabama Review* 33 (1980): 163–235; Flynt, *Montgomery*, p. 76.

3. Flynt, *Montgomery*, p. 76.

4. William Gunter, elected state senator from Montgomery County in 1919, managed to get legislation passed that returned power over the fire and police departments to the mayor's office and allowed the mayor to succeed himself. Elected to the Montgomery City Commission, Gunter served as mayor from 1919 until his death in 1940. *Montgomery Advertiser*, 23 March 1950.

5. Phillips interview. *Montgomery Advertiser*, 13 October 1916; 29 April 1917.

6. Phillips interview. *Birmingham Age-Herald*, 1 May 1949. "Address of welcome by J. Lister Hill in behalf of the Board of Education of the City of Montgomery to the Colored Alabama Education Association," 4 April 1917, copy in Hill Papers.

7. Flynt, *Montgomery*, pp. 81–83; Phillips interview.

8. Marguerite Johnston, "Alabama's Sen. Hill One of Leaders Guiding Way to World Tomorrow," *Birmingham News*, 13 January 1946.

9. Phillips interview.

10. *Current Biography* (New York: H. W. Wilson, 1943), pp. 297–300; Johnston, "Alabama's Sen. Hill."

11. For coverage of the controversy over Feagin, see *Montgomery Advertiser*, 4–25 April 1920.

12. *Montgomery Advertiser*, 20 April 1920; a pamphlet entitled "Mass Meeting Held at Montgomery County Court House, April 19, 1920 That Drove W. F. Feagin from the County Superintendency of Education of Montgomery County, Alabama," a stenographic report, contains details of the accusations that the *Advertiser* chose not to publish. Hill and his group had the pamphlet printed to refute Governor Kilby's description of the mass meeting as a "character lynching bee." Copy in Hill Papers.

13. "Mass Meeting" pamphlet, Hill Papers; *Montgomery Advertiser*, 23, 25 April 1920, 10 June 1920.

14. Recalling the school board controversy, *Alabama*, a magazine published by antagonists of Hill, reported that Feagin, who had not been on speaking terms with Hill for many years, was working in the senator's behalf in 1943. *Alabama*, 26 November 1943. Senator Hill's correspondence with Roy Nolen in 1944 confirms this. Hill Papers.

15. *Montgomery Advertiser*, 24, 28 June 1919. Although Alabama women became entitled to vote when the Nineteenth Amendment was ratified in August 1920, their state did not ratify this amendment until 1953.

16. Luther Lyons Hill Jr. interview.

17. Hubbard, Laslie, and Luther Lyons Hill Jr. interviews.

18. Lister Hill to Jesse B. Hearin, 1 September 1948, Hill Papers.

19. Laslie and Davis interviews.

20. Lister Hill to Dr. L. L. Hill, 8 February 1926, Hill Papers. For a more detailed description of the Alabama Klan during the 1920s, see Virginia Van der Veer Hamilton, *Hugo Black: The Alabama Years* (Baton Rouge: Louisiana State University Press, 1972), pp. 70–140.

21. *Montgomery Advertiser*, 14–15 May 1927. Beech interview. Interview with Robert Frazer (henceforth, Frazer interview), Arlington, Va., 16–17 March 1985.

22. *Montgomery Advertiser*, 24 June 1919. Campaign Correspondence, 1923 Congressional campaign; Kenneth Murphy to "Dear Friend," 12 May 1923, Hill Papers.

23. Counties making up the Second District in 1923 were Montgomery, Pike, Wilcox, Crenshaw, Butler, Baldwin, Conecuh, Covington, and Escambia.

24. Interview with Lister Hill in *Birmingham Post-Herald*, 22 January 1968. The Second District's Populist heritage is traced in William Warren Rogers, *The One-Gallused Rebellion* (Baton Rouge: Louisiana State University Press, 1970), and Francis Sheldon Hackney, *From Populism to Progressivism in Alabama, 1890–1910* (Princeton: Princeton University Press, 1969).

25. U.S. Commerce Department, Bureau of the Census, *Fifteenth Census of the United States* (1930), 3:101–8; Hamilton, *Hugo Black*, pp. 147–48.

26. Phillips interview.

27. Campaign Correspondence, 1923 Congressional campaign, Hill Papers.

28. Owen, *History of Alabama*, 4:1478; Phillips interview.

29. Campaign Correspondence, 1923 Congressional campaign, Hill Papers.

30. Campaign Correspondence, 1923 Congressional campaign, Hill Papers.

31. Phillips interview.

32. Interview with George Le Maistre (henceforth, Le Maistre interview), Tuscaloosa, 15 December 1983; Thomas S. Duncan to Dr. L. L. Hill, 17 July 1923; C. T. Livingston to Dr. L. L. Hill, 5 April 1923; J. T. Dale to Dr. L. L. Hill, 17 April 1923, Hill Papers.

33. Beech interview.

34. Ulay Black to Lister Hill, 12 June 1923; Ulay Black to J. Lee Holloway, 12 June 1923; W. J. Ray to O. P. Spiegel, 2 July 1923; Waverly Kendrick to Dr. L. L. Hill, 11 June 1923, Hill Papers.

35. The Hill Papers contain numerous communications to voters from Dr. Hill and William Wallace Hill stressing their Methodist heritage. J. E. Terry to Dr. L. L. Hill, 26 June 1923, Hill Papers.

36. Lister Hill to A. R. Woodham, 2 May 1923; Kenneth Murphy to B. F. Beasley, 7 July 1923; Kenneth Murphy to B. M. Archibald, 6 July 1923; Kenneth Murphy to J. T. Carter, 3 July 1923; Kenneth Murphy to M. M. Bentley, 16 June 1923. Lister Hill stressed his Methodist affiliation in numerous other letters. Hill Papers.

37. Dr. A. P. Webb to John B. O'Bannon, 20 July 1923, Hill Papers.

38. Lister Hill to Dr. A. P. Webb, 23 July 1923, Hill Papers.

39. Johnston, "Alabama's Sen. Hill." *Montgomery Advertiser*, 14, 15 July 1923.

40. *Montgomery Advertiser*, 14, 15 July 1923; *Birmingham Age-Herald* 17 July 1923; Lister Hill to Dr. Wayne B. Wheeler, 26 April 1923; Lister Hill to Joe Raley, River Falls, 16 May 1923, Hill Papers.

41. *Montgomery Advertiser*, 14 July 1923, 7 October 1956.

42. *Montgomery Advertiser*, 15 July 1923. Cato D. Glover to Lister Hill, 18 July 1923, Hill Papers.

43. Hamilton, *Hugo Black*, pp. 133–34.

44. *Alabama Journal*, 17 July 1923; *Montgomery Advertiser*, 17 July 1923. Official returns were: Hill, first choice, 9,403, second choice, 908; Sanders, first choice, 4,001, second choice, 1,724; Rushton, first choice, 4,184, second choice, 1,089.

45. Joseph Lyons to Dr. L. L. Hill, Jr., 19 December 1923, Hill Papers.

46. See V. O. Key Jr., *Southern Politics in State and Nation* (New York: Alfred A. Knopf, 1950), pp. 37–38.

47. Phillips interview.

48. In a light turnout, voters cast 4,483 votes for Hill to 1 for a nominal opponent, S. H. Yarbrough. *Montgomery Advertiser*, 15 August 1923.

CHAPTER 3

1. The National Park Service, which oversees President Coolidge's birthplace in Plymouth, Vt., uses his father's quotation in its literature and lectures. In his interview with Phillips, Hill recalled having seen Longworth in his car.

2. Ben May to Margaret Lyons, undated letter, Hill Papers.

3. Laslie interview. Numerous notes from Dr. Hill to Lister Hill are to be found in the Hill Papers.

4. Undated (probably December 1925) memorandum, Lister Hill to Kenneth Murphy; Hill to Cadet Frank Melton, 9 December 1925, Hill Papers. Walling Keith, a former member of Hill's staff, recalled the senator's office procedures in an article in the *Birmingham News*, undated clipping, Lister Hill Clipping File, Alabama Department of Archives and History, Montgomery. Interview with John T. Walden (henceforth, Walden interview), Washington, D.C., 17 April 1978. Cronin and Jones interviews. Hill's office files provide ample evidence of this activity. Hill Papers.

5. Frazer interview.

6. Phillips interview.

7. *Congressional Record*, 68th Cong., 2nd Sess., 27 January 1925, p. 2544.

8. Lister Hill to Mark W. Wilson, president of the Chattanooga Chamber of Commerce, 9 February 1924, Hill Papers.

9. Preston J. Hubbard, *Origins of the TVA: The Muscle Shoals Controversy, 1920–1932* (1961; reprint ed., New York: W. W. Norton, 1968), pp. 273–75.

10. Lister Hill to O. C. Hackworth, 23 March 1928. Copy of minority report on TVA, intended to be submitted by Hill but withheld, Hill Papers.

11. Phillips interview.

12. Hubbard, *Origins of the TVA*, pp. 307–9.

13. Daisy V. Smith to Lister Hill, 18 April 1926; Lister Hill to Dr. L. L. Hill, 20 January 1928, Hill Papers. Frazer interview.

14. Robert Frazer recollected their early years in Washington in a letter to Lister Hill, 6 March 1957; Lister Hill to Joe B. Perry, 4 February 1928; Lister Hill to W. M. Brunson, 6 February 1928, Hill Papers.

15. *Montgomery Advertiser*, 17, 21 February 1928. *Birmingham Age-Herald*, 19 February 1928.

16. Henrietta Hill described her family, background, childhood, and wedding in her book, Henrietta Fontaine Hill, *The Family Skeleton* (Montgomery: Paragon Press, 1958).

17. Hubbard interview.

18. Frazer interview.

19. *Montgomery Advertiser*, 21 February 1928.

20. Hill, *The Family Skeleton*. Frazer interview.

21. Interviews with former Representative Carl Elliott (henceforth, Elliott interview), Birmingham, 21 April 1983, and Judge Clarence Allgood (henceforth, Allgood interview), Birmingham, 20 November 1982. Jones and Rains interviews. Lister Hill to William W. Hill, 8 May 1937, Hill Papers.

22. Laslie, Hubbard, and Durr interviews.

23. Phillips interview.

24. Lister Hill to C. M. Stanley, 31 January 1928; John C. Frazer to Lister Hill, 16 December 1925, Hill Papers. Flynt, *Montgomery*, pp. 102–3, 109–15, 129. *Montgomery Advertiser*, 2 March 1936.

25. *Opp News*, 1 May 1933. *Montgomery Advertiser*, 2 March 1936. Statistics for these Second District primaries and elections may be found in the 1927, 1931, 1935, and 1939 volumes of the *Alabama Official and Statistical Register*.

26. J. Mills Thornton III, "Alabama Politics: J. Thomas Heflin and the Expulsion Movement of 1929," *Alabama Review* 21 (April 1968): 83–112.

27. Hamilton, *Hugo Black*, pp. 119–39.

28. The Hill Papers contain a copy of Dr. Hill's radio address. Hamilton, *Hugo Black*, pp. 140–57; Thornton, "Alabama Politics," p. 101.

29. Lister Hill to J. Bibb Mills, 24 August 1928; Marion E. Lazenby to Lister Hill, 28 August 1928; Dr. L. L. Hill to Lister Hill, 14 February 1927, Hill Papers.

30. Lister Hill to R. H. Jones, 12 September 1928; Lister Hill to W. C. Beebe, 10 September 1928; Lister Hill to Senator Millard Tydings, 9 September 1928; Lister Hill to P. A. Sansom, 10 September 1928; Marie Bankhead Owen to Lister Hill, 26 September 1928, Hill Papers.

31. Lister Hill to J. W. Caldwell, 25 October 1928. A copy of this circular is included in the 1928 Campaign Correspondence, Hill Papers.

32. A copy of Hill's statement is included in the 1928 Campaign Correspondence, Hill Papers. See also *Montgomery Advertiser*, 19 October 1928.

33. W. B. Oliver to Robert Frazer, 12 September 1928; Jesse B. Hearin to Lister Hill, 8 November 1928; W. A. Gunter Jr. to Senator Joseph T. Robinson, 28 November 1928, Hill Papers.

34. John C. Frazer to Lister Hill, 16 December 1925; J. Bibb Mills to Lister Hill, 28 January 1926, Hill Papers.

35. The Hill Papers contain an undated draft of an announcement against Heflin in

Lister Hill's handwriting. Dr. L. L. Hill to Lister Hill, 5 June 1929, Hill Papers.

36. S. W. Lambeth to Dr. L. L. Hill, 1 January 1929, Hill Papers.

37. Jesse B. Hearin to Lister Hill, 22 May 1929; Harry M. Ayers to Lister Hill, 28 January 1930; R. J. U. Ray to Lister Hill, 3 January 1930; R. M. McCann to Lister Hill, 10 February 1930, Hill Papers.

38. Lister Hill to William W. Hill, 2 March 1930, Hill Papers.

39. Hamilton, *Hugo Black*, pp. 181–96.

CHAPTER 4

1. Lister Hill to William W. Hill, 14 January 1933; Lister Hill to Amelie Hill, 17 January 1933; Walter McAdory to Lister Hill, 23 January 1933; Hill's undated, handwritten comment on Roosevelt's visit, Hill Papers.

2. Lister Hill to T. J. Kidd, 2 June 1932; Lister Hill to Wallace D. Malone, 28 September 1932; Lister Hill to Luther Lyons Hill, 27 October 1932; Lister Hill to A. M. Tunstall, 14 March 1933; Lister Hill to Col. Samuel G. Jones, 30 March 1933; Lister Hill to Dr. L. L. Hill, 5 May 1933, Hill Papers.

3. Lister Hill to W. M. Richardson, 9 January 1933; Lister Hill to Franklin D. Roosevelt, 3 February 1933, Hill Papers. Phillips interview. Richard Lowitt, *George W. Norris: The Triumph of a Progressive, 1933–1944* (Urbana: University of Illinois Press, 1978), p. 21.

4. Lister Hill to James L. Davidson, 31 March 1933, Hill Papers. Lowitt, *Norris: Triumph*, pp. 21–22.

5. Wilmon Henry Droze, *High Dams and Slack Waters: TVA Rebuilds a River* (Baton Rouge: Louisiana State University Press, 1965), pp. 30–31.

6. For Hill's voting record on major New Deal programs, see *Congressional Record*, 73d Cong., 1st and 2nd Sess. Lister Hill to Wiley C. Hill, 15 March 1934, Hill Papers.

7. Interview with Charles Dobbins (henceforth, Dobbins interview), Washington D.C., 20 April 1978.

8. Hamilton, *Hugo Black*, pp. 215–21. Frazer interview. Lister Hill to Roy Nolen, 1 February 1935, Hill Papers.

9. Correspondence between Lister Hill and Francis Pickens Miller, Hill Papers. Morton Sosna, *In Search of the Silent South: Southern Liberals and the Race Issue* (New York: Columbia University Press, 1977), p. 89. For a contemporary view of the Southern Policy Committee, see Donald Davidson, "Where Are the Laymen? A Study in Policy-Making," *American Review* 9 (October 1937): 456–81.

10. Representative Malcolm Tarver to Lister Hill, 2 June 1937, Hill Papers; Henry Wallace Interview, Oral History Collection, Columbia University, New York City, pp. 481–82. Hill's correspondence on these meetings is contained in the Hill Papers. Frazer interview.

11. Lister Hill to Franklin Roosevelt, 19 September 1936, Franklin D. Roosevelt

Papers, Roosevelt Library, Hyde Park, N.Y. *Congressional Record*, 75th Cong., 1st Sess., 7 April 1937, pp. 3562–63. George B. Tindall, *The Emergence of the New South, 1913–1945* (Baton Rouge: Louisiana State University Press, 1967), pp. 593–94. *Birmingham News*, 20 December 1939. *Montgomery Advertiser*, 20 December 1939.

12. *Baltimore Sun*, 8 January 1932. *New York Herald-Tribune*, 8 January 1937. *Foley Onlooker*, 7 January 1937. *Alabama Journal*, 2 February 1937.

13. *Alabama Journal*, 12 June 1937. *Greenville Advocate*, 10 June 1937.

14. *Birmingham Post*, 22 June 1937.

15. *Montgomery Advertiser*, 13 August 1937. *Birmingham News*, 21 August 1937.

16. Charles W. Williams, a former official of the Federal Land Bank, was a third candidate. The Hills believed that Williams had been urged to enter the race by certain lumber and business interests dissatisfied with either Hill or Heflin. Others mentioned as possible candidates did not enter. Representative William Bankhead had been elected Speaker of the House in 1936, a post higher than that of a freshman senator. John Sparkman, Luther Patrick, and Pete Jarman were all serving their first terms in the House. 1938 Campaign Correspondence, Hill Papers. "Tom Heflin: Story of an Old Schooler's Fight against a New Dealer," *Newsweek* 11 (3 January 1938): 15–18.

17. *Birmingham News*, 21 August 1937; Dr. L. L. Hill to Lister Hill, 21 August 1937, Hill Papers.

18. For a description of Heflin's campaign oratory, see Jama Davis Rogers, "The 1938 Senatorial Election in Alabama between J. Thomas Heflin and J. Lister Hill" (M.A. thesis, Samford University, 1975).

19. Rogers, "1938 Senatorial Election," p. 15. Heflin's senatorial career is examined in detail in Norma Jean Short, "The Senatorial Career of James Thomas Heflin, 1920–1931" (Ph.D. dissertation, Vanderbilt University, 1954), and Ralph M. Tanner, "J. Thomas Heflin: U.S. Senator, 1920–1931" (Ph.D. dissertation, University of Alabama, 1967).

20. For detailed treatment of the 1928 election in Alabama, see Vincent J. Dooley, "United States Senator J. Thomas Heflin and the Democratic Party Revolt in Alabama" (M.A. thesis, Auburn University, 1963); Hugh Dorsey Reagan, "Race as a Factor in the Presidential Election of 1928 in Alabama," *Alabama Review* 19 (January 1966): 5–18; and Thornton, "Alabama Politics," *Alabama Review*. For a briefer overview, see Hamilton, *Hugo Black*, pp. 171–96.

21. 1938 Campaign Correspondence, Hill Papers.

22. Frazer, Davis, and Allgood interviews. The figure of $3,000 for Hill's 1938 campaign expenditures was reported in Jasper B. Shannon, "Presidential Politics in the South: 1938, I," *Journal of Politics* 1 (May 1939): 146–70.

23. Roy Nolen to William W. Hill, 16 August 1937, Hill Papers. *Montgomery Advertiser*, 7 October 1944.

24. See Roy Nolen file, Hill Papers, for examples of this terminology.

25. Allgood, Le Maistre, Jones, Rains, and Duncan interviews.

26. Le Maistre and Elliott interviews. Tindall, *Emergence of the New South*, pp. 81–82.

27. Frazer, Elliott, and Godbold interviews. Louise Charlton to Alice Doyle, 5 November 1937; Robert Frazer to Lister Hill, 3 October 1944; *Montgomery Advertiser*, undated (probably 1934) clipping, Hill Papers.

28. Rogers, "1938 Senatorial Election," pp. 60–62; "Tom Heflin," *Newsweek* 11 (3 January 1938): 15–18. *Asbury Park* (N.J.) *Evening News*, 28 December 1937.

29. Tindall, *Emergence of the New South*, pp. 533–35.

30. *Troy Messenger*, 10 September 1937. *Lee County Bulletin*, undated (1937) clipping; Lister Hill to Hugo Black, 28 September 1937, Hill Papers.

31. 1938 Campaign Correspondence, Hill Papers.

32. William Nicrosi to Lister Hill, 25 September 1937; Harwell Davis to Lister Hill, 22 October 1937, Hill Papers. Rogers, "1938 Senatorial Election," pp. 45, 69–71. "Tom Heflin."

33. *Montgomery Advertiser*, 10, 15 December 1937.

34. Voting to kill the wage-hour bill were Alabama Congressmen Frank Boykin, Sam Hobbs, Pete Jarman, Luther Patrick, John Sparkman, Joe Starnes, and Henry Steagall. *New York Times*, 18 December 1937.

35. Lee Robinson to J. Thomas Heflin, 21 October 1937, J. Thomas Heflin Papers, University of Alabama Library, Tuscaloosa. Viola McCarty to Alice N. Doyle, 4 November 1937, Hill Papers; Thomas Corcoran to James Roosevelt, 4 December 1937, Roosevelt Papers; Rogers, "1938 Senatorial Election," pp. 73–76; *New York Times*, 6 December 1937. *Washington Herald*, 2 December 1937.

36. The total vote was Hill, 90,601 (61.8%); Heflin, 50,189 (34.2%); and Williams, 5,573 (4%). Alexander Heard and Donald S. Strong, eds., *Southern Primaries and Elections, 1920–1947* (University: University of Alabama Press, 1950), pp. 17–18. Heflin never again held elective office although he unsuccessfully sought a congressional seat in the spring of 1938. He died in April 1951 at the age of eighty-two.

37. *Birmingham News*, 6 January 1938. Rogers, "1938 Senatorial Election," p. 78. Bibb Graves to Franklin D. Roosevelt, 4 January 1938, Roosevelt Papers. Press release, 5 January 1938, Hill Papers. *Washington Evening Star*, 7 January 1938.

38. *Pittsburgh Amalgamated Journal*, 19 May 1938.

39. The results of the November election were Hill, 113,413 and J. M. Pennington, 17,885. Heard and Strong, *Southern Primaries*, pp. 9, 17.

40. Lister Hill to Roy Nolen, 1 February, 30 April 1940, Hill Papers.

41. Dobbins, Walden, Beech, and Davis interviews.

CHAPTER 5

1. *Montgomery Advertiser*, 19 October 1941. *Washington Post*, 21 June 1938, 12 June 1939. *Florala News* (undated) September 1937, Hill Papers.

2. Albert A. Carmichael to Lister Hill, 12 February 1940; Roy Nolen to Lister Hill, 26 January 1940; Gould Beech to Roy Nolen, 27 June 1941; James E. Folsom to Lister Hill, 13 August 1942, Hill Papers. Frazer interview.

3. *Montgomery Advertiser*, 7 January 1938.

4. Hill's concluding sentence was quoted by Ralph Smith, a Washington correspondent, in the *Atlanta Journal*, 31 January 1938, and reprinted with approbation in *Dixie Business* (1938), p. 7. Copy in Hill Papers.

5. Lister Hill to Jonathan Daniels, 29 July 1939, Hill Papers.

6. Lister Hill to Roy Nolen, 20 October 1939; Roy Nolen to Lister Hill, 2 February 1940, Hill Papers.

7. Lister Hill to Roy Nolen, 3 February 1940, Hill Papers.

8. Lister Hill to Roy Nolen, 7, 15 February, 1940; Roy Nolen to Lister Hill, 18, 23 February 1940, Hill Papers.

9. Hill's news release backing Bankhead's candidacy, 31 December 1939; copy of Bankhead's statement of 3 March 1940; Lister Hill to Roy Nolen, 2 March 1940, Hill Papers.

10. Statement by Lister Hill, 5 March 1940, Hill Papers.

11. Lister Hill to Roy Nolen, 28 February 1940, Hill Papers.

12. Lister Hill to Roy Nolen, 17 May 1940, Hill Papers. Statement by Harry M. Ayers, 10 May 1940, copy in Hill Papers. *Anniston Star*, 12 May 1940. *Alabama Journal*, 15 May 1940.

13. Frazer interview. Roy Nolen to Lister Hill, 26 May 1940, Hill Papers.

14. Frazer interview. John C. Godbold remembered that Richard Rives described to him Hill's extreme nervousness. Godbold interview. *New York Times*, 18 July 1940.

15. A copy of the nominating speech may be found in the Roosevelt Papers. A tape recording is in the possession of the author.

16. *Montgomery Advertiser*, 19 July 1940.

17. Many unfavorable newspaper reactions to Hill's speech were reprinted by *Alabama Magazine* on 29 July and 5 August 1940. Interview with Douglass Cater (henceforth, Cater interview), Aspen, Colo., 10 August 1979. Davis and Le Maistre interviews. *Pell City News*, 1 August 1940.

18. Franklin D. Roosevelt to Lister Hill, 2 August 1940, Roosevelt Papers. Frazer interview.

19. Lister Hill to Roy Nolen, 21 August 1940, 23 October 1943; Roy Nolen to Lister Hill, 16 March 1944, Hill Papers.

20. Lister Hill to Franklin D. Roosevelt, 22 October 1940, Hill Papers.

21. *Montgomery Advertiser*, 29 October 1940. Roy Nolen to Lister Hill, 10 July 1940, Hill Papers.

22. *Alabama Journal*, 30 January 1939. Lister Hill to Roy Nolen, 1 May 1940; Lister Hill to Joseph Lyons, 1 May 1940, Hill Papers.

23. Phillips interview. Tindall, *Emergence of the New South*, pp. 601–3. *Atlanta Constitution*, 30 March 1940.

24. Phillips interview.

25. Lister Hill to Barrett Shelton, 28 August 1940; Lister Hill to Roy Nolen, 26 May 1941, Hill Papers. *Montgomery Advertiser*, 24 October 1941; David L. Cohn, "The Gentleman from Alabama: Lister Hill," *Atlantic Monthly* 173 (1944): 63–67. Phillips interview.

26. *New York Times*, 8 January 1937, 5 August 1940, 17 July 1941; Cohn, "Gentleman from Alabama," pp. 63–67; Tindall, *Emergence of the New South*, p. 691; *Congressional Record*, 19 August 1940, p. 10472.

27. *Montgomery Advertiser*, 27 April 1941; *Alabama Journal*, 29 September 1941, 6 November 1941; *Birmingham News*, 2 March 1941. For Hill's speeches on these issues, see also *Congressional Record*, 19 February 1944, pp. 1165–66; 1 March 1941, pp. A–921–22; 6 November 1941, pp. 8566–67,

28. *Montgomery Advertiser*, 1 March 1941.

29. Lister Hill to Franklin D. Roosevelt, 14 March 1942; Franklin Roosevelt to Lister Hill, 7 March 1942, Roosevelt Papers. James MacGregor Burns, *Roosevelt: The Soldier of Freedom* (New York: Harcourt Brace Jovanovich, 1970), pp. 183, 415, 494.

30. After the war, Hill co-authored the law making the Women's Army Corps a permanent part of the army. *Birmingham News*, 21 September 1942; Lister Hill to R. H. Long, 27 January 1945; Lister Hill to Walter Bragg Smith, 8 February 1943, Hill Papers. *Congressional Record*, 22 June 1942, p. 5403.

31. Lister Hill to Evelyn Hicks, 9 December 1941, Hill Papers.

32. Foots Clement to Lister Hill, 5 November 1942; Lister Hill to Foots Clement, 6 November 1942, Hill Papers.

33. *Montgomery Advertiser*, 20 January 1943. *Alabama Journal*, 20 January 1943. *Birmingham News*, 20 January 1943.

34. Statement by Senators Hill, Ball, Hatch, and Burton, Hill Papers. Burns, *Soldier of Freedom*, p. 427.

35. *New York Times*, 16 March 1943. Robert Divine, *Second Chance* (New York: Atheneum, 1971), pp. 93–95.

36. Undated text of speech by Lister Hill to University of Alabama Alumni Association, Hill Papers. *New York Times*, 17 March 1943. *New Republic*, 31 May 1943, pp. 727–28; *Congressional Record*, 16 March 1943, pp. A–1298–99.

37. Divine, *Second Chance*, pp. 110–11.

38. Divine, *Second Chance*, pp. 144–45; Burns, *Soldier of Freedom*, p. 428.

39. Letters to several constituents, November 1943, Hill Papers.

40. Lister Hill, "Nation's Responsibility for Education," *National Education Association Journal* 30 (September 1941): 165.

41. *Montgomery Advertiser*, 3 September 1941, 11 October 1943.

42. *Montgomery Advertiser*, 20 October 1943; Lister Hill, "The Fifth Freedom Is Freedom from Ignorance," *Alabama School Journal*, May 1943, p. 30.

43. Steven F. Lawson, *Black Ballots: Voting Rights in the South, 1944–1969* (New York: Columbia University Press, 1976), p. 66.

44. Lawson, *Black Ballots*, p. 67; "Report of the Thirteenth Annual Policy Conference on Democracy and the Constitution" (Montgomery: Alabama Policy Committee, 1945), pp. 26–47. V. O. Key, *Southern Politics*, p. 580.

45. *Birmingham News*, 13 September 1942; Lawson, *Black Ballots*, p. 66.

46. Lawson, *Black Ballots*, p. 69; *New York Times*, 15–21 November 1942.

47. Lawson, *Black Ballots*, pp. 70–71; *Congressional Record*, 21 November 1942, pp. 9043–45.

48. Virginia and Clifford Durr interview, Columbia Oral History Collection, Columbia University, New York City.

49. Stanton Durr to Lister Hill, 3 March 1943, Hill Papers.

50. Jones, Le Maistre, and Elliott interviews.

51. Interview with John Horne (henceforth, Horne interview), Washington, D.C., 1 August 1983.

52. Jones interview.

53. Le Maistre interview.

54. Allgood and Cronin interviews.

55. Thomas A. Krueger, *And Promises to Keep: The Southern Conference for Human Welfare, 1938–1948* (Nashville: Vanderbilt University Press, 1967), pp. 21–39.

56. Duncan and Keith each served brief terms as administrative assistants in Hill's Washington office. Frazer, Davis, Duncan, Beech, Dobbins, and Godbold interviews. Interviews with Barrett Shelton (henceforth, Shelton interview), Decatur, 15 June 1983, and Barney Weeks (henceforth, Weeks interview), Birmingham, 15 November 1982. Lister Hill to Grover Hall, 10 December 1948, Hill Papers.

57. Lister Hill to Roy Nolen, 2 October 1939, Hill Papers.

58. Correspondence Files, Hill Papers. Allgood interview.

59. Correspondence Files, Hill Papers.

60. Hubbard and Durr interviews.

61. Lister Hill to Roy Nolen, 1 January 1938, 10 March 1939, Hill Papers.

62. Robert Frazer to Lister Hill, 8 August 1946, Hill Papers.

63. Walling Keith to Roy Nolen, 2 February 1942, Hill Papers.

64. Lister Hill to Roy Nolen, 6 June, 27 September 1940; 10 February 1942, Hill Papers.

65. Interview with Carroll Kilpatrick (henceforth, Kilpatrick interview), Amissville, Va., 30 July 1983. Allgood and Cronin interviews. Lister Hill to Roy Nolen, 6 April 1940; Hugo Black to Lister Hill, 14 November 1946, Hill Papers.

66. Walden, Jones, Elliott, Cronin, Davis, and Duncan interviews.

67. Lister Hill to Roy Nolen, 5 December 1941, Hill Papers.

68. Lister Hill to Josephus Daniels, undated letter, Hill Papers. Duncan, Beech, Cronin, and Kilpatrick interviews.

69. Weeks, Jones, Elliott, Walden, Cater, Beech, and Davis interviews. Lee Hawthorne to Lister Hill, 26 August 1965, Hill Papers.

CHAPTER 6

1. Jesse B. Hearin to Lister Hill, 2 October 1943, Hill Papers.

2. "Hill of Alabama," *New Republic* 110 (1 May 1944): 602.

3. Jesse B. Hearin to Lister Hill, 2 October 1943, Hill Papers.

4. Jesse B. Hearin to John P. Figh, 11 February 1943, copy in Hill Papers.

5. Howard C. Smith to Lister Hill, 4 January 1943, Hill Papers.

6. John Temple Graves II to Lister Hill, 22 June 1942; Jimmy Faulkner to Lister Hill, 21 November 1942; James E. Folsom to Lister Hill, 13 August 1942; Frederick I. Thompson to Lister Hill, 19 February 1943; Roy Nolen to Lister Hill, 16, 21, 22, 25 June 1942, 13, 16 September 1945, Hill Papers.

7. John Temple Graves II to Lister Hill, 19 June 1942, Hill Papers. Graves's reference was to Thomas Dixon, an uncle of Frank Dixon, whose popular novel, *The Clansman*, was the basis of the enormously popular motion picture, *Birth of a Nation*, which in 1915 glorified the role of the Ku Klux Klan in bringing an end to Reconstruction.

8. Edgar M. Steed (pseudonym for Charles G. Dobbins), "Yankee Dollars Fight Hill," *Nation*, 158 (29 April 1944): 506–7.

9. Allgood interview.

10. Lister Hill to Robert Frazer, 16 December 1943, Hill Papers. 1944 Campaign Notes, James A. Simpson Papers, Alabama Department of Archives and History, Montgomery. Jonathan Daniels to Josephus Daniels, 4 December 1943, Jonathan Daniels Papers, University of North Carolina, Chapel Hill, N.C.

11. *Birmingham Age-Herald*, 21 December 1943.

12. *Birmingham News*, 8, 20, 21 January 1944.

13. The stand of a number of Alabama newspapers was enumerated in an editorial in the *Birmingham News*, undated clipping, Hill Clipping File, Alabama Department of Archives and History, Montgomery. Roy Nolen to Lister Hill, 6 February 1945; Grover Hall Jr. to Roy Nolen, 4 March 1944; Walling Keith to Lister Hill, 16 February 1944, Hill Papers. Charles G. Dobbins to the author, 23 May 1984. See also Daniel Webster Hollis III, *An Alabama Newspaper Tradition: Grover C. Hall and the Hall Family* (University: University of Alabama Press, 1983), pp. 142, 148.

14. Allgood interview. Simpson's advertisements appeared in the *Birmingham News* and *Age-Herald*, 16 April 1944. The special series by Van der Veer appeared in the *Birmingham News*, 23 February–2 March 1944. John Temple Graves II to Lister Hill, 13 March 1944, Hill Papers.

15. The *Birmingham News*, on 19 March 1944, listed a number of Hill's opponents. Included in the Hill Papers is a file of the senator's political opponents in which many of these names appear. A letter from Donald Comer to Lister Hill, 16 February 1944, declaring "I am going to vote for you," is in the Hill Papers. B. C. Whitton to Lister Hill, 25 January 1944, Hill Papers.

16. Allgood interview. Joseph Lyons to Roy Nolen, 16 March 1944, Hill Papers.

17. *The Progressive*, 4 December 1944, copy in Hill Papers.

18. 1944 Campaign Files, Hill Papers. M. E. Lazenby to Lister Hill, 28 January 1944; Dr. L. L. Gwaltney to Lister Hill, 3 February 1944, Hill Papers.

19. J. Thomas Heflin to Lister Hill, 4 March 1944; John Bankhead Jr. to Lister Hill, 11 April 1944, Hill Papers. Victor Hanson to John Bankhead Jr., 25 March 1944, copy in Hill Papers.

20. Allgood interview. Lister Hill to Roy Nolen, 27 May 1944, Hill Papers.

21. Lister Hill to Senator George W. Norris, 16 May 1944; Lister Hill to Capt. Gould Beech, 26 May 1944; E. E. South to Lister Hill, 16 May 1942, Hill Papers. Henry Wallace interview, 8 May 1944, Columbia Oral History Collection, New York City. Allgood interview.

22. Dr. Hill, at eighty-three, again wrote numerous letters to druggists and fellow physicians. Nolen estimated that not more than 50 to 100 "Big Mule Doctors" opposed Hill in 1944. Roy Nolen to Lister Hill, 11 April 1944; Lister Hill to A. A. Carmichael, 10 January 1944; Hill campaign document, 1944 Campaign Files, Hill Papers. *Montgomery Advertiser*, 20 January 1944. Jonathan Daniels to Lister Hill, 16, 29 March 1944, Daniels Papers.

23. Dr. L. L. Hill to Lister Hill, 1 November 1943, Hill Papers.

24. Hollis, *An Alabama Newspaper Tradition*, p. 148. Allgood interview. J. Thomas Heflin to Lister Hill, undated, Hill Papers.

25. Lawson, *Black Ballots*, pp. 74–75.

26. Hill press releases, 25 March, 15 April 1944, Hill Papers. Jonathan Daniels to Samuel I. Rosenman, 4 April 1944, Daniels Papers.

27. Gerald T. Dunne, *Hugo Black and the Judicial Revolution* (New York: Simon and Schuster, 1977), p. 220. Clarence Allgood to "Mr. X" [Roy Nolen], undated, Hill Papers. *Birmingham Age-Herald*, 6 April 1944.

28. *Alabama*, 17, 21 March 1944, p. 3. *Southern Watchman*, 25 March 1944.

29. William W. Hill to Lister Hill, 27 October 1943; Clarence Allgood to Roy Nolen, undated 1944 campaign memorandum; Lister Hill to Roy Nolen, 14 March 1944, Hill Papers. Steed, "Yankee Dollars," p. 508. *Montgomery Advertiser*, 16 April 1944.

30. *Birmingham News*, 11, 14 April 1944.

31. Simpson had voted *against* the Tunstall amendment, which removed the language "after the fifth generation inclusive" from the Alabama Code and attempted to ensure that mulattoes should always be legally classified as black by substituting the words "without reference to . . . number of generations removed." Explaining this vote in 1944, Simpson said: "We had gotten along very well under [the original statute] . . . for something like 100 years." *Birmingham News*, 21, 25, 26 April 1944. *Houston Herald*, 20 April 1944. John Bankhead Jr. to Roy Nolen, 13 April 1944; Joseph Lyons to Roy Nolen, 16 March 1944, Hill Papers.

32. *Birmingham News*, 30 April 1944. *Montgomery Advertiser*, 28 April 1944. John Bankhead Jr. to Roy Nolen, 13 April 1944, Hill Papers.

33. Roy Nolen's analysis of the campaign results is included in the 1944 campaign files of the Hill Papers. Roy Nolen to Lister Hill, 19 May 1944, Hill Papers. Of the total 227,548 votes cast, Hill received 126,372 to Simpson's 101,176. Barrett Shelton's editorial was quoted in the *Alabama Journal*, 9 May 1944.

34. Lister Hill to Roy Nolen, 13 May 1944; Roy Nolen to Lister Hill, 12 May 1944, Hill Papers.

35. Roy Nolen to Lister Hill, 12 May 1944, Hill Papers.

36. Frank Dixon to Lt. Grover Hall Jr., 2 August 1944, Frank M. Dixon Papers (henceforth, Dixon Papers), Alabama Department of Archives and History, Montgomery. Hollis, *An Alabama Newspaper Tradition*, p. 148.

37. Stephen Early to Lister Hill, 5 May 1944, Roosevelt Papers. Harry Truman to Lister Hill, 4 May 1944, Harry S Truman Papers, Truman Library, Independence, Mo.

38. Frank Dixon to Grover Hall Jr., 2 August 1944, Dixon Papers.

39. Lister Hill to George W. Norris, 16 May 1944; Lister Hill to Roy Nolen, 25, 27 May 1944; 25 May 1945, Hill Papers. Davis interview.

40. The results of the Alabama general election for United States senator, 7 November 1944, were: Hill, 202,604; John A. Posey, Republican, 41,963; Hollis B. Parrish, Prohibitionist, 3,162. In the presidential race, Roosevelt electors polled 199,000 to 45,000 for Dewey. Heard and Strong, *Southern Primaries*, p. 18. Lawson, *Black Ballots*, p. 47. Jonathan Daniels to Franklin D. Roosevelt, 28 September 1944, Daniels Papers.

41. Lister Hill to Franklin Roosevelt, 6 October 1944, Roosevelt Papers.

42. Crampton Harris to Lister Hill, 13 January 1945, Hill Papers.

43. Frank M. Dixon to Gessner McCorvey, 12 October 1944, Dixon Papers. *Birmingham News*, 9 February 1945. *Birmingham Age-Herald*, 10 February 1945.

44. *Montgomery Advertiser*, 15 February 1945. James A. Simpson to J. H. Sanders, 21 February 1945, Simpson Papers.

45. *Montgomery Advertiser*, 18 January 1945. "People in the Limelight," *New Republic*, 26 March 1945, p. 407. *Birmingham News*, 16, 17 May 1945. Claribel McCann to Lister Hill, 26 February 1945, Hill Papers.

46. *Mobile Press-Register*, 2 March 1945. John Salmond, *A Southern Rebel: The Life and Times of Aubrey Willis Williams, 1890–1965* (Chapel Hill: University of North Carolina Press, 1983), pp. 179–83.

47. Salmond, *A Southern Rebel*, p. 192.

48. Salmond, *A Southern Rebel*, pp. 193, 195.

49. A copy of Hill's statement on Roosevelt's death is contained in the Hill Papers.

50. Lister Hill to Roy Nolen, 14 April, 1 May 1945, Hill Papers.

51. Elliott interview.

CHAPTER 7

1. In his distrust for some former Roosevelt associates, Truman evidently acquiesced in the taping of Corcoran's telephone conversations from 1 June 1945 through May 1947. See Robert J. Donovan, *Conflict and Crisis: The Presidency of Harry S Truman, 1945–1948* (New York: W. W. Norton, 1977), pp. 29–30. Telephone conversation, Thomas Corcoran and Lister Hill, 9:45 P.M., 19 June 1945. "Summaries of Conversations (Thomas G. Corcoran)," President's Secretary's Files, Truman Papers.

2. *Nashville Tennesseean*, 2 May 1945; *Birmingham News*, 31 December 1945, 13 January 1946.

3. Donovan, *Conflict and Crisis*, p. 125; Alonzo L. Hamby, *Beyond the New Deal: Harry S. Truman and American Liberalism* (New York: Columbia University Press, 1973), pp. 61–62.

4. Undated newspaper clipping, Hill Clipping File, Department of Archives and History, Montgomery.

5. Telephone conversation, Lister Hill and Thomas Corcoran, 8:26 A.M., 13 December 1945, Truman Papers.

6. Donovan, *Conflict and Crisis*, pp. 138–40. Telephone conversation, Thomas Corcoran and Lister Hill, 9:25 P.M., 25 November 1945, Truman Papers.

7. *Alabama Journal*, 30 November 1948. Donovan, *Conflict and Crisis*, pp. 264–65.

8. Drew Pearson, "Washington Merry-Go-Round: Medicos Battle Politicos on National Health," *Alabama Journal*, 27 November 1945.

9. Paul Starr, *The Social Transformation of American Medicine* (New York: Basic Books, 1982), pp. 280–82. Donovan, *Conflict and Crisis*, p. 125.

10. Donovan, *Conflict and Crisis*, p. 126. Pearson, "Medicos Battle Politicos," *Alabama Journal*, 27 November 1945.

11. Dan Feshbach, "What's Inside the Black Box: A Case Study of Allocative Politics in the Hill-Burton Program," *International Journal of Health Services* 9 (1979): 315–17.

12. Feshbach,"What's Inside the Black Box," pp. 314–16. Starr, *Social Transformation of American Medicine*, pp. 282–83.

13. Feshbach, "What's Inside the Black Box," pp. 318–19.

14. L. L. Hill Jr., "Family Record," pp. 295–304. *Montgomery Advertiser*, 14 August 1947. Before World War II, Luther Hill had joined the *Des Moines* (Ia.) *Register and Tribune*. He rejoined this newspaper after the war, eventually becoming its publisher.

15. Starr, *Social Transformation of American Medicine*, pp. 348–49.

16. Starr, *Social Transformation of American Medicine*, p. 350. U.S. Congressional Quarterly, *Congress and the Nation* (Washington, D.C.: Government Printing Office), 3 (1965): 1130.

17. Michael Balter, "The Best-Kept Secret in Health Care," *The Progressive* (April

1981): 34–37. Feshbach, "What's Inside the Black Box," pp. 327–28.

18. *Mobile Press-Register*, 17 November 1949. *Montgomery Advertiser*, 21 August 1977.

19. Feshbach, "What's Inside the Black Box," pp. 313–14. "Lister Steps Down from the Hill," *Medical World News*, 1 November 1968, pp. 56–58.

20. Starr, *Social Transformation of American Medicine*, pp. 350–51. Judith R. Lave and Lester B. Lave, *The Hospital Construction Act: An Evaluation of the Hill-Burton Program, 1948–1973* (Washington, D.C.: American Enterprise Institute for Public Policy Research, 1974), pp. 41–43, 47. "Lister Steps Down from the Hill," *Medical World News*, pp. 56–58.

21. Starr, *Social Transformation of American Medicine*, pp. 349–50. Feshbach, "What's Inside the Black Box," pp. 313–16.

22. *Mobile Register*, 12 May 1949; *Birmingham News*, 31 March, 24 April 1949, 21 April 1950. Lister Hill to Roy Nolen, 26 January 1949, Hill Papers. Starr, *Social Transformation of American Medicine*, p. 285.

23. To salute Truman for his early and courageous advocacy, President Lyndon Johnson signed the Medicare legislation into law in July 1965 in the presence of the former president at the Truman Library in Independence, Mo. Donovan, *Conflict and Crisis*, pp. 125–26. Feshbach, "What's Inside the Black Box," pp. 320–21, 336–37.

24. Folsom's rise to power in 1946 is chronicled in William D. Barnard, *Dixiecrats and Democrats: Alabama Politics, 1942–1950* (University: University of Alabama Press, 1974), and in Carl Grafton and Anne Permaloff, *Big Mules and Branchheads: James E. Folsom and Political Power in Alabama* (Athens: University of Georgia Press, 1985). Other treatments may be found in George E. Sims, "The Little Man's Big Friend: James E. Folsom in Alabama Politics, 1946–1958" (Ph.D. dissertation, Emory University, 1981), and Thomas J. Gilliam, "The Second Folsom Administration: The Destruction of Alabama Liberalism 1954–1958" (Ph.D. dissertation, Auburn University, 1975).

25. Lister Hill to Roy Nolen, 29 September 1945; telegram, Lister Hill to Bill Graham, 23 May 1946, Hill Papers. Barnard, *Dixiecrats and Democrats*, p. 39.

26. Roy Nolen to Lister Hill, 25 February, 18 March 1946; Lister Hill to Roy Nolen, 24 March 1945; Roy Nolen to Joseph Lyons, 11 July 1946, Hill Papers.

27. Barnard, *Dixiecrats and Democrats*, pp. 8, 33–34. Sims, "The Little Man's Big Friend," p. 47. Gilliam, "The Second Folsom Administration," p. 41.

28. Jesse Hearin to Lister Hill, 20 May 1946; Richard Rives to Lister Hill, 14 May 1946, Hill Papers. Frank M. Dixon to B. B. Gossett, 16 May 1946, Dixon Papers.

29. *Alabama Journal*, 16 October 1948.

30. Roy Nolen to Lister Hill, 15 March 1947, Hill Papers. Beech interview.

31. Evelyn Hicks to Lister Hill, 17 September 1945; Lee B. Burroughs to Lister Hill, 6 June 1946, Hill Papers. Beech interview.

32. Roy Nolen to Lister Hill, 7 June 1946, Hill Papers.

33. Allgood and Horne interviews. *Montgomery Examiner*, 3 November 1954.

34. Lister Hill to Jesse B. Hearin, 29 June 1946; Lister Hill to J. C. Pope, 29 June 1946; Dr. Worcester (no first name given) to Lister Hill, 31 July 1946, Hill Papers. *Alabama Journal*, 25 July 1946.

35. Barnard, *Dixiecrats and Democrats*, p. 57. Roy Nolen to Mrs. Albert Thomas, 27 February 1947; John D. Hill to Roy Nolen, 6 August 1946, Hill Papers.

36. Horne and Cronin interviews.

37. Interview with John Sparkman (henceforth, Sparkman interview), Huntsville, Ala., 10 November 1979. Cronin interview.

38. Rains, Jones, and Elliott interviews. Other members of Alabama's House delegation were Sam Hobbs, George Grant, George Andrews, and Frank Boykin.

39. Barnard, *Dixiecrats and Democrats*, pp. 59–61.

40. Barnard, *Dixiecrats and Democrats*, p. 61.

41. Gessner McCorvey to members of the Alabama legislature, 10 May 1945, copy in Hill Papers. Barnard, *Dixiecrats and Democrats*, p. 62.

42. Barnard, *Dixiecrats and Democrats*, p. 65.

43. Richard T. Rives, "An Argument against the Adoption of the Boswell Amendment," copy of speech delivered at Montgomery Museum of Fine Arts, 18 April 1946, Hill Papers. Horace Wilkinson, "Argument for Adoption of Boswell Amendment," *Alabama Lawyer* 7 (October 1946): 375–82.

44. Hill undated (approximately September 1946) press release on Boswell amendment, copy in Hill Papers. Key, *Southern Politics*, p. 634.

45. Lawson, *Black Ballots*, p. 93; Key, *Southern Politics*, pp. 634–35.

46. This case was *Davis v. Schnell*, 81 F. Supp. (U.S.) 872 (1949).

47. Donovan, *Conflict and Crisis*, p. 173.

48. Telephone conversation, Lister Hill and Thomas Corcoran, 8:30 P.M., 29 April 1946, Truman Papers.

49. Duncan interview.

50. *Birmingham News*, 24 December 1946.

51. *Montgomery Advertiser*, 5 November 1948.

52. *Montgomery Advertiser*, 25 November 1950.

CHAPTER 8

1. Harvard Sitkoff, "Harry Truman and the Election of 1948: The Coming of Age of Civil Rights in American Politics," *Journal of Southern History* 37 (November 1971): 597–616.

2. Sitkoff, "Harry Truman and the Election of 1948," p. 598. E. D. Nixon to Lister Hill, 29 February 1948, Hill Papers.

3. "Crossroads Democracy," text of a speech by Frank Dixon before the Southern Society of New York, 11 December 1942, Dixon Papers. Barnard, *Dixiecrats and Democrats*, pp. 98–99.

4. Frank Dixon to Frank R. Broadway, 12 June 1945, Dixon Papers.

5. Roy Nolen to Lister Hill, (undated) 1948, Hill Papers.

6. Barnard, *Dixiecrats and Democrats*, pp. 102–3.

7. Sims, "The Little Man's Big Friend," pp. 218–19; William M. Beck to Lister Hill, 10 February 1948; Clarence Allgood to Lister Hill, 15 March 1948, Hill Papers.

8. Lister Hill to Roy Nolen, 21 February 1948. Roy Nolen to Lister Hill, (undated) 1948, Hill Papers.

9. *Birmingham News*, 3 January 1948. Text of Hill's announcement as a delegate candidate, 1 March 1948; Lister Hill to Curtis E. Hill, 1 March 1948, Hill Papers.

10. *Birmingham News*, 3 March 1948. *Birmingham Post*, 12 March 1948. *Mobile Press*, 9 March 1948. Jesse Hearin to Lister Hill, 3 March 1948; William H. Beck to Lister Hill, 15 March 1948; Clarence Allgood to Lister Hill, 15 March 1948; Richard Rives to Lister Hill, 14 March 1948; Fred H. Foy to Lister Hill, 25 March 1948, Hill Papers.

11. Lister Hill to Richard Rives, 26 March 1948; Lister Hill to Dr. H. C. Fountain, 8 April 1948, Hill Papers.

12. Lister Hill to Michael Straight, 3 April 1948; Lister Hill to Marion Rushton, 21 April 1948; J. C. Yarbrough to Lister Hill, 3 April 1948, Hill Papers.

13. For a detailed account of the 1948 campaign in Alabama, see Gladys King Burns, "The Alabama Dixiecrat Revolt of 1948" (M.A. thesis, Auburn University, 1965). Paul Maxwell Smith Jr."Loyalists and States' Righters in the Democratic Party of Alabama, 1949–1954" (M.A. thesis, Auburn University, 1966), pp. 16–18.

14. Barnard, *Dixiecrats and Democrats*, pp. 108–9. *Birmingham Post*, 12 March 1948. Lister Hill to Horace Wilkinson, 21 April 1948, Hill Papers.

15. Frank Dixon to Laurie Battle, 6 July 1948, Dixon Papers.

16. *Alabama Journal*, 24 April 1948. Davis interview.

17. Sibyl Pool to Lister Hill, 14 May 1948; Jesse Hearin to Lister Hill, 5 May 1948, Hill Papers. Barnard, *Dixiecrats and Democrats*, p. 110.

18. Elected in the 4 May primary race for delegates-at-large were: Hill, 161,629; Chauncey Sparks, 143,065; Handy Ellis, 137,601; and Eugene ("Bull") Connor, 125,614. Forced into a runoff were J. M. Bonner, 121,001; D. H. Riddle, 118,047; Albert Stapp, 116,174; Albert A. Carmichael, 112,011; Gessner McCorvey, 111,276; Joe Money, 96,296, and James E. Folsom, 80,540. Marie B. Owen, *Alabama Official and Statistical Register, 1951* (Alexander City: Outlook Publishing Company, 1951), pp. 581–82. Sims, "The Little Man's Big Friend," pp. 214–15, 220–22.

19. For a more detailed explanation of the race for presidential electors, see Barnard, *Dixiecrats and Democrats*, p. 121.

20. Roy Nolen to Lister Hill, 3 May 1947; Lister Hill to Roy Nolen, 6 May 1948; Lister Hill to Foots Clement, 7 May 1948, Hill Papers.

21. *Birmingham News*, 6 July 1948.

22. *Montgomery Advertiser*, 13 July 1948. Letter from George C. Wallace to the author (henceforth, Wallace letter), 22 September 1983.

23. Frank Dixon to J. O. Emmerich, 24 June 1948, Dixon Papers.

24. Barnard, *Dixiecrats and Democrats*, p. 111. Wallace explained later that he had run for delegate as a Russell supporter and had remained in the committee convention to carry out that commitment. Wallace letter.

25. Emile B. Adler, "Why Dixiecrats Failed," *Journal of Politics* 15 (August 1953): 357. Barnard, *Dixiecrats and Democrats*, p. 114.

26. Paul Maxwell Smith Jr., "Loyalists and States' Righters," pp. 14–15.

27. Gessner McCorvey to Albert Stapp, 31 July 1948, copy in Dixon Papers.

28. James E. Folsom to Lister Hill, 31 October 1948. Horace Wilkinson to James E. Folsom, 5 November 1948, copy in Hill Papers. Barnard, *Dixiecrats and Democrats*, p. 123.

29. *Montgomery Advertiser*, 8 August 1948.

30. Typical of many replies to constituents on the issue of the 1948 election is Lister Hill to A. L. Hawley, 14 September 1948, Hill Papers. *Montgomery Advertiser*, 7 September 1948.

31. E. Q. Hawk to Lister Hill, 19 July 1948; *Opelika Daily News*, (undated) August 1948 clipping; Ralph McGill, "The Lean Wind from Alabama," undated clipping, *Atlanta Journal*, Hill Papers.

32. Cater interview. Smith, "Loyalists and States' Righters," p. 11.

33. Adler, "Why the Dixiecrats Failed," pp. 358–60.

34. Lister Hill to Carroll Kilpatrick, 13 November 1948; Guy A. Matlock to John R. Steelman, 18 November 1948, Hill Papers. Lyndon B. Johnson to Lister Hill, 15 November 1948, Lyndon B. Johnson Papers (henceforth, Johnson Papers), Lyndon B. Johnson Library, Austin, Tex.

35. S. A. Lynne to Lister Hill, 6 November 1948; R. A. Reid to Lister Hill, 9 November 1948, Hill Papers.

36. Cronin and Jones interviews.

37. The name of the Senate Committee on Education and Labor had been changed in 1946 to Labor and Public Welfare, and Military Affairs had become Armed Services. *Birmingham News*, 6 January, 9 February, 6 March 1949.

38. When the Senate passed Taft-Hartley in 1947 Hill voted against it, Sparkman voted for it. Both Hill and Sparkman voted against overriding Truman's veto. *Congressional Record* (June 1947), p. 7538. *Alabama Digest*, 15 May 1947. Lister Hill to Roy Nolen, 27 July 1949, Hill Papers.

39. Lister Hill, "Should Congress Approve Current Plans for Federal Aid to Education?" *Congressional Digest*, November 1949, p. 270.

40. Jean Begeman, "The Vanishing Farm Phones," *New Republic* 120 (28 March 1949): 10–11.

41. Begeman, "The Vanishing Farm Phones," pp. 10–11.

42. *Birmingham News*, 14 November 1949. *Birmingham Age-Herald*, 23 November 1949.

43. *Birmingham News*, 23 October 1949.

44. *Lee County Bulletin*, Auburn, Ala., 30 June 1955.

45. *Montgomery Advertiser*, 5 December 1948; *Birmingham News*, 10 April 1949, 21 February 1950. Roy Nolen to Lister Hill, 14 April 1949; Luther Patrick to Lister Hill, 21 February 1950, Hill Papers.

46. Roy Nolen (quoting Douglas Clark) to Lister Hill, 15 February 1950; Waights M. Taylor to Lister Hill, 10 January 1950, Hill Papers. Smith, "Loyalists and States' Righters," pp. 16–17, 24–26.

47. Smith, "Loyalists and States' Righters," pp. 16–17, 24–26.

48. *Birmingham News*, 14 February 1950. L. F. Jeffers to Lister Hill, 23 February 1950, Hill Papers.

49. Charles Dobbins to Lister Hill, 1 February 1950, Hill Papers.

50. Smith, "Loyalists and States' Righters," pp. 24–27.

51. Richard Rives to Lister Hill, 10 February 1950, 22 January 1950; Foots Clement to Lister Hill, 14 February 1950, Hill Papers.

52. Copy of McNeil announcement; William Mitch to Lister Hill, 13 March 1950; Ben F. Ray to Lister Hill, 1 March 1950; Luther Patrick to Lister Hill, 14 March 1950; Joe B. Sarver to Lister Hill, 2 March 1950, Hill Papers.

53. Political Correspondence, 1950 Campaign, Hill Papers.

54. Smith, "Loyalists and States' Righters," pp. 30–33. Herbert J. Meighan, Gadsden mayor, was titular head of the loyalist campaign.

55. Smith, "Loyalists and States' Righters," pp. 34–48.

56. Smith, "Loyalists and States' Righters," pp. 35–36. Ed E. Reid to Lister Hill, 7 April 1950, Hill Papers.

57. *Montgomery Advertiser*, 13 April 1950. Smith, "Loyalists and States' Righters," p. 45. Roy Nolen to Lister Hill, 5 April 1950, Hill Papers.

58. *Montgomery Advertiser*, 13 April 1950. Smith, "Loyalists and States' Righters," pp. 39–44. Albert Carmichael to Lister Hill, 21 July 1949, Hill Papers.

59. Smith, "Loyalists and States' Righters," p. 33. Lister Hill and John Sparkman to Harry Truman, 30 March 1950, Truman Papers.

60. Smith, "Loyalists and States' Righters," pp. 50–52. Richard Bunch to Lister Hill, 5 May 1950, Hill Papers.

61. Foots Clement to Lister Hill, 20 May 1950, Hill Papers. For a detailed analysis of the outcome of the committee race, see Smith, "Loyalists and States' Righters," pp. 49–63.

62. Smith, "Loyalists and States' Righters," p. 62.

63. Smith, "Loyalists and States' Righters," pp. 58–61.

64. Hill polled 228,524 votes to McNeil's 112,615. Numan V. Bartley and Hugh D. Graham, *Southern Elections: County and Precinct Data, 1950–1972* (Baton Rouge: Louisiana State University Press, 1978), p. 8. Owen, *Alabama Official and Statistical Register, 1951*, pp. 581–82.

65. William Beck to Lister Hill, 31 May 1950; J. Guy Daniels to Lister Hill, 21 March 1950; Frank C. Heard to Lister Hill, 17 March 1950, Hill Papers.

66. Sosna, *In Search of the Silent South*, p. 165.

67. Hill's statement to the United Press, Washington, D.C., 11 June 1950, Hill Papers. *Birmingham News*, 10 May 1950.

68. *Birmingham News*, 5 November 1950.

69. Lister Hill to Daniel H. Thomas, 3 October 1950; Roy Nolen to Lister Hill, 15 April 1950, Hill Papers.

70. Ben F. Ray to Gessner McCorvey, 30 October 1950, copy in Hill Papers; Lester F. Larence [*sic*] to Lister Hill, 16 August 1950, Hill Papers. *Birmingham News*, 5 November 1950.

71. Hill received 125,534 votes to Crommelin's 38,477. Owen, *Alabama Official and Statistical Register, 1951*, pp. 581–82.

72. A copy of Nolen's 1944 affidavit is in the Hill Papers. Roy Nolen to Joseph Lyons, 11 July 1946; Lister Hill to Curtis McPherson, 8 August 1952, Hill Papers. *Montgomery Advertiser*, 7 October 1941.

73. Foots Clement to Lister Hill, 6 June 1950, Hill Papers.

74. Jesse B. Hearin to Hugo Black, 8 May 1950, copy in Hill Papers.

CHAPTER 9

1. Ronald C. Hood to Lister Hill, 7 May 1950, Hill Papers.

2. Lister Hill, "A Bonanza for Education," *Harper's* 204 (March 1958): 28–31.

3. Jack Bass, *Unlikely Heroes* (New York: Simon and Schuster, 1981), pp. 67–74. Later that same year, Hill engineered the selection of Daniel H. Thomas, of Mobile, a Democratic loyalist in 1950 and a law partner of his uncle, Joseph Lyons, to be federal district judge for Alabama's southern district. Judge Thomas was to prove decidedly more moderate than Rives in his initial approach to civil rights issues, especially that of voting rights discrimination in the Black Belt area surrounding Selma. Tinsley E. Yarbrough, *Judge Frank Johnson and Human Rights in Alabama* (University: University of Alabama Press, 1981), p. 86. Smith, "Loyalists and States' Righters," pp. 64–68. Bass, *Unlikely Heroes*, pp. 69–74, 82. Lister Hill to Joseph Lyons and Daniel Thomas, 1 March 1951, Hill Papers. Hugo Black Jr., "Richard Taylor Rives, 1895–1982," *Alabama Lawyer* 44 (January 1983): 59–60.

4. Smith, "Loyalists and States' Righters," pp. 64–67.

5. Quietly and behind the scenes, Hill opposed McCarthy's tactics as a challenge to "our traditional American principle of 'innocent until proved guilty.' " In November 1954, he voted in favor of censuring McCarthy. Lister Hill to Mrs. William P. Duvall, 25 March 1952, Hill Papers. *Christian Science Monitor*, 2 November 1954.

6. Smith, "Loyalists and States' Righters," pp. 68–71.

7. Smith, "Loyalists and States' Righters," pp. 72–73. Elliott interview.

8. Smith, "Loyalists and States' Righters," pp. 74–75.

9. Smith, "Loyalists and States' Righters," p. 74, 76–77.

10. Smith, "Loyalists and States' Righters," p. 77.

11. Smith, "Loyalists and States' Righters," pp. 80–83.

12. Smith, "Loyalists and States' Righters," pp. 84–85.

13. The case was *Ray v. Blair*, 353, U.S. 231 (1952).

14. Lister Hill to Lecil [*sic*] Gray, 28 January 1952, Hill Papers.

15. Smith, "Loyalists and States' Righters," pp. 78, 83–84, 92–94.

16. Ben May to Lister Hill, 21 January 1952; Joseph Lyons to Lister Hill, 29 March 1952; Jesse B. Hearin to Lister Hill, 18 January 1952, Hill Papers.

17. Jonathan Daniels, *The Man from Independence* (Philadelphia: J. B. Lippincott, 1950), p. 345.

18. Lister Hill to Harry Truman, 15 January 1953, 4 June 1953, 26 November 1954, Truman Papers.

19. Smith, "Loyalists and States' Righters," p. 79. 1952 Democratic campaign folder, Hill Papers.

20. *Birmingham Post-Herald*, 21 May 1952; Smith, "Loyalists and States' Righters," p. 89.

21. Joint statement by Hill and Sparkman, 11 May 1952, Hill Papers.

22. William Mitch, E. M. Wells, J. P. Knight to Lister Hill, 23 May 1952; Harold M. Lee to Lister Hill, 12 May 1952; Ben Leader to Lister Hill, 13 June 1952, Hill Papers.

23. *Mobile Register*, 24 July 1952.

24. *Mobile Register*, 24 July 1952.

25. *Montgomery Advertiser*, 6 March 1949; *Birmingham News*, 18 May 1952; *Gadsden Times*, 26 February 1952.

26. Lister Hill to Jesse Hearin, 1 April 1954, Hill Papers. Godbold interview.

27. Weeks, Godbold, Allgood, Davis, and Elliott interviews.

28. Duncan, Jones, Shelton, Davis, Rains, Horne, and Le Maistre interviews.

29. Davis, Duncan, Jones interviews.

30. Ed E. Reid to Ben Ray, 4 August 1952, copy in Hill Papers.

31. *Montgomery Advertiser*, 4 October 1952.

32. Smith, "Loyalists and States' Righters," pp. 89–95.

33. Lister Hill to E. Jean Willett, 29 July 1952; Lister Hill to Adlai Stevenson, 5 August 1952, Hill Papers.

34. *Montgomery Advertiser*, 4 October 1952.

35. Smith, "Loyalists and States' Righters," p. 94. *Montgomery Advertiser*, 9 November 1952.

36. Gilliam, "Second Folsom Administration," p. 55. Smith, "Loyalists and States' Righters," p. 106.

37. Smith, "Loyalists and States' Righters," pp. 104–12. Lister Hill to a number of constituents, Hill Papers.

38. Battle, a war veteran, the son of a widely known Methodist minister, and a member of a large, professionally oriented Alabama family, made an attractive candi-

date for the States' Righters. The *Montgomery Advertiser*, *Alabama Journal*, and *Dothan Eagle* endorsed Battle. The *Eagle* published a photograph of Sparkman with three black leaders under the caption "Alabama's non-deviating senator." The *Birmingham News* gave Sparkman its belated endorsement. Charles Feidelson, an Alabama editor writing for the *Washington Times-Herald*, 25 April 1954, reported that Battle had considerable financial support from Texas oil financiers. See also Doris Fleeson, *Washington Star*, 12 April 1954. Gilliam, "Second Folsom Administration," pp. 74–77.

39. Gilliam, "Second Folsom Administration," pp. 74–77. John G. Crommelin to Dwight Eisenhower, 29 April 1954, Eisenhower Papers, Eisenhower Library, Abilene, Kan.

40. Gilliam, "Second Folsom Administration," pp. 72–80. Smith, "Loyalists and States' Righters," pp. 109–10.

41. Smith, "Loyalists and States' Righters," pp. 115–16. *Montgomery Advertiser*, 6 May 1954.

42. *Washington Evening Star*, 7 May 1954.

43. Frederic D. Ogden, *The Poll Tax in the South* (University: University of Alabama Press, 1958), pp. 234–35.

44. Ogden, *Poll Tax in the South*, pp. 234–35.

45. Ogden, *Poll Tax in the South*, p. 135; Gilliam, "Second Folsom Administration," pp. 29–30

46. Gilliam, "Second Folsom Administration," p. 51.

47. Gilliam, "Second Folsom Administration," pp. 56–80. *Andalusia Star-News*, 6 May 1954.

48. Smith, "Loyalists and States' Righters," p. 111.

CHAPTER 10

1. Interview with Mike Gorman (henceforth, Gorman interview), Washington, D.C., 17 April 1978.

2. Edward G. Holley and Robert F. Schremser, *The Library Services and Construction Act: A Historical Overview from the Viewpoint of Major Participants* (Greenwich, Conn.: JAI Press, 1983), p. 84. William W. White, "Democrats' Board of Directors," *New York Times Magazine*, 10 July 1955, pp. 10–11.

3. For an overview of this committee's history, see *Committee on Labor and Public Welfare, United States Senate, 100th Anniversary: 1869–1969* (Washington, D.C.: Senate Documents No. 90–108), 24 September 1968.

4. In his interview with Phillips, Hill recalled having seen Taft, Hughes, and Stone in the old Supreme Court chamber. Later Hill suggested that this room be restored to its original appearance. At first he thought that it should be arranged as used by the Court. But with the Court unpopular in the South at that time, he decided that the room would

be better received if restored as the Senate had used it. *Stewart McClure, Chief Clerk of the Senate Committee on Labor, Education, and Public Welfare: Oral History Interviews, December 1982-May 1983* (Washington, D.C.: Senate Historical Office, 1984), pp. 67–68 (henceforth, *Stewart McClure*).

5. *Stewart McClure*, pp. 81–82.

6. Gorman interview. *Stewart McClure*, pp. 77–78.

7. *Stewart McClure*, pp. 79–81. Gorman interview.

8. *Congressional Record*, 18 April 1953, p. 3286.

9. *Stewart McClure*, p. 173.

10. Interview with Stewart McClure (henceforth, McClure interview), Washington, D.C., 18 March 1985.

11. *Stewart McClure*, p. 81.

12. Lister Hill to Richard Rives, 19 March 1955, Hill Papers.

13. Phillips interview. Daniels, *Frontier on the Potomac*, pp. 61–62.

14. *Birmingham News*, 19 June 1946.

15. *Birmingham News*, 1 August 1954.

16. David A. Frier, *Conflict of Interest in the Eisenhower Administration* (Ames: University of Iowa Press, 1969), pp. 54–57.

17. Frier, *Conflict of Interest*, pp. 61–67. For a more detailed study of the Dixon-Yates controversy, see Aaron Wildavsky, *Dixon-Yates: A Study in Power Politics* (New Haven: Yale University Press, 1962).

18. *Montgomery Examiner*, 12 July 1955; Lister Hill to Joe Marshall, 5 October 1956, Hill Papers.

19. Interview with Florence Mahoney (henceforth, Mahoney interview), Washington, D.C., 6 September 1985. Lister Hill to Dwight Eisenhower, 16 April 1955, Eisenhower Papers.

20. *Congressional Record*, 17 June 1955, p. 8677. *Birmingham News*, 6 May 1955.

21. Dr. Leonard A. Scheele, former surgeon general of the U.S. Public Health Service, oral history interview, Columbia Oral History Research Office, Columbia University, New York City. Copy in Eisenhower Papers.

22. Quoted in *Congressional Record*, 17 June 1955, p. 8677.

23. *Birmingham News*, 17, 18 May 1955. *Congressional Record*, 29 June 1955, p. A–4765.

24. *Stewart McClure*, pp. 71–73; Phillips interview.

25. Charles L. Fontenay, *Estes Kefauver: A Biography* (Knoxville: University of Tennessee Press, 1980), pp. 312–30.

26. Yarbrough, *Judge Frank Johnson*, p. 35. Bass, *Unlikely Heroes*, p. 68. *Alabama Journal*, 9 July 1955.

27. Yarbrough, *Judge Johnson*, p. 35. *Birmingham News*, 9 June 1952.

28. *Montgomery Advertiser*, 7 September 1955; Yarbrough, *Judge Johnson*, pp. 35–36.

29. *Alabama Journal*, 9 July 1955; Yarbrough, *Judge Johnson*, p. 35.

30. Gilliam, "Second Folsom Administration," pp. 263–68. The Montgomery bus case was *Gayle v. Browder*, 352 U.S. 903 (1956).

31. Mahoney interview. Interview with Mary Lasker (henceforth, Lasker interview), New York City, 24 April 1978.

32. Stephen P. Strickland, *Politics, Science, and Dread Disease: A Short History of United States Medical Research Policy* (Cambridge: Harvard University Press, 1972), pp. ix–x. Elizabeth Brenner Drew, "The Health Syndicate: Washington's Noble Conspirators," *Atlantic Monthly*, December 1967, p. 75. Lasker interview.

33. Strickland, *Politics*, pp. 101–6. Phillips and Lasker interviews.

34. Phillips interview. Strickland, *Politics*, p. 106.

35. Lasker, Cronin, and Mahoney interviews. *Stewart McClure*, pp. 71–72.

36. Milton Viorst, "The Political Good Fortune of Medical Research," *Science*, 17 April 1964, pp. 267–70.

37. Drew, "The Health Syndicate," pp. 80–81. Strickland, *Politics*, p. 187.

38. Lasker and Mahoney interviews. Strickland, *Politics*, pp. 122, 225–26.

39. *Birmingham News*, 19 April 1959.

40. *Mobile Press-Register*, 17 November 1944. Holley and Schremser, *Library Services Act*, pp. 8–19.

41. Holley and Schremser, *Library Services Act*, pp. 17–20.

42. Holley and Schremser, *Library Services Act*, pp. 15–18, 84. Jerome Levy to editor of *Montgomery Advertiser*, 20 February 1968.

43. Holley and Schremser, *Library Services Act*, pp. 25–26, 83.

44. Holley and Schremser, *Library Services Act*, p. 53.

45. Holley and Schremser, *Library Services Act*, p. 66.

46. Phillips interview. Dr. Brad Rogers, "Senator Lister Hill and the Beginnings of Medlars," *Alabama Librarian* 34, No. 8–9 (1983): 10–11.

47. First chairman of this new library's board would be Dr. Worth Daniels, son of Hill's old mentor, Josephus Daniels; its second chairman would be Hill's cousin, Dr. Champ Lyons. Interview with Dr. Frank B. Rogers (henceforth, Rogers interview), Denver, 4 August 1984.

CHAPTER 11

1. Hollinger F. Barnard, ed., *Outside the Magic Circle: The Autobiography of Virginia Foster Durr* (University: University of Alabama Press, 1985), pp. 254–75. Aubrey Williams to Lister Hill, 15 February 1954, Aubrey Williams Papers, Franklin D. Roosevelt Library, Hyde Park, N.Y. For a detailed treatment of this era, see James Tyra Harris, "Alabama Reaction to the *Brown* Decision, 1954–1956: A Case Study in Massive Resistance" (D.A. dissertation, Middle Tennessee State University, 1978).

2. *Montgomery Advertiser*, 19 May 1954. Davis, Durr, and Hubbard interviews.

3. Sims, "Little Man's Big Friend," pp. 400–414. Gilliam, "Second Folsom Administration," p. 254.

4. Neil R. McMillen, *The Citizens' Council: Organized Resistance to the Second Reconstruction, 1954–64* (Urbana: University of Illinois Press, 1971), p. 45.

5. *Montgomery Advertiser*, 3 October 1956. Hill's memorandum on nullification is in the Hill Papers. McMillen, *Citizens' Council*, p. 45.

6. *Washington Post*, 3 March 1956.

7. Sam M. Engelhardt Jr. to Lister Hill, 15 March 1956; Lister Hill to Sam Engelhardt Jr., 20 March 1956; Jo Richardson to Lister Hill, 13 March 1956; Lister Hill to Jo Richardson, 19 March 1956, Hill Papers.

8. Senator Lehman's friendship with Hill also resulted from the fact that Lehman's father, Mayer Lehman, a Bavarian by birth, had settled in Montgomery before the Civil War and had supported the Confederacy. The family had moved to New York after this war. *Birmingham News*, 3 December 1955. *Time*, 3 June 1957, p. 16.

9. The *Advertiser* editorial was reprinted in the *Birmingham News*, 8 January 1956.

10. *Andalusia Star-News*, 25 January 1956. *Lee County Bulletin*, 13 October 1955.

11. *Birmingham News*, 30 March 1956.

12. Harry M. Ayers to Lister Hill, 2 March 1956; Billy Partlow to Lister Hill, 1 March 1956, Hill Papers. *Opelika Daily News*, undated clipping, Hill Papers.

13. McMillen, *Citizens' Council*, pp. 50–57. Gilliam, "Second Folsom Administration," pp. 360–79.

14. Gilliam, "Second Folsom Administration," p. 370. Clarence Allgood to Charles S. Brewton, 29 March 1956, Hill Papers.

15. Sims, "Little Man's Big Friend," pp. 422–23. Lawson, *Black Ballots*, p. 134.

16. A copy of Hill's handwritten response to the Citizens' Council questionnaire is in the Hill Papers.

17. Hill's campaign advertisements appeared frequently in the *Birmingham News* during April 1956.

18. *Alabama Journal*, 9 May 1956. Gilliam, "Second Folsom Administration," p. 45.

19. *Birmingham Post-Herald*, 4 May 1956.

20. Numan V. Bartley and Hugh D. Graham, *Southern Elections: County and Precinct Data, 1950–1972* (Baton Rouge: Louisiana State University Press, 1978), pp. 11–12. Hill polled 249,271 votes (68.5%) to 115,440 (31.5%) for Crommelin.

21. Bartley and Graham, *Southern Elections*, pp. 7–8. Weeks interview. *Andalusia Star-News*, 3 May 1956. Crommelin won Bullock, Elmore, Dallas, Wilcox, and Pickens counties.

22. Bartley and Graham, *Southern Elections*, p. 6.

23. *Montgomery Advertiser*, 4 October 1956.

24. *Birmingham News*, 25 July 1956. *Montgomery Advertiser*, 23 January 1957. James L. Sundquist, *Politics and Policy: The Eisenhower, Kennedy, and Johnson Years* (Washington, D.C.: Brookings Institution, 1968), p. 229.

25. Sundquist, *Politics and Policy*, p. 223. *Montgomery Advertiser*, 23 January 1957.

26. *Birmingham Post-Herald*, 9, 10 May 1957.

27. *Congressional Record*, 11 July 1957, pp. 11357–66.

28. *Montgomery Advertiser*, 9, 30 August 1957. *Birmingham News*, 24, 29 September 1957.

29. *Birmingham Post-Herald*, 2 August 1957.

30. Fleeson's column ran in the *Tuscaloosa News*, 7 August 1957. Sundquist, *Politics and Policy*, p. 238.

31. *Montgomery Advertiser*, 12, 18 June 1957. *Chattanooga Times*, 16 June 1957. *Birmingham News*, 10 August 1957.

32. *Fairhope Courier*, 20 June 1957.

33. Clarence Allgood to Lister Hill, 22 October 1957, Hill Papers. *Montgomery Advertiser*, 13 October 1957. *Birmingham News*, 16 November 1957.

34. Undated clipping, *Birmingham News*, Hill Papers.

35. *Montgomery Advertiser*, 14 December 1957. *Birmingham News*, 14 December 1957. *Alabama Journal*, 15 December 1957.

36. Ingram's interview was reprinted in the *Butler County News*, 24 December 1957.

CHAPTER 12

1. For a comprehensive study of the events leading to passage of the National Defense Education Act, see Barbara Barksdale Clowse, *Brainpower for the Cold War: The Sputnik Crisis and the National Defense Act of 1958* (Westport, Conn.: Greenwood Press, 1981).

2. *Stewart McClure*, pp. 113–14.

3. Sundquist, *Politics and Policy*, p. 176.

4. *Current Biography* (1943) (New York: H. W. Wilson, 1944) pp. 21–24.

5. *Birmingham News*, 6 December 1946. *Catholic Week*, 9 August 1946. Clowse, *Brainpower*, p. 44.

6. Lister Hill, "Should Congress Approve Current Plans for Federal Aid to Education? PRO," *Congressional Digest*, November 1949, p. 270.

7. Hill pressed the idea of "oil-for-education" in articles in two national publications. See Lister Hill, "A Bonanza for Education," *Harper's* 204 (20 May 1952): 28–31; Lister Hill, "Oil for Learning," *Nation* 179 (2 October 1954): 288. *Montgomery Advertiser*, 3 January 1954.

8. *Dallas Morning News*, 8 June 1951. The Hill Papers contain numerous letters of protest from Alabamians opposed to "oil-for-education." Jones interview.

9. *Birmingham News*, 30 June, 16 August 1953. Lister Hill to John Godbold, 4 May 1953, Hill Papers.

10. *Montgomery Advertiser*, 3 January 1955, 23 March 1957. *Church and State: A Monthly Review* 8 (3 March 1955): 1–7. Clowse, *Brainpower*, p. 47. Crampton Harris to Lister Hill, 15 January 1957, Hill Papers.

11. Clowse, *Brainpower*, p. 53.

12. *New York Times*, 22 August 1958.

13. *New York Times*, 22 August 1958.

14. Elliott interview. Clowse, *Brainpower*, pp. 66–76.

15. Elliott interview. Clowse, *Brainpower*, pp. 71–77; Sundquist, *Politics and Policy*, p. 178.

16. Clowse, *Brainpower*, pp. 75–76. *New York Times*, 22 August 1958.

17. Clowse, *Brainpower*, pp. 83–92. *Stewart McClure*, p. 16.

18. Clowse, *Brainpower*, pp. 86–87.

19. Clowse, *Brainpower*, p. 131. *Stewart McClure*, pp. 120–22.

20. Clowse, *Brainpower*, pp. 135–36. Elliott interview.

21. Sundquist, *Politics and Policy*, p. 179. Clowse, *Brainpower*, pp. 136–39. Among the fifteen senators who voted against the conference report on NDEA were six southern Democrats: Byrd of Virginia, Eastland and Stennis of Mississippi, Russell and Talmadge of Georgia, and Thurmond of South Carolina. Eight members of Alabama's House delegation voted in favor of NDEA; Frank Boykin did not vote. *Congressional Record*, 85th Cong., pp. 19090–92.

22. Sundquist, *Politics and Policy*, p. 179. Clowse, *Brainpower*, pp. 139–48.

23. *New York Times*, 22 August 1958. Clowse, *Brainpower*, p. 138.

24. Clowse, *Brainpower*, pp. 137, 146.

25. *Butler County News*, 24 April 1958.

26. *Birmingham News*, 4 May 1958. *Florence Times*, 3 May 1958.

27. *Birmingham Post-Herald*, 7 January 1958. *Birmingham News*, 29 March 1958.

28. *Birmingham News*, 7 January, 4 May 1958. *Florence Times*, 3 May 1958. Clarence Allgood to Lister Hill, 14 February 1958, Hill Papers.

29. Sims, "Little Man's Big Friend," pp. 474–76. A. E. Thomas, M.D. to Lister Hill, 27 March 1958; I. Berman to Lister Hill and John Sparkman, 16 April 1958, Hill Papers.

30. John Horne to Lister Hill, 5 November 1958, Hill Papers. *Anniston Star*, 6 April 1958. *Birmingham Post-Herald*, 7 June 1958. *Birmingham News*, 2 October 1958.

31. The International Health and Medical Research Act won House approval in July 1960, despite objections to another National Institute and an expensive program to be funded almost entirely by the United States. *Birmingham News*, 4, 21 May 1959.

32. *Montgomery Advertiser*, 12, 23 October 1959. *Birmingham News*, 29 April, 8 October 1959; 10 July 1960.

33. *Birmingham News*, 27 August 1959. *Birmingham Post-Herald*, 14 September 1959.

34. *Washington Post*, 28 August 1959. *Birmingham News*, 28 August 1959.

35. *Decatur Daily*, 26 May 1960.

36. Zeke Calhoun, of Fort Mitchell, was Sparkman's second opponent. *Washington Post*, 19 April 1960. *Birmingham News*, 29 May 1960.

37. *Montgomery Advertiser*, 28 May 1960. McMillen, *Citizens' Council*, pp. 328–32.

38. Lister Hill to C. W. McKay Jr., 26 January 1960; Lister Hill to H. Coleman Long, 3 March 1960, Hill Papers. *Birmingham News*, 6 March, 10 April 1960.

39. Bartley and Graham, *Southern Elections*, p. 4. The *Dothan Eagle* quotation was reprinted in the *Birmingham News*, 13 June 1960. Foots Clement to Lister Hill, 22 June 1960, Hill Papers.

40. *Andalusia Star-News*, 14 July 1960. *Birmingham News*, 23 January 1960. The *Atlanta Constitution* comment was reprinted in the *Montgomery Advertiser*, 22 July 1960.

41. *Washington Post*, 14 August 1960. *Stewart McClure*, pp. 64, 88–89.

42. *Stewart McClure*, pp. 120–22, 159–72. Cronin interview.

43. *Birmingham News*, 25 August 1960. *Butler County News*, 8 September 1960.

44. *Birmingham News*, 29 May 1960. *Montgomery Advertiser*, 6 November 1960.

45. *Tuscaloosa News*, 27 September 1960.

46. *Decatur Daily*, 13, 23 October 1960.

47. McMillen, *Citizens' Council*, p. 333. Bartley and Graham, *Southern Elections*, p. 6.

48. Bartley and Graham, *Southern Elections*, p. 6.

49. *Birmingham News*, 16 November 1960.

50. *Birmingham News*, 11 February 1961.

51. *Birmingham News*, 18 January 1961. *Bessemer Advertiser*, 27 January 1961.

52. Bass, *Unlikely Heroes*, pp. 206–8

53. Bass, *Unlikely Heroes*, pp. 159–60

54. *Birmingham News*, 21 September 1961. Julia Marks Young, "A Republican Challenge to Deep South Progressivism: Alabama's 1962 United States Senatorial Contest" (Ph.D. dissertation, Auburn University, 1978), p. 94.

CHAPTER 13

1. Cronin interview. *Birmingham News*, 25 January 1962.

2. *Decatur Daily*, 16 March 1962.

3. *Atlanta Journal*, 18 April 1962. *Florence Times*, 27 March 1962. *Birmingham News*, 27 March 1962. *Alabama Journal*, 18 April 1962. Richard Rovere, "Letter from Washington," *New Yorker* 36 (26 March 1960): 138–45.

4. Young, "A Republican Challenge," p. 31. The Democratic primary vote in 1962 was Hill, 363,613 (73.7%); Hallmark, 72,855 (14.8%); Crommelin, 56,822 (11.5%). Bartley and Graham, *Southern Elections*, p. 16.

5. Ed Leigh McMillan to Lister Hill, 3 May 1962, Hill Papers. Young, "A Republican Challenge," p. 25.

6. For a detailed assessment of Folsom's lack of success as governor, see Grafton and Permaloff, *Big Mules and Branchheads*, pp. 242–63.

7. Cronin, Le Maistre, and Elliott interviews. Young, "A Republican Challenge," p. 26.

8. *Montgomery Advertiser*, 10 June 1962.

9. In accordance with the 1960 census, Alabama was ordered to reduce its membership in the House from nine to eight. In the May Democratic primary, all nine ran statewide. Frank Boykin, who received the fewest votes, lost his seat. The remaining eight nominees were required to run statewide in November against nominees of other parties. Republicans selected Thomas Abernathy of Talladega, John Buchanan of Birmingham, and Evan Foreman of Mobile as their candidates. They hoped that these men could defeat Jones, Elliott, and Rains, considered the most progressive of the Democratic congressmen. Young, "A Republican Challenge," pp. 35–49.

10. Young, "A Republican Challenge," pp. 46–48. W. M. Hodgson to Lister Hill, 12 September 1982, Hill Papers.

11. Young, "A Republican Challenge," pp. 71–88.

12. Young, "A Republican Challenge," pp. 58, 69, 114.

13. Included in Martin's official list of contributors were the names of Joseph Simpson, son of his 1944 opponent, and Mrs. Herbert Stockham, wife of the wealthy Birmingham industrialist who had been a Simpson backer in that race. Young, "A Republican Challenge," pp. 75–86. Weeks interview. *Birmingham News*, 19 August 1962.

14. After the campaign, Hill returned to Mary Lasker what remained of her contribution. Young, "A Republican Challenge," pp. 126–36. Cronin, Lasker, and Allgood interviews.

15. Young, "A Republican Challenge," pp. 125–26. Will Hill Tankersley to Lister Hill, 3 October 1962, Hill Papers.

16. Young, "A Republican Challenge," pp. 66–69.

17. James L. Lawson to Lister Hill, 14 November 1962, Hill Papers. Young, "A Republican Challenge," pp. 147–48.

18. Young, "A Republican Challenge," pp. 144–51.

19. Sam W. Pipes III to Lister Hill, 8 October 1962; C. LeNoir Thompson to Lister Hill, 13 October 1962; Lister Hill to Charles H. Bradley and others, 7 March 1963, Hill Papers. The Hill Papers also contain numerous letters urging the impeachment of Justice Warren and other members of the Supreme Court.

20. Truman Hobbs to Lister Hill, 8 August 1962; E. L. Holland Jr. to Lister Hill, 30 June 1962; Marie Stokes Jemison to Lister Hill, undated (1962), Hill Papers.

21. Leaflet to all physicians in the Sixth District from two Tuscaloosa doctors, copy in Hill Papers. Winston Grooms to Lister Hill, 13 October 1962; William S. Hurst to Lister Hill, 10 September 1962; William M. Parker Jr. to Lister Hill, 2 June 1962, Hill Papers. Cronin interview.

22. Sundquist, *Politics and Policy*, pp. 306–7; *Congress and the Nation, 1945–1965* (Washington, D.C.: Congressional Quarterly Service, 1965) (I–II), 1154 and appendix, p. 81.

23. *Birmingham News*, 25 November 1962. Robert M. Killgore to Lister Hill, 28 July 1962; Frank J. Mizell Jr. to Lister Hill, 23 August 1962; Augustine Meaher Jr. to Lister Hill, 2 August 1962, Hill Papers.

24. Bass, *Unlikely Heroes*, pp. 182–91.

25. Young, "A Republican Challenge," p. 180; Ted Sorensen to John F. Kennedy, taped conversation, Kennedy Papers; *Birmingham Post-Herald*, 20 October 1962.

26. *Decatur Daily*, 4 July 1962.

27. Ralph Silver to Lister Hill, 15 September 1962; Ed Reid to Milton Cummings, 12 September 1962 (copy in Hill Papers); Marshall Hester to Lister Hill, 13 September 1962, Hill Papers.

28. Young, "A Republican Challenge," p. 91.

29. Isadore Pizitz to Lister Hill, 9 May 1962, Hill Papers.

30. Mrs. John M. Ward to Lister Hill, 17 September 1962; A. L. Harrell to Lister Hill, 14 October 1962; Ralph Silver to Don Cronin, 23 September 1962, Hill Papers.

31. Fourth grade class of Dean Road School, Auburn, to Lister Hill, 3 May 1962; T. B. Lewis to Lister Hill, 14 August 1962; John C. Persons to Lister Hill, 20 July 1962, Hill Papers. *Valley Voice*, 10 August 1962. *Piedmont Journal*, 2 November 1962.

32. Cronin interview.

33. Young, "A Republican Challenge," pp. 104–6.

34. Cronin interview. Drew Pearson, *Huntsville Times*, 6 November 1962. Young, "A Republican Challenge," p. 110.

35. Bob Ingram, "The Titleholder in Action," *Montgomery Advertiser*, 2 November 1962.

36. *Birmingham Post-Herald*, 20 October 1962.

37. Duncan and McClure interviews. Julian D. Butler to Don Cronin, 24 October 1962, Hill Papers.

38. Weeks interview.

39. Young, "A Republican Challenge," pp. 194–200.

40. Don Cronin to John E. Horne, 23 October 1962; Virgil Pittman to Lister Hill, 30 October 1962, Hill Papers. Young, "A Republican Challenge," pp. 200–201. *Birmingham News*, 28 October 1962.

41. *Huntsville Times*, 6 November 1962.

42. The official vote showed Hill, 201,937 (50.9%); Martin, 195,134 (49.1%). Hill carried 37 counties to Martin's 30. Republicans later filed charges of irregularities in the 1962 senatorial election but failed to present sufficient evidence to convince a Senate subcommittee that Martin had been defrauded of almost 7,000 votes. Young, "A Republican Challenge," pp. 210–28. *Birmingham Post-Herald*, 6 February 1963. For one political scientist's analysis, see Walter Dean Burnham, "The Alabama Senatorial Election of 1962: Return of Inter-Party Competition," *Journal of Politics* 26 (1964): 798–829.

43. Harry S Truman to Lister Hill, 20 November 1962, Truman Papers. Lawrence F. O'Brien to Lister Hill, 7 November 1962, Kennedy Papers.

44. Montgomery County gave Hill only 42% of its vote. Burnham, "Alabama Senatorial Race," p. 818. *Alabama Journal*, 9 November 1962. W. G. Hardwick to Lister Hill, 25 June 1962, Hill Papers.

45. *Alabama Journal*, 9 November 1962. Luther Lister Hill interview.

46. Barrett Shelton to Lister Hill, 2 January 1963, Hill Papers. *Alabama Journal*, 9 November 1962. *Birmingham News*, 9 November 1962.

47. Key, *Southern Politics*, pp. 280–85. Young, "A Republican Challenge," p. 249.

48. Young, "A Republican Challenge," p. 252. Harvey H. Jackson to Lister Hill, 10 December 1962, Hill Papers.

49. Young, "A Senatorial Challenge," p. 255.

50. The total vote in the first Democratic gubernatorial primary was 630,799, and the total vote in the general election was 397,071. The vote in the 1960 senatorial election was Sparkman, 389,196; Elgin, 164,868. Bartley and Graham, *Southern Elections*, p. 14. *Birmingham News*, 16 December 1962.

51. Alex L. Herman to Drew Pearson in *Birmingham News*, 4 December 1962. W. C. Patton to Lister Hill, 2 February 1963; Arthur D. Shores to Lister Hill, 15 November 1962, Hill Papers. Allgood interview. Burnham, "The Alabama Senatorial Election," pp. 816–17; Young, "A Republican Challenge," p. 267.

52. Barney Weeks to Lister Hill, 16 March 1962; Ben Ray to Lister Hill, 9 January 1963; Karl Harrison to Lister Hill, 16 February 1962; Ralph Silver to Don Cronin, 13 August 1962; Walter Gewin to Lister Hill, 12 November 1962; James L. Lawson to Lister Hill, 26 November 1962, Hill Papers. Young, "A Republican Challenge," pp. 260–69.

53. Young, "A Republican Challenge," p. 242.

54. Dr. J. H. Little to Lister Hill, 3 November 1962, Hill Papers. South Carolina's Olin Johnston, a senator with generally progressive views, won reelection over a strong Republican opponent in 1962 despite the fact that he had voted in favor of Medicare.

55. *Atlanta Constitution*, 16 November 1962.

56. Robert S. Vance to Don Cronin, 10 August 1962, Hill Papers.

CHAPTER 14

1. Cronin interview. *Stewart McClure*, p. 86. Dr. John Carter to Lister Hill, 12 December 1962, Hill Papers.

2. Mike Manatos to Larry O'Brien, 5 February 1963, Kennedy Papers.

3. *Birmingham Post-Herald*, 11 January 1963. *Louisville Times*, 26 February 1963. John F. Kennedy to Lister Hill, 11 January 1963, Kennedy Papers.

4. Carl Brauer, *John F. Kennedy and the Second Reconstruction* (New York: Columbia University Press, 1977), pp. 62, 270.

5. Jones interview.

6. C. H. Erskine Smith to Lister Hill, 22 October 1963, Hill Papers. *Birmingham Post-Herald*, 9 December 1963.

7. *Washington Post*, 28 November 1963.

8. Barrett Shelton to Lister Hill, 7 April 1964. Lister Hill to Barrett Shelton, 9 April 1964, Hill Papers.

9. Lister Hill to Barrett Shelton, 9 April 1964, Hill Papers. The *Birmingham News* published Hill's speech in its entirety on 11 March 1964.

10. *Alabama Journal*, 29, 30 April 1964. *Montgomery Advertiser*, 3 March 1964.

11. *Birmingham News*, 31 January 1964. *Florence Times*, 1 February 1964. *Montgomery Advertiser*, 1 March 1964.

12. *Florence Times*, 1 February 1964.

13. Cronin interview. *Florence Times*, 31 March 1964. *Lee County Bulletin*, reprinted in *Birmingham News*, 6 June 1964.

14. *Lee County Bulletin*, 5 November 1964; Clifford Fulford to Bill Brawley, Democratic National Committee, 3 September 1964, copy in Hill Papers.

15. *Lee County Bulletin*, 5 November 1964.

16. *Birmingham News*, 30, 31 May, 1 April 1965; *Lee County Bulletin*, 5 November 1964.

17. *Birmingham News*, 10 January 1965.

18. *Montgomery Advertiser*, 20, 27 May 1965. *Birmingham News*, 6, 27 May 1965.

19. Jack Valenti to President Johnson, 4 August 1966; Mike Manatos to President Johnson, 17 August 1966; Claude Desautels to Perry Barber, 5 October 1965, Johnson Papers.

20. Cronin interview. Madelyn Pearson to Lister Hill, 14 July 1965, Hill Papers.

21. Strickland, *Politics, Science, and Dread Disease*, p. 213; *New York Times*, 7 September 1965. U.S Congressional Quarterly, *Congress and the Nation, 1945–1965*, p. 752. Phillips interview.

22. The Supreme Court refused to review a decision by the Fourth Circuit Court of Appeals (*Simpkins v. Moses H. Cone Memorial Hospital*) forbidding racial discrimination in hospitals receiving federal aid.

23. For more detailed treatment of this subject, see Strickland, *Politics, Science, and Dread Disease*, pp. 158–83.

24. Strickland, *Politics, Science, and Dread Disease*, pp. 168–69.

25. Strickland, *Politics, Science, and Dread Disease*, pp. 178–83.

26. Holley and Schremser, *Foundations in Library and Information Science*, pp. 74–76.

27. Mike Manatos to Larry O'Brien, 9 January 1965, Johnson Papers. Clowse, *Brainpower*, pp. 157–58.

28. Clowse, *Brainpower*, pp. 156–58.

29. Strickland, *Politics, Science, and Dread Disease*, pp. 182–222.

30. *Washington Post*, 30 December 1967.

31. *Birmingham News*, 30 November 1967.

32. The *Foley Onlooker*'s comment was reprinted in the *Birmingham News*, 31 December 1967.

33. *Birmingham News*, 15 July, 20 November 1966. James L. Lawson to Lister Hill, 8 May 1967, Hill Papers. Sparkman assumed the chair of the Senate Banking and Currency Committee after his reelection. After Fulbright's defeat in 1974, Sparkman

took over the chairmanship of the Senate Foreign Relations Committee; Proxmire then succeeded to the chairmanship of Banking and Currency.

34. Lurleen Wallace defeated her nine opponents, including Carl Elliott, by winning 54% of the votes in the Democratic primary. She swamped Martin in November by a margin of 2 to 1. Donald Strong's analysis of rich and poor segregationists is quoted in Young, "A Republican Challenge," p. 282. *Birmingham News*, 26 November 1967.

35. Bartley and Graham, *Southern Elections*, p. 4. *Andalusia Star-News*, 14 July 1966. *Montgomery Advertiser-Journal*, 10 July 1966.

36. James R. Jones to W. Marvin Watson, 17 November 1967, Hill Papers. *Huntsville Times*, 17 December 1967.

37. *Huntsville Times*, 17 December 1967. Barrett Shelton to Lister Hill, 24 March 1967, Hill Papers.

38. Cronin interview.

39. *Birmingham News*, 20, 21 January 1968.

40. Weeks interview. *Birmingham News*, 21 January 1968. *Birmingham Post-Herald*, 10 November 1967. *Montgomery Advertiser*, 2 November 1967. *Lee County Bulletin*, 18 January 1968.

41. *Montgomery Advertiser*, 22 January 1968. *Alabama Journal*, 22, 27 January 1968. *Mobile Register*, 15 February 1968.

42. *Winston-Salem Journal*, 26 January 1968. *Greensboro Daily News*, 30 January 1968.

43. *New York Times*, 27 January 1968. Lyndon B. Johnson to Lister Hill, 22 May 1968, Johnson Papers.

44. Weeks interview. Allen defeated Selden in the runoff by 196,511 (50.5%) to 192,448 (49.5%). In the November election, Allen (533,327) defeated Republican Perry Hooper (171,320) and Robert Schwenn (61,898) who campaigned under the label of the National Democratic party. In the first primary, Folsom polled only 32,000 votes (6%). Bartley and Graham, *Southern Elections*, p. 4. *Birmingham News*, 6 November 1968.

45. Announcing plans to retire at the end of 1968, in addition to Hill and Carlson, were Bourke Hickenlooper of Iowa, Carl Hayden of Arizona, Thruston Morton of Kentucky, and George Smathers of Florida. *Washington Evening Star*, 1 August 1968. *Montgomery Advertiser*, 22 January 1968.

46. Lasker interview. Tributes to Hill appear in the *Congressional Record*, 11, 12, 14 October 1968, House, pp. 30802–3, 31841–42; Senate, pp. 30874, 31012, 31031, 31291, 31298–99, 31918–19, 32058. *Stewart McClure*, pp. 216–20.

47. *Medical World News*, 1 November 1968, pp. 56–58.

48. Clowse, *Brainpower*, p. 159. Wilbur Cohen to Lister Hill, 20 August 1968, Johnson Papers.

49. *Birmingham News*, 20 November 1968. *Washington Post*, 20 November 1968.

CHAPTER 15

1. Elliott, Cronin, Luther Lister Hill, and Phillips interviews. Lister Hill to Curtis McPherson, 19 March 1957, Hill Papers.

2. *Birmingham News*, 19 April 1970, 2 April 1972.

3. Lister Hill to Harry Truman, 11 May 1970, Truman Papers.

4. Richard Rives to Lister Hill, 12 May 1958, Hill Papers. Durr interview.

5. Elizabeth S. Black, *Mr. Justice and Mrs. Black: The Memoirs of Hugo L. Black and Elizabeth Black* (New York: Random House, 1986), p. 166.

6. Lister Hill to Dr. Joseph L. Selden Jr., 26 July 1968, Hill Papers.

7. *Medical World News*, 1 November 1968, pp. 56–58.

8. Jerome Levy, chairman of the executive board of the Alabama Public Library Service, to *Montgomery Advertiser*, 20 February 1968. Holley and Schremser, *Library Services Act*, pp. 80–81.

9. Clowse, *Brainpower*, p. 159.

10. Strickland, *Politics, Science, and Dread Disease*, pp. 243–48.

CODA

1. *Birmingham News*, 2 April 1972.

2. Jones interview.

3. *Montgomery Advertiser*, 3 June 1962.

4. Lister Hill to Jesse B. Hearin, 2 May 1945, Hill Papers. The reference was to Thomas B. Martin, then head of the Alabama Power Company.

5. Norris's inscribed photograph is in the Hill Papers. *Congressional Record*, S. 11056, 6 February 1985.

6. Cronin and Gorman interviews. *Stewart McClure*, p. 78.

7. Durr interview.

8. Beech interview.

9. Davis interview.

10. Weeks, Elliott, Rains, Jones, and Beech interviews.

11. *Montgomery Advertiser*, 21 August 1977.

12. For a thorough exploration of southern progressivism, see Dewey Grantham, *Southern Progressivism*.

13. *Medical World News*, 1 November 1968, p. 57.

14. *Alabama Journal*, 4 October 1961.

15. Douglas Kiker, "Those Solid Southern 'Conservatives,' " reprinted from *Atlanta Journal* in *Montgomery Advertiser*, 10 February 1962.

16. Sparkman interview.

BIBLIOGRAPHICAL

ESSAY

Lister Hill provided the major source for a study of his career in the Papers collected over the course of his forty-five years in Congress. This 1,875,000-piece collection contains originals or copies of letters, memoranda, invitations, and other written communications received or sent out by one who took pride in the promptness and thoroughness of his responses to constituents. It also includes Hill's correspondence with members of his family and a number of close associates. The Hill Papers contain detailed files on legislative issues in which Hill involved himself as well as 162,000 pieces of correspondence relating to his campaigns for the House and Senate from 1923 through 1962. This latter segment proved especially useful.

For the most part, Hill used carefully guarded language in responding to constituents and friends. One of the few persons to whom he wrote freely was his longtime campaign manager, Roy Nolen. After Hill's death, hundreds of letters from Nolen were found in the senator's Montgomery office along with a large number of unusually frank responses from Hill. This correspondence is a rich source of background on Alabama politics in the 1930s and 1940s. The Lister Hill Papers are housed in the Gorgas Library of the University of Alabama, Tuscaloosa.

An immense clipping file on Senator Hill, located in the Alabama Department of Archives and History in Montgomery, complements the Papers. A small collection of Papers of Senator Hill's father, Dr. L. L. Hill, is housed in the Reynolds Historical Collection of the Lister Hill Library at the University of Alabama at Birmingham. Material relating to Hill's maternal ancestry is contained in the Horsler File of the Pensacola Historical Society, as well as in the Probate Records, Historical Documents Section, Escambia County Courthouse, Pensacola, Florida; the Minute Books of the Department of Archives and Manuscripts in the Judicial Building, Pensacola, and the early records of St. John the Evangelist Church in Warrington, Florida, St. Michael's Church in Pensacola, and St. Peter's Church in Montgomery.

The Papers of Hill's political adversaries, James A. Simpson and Frank M. Dixon, are housed in the Alabama Department of Archives and History in Montgomery. Those of Senator J. Thomas Heflin are available, with the permission of his nephew, Senator Howell Heflin, at the Gorgas Library of the University of Alabama. The Aubrey Williams Papers in the Franklin D. Roosevelt Library at Hyde Park, New York, and the

345

Jonathan Daniels Papers at the University of North Carolina in Chapel Hill contain small amounts of correspondence with Hill.

Hill served in Congress during the administrations of seven presidents; thus materials relating to him are to be found in the Herbert Hoover Papers at the Hoover Library, West Branch, Iowa; the Franklin Roosevelt Papers; the Harry Truman Papers at the Truman Library, Independence, Missouri; the Dwight Eisenhower Papers at the Eisenhower Library, Abilene, Kansas; the John F. Kennedy Papers at the Kennedy Library, Boston, Massachusetts; and the Lyndon B. Johnson Papers at the Johnson Library, Austin, Texas. Research at the Truman Library revealed the transcripts of taped conversations of Hill's longtime friend and fellow New Dealer, Thomas Corcoran. For about one year after he assumed the presidency, Truman evidently acquiesced in the FBI's taping of Corcoran's telephone conversations. This collection contains a number of frank conversations between Corcoran and Hill, mostly dealing with the effects of the changeover from the Roosevelt to the Truman administration.

The Oral History Collection at Columbia University contains a number of references to Hill by contemporaries, including Henry Wallace and Virginia and Clifford Durr.

Oral history was a major research tool for this biography. On one occasion, shortly after assuming the task of biographer, the author had an interview with Senator Hill in Montgomery. By that time, however, the senator's memory was faltering and he asked his longtime administrative assistant Don Cronin, who was present, to answer most of the questions. Hill had been interviewed at length in 1967 by Harlan B. Phillips, Ph.D. The transcript of these interviews at the History of Medicine Division, National Library of Medicine, Bethesda, Maryland, contains a few useful insights.

Members of Senator Hill's family were most cooperative in submitting to interviews. In Montgomery, this researcher talked to Hill's sister, Amelie Hill Laslie; his daughter, Henrietta Hill Hubbard, and son, L. Lister Hill; and his cousin, Will Hill Tankersley. In Birmingham, his sister, Lillian Hill Rucker, granted an interview. In Mobile, another cousin, Mark Lyons Jr., and an aunt, Reba Lyons, were cordial and receptive. Senator Hill's nephew, Luther Lyons Hill Jr. of Des Moines, Iowa, not only granted an informative interview but supplied a copy of his unpublished manuscript of family history, entitled "A Family Record."

This author was fortunate in having the opportunity to interview three persons who served as members of Hill's staff over long periods of time: his first congressional secretary, Robert Frazer of Arlington, Virginia; his last and longest administrative assistant, Don Cronin of Washington, D.C.; and the chief clerk of the Senate Committee on Labor and Public Welfare, Stewart McClure of Washington, D.C. McClure is also the subject of an intensive oral history interview conducted by the Senate Historical Office in 1984. This document contains insightful views of Hill as a committee chairman. Other former members of Hill's office staff who contributed their oral recollections were Paul Duncan of Magnolia Springs, Alabama, and John T. Walden of Washington, D.C. This researcher also interviewed Senator John Sparkman's longtime administrative assistant, John E. Horne of Washington, D.C.

Many Alabamians who had been closely associated with Hill provided valuable oral recollections. These included former Senator Sparkman of Huntsville and former Representatives Carl Elliott of Jasper, Bob Jones of Scottsboro, and Albert Rains of Gadsden. Longtime friends and associates interviewed for this biography included Judge Clarence Allgood and Barney Weeks, both of Birmingham; George Le Maistre of Tuscaloosa; and Judge John C. Godbold and Virginia Foster Durr, both of Montgomery. Native Alabamians in the field of journalism who contributed their knowledge of Hill included Charles Dobbins of Washington, D.C.; Douglass Cater and Stephen P. Strickland, both then residents of Aspen, Colorado; Carroll Kilpatrick of Amissville, Virginia; Gould Beech of Magnolia Springs, Alabama; Neil Davis of Auburn; and Barrett Shelton of Decatur.

By virtue of a grant from the National Library of Medicine, this researcher was able to interview a number of persons who had been closely connected with Hill in the field of national health, including Mary Lasker, New York City; Florence Mahoney, Washington, D.C.; Dr. Michael DeBakey, Houston, Texas (telephone interview); Dr. Howard Rusk, New York City; Dr. Frank B. Rogers, Denver, Colorado; Dr. Robert Q. Marston, Gainesville, Florida; Boisfeuillet Jones, Atlanta, Georgia; Dr. Howard L. Holley, Birmingham, and in Washington, D.C., Kenneth Williamson, Dr. Luther Terry, Dr. Matthew F. McNulty Jr., Mike Gorman, and Hal M. Christensen.

Original research in the area of twentieth-century Alabama politics has been relatively sparse. However, a number of unpublished theses and dissertations help to shed light on various aspects of this period, including: Gladys King Burns, "The Alabama Dixiecrat Revolt of 1948," Master's thesis, Auburn University, 1965; Vincent J. Dooley, "United States Senator J. Thomas Heflin and the Democratic Party Revolt in Alabama," Master's thesis, Auburn University, 1963; Thomas J. Gilliam, "The Second Folsom Administration: The Destruction of Alabama Liberalism, 1954–1958," Ph.D. dissertation, Auburn University, 1975; James Tyra Harris, "Alabama Reaction to the Brown Decision, 1954–1956: A Case Study in Massive Resistance," D.A. dissertation, Middle Tennessee State University, 1978; Jama Davis Rogers, "The 1938 Senatorial Election in Alabama between J. Thomas Heflin and J. Lister Hill," Master's thesis, Samford University, 1975; Norma Jean Short, "The Senatorial Career of James Thomas Heflin, 1920–1931," Ph.D. dissertation, Vanderbilt University, 1954; Paul Maxwell Smith Jr., "Loyalists and States' Righters in the Democratic Party of Alabama, 1949–1954," Master's thesis, Auburn University, 1966; Ralph M. Tanner, "J. Thomas Heflin: U.S. Senator, 1920–1931," Ph.D. dissertation, University of Alabama, 1967; and Julia Marks Young, "A Republican Challenge to Deep South Progressivism: Alabama's 1962 Senatorial Contest," Ph.D. dissertation, Auburn University, 1978.

Alabama newspapers of the period, 1923–68, contain innumerable accounts of Senator Hill's political and legislative career. Over the years, Hill's staff made this enormous resource more accessible by keeping scrapbooks of press clippings relating to him. Around seventy of these scrapbooks are now part of the Hill Papers. The richest sources for journalistic coverage of Hill are his hometown newspapers, the *Montgomery Advertiser*, the *Alabama Journal*, and two shorter-lived newspapers, the *Montgomery Independent* and the *Montgomery Examiner*, as well as his most consistent press supporters, the *Birmingham Age-Herald* and the *Birmingham News*. This researcher also sampled the coverage of Hill by friendly newspapers such as the *Andalusia Star-News*, the *Anniston Star*, the *Decatur Daily*, the *Florence Times*, the *Huntsville Times*, and the *Lee County Bulletin*, as well as opposition newspapers such as the *Mobile Press*, the *Mobile Register*, the *Birmingham Post*, the *Southern Watchman* of Greensboro, Alabama, and the *Pell City News*. The *New York Times*, as always, proved a helpful source, as did the *Washington Post*, the *Washington Evening Star*, and the perceptive comments of Ralph McGill in the *Atlanta Journal*.

Standard sources in the area of government documents were the *Congressional Record* and the *Congressional Directory*; *Congress and the Nation*, published by the *U.S. Congressional Quarterly*; hearings of the Senate Committee on Labor and Public Welfare; and the *Alabama Official and Statistical Register*. Hill was the author of an article, "Health in America: A Personal Perspective," in a pamphlet entitled *Health in America, 1776–1976*, published by the U.S. Department of Health, Education, and Welfare in 1976. After Hill's death, many of his Senate colleagues paid tribute to his long service in that body. Their remarks were published in *Lister Hill: Late a Senator from Alabama; Memorial Addresses and Tributes in the Congress of the United States* (Washington, D.C.: Government Printing Office, 1985).

Periodicals also proved a prolific source of information. A number of articles appeared under Lister Hill's name, including: "A Bonanza for Education," *Harper's* 204 (March 1958); "My Father: Dr. Luther Leonidas Hill," *Alabama Review* 24 (April 1971); "Nation's Responsibility for Education," *National Education Association Journal*, 30 September 1941; "Oil for Learning," *Nation* 179 (2 October 1954); "Should Congress Approve Current Plans for Federal Aid to Education?" *Congressional Digest* 270 (November 1949); "The Fifth Freedom Is Freedom from Ignorance," *Alabama School Journal* 30 (May 1943).

Articles about Hill in periodicals include: Robert Barkdoll, "Lister Hill: Statesman for Health," *Today's Health* 79 (June 1962); David L. Cohn, "The Gentleman from Alabama: Lister Hill," *Atlantic Monthly* 173 (May 1944); Martin M. Cummings, M.D., "Senator Lister Hill: Statesman for Health and Patron of Medical Libraries," *Alabama Journal of the Medical Sciences* 9 (January 1972); Elizabeth Brenner Drew, "The Health Syndicate: Washington's Noble Conspirators," *Atlantic Monthly* 220 (December 1967); Dan Feshbach, "What's Inside the Black Box: A Case Study of Allocative Politics in the Hill-Burton Program," *International Journal of Health Services* 9 (1979); "Hill of Alabama," *New Republic* 110 (1 May 1944); "Lister Steps Down from the Hill," *Medical World News* 9 (1 November 1968); "People in the Limelight," *New Republic* 112 (26 March 1945); Dr. Brad Rogers, "Senator Lister Hill and the Beginnings of Medlars," *Alabama Librarian* 34 (November–December 1983); Edgar M. Steed (pseudonym for Charles G. Dobbins), "Yankee Dollars Fight Hill,"

Nation 158 (29 April 1944); "Tom Heflin: Story of an Old Schooler's Fight against a New Dealer," *Newsweek* 11 (3 January 1938); Milton Viorst, "The Political Good Fortune of Medical Research," *Science* 17 (April 1944); William S. White, "Democrats' Board of Directors," *New York Times Magazine* (10 July 1955).

Alabama magazine published numerous articles critical of Hill during the late 1930s and 1940s.

Useful background articles in periodicals include: Emile B. Adler, "Why Dixiecrats Failed," *Journal of Politics* 15 (August 1953); Lee N. Allen, "The Woman Suffrage Movement in Alabama, 1910–1920," *Alabama Review* 11 (April 1958); Michael Balter, "The Best-Kept Secret in Health Care," *Progressive* 45 (April 1981); Jean Begeman, "The Vanishing Farm Phones," *New Republic* 150 (28 March 1949); Hugo L. Black Jr., "Richard Taylor Rives, 1895–1982," *Alabama Lawyer* 44 (1983); Walter Dean Burnham, "The Alabama Senatorial Election of 1962: Return of Inter-Party Competition," *Journal of Politics* 26 (1964); Donald Davidson, "Where Are the Laymen?: A Study in Policy-Making," *American Review* 9 (October 1937); Hugh Dorsey Reagan, "Race as a Factor in the Presidential Election of 1928 in Alabama," *Alabama Review* 9 (January 1966); Richard Rovere, "Letter from Washington," *New Yorker* 36 (26 March 1960); Jasper B. Shannon, "Presidential Politics in the South: 1938, I," *Journal of Politics* 1 (May 1939); Harvard Sitkoff, "Harry Truman and the Election of 1948: The Coming of Age of Civil Rights in American Politics," *Journal of Southern History* 37 (November 1971); J. Mills Thornton III, "Alabama Politics: J. Thomas Heflin and the Expulsion Movement of 1929," *Alabama Review* 21 (April 1968); J. Mills Thornton III, "Challenge and Response in the Montgomery Bus Boycott of 1955–1956," *Alabama Review* 33 (March 1980); Horace Wilkinson, "Argument for Adoption of the Boswell Amendment," *Alabama Lawyer* 7 (October 1946).

In the secondary literature, two works by family members shed light on Hill's background: *Sermons, Addresses and Papers of Rev. Luther Leonidas Hill, Published for Private Circulation by His Children* (New York: Fleming H. Revell, 1919), and his wife's book about her family background, Henrietta Fontaine Hill, *The Family Skeleton* (Montgomery: Paragon Press, 1958). Elizabeth Black, in *Mr. Justice Black and Mrs. Black: The Memoirs of Hugo L. Black and Elizabeth Black* (New York: Random House, 1986), testifies to the severing of the once close relationship between Black and Hill.

Hill's career encompassed such a lengthy and historically significant portion of the twentieth century that, of necessity, the author turned to the work of others for assistance and background, among them: Jack Bass, *Unlikely Heroes* (New York: Simon and Schuster, 1981); Carl M. Brauer, *John F. Kennedy and the Second Reconstruction* (New York: Columbia University Press, 1977); James MacGregor Burns, *Roosevelt: The Soldier of Freedom* (New York: Harcourt Brace Jovanovich, 1970); Jonathan Daniels, *Frontier on the Potomac* (New York: Macmillan, 1946) and *The Man from Independence* (Philadelphia: J. B. Lippincott, 1950); Robert Divine, *Second Chance* (New York: Atheneum, 1971); Robert J. Donovan, *Conflict and Crisis: The Presidency of Harry S Truman, 1945–1948* (New York: W. W. Norton, 1977); Gerald T. Dunne,

Hugo Black and the Judicial Revolution (New York: Simon and Schuster, 1977); David A. Frier, *Conflict of Interest in the Eisenhower Administration* (Ames: University of Iowa Press, 1969); Alonzo L. Hamby, *Beyond the New Deal: Harry S. Truman and American Liberalism* (New York: Columbia University Press, 1973); Richard Lowitt, *George W. Norris: The Triumph of a Progressive, 1933–1944* (Urbana: University of Illinois Press, 1978); James L. Sundquist, *Politics and Policy: The Eisenhower, Kennedy, and Johnson Years* (Washington, D.C.: Brookings Institution, 1969); Aaron Wildavsky, *Dixon-Yates: A Study in Power Politics* (New Haven: Yale University Press, 1962).

Several authors have dealt in depth with programs in which Hill played a major role; their works provided much-needed background to help interpret his work in these areas. For the history of the Tennessee Valley Authority, Preston J. Hubbard, *Origins of the TVA: The Muscle Shoals Controversy, 1920–1932* (New York: W. W. Norton, 1969), and Wilmon Henry Droze, *High Dams and Slack Waters: TVA Rebuilds a River* (Baton Rouge: Louisiana State University Press, 1965), are indispensable. For the National Defense Education Act, Barbara Barksdale Clowse, *Brainpower for the Cold War: The Sputnik Crisis and the National Defense Act of 1958* (Westport, Conn.: Greenwood Press, 1981), is a thorough and enlightening case study. In the area of federal assistance to libraries, Edward G. Holley and Robert F. Schremser, *The Library Services and Construction Act: A Historical Overview from the Viewpoint of Major Participants* (Greenwich, Conn.: JAI Press, 1983), gives valuable insights into Hill's role. In the area of federal assistance to health programs, Paul Starr, *The Social Transformation of American Medicine* (New York: Basic Books, 1982), and Stephen P. Strickland, *Politics, Science, and Dread Disease: A Short History of United States Medical Research Policy* (Cambridge: Harvard University Press, 1972), are important overviews. The Hill-Burton hospital construction program has been the subject of an immense amount of secondary literature in periodicals. The most useful one-volume study is Judith R. Lave and Lester B. Lave, *The Hospital Construction Act: An Evaluation of the Hill-Burton Program, 1948–1973* (Washington, D.C.: American Enterprise Institute, 1974).

For Alabama background, the following were useful: Hollinger F. Barnard, ed., *Outside the Magic Circle: The Autobiography of Virginia Foster Durr* (University: University of Alabama Press, 1985); William D. Barnard, *Dixiecrats and Democrats: Alabama Politics, 1942–1950* (University: University of Alabama Press, 1974); John Witherspoon Dubose and James Greer, eds., *Alabama's Tragic Decade: Ten Years of Alabama, 1865–1874* (Birmingham: Webb Book Company, 1940); Walter L. Fleming, *Civil War and Reconstruction in Alabama* (New York: Macmillan, 1905); Wayne Flynt, *Montgomery: An Illustrated History* (Windsor Hills, Calif.: Windsor Publications, 1980); Carl Grafton and Anne Permaloff, *Big Mules and Branchheads: James E. Folsom and Political Power in Alabama* (Athens: University of Georgia Press, 1985); Francis Sheldon Hackney, *From Populism to Progressivism in Alabama, 1890–1910*

(Princeton: Princeton University Press, 1969); Virginia Van der Veer Hamilton, *Hugo Black: The Alabama Years* (Baton Rouge: Louisiana State University Press, 1972); Daniel Webster Hollis III, *An Alabama Newspaper Tradition: Grover C. Hall and the Hall Family* (University: University of Alabama Press, 1983); Marion Elias Lazenby, *History of Methodism in Alabama and West Florida* (North Alabama and Alabama West-Florida Conferences of the Methodist Church, 1960); Thomas Chalmers McCorvey, *Alabama Historical Sketches* (Charlottesville: University of Virginia Press, 1960); A. B. Moore, *History of Alabama and Her People*, 2 vols. (Chicago and New York: American Historical Society, 1927); Thomas McAdory Owen, *History of Alabama and Dictionary of Alabama Biography*, 6 vols. (Chicago: S. J. Clarke Company, 1921); William Warren Rogers, *The One-Gallused Rebellion* (Baton Rouge: Louisiana State University Press, 1970); Sarah Woolfolk Wiggins, *The Scalawag in Alabama Politics, 1865–1881* (University: University of Alabama Press, 1977); Tinsley E. Yarbrough, *Judge Frank Johnson and Human Rights in Alabama* (University: University of Alabama Press, 1981).

To assess Hill's family background, the following studies were helpful: Leonard Dinnerstein and Mary Dale Polsson, eds., *Jews in the South* (Baton Rouge: Louisiana State University Press, 1973), and William Warren Sweet, *Methodism in American History* (Nashville: Abingdon Press, 1953). Among studies of Hill's southern contemporaries consulted were: Charles L. Fontenay, *Estes Kefauver: A Biography* (Knoxville: University of Tennessee Press, 1982), and John Salmond, *A Southern Rebel: The Life and Times of Aubrey Willis Williams, 1890–1965* (Chapel Hill: University of North Carolina Press, 1983).

Secondary literature on southern politics abounds. As have many others, this author has leaned on these major overviews: V. O. Key Jr., *Southern Politics in State and Nation* (New York: Alfred A. Knopf, 1950); George B. Tindall, *The Emergence of the New South, 1913–1945* (Baton Rouge: Louisiana University Press, 1967), and Dewey W. Grantham, *Southern Progressivism: The Reconciliation of Progress and Tradition* (Knoxville: University of Tennessee Press, 1983). Among more specialized studies consulted were: Thomas A. Krueger, *And Promises to Keep: The Southern Conference for Human Welfare, 1938–1948* (Nashville: Vanderbilt University Press, 1967); Steven F. Lawson, *Black Ballots: Voting Rights in the South, 1944–1969* (New York: Columbia University Press, 1976); Neil R. McMillen, *The Citizens' Council: Organized Resistance to the Second Reconstruction, 1954–64* (Urbana: University of Illinois Press, 1971); Frederick D. Ogden, *The Poll Tax in the South* (University: University of Alabama Press, 1958), and Morton Sosna, *In Search of the Silent South: Southern Liberals and the Race Issue* (New York: Columbia University Press, 1977). Also useful were these studies of electoral results: Numan V. Bartley and Hugh D. Graham, *Southern Elections: County and Precinct Data, 1950–1972* (Baton Rouge: Louisiana State University Press, 1978), and Alexander Heard and Donald S. Strong, eds., *Southern Primaries and Elections, 1920–1947* (University: University of Alabama

Press, 1950). Other useful works on the topic of politics are Numan V. Bartley and Hugh D. Graham, *Southern Politics and the Second Reconstruction* (Baltimore and London: Johns Hopkins University Press, 1975); Numan V. Bartley, *The Rise of Massive Resistance: Race and Politics in the South during the 1950s* (Baton Rouge: Louisiana State University Press, 1969); and Alexander P. Lamis, *The Two-Party South* (New York: Oxford University Press, 1984).

I N D E X

236, 247, 254
Hopkins, Harry, 74
Horne, John, 105, 144, 145, 189, 232
Horseshoe Bend, battle of, 41, 51
Horsler, Amelia. *See* Lyons, Amelia
  Horsler
Horsler, Andrew (great-grandfather of
  Lister Hill), 9
Horsler, Bela Weil. *See* Langley, Barbet
  (Bela, Bertha) Weil Stein Horsler
Howard College (Marion, Ala.), 15
Huddleston, George, Jr., 270, 294
Hughes, Charles Evans, 196
Hull, Cordell, 91, 101
Humphrey, George, 205
Humphrey, Hubert, 158, 200, 214, 236,
  269, 293
Huntsville, Ala., 59, 97, 229, 277, 286
Huntsville Times, 118, 168, 170, 246
Hyde Park, N.Y., 84, 86

Inge, Francis, 119
Ingersoll, Robert, 12, 15, 16, 39, 137,
  138
Ingram, Robert ("Bob"), 223
Interstate Commerce Commission (ICC),
  96

Jackson, Andrew, 41, 51, 284, 293
Jackson, Robert, 184
Jackson County, Ala., 105, 249
Jasper, Ala., 253
Javits, Jacob, 247, 281, 293
Jefferson, Thomas, 46, 50, 109, 213,
  224, 290, 293
Jefferson County, Ala., 126, 258
Jefferson County Democratic Executive
  Committee, 193, 277
Jefferson Davis Hotel (Montgomery),
  190
Jefferson Medical College (Philadel-
  phia), 16

Jemison, Marie Stokes, 248
Jerome, Jennie, 5
Jews, 3, 8, 9, 11, 12, 13, 14, 39, 40,
  45, 47, 80, 86, 94, 125, 192, 216,
  251, 291
Johnson, Frank M., Jr., 24, 182, 292;
  appointment to federal court, 203–4;
  on *Browder v. Gayle*, 219
Johnson, Hiram, 129
Johnson, Hugh, 94
Johnson, Lady Bird (Mrs. Lyndon), 284
Johnson, Lyndon, 74, 150, 161, 195,
  196, 211, 219, 236, 277; suffers heart
  attack, 206; and "Southern Manifesto," 213; and civil rights, 220–21;
  and offshore oil, 226; at 1960 Democratic convention, 237; as 1960 vice
  presidential candidate, 238; elected
  vice president, 239; presidency of,
  268–71, 273–75, 279–80; and 1964
  presidential campaign, 270; and Great
  Society, 271, 275; relations with Hill,
  272; and funding for health research,
  273; comments on Hill's retirement,
  279–80; honors Hill, 284
Johnston, Forney, 120
Johnston, Olin, 294
Jones, Bob (congressman), 105, 106,
  112, 146, 168, 170, 183, 256, 257,
  267, 270, 280, 292, 294
Jones, Bob (evangelist), 43, 59
Jones, Catesby ap R, 21
Jordan, Mortimer, 165
Junior League, 2
Justice Department, 151

Kappa Alpha fraternity, 105
Kefauver, Estes, 103, 187, 203, 213,
  221, 232, 293
Keith, Walling, 107, 110
Kennedy, John F., 196, 214, 236, 267;
  and Library Services Act, 208; assas-

retirement, 279–80
Montgomery Anti-Ratification Association, 38
Montgomery Chamber of Commerce, 60, 75, 114
Montgomery City Board of Education, 35, 37, 163, 224
Montgomery County, Ala., 36–37, 46–47, 126, 255
Montgomery County Democratic Executive Committee, 43
Montgomery Examiner, 166
Montgomery Independent, 8
Montgomery Kiwanis Club, 248
Montgomery Light and Traction Company, 46
Montgomery Medical and Surgical Society, 18
Montgomery Rotary Club, 185
Morgan, John Tyler, 59, 80
Morrill Act, 226
Morse, Wayne, 200, 222, 281, 290
Mother's Day, 44, 55, 77, 196
Mountain Brook, Ala., 258
Mullin, Atticus, 79, 130
Mullins, Clarence, 153
Murphy, Kenneth, 41, 43, 45, 50, 59
Murray, James, 196
Muscle Shoals, Ala., 42, 45, 46, 51, 53, 70, 246, 252
Myrick, Henry, 19

Nation, 192
National Association for the Advancement of Colored People (NAACP), 148, 151, 169, 218
National Defense Education Act (NDEA): genesis of, 224–31, 266, 286, 290, 293; extension of, 274–75; tenth anniversary of, 281–82
National Democratic Committee, 84

National Democratic party. *See* Democratic party, national
National Education Association, 101, 281
National health insurance. *See* Health insurance; Medicaid; Medicare
National Heart Institute, 281
National Industrial Recovery Act (NIRA), 72
National Institutes of Health (NIH), 210, 220, 281, 290; appropriations for, 205–7, 221, 239, 248, 272–73, 275; appropriations criticized, 274; research achievements of, 286–87
National Labor Relations Board, 81
National Library of Medicine, 210, 237, 286
National Physicians Committee, 136
National Policy Committee, 73
National Recovery Administration (NRA), 73
National Service Act, 99, 100
National Youth Administration, 131
Neuberger, Richard, 22
Neutrality Act of 1937, 98
New Deal, 14, 70, 72, 73, 79, 80, 81, 82, 84, 85, 86, 100, 112, 114, 115, 116, 131, 133, 134, 137, 142, 146, 152, 185, 192, 195, 196, 214, 217, 244, 268, 287; anti-New Dealers in 1940, 38, 75, 79, 89, 90–91, 93, 95, 97; issue of in 1940 Democratic convention, 90–92; in 1942 congressional election, 99; support for Southern Conference for Human Welfare, 107; anti-New Dealers in 1944, 117, 125, 127, 129; impact on 1944 campaign, 127–28; impact on 1946 campaign, 141; anti-New Dealers in 1948, 151–62
New England Journal of Medicine, 266

220; and NDEA, 224, 228–30; Select Committee on Small Business, 276; Banking and Currency Committee, 276, 342 (n. 33)

United States Steel Corporation, 120, 169

U.S. Supreme Court, 73, 76, 81, 82, 84, 124, 149, 196, 222, 227, 285, 332 (n. 4), 342 (n. 22); on offshore oil, 181, 190; on loyalty oath, 184–85; on *Brown v. Board of Education*, 194, 213; on *Browder v. Gayle*, 219; on school prayer, 244, 247; on James Meredith, 244, 250; impeachment threats to members, 248

U.S. War Department, 56, 57, 74, 134

University of Alabama (Tuscaloosa), 24, 25, 227, 276; student government association, 26; School of Law, 27, 39, 106; student politics at, 104–6, 144; Crimson Tide, 105, 254; integration controversy at, 212–13

University of Alabama at Birmingham, 285

University of Michigan Law School, 27

University of Mississippi (Oxford), 244, 250, 254, 257

Valenti, Jack, 272

Valley Voice (Muscle Shoals, Ala.), 246, 252

Vance, Robert, 259

Vandenberg, Arthur, 206

Vanderbilt Agrarians, 73

Van der Veer, McClellan ("Ted"), 107, 119

Vardaman, Claude, 204, 244

Vaughn, Harry, 133

Vietnam War, 275

Vocational education, 225

Von Braun, Wernher, 229

Vredenburgh, Dorothy, 108, 168

Wage and hour regulations. *See* Fair Labor Standards Act

Wagner, Robert, 139

Wagner Act, 136, 220, 234

Wagner-Murray-Dingell bill, 136

Walker County, Ala., 127

Wallace, George C., 1, 24, 116, 204, 276, 280, 287, 291, 295; at 1948 Democratic convention, 158; at 1956 Democratic convention, 217; in 1962 gubernatorial race, 242–43; elected governor, 246–47; in 1962 Senate campaign, 252–54; and John F. Kennedy, 267; and "stand in the schoolhouse door," 267; dominates SDEC, 268–69; and James Martin, 271; and 1966 Democratic primary, 276–77; backs James B. Allen, 278; at Hill's funeral, 287

Wallace, Henry A., 74, 86, 92, 109, 131, 133; presidential campaign of, 151–54, 160

Wallace, Lurleen (Mrs. George C.), 227–78, 343 (n. 34)

Wall Street Journal, 98

Walton, Mary Helener. *See* Hill, Mary Helener Walton

Warm Springs, Ga., 70

War of 1812, 21

Warren, Earl, 248

Washington, Booker T., 23, 36

Washington, George, 95, 129, 284

Washington Herald, 84

Washington Post, 87, 101, 202, 213, 233, 275, 280

Washington Star, 85, 193

Watson, Edwin ("Pa"), 93

Webb, A. P., 45

Webb, Walter Prescott, 109

Webster, Daniel, 20, 21, 196

Weeks, Barney, 107, 188, 246, 258, 278, 280, 291